The Person of Christ

John Owen's *The Person of Christ* is the richest book on Christology I have ever read and one to which I return on a regular basis. Systematic in scope and doxological in aim, Owen's treatise is impossible to read without having one's mind enlarged and one's heart enamored by the glory of Jesus Christ. The new Christian Heritage edition, which makes the argument more transparent through the introduction of headings — all the while preserving Owen's rewarding content without abridgement — will be a great benefit to contemporary readers. Take up and read, and relish in the glory of Christ!

SCOTT R. SWAIN,
Professor of Systematic Theology, Academic Dean,
Reformed Theological Seminary, Orlando, Florida

The Apostle Paul told Timothy to "rightly divide" the word of truth (2 Tim. 2:15). He meant more than simply cutting it into paragraphs and chapters of course, though that can be a useful aid to understanding. John Owen's magnificent book on the person of Jesus Christ rightly handles the word about Truth Himself, in the midst of much confusion and controversy. And this edition presents that teaching in a helpfully divided up format — with chapter headings and simplified structures — that make it even more of a joy to read. This is not a superficial book, and superficial Christians will not read it. But those that do can expect meaty theology and practical piety of an exhilarating and challenging kind.

LEE GATISS,
Director of Church Society,
and Adjunct Lecturer in Church History,
Wales Evangelical School of Theology, Bridgend, Wales

I don't always read the same book five times, but when I do, it is this one by John Owen. If there is a richer book on Christology in the English language, I am not aware of it.

MARK JONES,
Minister, Faith Reformed Presbyterian Church (PCA),
Vancouver, Canada

The Person of Christ

Declaring a Glorious Mystery—God and Man

John Owen

'Yea doubtless, and I count all things but loss for the excellency of the knowledge of Christ Jesus my Lord: for whom I have suffered the loss of all things, and do count them but dung, that I may win Christ.' —(Phil. 3:8)

CHRISTIAN
HERITAGE

Introduction © Sinclair B. Ferguson 2015
Copyright © Christian Focus Publications 2015

paperback ISBN 978-1-78191-603-2
epub ISBN 978-1-78191-712-1
mobi ISBN 978-1-78191-713-8

This edition first published in 2015
in the
Christian Heritage Imprint
by
Christian Focus Publications,
Geanies House, Fearn, Ross-shire,
IV20 1TW, Scotland
www.christianfocus.com

Cover design by Alister MacInnes
Printed by Bell & Bain, Glasgow

MIX
Paper from
responsible sources
FSC® C007785
FSC
www.fsc.org

CONTENTS

CONTENTS

Contents

THIS EDITION

The contents of this book first appeared under the splendid title *Christologia: or, a Declaration of the Glorious Mystery of the Person of Christ—God and Man: with the Infinite Wisdom, Love, and Power of God in the Contrivance and Constitution thereof; as also, of the Grounds and Reasons of His Incarnation; the Nature of His Ministry in Heaven; the Present State of the Church above thereon;and the Use of His Person in Religion: with an Account and Vindication of the Honour, Worship, Faith, Love, and Obedience due to Him, in and from the Church*. The text in this edition is unchanged apart from the following features, designed to make the book more user-friendly:

1. The text has been divided into nine chapters.
2. Subheadings, sometimes extending to four levels and mainly based on the original numeric structure, have been inserted. The contents pages include primary and secondary subheadings to aid navigation.
3. Sentences enumerating more than five or six items, lists of more than one sentence, selected notes, and some 'digressions' are broken off from the main text and displayed.
4. The style and placement of biblical references has been made consistent with modern practice and Roman numerals have been changed to Arabic.
5. Words such as 'unto' become 'to' or 'doth consist' becomes 'consists'.

INTRODUCTION

You are holding in your hand probably one of the most important books you could ever read.

That may seem an astonishing claim to make for a work that is now well over three hundred years old. Not least since sixty years ago you might have been a graduate in theology and yet not known such a book existed or recognized the name of the author. Thankfully this is no longer true.

Even so, how can such a claim—'probably one of the most important books you could ever read'—possibly be made for an old, not to say antiquarian book on Jesus Christ? Is this 'publisher-speak'?

A moment's reflection and some self-catechetical questions may point you in the direction of an answer.

Q 1 Can I remember when I last read a substantial book on the Person of Jesus Christ?
Q 2 Can I name three or four really great books about Christ written during my lifetime, or in the past hundred years?

Perhaps you can. But if so you are almost certainly in the minority—

and not necessarily because you lack knowledge or read little. For despite the fact that Christ-centredness has been understood to be a hallmark of evangelical Christianity (and indeed in recent years has become almost a 'buzz-word') it has not led to a multitude of outstanding books about the Person of Christ.

The judgment of charity would suggest that this is not due to a conspiracy of silence among publishers and authors, but simply that it has been assumed that evangelical Christianity is Christ-centred and suffused with a real and deep familiarity with him and what the Scriptures teach about him. After all, such exhortations as 'Consider Jesus' and 'let us run with endurance the race that is set before us, looking to Jesus' (Heb. 3:1; 11:1–2, ESV) must be among the most commonly heard words in Sunday Schools, Bible Classes and in sermons.

So what is the problem?

The presenting symptom is that most of us find these exhortations difficult to put into practice for any length of time. Indeed, honesty might lead us to confess that we find it much easier to '*consider*' the sports, or music, or hobby that we enjoy; and as for '*looking to*' someone, we find our minds and affections more easily captured by others than by the Lord Jesus.

This, however, simply leads to another question: what is the problem that creates 'the problem'? It may be manifold, but at its heart lies a lack of knowledge. We cannot sustain either admiration or reflection where there is ignorance of the object.

'But' it might be said, 'surely knowledge of Jesus is *personal* knowledge, not academic, factual, cerebral knowledge?' True. But *personal* knowledge requires *knowledge* of the person in order to be sustained. So any antithesis between informational knowledge and personal knowledge is poorly grounded. We need to know as much as we possibly can about Jesus Christ if we are to enjoy knowing him as much as we can!

Think of a young man who has recently developed a special friendship with a young woman and 'fallen in love'. Does he have a problem 'looking to' her? Why is it almost redundant to tell him to 'consider' her? The instinctive answer may be 'sight'; but the deeper answer is 'knowledge'. Sight may create interest, but on its own it cannot sustain attention unless it is accompanied by knowledge. Here is—from a distance—a beautiful young woman. Get closer and learn more about her attitude, her language, her habits, the way she treats others. Knowledge may now feed attraction; on the other hand it may dispel it! Knowledge and affections go hand in glove.

Personal knowledge of Christ similarly requires knowledge and understanding in order to develop into ongoing love for him. Indeed by its very nature it desires more and more knowledge.

We could here paraphrase the famous phrase of Anselm of Canterbury: *Fides quaerens intellectum* ('faith always seeks understanding'): love also seeks understanding. We cannot love what we do not know. To be able to admire Jesus Christ with the love of faith requires a growing understanding of who he is and what he has done for us.

OWEN'S TEACHING

The genius of John Owen lay in his ability to combine profound theological understanding with deep pastoral and personal insight. Like many of his works, *The Person of Christ* is designed to help us grow in knowledge *in order that we may grow in faith and hope and love*. Thus as a patient and prayerful reading of it fills the mind with fresh understanding, the will is drawn to a deeper devotion to him, and the affections are filled with a deeper joy in him. This is theology (or, to be more precise, Christology) of the best and richest kind. It breathes the atmosphere of an author who loved the Scriptures, and both knew and appreciated the writings of the early fathers of the church who wanted to describe Christ biblically and accurately not because they were academics but because they were, to coin a term, Christophileans—lovers of Christ. Should a Christian have less zeal for a true and full description of the Saviour, Lord and God than a young man has for the girl he loves, or a married man for his wife?

Once we grasp the real nature of personal knowledge of Christ, not only does the rationale behind Owen's book make sense, but we will appreciate every page of it. For his stated goal is to reach the heart and conscience by instructing the mind: 'The re-enthroning of the Person, Spirit, Grace, and Authority of Christ, in the hearts and consciences of men.'[1] Owen well grasped Paul's principle that it is through the renewal of the mind that the transformation of our lives is effected.[2]

A minister who had read an earlier volume of the Christian Focus editions of Owen once contacted me to ask if there were any more books in print like it. It is therefore quite possible that some readers will be unfamiliar not only with this particular title but also know little of its author. It may be helpful, therefore, to introduce John Owen himself, and to set the context for *The Person of Christ*.

JOHN OWEN—A SEVENTEENTH CENTURY LIFE

John Owen was born at Stadhampton, near Oxford, in 1616, the second son of Henry Owen, the local vicar. Educated first in a small grammar school, his immense intellectual ability must have been apparent early in his life. He entered the University of Oxford at the age of twelve and graduated with a BA in 1632 (aged either 15 or 16!). A lifetime later would see him bequeath to the church materials which now fill twenty four volumes each around 600 pages in length. We are rightly awestruck by how this was possible—not least considering the poverty of writing materials in bygone generations.

Life was not all study for Owen. In his teens he threw the javelin and he enjoyed playing the lute. Nevertheless, towards the end of his life he lamented that elements of his ill health were the result of the indifference he had shown to his physical well-being in earlier days—in particular deliberately depriving himself of sleep to permit more time for study (plus his College day began with a Latin sermon at 6.00 a.m.!). There can be little doubt that in his youth he was driven to pursue great learning—a pursuit in which he obviously enjoyed considerable success.

---

1 From Owen's Preface in this edition, p. 25.
2 Romans 12:1-2.

Owen later became a master scholar, writing and lecturing in Latin as well as English, commanding encyclopedic learning in a variety of theological disciplines. He was a consummate intellectual, but by no means an 'ivory-tower theologian'. As was said of John Calvin before him, he became a theologian in order to be a better pastor. Throughout his writings it is clear that the heartbeat of his life was not ultimately the pursuit of learning for its own sake but a desire to love and serve Jesus Christ.

We know relatively little of an intimate nature about Owen's personal life and habits. Like many of his Puritan contemporaries he may have kept a personal journal—but if so, like them, he also insisted on its destruction at the time of his death. Only occasionally, even in his correspondence, are we given an insight into his domestic life. But occasionally his biographers are able to give us a glimpse of the inner workings of his soul.

Born and reared in an English vicarage with deep Puritan sympathies, Owen knew the gospel from his infancy. But although he must have 'drunk in godliness with their mother's milk' (as John Calvin once aptly wrote of Timothy), his own faith flourished only after a period of some personal struggle.

Following his student days in Oxford and a period serving as a domestic chaplain, Owen moved to London in 1642. An early biography suggests that for several years he had struggled with melancholy and lacked a sense of assurance of his own salvation. But soon after his arrival in the capital he was to have an experience that would leave its mark on the rest of his life.

Accompanied by a cousin, Owen went one Sunday to St Mary's, Aldermanbury to hear the famous Edmund Calamy (1600-1666), only to be disappointed that a substitute was to occupy the pulpit. Yet, in the providence of God, the anonymous preacher's sermon, on the words of Jesus, 'Why are ye fearful, O ye of little faith' (Matthew 8:26 Geneva Bible), were the means of bringing Owen to a settled assurance of faith.

During the years that followed Owen gradually rose to public prominence in both ecclesiastical and national life. But prominence does not protect us from trials or sorrows. While he enjoyed

31 years of marriage to Mary Rooke, and together they had eleven children, only one of them survived into adult life. Both personally and politically he knew high points and low points.

Called to the ministry he served parishes at Fordham in Essex and later at Coggeshall. He was only thirty years old when he first preached before Parliament. Later, still only thirty two, in January 1649 he was appointed to preach before Parliament on the day following the execution of King Charles I (which he may well have witnessed. It was not long before he was on relatively intimate terms with some of the most significant figures in the body-politic, including Oliver Cromwell, the Lord Protector (whose granddaughter would later in the 1670s be a member of his London congregation). In 1651 he was appointed Dean of Christ Church, Oxford and in 1652 Vice-Chancellor of the University (in American terms, the President).

The heady days of the Cromwellian period passed within the decade. By that time, however, Owen's star was already on the wane, since in 1657 he had opposed moves to make Cromwell king.

Owen was, of course, a nonconformist. Following the restoration of the monarchy in 1660 and the Act of Uniformity in 1662 his service was largely of an unofficial nature, writing and ministering privately (congregations would gather in his own residences—in which from time to time he experienced government raids!). Only in the last decade or so of his life was it possible for ministers with his Puritan convictions to serve churches in a more public way. The forty or so members of the fellowship he cared for united in 1673 with a larger group of more than one hundred worshippers meeting in Leadenhall Street in London. During the next decade another hundred people became members. Thus, towards the end of his life, when strong enough to preach, he ministered to a congregation of perhaps two hundred and fifty members and a number of adherents and visitors. He continued to write and preach in London as his health allowed until his death in 1683 in the then 'quiet village of Ealing'.

Owen was an intellectual, a scholar, an academic leader, a figure moving for a season in the corridors of power. He was a sufficiently influential figure to have his name linked with various plots—including one to bring down Richard the son and (inefficient) successor of Oliver Cromwell. But Owen had a deeper passion than either political influence or the pursuit of knowledge for its own sake. His concern was for the church of Christ and for the life-changing ministry of the word of God. This explains the friendship he cultivated and the help he sought to give to John Bunyan—who clearly belonged educationally and socially to a different sphere. It was Owen who sought to influence his former Oxford tutor Thomas Barlow, now Bishop of Lincoln, to petition for Bunyan's release from prison. Thereafter Bunyan probably preached for Owen's congregation at its meetings in White's Alley in Moorfields whenever he was in London. King Charles II is reported to have asked Owen why he would listen to the preaching of an uneducated tinker like John Bunyan. The learned Doctor responded, 'Could I possess the tinker's abilities for preaching, please your majesty, I would gladly relinquish all my learning.'

In fact Owen was almost certainly one of the very first people ever to read Bunyan's immortal work *The Pilgrim's Progress*. At his suggestion Bunyan took his manuscript to his own publisher, Nathaniel Ponder. The rest, as they say, is history. Ponder—who must have had a special empathy for Bunyan since he himself had been imprisoned earlier in the same year Bunyan brought his manuscript to him—had a best seller on his hands and soon became known as 'Bunyan Ponder'!

These incidents, coupled with his voluminous writings, give us important clues to Owen's deep love for God's people and his devotion to the church. His last assistant David Clarkson underlined this in the funeral sermon he preached following his death:

> I need not tell you of this who knew him, that it was his design to promote holiness in the life and exercise of it . . . He was a burning and a shining light, and you for a while rejoiced in his light. Alas! It was but for a while; and we may rejoice in it still.

CONTEXT

In many ways John Owen held a unique position in the critical third quarter of seventeenth century English political and religious life. His profound learning, his connections to some of the most influential people in the country, the positions he had held in academia combined to make him a force to be reckoned with, or on occasion to seek as a co-belligerent. For that reason a considerable proportion of his writing was devoted to controversial issues. While *The Person of Christ* constitutes one of Owen's substantial works of theology it too needs to be read against the background of a developing crisis for theological orthodoxy.

The crisis had in fact been simmering for a century. While we usually think of the mainstream sixteenth century reformers as engaged in controversy with the Roman Catholic Church they were also fighting a battle on their left flank with a multi-faceted and radical movement marked by Arianism[3] and anti-Trinitarianism. John Calvin had unhappy contacts with some of these figures (Michael Servetus being the best known), including Laelius Socinus whom he sought to recover from his tendency to embrace unbiblical teaching. His nephew Fausto Sozzini became a major figure among anti-Trinitarians in Poland in what came to be known as The Minor Church which developed not only an academic institution and a printing house but also published the internationally influential *Racovian Catechism*. This had been translated into English and published in Amsterdam in 1652 by John Biddle (or Bidle, 1615-1662) who must have been a student at Oxford when Owen was still there as a graduate. The Council of State called Owen into service to refute the Socinian teaching. This he did in his *Vindiciae Evangelicae*, published in 1655, and also later in his great series of 'Exercitations' on the Priesthood of Christ prefaced to his massive *Commentary on Hebrews*. Thus by 1679 when Owen published *The Person of Christ* he had already engaged

---

3 Arianism is the heresy which denies the full deity of Christ. It is named after Arius (died 336 AD).

in polemics with Socinianism's denial of the deity of Christ and its rejection of the necessity of his priestly ministry in substitutionary atonement.

We rarely hear the term 'Socinianism' today. In its English dress it soon morphed into Deism and Unitarianism in both old and new England—a professed Christianity eviscerated of everything that makes Christianity distinctive. Its father figure was Edward, Lord Herbert of Cherbury (1582-1648), the older brother of the great metaphysical poet George Herbert.[4] For him true religion could be summarized as an expression of five building blocks:

1. Belief in the existence of a Supreme Being
2. Worship of this great Being
3. Virtue coupled with piety as the chief elements in that worship
4. Sin expiated by repentance
5. Rewards and punishments in the afterlife.[5]

Owen's world was therefore one in which other figures like Thomas Hobbes were raising questions about the classical view of Scripture (as he did in his *Leviathan*, 1650) so that the Bible was being brought down to the level of other texts. The principles of Deism would slowly take hold in, for example, John Locke's *The Reasonableness of Christianity* (1695). Here, influenced by Herbert, Locke maintained that while Christianity transcends reason—the plain man must not be expected to believe anything that does not harmonize with natural religion. In his *Essay on Human Understanding* (published in 1689) he had already argued that reason is to our ultimate court of appeal.

Such Deism would soon find vivid expression in the title of John Toland's book: *Christianity Not Mysterious* (1696) and flower

---

4 Intriguingly Owen had a brief correspondence in 1653 with Lord Herbert's son Richard, the second Baron Cherbury over an unpaid bill for his son who was a student at Christ Church, Oxford when Owen was Dean. Even more intriguingly his letter (which the editor notes is not only 'now badly faded but it is also written in poor English'!) is signed 'Your affectionate friend and humble servant'. P. Toon, ed., *The Correspondence of John Owen* (Cambridge: James Clarke, 1970), 61-2.

5 Herbert had published his influential *De Veritate* in 1624.

in such works as Matthew Tindal's *Christianity as Old as Creation; or, the Gospel a Republication of the Religion of Nature* (1730). Tindal essentially removed the fall, sin and guilt and the necessity of the atonement. Moderation and acting consistently with one's nature summarized true religion.

Thus the context in which Owen was writing in the late 1670s was one in which the essential elements of the gospel surrounding both the Person and the Work of Christ were under threat. Deism was essentially reductionist, denying supernaturalism and the necessity of redemption—and therefore inevitably the Christ-centredness of the Bible and of the gospel. A new agenda was being set—in which man was becoming the measure of all things, reason autonomous, and the uniqueness of Christ discounted.

Significantly however, although Owen challenges false views of Christ, *The Person of Christ* well illustrates his deep conviction that the best antidote to error is not to be found so much in polemic *per se* as it is in the exposition and application of the truth. And this he does in rich abundance. The result is that these pages transcend the narrow context of late seventeenth century England and continue to instruct us today.

This said, however, we too are living in a time when forms of Socinianism and Deism abound—today, as in Owen's day—sadly also within the professing Christian Church. So there is not only a certain timelessness attached to Owen's positive exposition but also a relevance in his polemics.

THIS EDITION

This new edition of *The Person of Christ* is now the sixth volume selected from the massive corpus of Owen's *Works* which *Christian Focus* have published under the careful and skilled editorship of Dr Philip Ross. His aim has been to highlight the value of this particular book and to present it in a way that is both attractive and helpful to the modern reader.

Owen himself would surely have approved. For he had a passion not only to defend the truth about Christ against attacks, but to communicate it to ordinary Christians like ourselves. This was a deeply-held pastoral conviction and commitment. As early as 1645 (when he was a young minister still under thirty years old) he wrote two catechisms for his congregation at Fordham in Essex. While engaging in theology at the highest of seventeenth century levels, he also held the conviction that all theology worth its name has a practical bearing on the Christian life. At the heart of this lies the knowledge of God in Christ. It is simply not possible to know too much about him! And the more and better we know, the greater our trust in him and love for him should grow.

READING THE PERSON OF CHRIST

Readers who are new to Owen may be glad of a few words of advice about approaching this work.

The Person of Christ has an extended Preface. Its history is interesting but also unexpectedly amusing.

Owen originally hoped to write a fully comprehensive study which would have included detailed exposition of the history of theological reflection and debate on the Person of Christ. Realizing this would stretch his work beyond limits he had then decided to provide a more condensed version. But even the great Owen had problems with publishers anxious to recoup their investment as quickly as possible! They had already printed the substance of the book, leaving Owen with both time and space only to provide his readers with some materials he already had to hand. This material he incorporated in the original publication in the form of a Preface.

Unless you are already familiar with Owen, my own suggestion is that you first only glance through this extensive introduction. In it Owen provides a map of the whole, but also numerous citations from classical theologians. Rather than be delayed by names that may be unfamiliar, it may be more helpful to leave them until you have worked your way through the whole book—and then return to them in due course. In fact Dr Ross's carefully laid out Contents pages will prove to be the simplest map for the first time reader.

However you approach this treatise you will meet profound reflections on many aspects of the Person of Christ and his Work.

Some elements of Owen's exposition of biblical truths may be quite new to you. But in all this he has one aim in view—to help you fix your gaze on Jesus Christ in such a way that your heart will be filled with faith and hope in him, and your love and affections will be fixed on him. His goal in writing is that you should feel, with Paul, 'the surpassing worth of knowing Christ Jesus my Lord.'[6]

If this goal is realized in any measure, then the editor Philip Ross, the Publisher Christian Focus, and I suspect the author John Owen himself will surely be satisfied.

So now, let your reading begin!

Sinclair B. Ferguson

6 Philippians 3:8.

PREFACE

It is a great promise concerning the person of Christ, as he was to be given to the church (for he was a child born, a son given to us, Isa. 9:6), that God would 'lay him in Zion for a foundation, a stone, a tried stone, a precious cornerstone, a sure foundation,' whereon 'he that believes shall not make haste' (Isa. 28:16). Yet was it also foretold concerning him, that this precious foundation should be 'for a stone of stumbling, and for a rock of offence, to both the houses of Israel; for a gin and for a snare to the inhabitants of Jerusalem;' so as that 'many among them should stumble, and fall, and be broken, and be snared, and be taken' (Isa. 8:14–15). According to this promise and prediction it has fallen out in all ages of the church; as the apostle Peter declares concerning the first of them (1 Pet. 2:6–8):

> Wherefore also, it is contained in the Scripture, Behold, I lay in Sion a chief cornerstone, elect, precious; and he that believes on him shall not be confounded. To you therefore which believe, he is precious; but to them which be disobedient, the stone which the builders disallowed, the same is made the head of the corner, and a stone of stumbling, and a rock of offence, even to them which stumble at the word, being disobedient: whereunto also they were appointed.

To them that believe to the saving of the soul, he is, he always has been, precious—the sun, the rock, the life, the bread of their souls—everything that is good, useful, amiable, desirable, here or to eternity. In, from, and by him, is all their spiritual and eternal life, light, power, growth, consolation, and joy here; with everlasting salvation hereafter. By him alone do they desire, expect, and obtain deliverance from that woeful apostasy from God, which is accompanied with—which contains in it virtually and meritoriously—whatever is evil, noxious, and destructive to our nature, and which, without relief, will issue in eternal misery. By him are they brought into the nearest cognation, alliance, and friendship with God, the firmest union to him, and the most holy communion with him, that our finite natures are capable of, and so conducted to the eternal enjoyment of him. For in him 'shall all the seed of Israel be justified, and shall glory' (Isa. 45:25) for 'Israel shall be saved in the Lord with an everlasting salvation;' they 'shall not be ashamed nor confounded, world without end' (v. 17).

On these and the like accounts, the principal design of their whole lives to whom he is thus precious, is to acquaint themselves with him—the mystery of the wisdom, grace, and love of God, in his person and mediation, as revealed to us in the Scripture, which is 'life eternal' (John 17:3)—to trust in him, and to him, as to all the everlasting concerns of their souls—to love and honour him with all their hearts—to endeavour after conformity to him, in all those characters of divine goodness and holiness which are represented to them in him. In these things consist the soul, life, power, beauty, and efficacy of the Christian religion; without which, whatever outward ornaments may be put upon its exercise, it is but a useless, lifeless carcass. The whole of this design is expressed in these heavenly words of the apostle (Phil. 3:8-12):

> Yea doubtless, and I count all things but loss for the excellency of the knowledge of Christ Jesus my Lord: for whom I have suffered the loss of all things, and do count them but dung, that I may win Christ, and be found in him, not having mine own righteousness, which is of the law, but that which is through

> the faith of Christ, the righteousness which is of God by faith:
> that I may know him, and the power of his resurrection, and
> the fellowship of his sufferings, being made conformable to his
> death; if by any means I might attain to the resurrection of the
> dead. Not as though I had already attained, either were already
> perfect; but I follow after, if that I may apprehend that for which
> also I am apprehended of Christ Jesus.

This is a divine expression of that frame of heart—of that design—
which is predominant and efficacious in them to whom Christ is
precious.

But, on the other hand (according to the fore-mentioned
prediction), as he has been a sure foundation to all that believe,
so he has in like manner been 'a stone of stumbling and a rock
of offence to them that stumble at the word, being disobedient:
whereunto also they were appointed.' There is nothing in him—
nothing wherein he is concerned—nothing of him, his person,
his natures, his office, his grace, his love, his power, his authority,
his relation to the church—but it has been to many a stone of
stumbling and rock of offence. Concerning these things have been
all the woeful contests which have fallen out and been managed
among those that outwardly have made profession of the Christian
religion. And the contentions about them do rather increase than
abate, to this very day; the dismal fruits whereof the world groans
under, and is no longer able to bear. For, as the opposition to the
Lord Christ in these things, by men of perverse minds, has ruined
their own souls—as having dashed themselves in pieces against this
everlasting rock—so in conjunction with other lusts and interests
of the carnal minds of men, it has filled the world itself with blood
and confusion.

The re-enthroning of the Person, Spirit, Grace, and Authority
of Christ, in the hearts and consciences of men, is the only way
whereby an end may be put to these woeful conflicts. But this is
not to be expected in any degree of perfection amongst them who
stumble at this stone of offence, whereunto they were appointed;
though in the issue he will herein also send forth judgment to

victory, and all the meek of the earth shall follow after it. In the meantime, as those to whom he is thus a rock of offence—in his person, his spirit, his grace, his office, and authority—are diligent and restless (in their various ways and forms, in lesser or higher degrees, in secret artifices, or open contradictions to any or all of them, under various pretences, and for divers ends, even secular advantages some of them, which the craft of Satan has prepared for the ensnaring of them) in all ways of opposition to his glory; so it is the highest duty of them to whom he is precious, whose principal design is to be found built on him as the sure foundation, as to hold the truth concerning him (his person, spirit, grace, office, and authority), and to abound in all duties of faith, love, trust, honour, and delight in him—so also to declare his excellency, to plead the cause of his glory, to vindicate his honour, and to witness him the only rest and reward of the souls of men, as they are called and have opportunity.

This, and no other, is the design of the ensuing treatise; wherein, as all things fall unspeakably short of the glory, excellency, and sublimity of the subject treated of (for no mind can conceive, no tongue can express, the real substantial glory of them), so there is no doubt but that in all the parts of it there is a reflection of failings and imperfections, from the weakness of its author. But yet I must say with confidence, that in the whole, that eternal truth of God concerning the mystery of his wisdom, love, grace, and power, in the person and mediation of Christ, with our duties towards himself therein, even the Father, Son, and eternal Spirit, is pleaded and vindicated, which shall never be shaken by the utmost endeavours and oppositions of the gates of hell.

And in the acknowledgment of the truth concerning these things consists, in an especial manner, that faith which was the life and glory of the primitive church, which they earnestly contended for, wherein and whereby they were victorious against all the troops of stumbling adversaries by whom it was assaulted. In giving testimony hereunto, they loved not their lives to the death, but poured out their blood like water, under all the pagan persecutions, which had no other design but to cast them down and separate them from this impregnable rock, this precious foundation. In the defence of these truths did they conflict, in prayers, studies, travels, and writings, against the swarms of seducers by whom they were opposed. And, for this cause, I thought to have confirmed the principal passages of the ensuing discourse with some testimonies from the most ancient writers of the first ages of the church; but I omitted that cause, as fearing that the interposition of such passages might obstruct instead of promoting the edification of the common sort of readers, which I principally intended. Yet, withal, I thought not good utterly to neglect that design, but to give at least a specimen of their sentiments about the principal truths pleaded for, in this preface to the whole. But herein, also, I met with a disappointment; for the bookseller having, unexpectedly to me, finished the printing of the discourse itself, I must be contented to make use of what lies already collected under my hand, not having leisure or time to make any farther inquiry.

I shall do something of this nature, the rather because I shall have occasion thereby to give a summary account of some of the principal parts of the discourse itself, and to clear some passages in it, which by some may be apprehended obscure.

CHAPTER ONE

The foundation of the whole is laid in the indication of those words of our blessed Saviour, wherein he declares himself to be the rock whereon the church is built: 'And I say also to you, That you are Peter, and upon this rock I will build my church; and the gates of hell shall not prevail against it' (Matt. 16:18). The pretended ambiguity of these words has been wrested by the secular interests of men, to give occasion to that prodigious controversy among Christians, viz., whether Jesus Christ or the Pope of Rome be the rock whereon the church is built. Those holy men of old to whom Christ was precious, being untainted with the desires of secular grandeur and power, knew nothing hereof. Testimonies may be—they have been—multiplied by others to this purpose. I shall mention some few of them.

Οὗτός ἔστιν ἡ πρὸς τὸν Πατέρα ἄγουσα ὁδὸς, ἡ πέτρα, ἡ κλεὶς, ὁ ποιμὴν, says Ignatius (*Epist. ad Philadelph*).—'He' (that is, Christ) 'is the way leading to the Father, the rock, the key, the shepherd'— wherein he has respect to this testimony.

And Origen expressly denies the words to be spoken of Peter, in Matthew 16 (Tract. i):

> Quod si super unum illum Petrum tantum existimes totam ecclesiam ædificari, quid dicturus es de Johanne, et apostolorum unoquoque? Num audebimus dicere quod adversus Petrum unum non prevalituræ sunt portæ inferorum?

> If you shall think that the whole church was built on Peter alone, what shall we say of John, and each of the apostles? What! shall we dare to say that the gates of hell shall not prevail against Peter only?

So he, according to the common opinion of the ancients, that there was nothing peculiar in the confession of Peter, and the answer made thereunto as to himself, but that he spake and was spoken to in the name of all the rest of the apostles (*Euseb. Præparat. Evang.*, lib. 1: cap. 3):

> Ἥτε ὀνομαστὶ προθεσπισθεῖσα ἐκκλεσία αὐτοῦ ἔστηκε κατὰ βάθους ἐρριζωμένη, καὶ μέχρις οὐρανίων ἀψίδων εὐχαῖς ὁσίων καὶ θεοφιλῶν ἀνδρῶν μετεωριζομένη—διὰ μίαν ἐκείνην, ἥν αὐτὸς ἀπεφήνατο λέξιν, εἴπων, Ἐπὶ τὴν πέτραν οἰκοδομήσω μου τὴν ἐκκλεσίαν, καὶ πύλαι ἄδου οὐ κατισχύσυσιν αὐτῆς.

He proves the verity of divine predictions from the glorious accomplishment of that word, and the promise of our Saviour, that he would build his church on the rock (that is, himself), so as that the gates of hell should not prevail against it. For 'Unum hoc est immobile fundamentum, una hæc est felix fidei Petra, Petri ore confessa, Tu es filius Dei vivi,' says Hilary (*de Trin.*, lib. 2): 'This is the only immovable foundation, this is the blessed rock of faith confessed by Peter, You are the Son of the living God.' And Epiphanius (*Hær.* 39): Ἐπὶ τῇ πέτρᾳ ταύτῃ τῆς ἀσφαλοῦς πίστεως οἰκοδομήσω μοῦ τὴν ἐκκλησίαν.—'Upon this rock of assured faith I will build my church.' For many thought that faith itself was metonymically called the Rock, because of its object, or the person of Christ, which is so.

One or two more out of Augustine shall close these testimonies: 'Super hanc Petram, quam confessus es, super meipsum filium Dei vivi, ædificabo ecclesiam meam. Super me ædificabo te, non me super te' (*De Verbis Dom.*, Serm. 13).—'Upon this rock which you have confessed—upon myself, the Son of the living God—I will build my church. I will build you upon myself, and not myself on you.' And he more fully declares his mind (*Tract.* 124, *in Johan*):

Universam significabat ecclesiam, quæ in hoc seculo diversis tentationibus, velut imbribus, fluminibus, tempestatibusque quatitur, et non cadit; quoniam fundata est supra Petram; unde et Petrus nomen accepit. Non enim a Petro Petra, sed Petrus a Petra; sicut non Christus a Christiano, sed Christianus a Christo vocatur. Ideo quippe ait Dominus, Super hanc Petram ædificabo ecclesiam meam,' quia dixerat Petrus, Tu es Christus filius Dei vivi.' Super hanc ergo' (inquit) Petram quam confessus es, ædificabo ecclaeism meam.' Petra enim erat Christus, super quod fundamentum etiam ipse ædificatus est Petrus. Fundamentum quippe aliud nemo potest ponere, præter id quod positum est, quod est Jesus Christus.

He (Christ) meant the universal church, which in this world is shaken with divers temptations, as with showers, floods, and tempests, yet falls not, because it is built on the rock (Petra) from whence Peter took his name. For the rock is not called Petra from Peter, but Peter is so called from Petra the rock; as Christ is not so called from Christian, but Christian from Christ. Therefore, said the Lord, Upon this rock will I build my church;' because Peter said, You are the Christ, the Son of the living God.' Upon this rock, which you have confessed, will I build my church. For Christ himself was the rock on which foundation Peter himself was built. For other foundation can no man lay, save that which is laid, which is Jesus Christ.

Chapter Two

Against this rock, this foundation of the church—the person of Christ, and the faith of the church concerning it—great opposition has been made by the gates of hell. Not to mention the rage of the pagan world, endeavouring by all effects of violence and cruelty to cast the church from this foundation; all the heresies wherewith from the beginning, and for some centuries of years ensuing, it was pestered, consisted in direct and immediate oppositions to the eternal truth concerning the person of Christ. Some that are so esteemed, indeed, never pretended to any sobriety, but were mere effects of delirant imaginations; yet did even they also, one way or other, derive from an hatred to the person of Christ, and centred therein. Their beginning was early in the church, even before the writing of the gospel by John, or of his Revelation, and indeed before some of Paul's epistles. And although their beginning was but small, and seemingly contemptible, yet, being full of the poison of the old serpent, they diffused themselves in various shapes and forms, until there was nothing left of Christ—nothing that related to him, not his natures, divine or human, not their properties nor acting, not his person, nor the union of his natures therein—that was not opposed and assaulted by them. Especially so soon as the gospel had subdued the Roman empire to Christ, and was owned by the rulers of it, the whole world was for some ages filled with uproars, confusion, and scandalous disorders about the person of Christ, through the cursed oppositions made thereunto by the gates of hell. Neither had the church any rest from these conflicts for about five hundred years. But near that period of time, the power of truth and religion beginning universally to decay among the outward professors of them, Satan took advantage to make that havoc and destruction of the church—by superstition, false worship, and profaneness of life—which he failed of in his attempt against the person of Christ, or the doctrine of truth concerning it.

It would be a tedious work, and, it may be, not of much profit to them who are utterly unacquainted with things so long past and gone, wherein they seem to have no concern, to give a specimen of the several heresies whereby attempts were made against this rock and foundation of the church. To those who have inquired into the records of antiquity, it would be altogether useless. For almost every page of them, at first view, presents the reader with an account of some one or more of them. Yet do I esteem it useful, that the very ordinary sort of Christians should, at least in general, be acquainted with what has passed in this great contest about the person of Christ, from the beginning. For there are two things relating thereunto

> *…I esteem it useful, that the very ordinary sort of Christians should, at least in general, be acquainted with what has passed in this great contest about the person of Christ, from the beginning.*

wherein their faith is greatly concerned. First, there is evidence given therein to the truth of those predictions of the Scripture, wherein this fatal apostasy from the truth, and opposition to the Lord Christ, are foretold: and, secondly, an eminent instance of his power and faithfulness, in the appointment and conquest of the gates of hell in the management of this opposition. But they have been all reckoned up, and digested into methods of time and matter, by many learned men (of old and of late), so that I shall not in this occasional discourse represent them to the reader again. Only I shall give a brief account of the ways and means whereby they who retained the profession of the truth contended for it, to a conquest over the pernicious heresies wherewith it was opposed.

The defence of the truth, from the beginning, was left in charge to, and managed by, the guides and rulers of the church in their several capacities. And by the Scripture it was that they discharged their duty confirmed with apostolic tradition consonant thereunto. This was left in charge to them by the great apostle (Acts 20:28–31; 1 Tim. 6:13–14; 2 Tim. 2:1–2, 15, 23–4, 4:1–5), and wherein any of them failed in this duty, they were reproved by Christ himself (Rev. 2:14–15, 20). Nor were private believers (in their places and capacities) either unable for this duty or exempt from it, but discharged themselves faithfully therein, according to commandment given to them (1 John 2:20, 27, 4:1–3; 2 John 8–9). All true believers, in their several stations—by mutual watchfulness, preaching, or writing, according to their calls and abilities—effectually used the outward means for the preservation and propagation of the faith of the church. And the same means are still sufficient to the same ends, were they attended to with conscience and diligence. The pretended defence of truth with arts and arms of another kind has been the bane of religion, and lost the peace of Christians beyond recovery. And it may be observed, that whilst this way alone for the preservation of the truth was insisted on and pursued, although innumerable heresies arose one after another, and sometimes many together, yet they never made any great progress, nor arrived to any such consistency as to make a stated opposition to the truth; but the errors themselves and their authors, were as vagrant meteors, which appeared for a little while, and vanished away. Afterwards it was not so, when other ways and means for the suppression of heresies were judged convenient and needful.

For in process of time, when the power of the Roman empire gave countenance and protection to the Christian religion, another way was fixed on for this end, viz., the use of such assemblies of bishops and others as they called General Councils, armed with a mixed power, partly civil and partly ecclesiastical—with respect to the authority of the emperors and that jurisdiction in the church which began then to be first talked of. This way was begun in the Council of Nice, wherein, although there was a determination of the doctrine concerning the person of Christ—then in agitation, and opposed, as to his divine nature therein—according to the truth, yet sundry evils and inconveniences ensued thereon. For thenceforth the faith of Christians began greatly to be resolved into the authority of men, and as much, if not more weight to be laid on what was decreed by the fathers there assembled, than on what was clearly taught in the Scriptures. Besides, being necessitated, as they thought, to explain their conceptions of the divine nature of Christ in words either not used in the Scripture, or whose signification to that purpose was not determined therein, occasion was given to endless contentions about them. The Grecians themselves could not for a long season agree among themselves whether οὐσία and ὑπόστασις were of the same signification or no (both of them denoting essence and substance), or whether they differed in their signification, or if they did, wherein that difference lay. Athanasius at first affirmed them to be the same (*Orat*. 5: *con*. *Arian*. and *Epist. ad African*). Basil denied them so to be, or that they were used to the same purpose in the Council of Nice (*Epist*. 78). The like difference immediately fell out between the Grecians and Latins about 'hypostasis' and 'persona.' For the Latins rendered 'hypostasis' by 'substantia,' and πρόσωπον by 'persona.' Hereof Jerome complains, in his Epistle to Damasus, that they required of him in the East to confess 'tres hypostases,' and he would only acknowledge 'tres personas' (*Epist*. 71). And Augustine gives an account of the same difference (*De Trinitate*, lib 5: cap. 8–9). Athanasius endeavoured the composing of this difference, and in a good measure effected it, as Gregory Nazianzen affirms in his oration concerning his praise. It was done by him in a synod at Alexandria, in the first year of Julian's reign. On this occasion many contests arose even among them who all pleaded their adherence to the doctrine of the Council of Nice. And as the subtle Arians made incredible advantage hereof at first, pretending that they opposed not the deity of Christ, but only the expression of it by ὁμοιούσιος, so afterwards they countenanced themselves in coining words and terms, to express their minds with, which utterly rejected it. Hence were their ὁμοιούσιος, ἑτερούσιος, ἐξ οὐκ ὄντων, and the like names of blasphemy, about which the contests were fierce and endless. And there were yet farther evils that ensued hereon. For the curious and serpentine wits of men, finding themselves by this means set at liberty to think and discourse of those mysteries of the blessed Trinity, and the person of Christ, without much regard to plain divine testimonies (in such ways wherein cunning and sophistry did much bear sway), began to multiply such new, curious, and false notions about them, especially about the latter, as caused new disturbances, and those of large extent and long continuance. For their suppression, councils were called on the neck of one another, whereon commonly new occasions of differences did arise, and most of them managed with great scandal to the Christian religion.

For men began much to forego the primitive ways of opposing errors and extinguishing heresies; betaking themselves to their interest, the number of their party, and their prevalence with the present emperors. And although it so fell out—as in that at Constantinople, the first at Ephesus, and that at Chalcedon—that the truth (for the substance of it) did prevail (for in many others it happened quite otherwise), yet did they always give occasions to new divisions, animosities, and even mutual hatreds, among the principal leaders of the Christian people. And great contests there were among some of those who pretended to believe the same truth, whether such or such a council should be received—that is, plainly, whether the church should resolve its faith into their authority. The strifes of this nature about the first Ephesian Council, and that at Chalcedon, not to mention those wherein the Arians prevailed, take up a good part of the ecclesiastical story of those days. And it cannot be denied, but that some of the principal persons and assemblies who adhered to the truth did, in the heat of opposition to the heresies of other men, fall into unjustifiable excess themselves.

We may take an instance hereof with respect to the Nestorian heresy, condemned in the first Ephesian Council, and afterwards in that at Chalcedon. Cyril of Alexandria, a man learned and vehement, designed by all means to be to it what his predecessor Athanasius had been to the Arian; but he fell into such excesses in his undertakings, as gave great occasion to farther tumults. For it is evident that he distinguishes not between ὑπόστασις and φύσις, and therefore affirms, that the divine Word and humanity had μία φύσιν, one nature only. So he does plainly in *Epist. ad Successum*: 'They are ignorant,' says he, ὅτι κατ' ἀλήθειαν ἐστὶ μία φύσις τοῦ λόγου σεσαρκωμένη. Hence Eutyches the Archimandrite took occasion to run into a contrary extreme, being a no less fierce enemy to Nestorius than Cyril was. For to oppose him who divided the person of Christ into two, he confounded his natures into one— his delirant folly being confirmed by that goodly assembly, the second at Ephesus. Besides, it is confessed that Cyril—through the vehemency of his spirit, hatred to Nestorius, and following the conduct of his own mind in nice and subtle expressions of the great mystery of the person of Christ—did utter many things exceeding the bounds of sobriety prescribed to us by the apostle (Rom. 12:3), if not those of truth itself. Hence it is come to pass, that many learned men begin to think and write that Cyril was in the wrong, and Nestorius by his means condemned undeservedly. However, it is certain to me, that the doctrine condemned at Ephesus and Chalcedon as the doctrine of Nestorius, was destructive of the true person of Christ; and that Cyril, though he missed it in sundry expressions, yet aimed at the declaration and confirmation of the truth; as he was long since vindicated by Theorianus (*Dialog. con. Armenios*).

However, such was the watchful care of Christ over the church, as to the preservation of this sacred, fundamental truth, concerning his divine person, and the union of his natures therein, retaining their distinct properties and operations, that—notwithstanding all the faction and disorder that were in those primitive councils, and the scandalous contests of many of the members of them; notwithstanding the determination contrary to it in great and numerous councils—the faith of it was preserved entire in the hearts of all that truly believed, and triumphed over the gates of hell.

I have mentioned these few things, which belong to the promise and prediction of our blessed Saviour in Matthew 16:18 (the place insisted on), to show that the church, without any disadvantage to the truth, may be preserved without such general assemblies, which, in the following ages, proved the most pernicious engines for the corruption of the faith, worship, and manners of it. Yea, from the beginning, they were so far from being the only way of preserving truth, that it was almost constantly prejudiced by the addition of their authority to the confirmation of it. Nor was there any one of them wherein 'the mystery of iniquity' did not work, to the laying of some rubbish in the foundation of that fatal apostasy which afterwards openly ensued. The Lord Christ himself has taken it upon him to build his church on this rock of his person, by true faith of it and in it. He sends his Holy Spirit to bear testimony to him, in all the blessed effects of his power and grace. He continues his Word, with the faithful ministry of it, to reveal, declare, make known, and vindicate his sacred truth, to the conviction of gainsayers. He keeps up that faith in him, that love to him, in the hearts of all his elect, as shall not be prevailed against. Wherefore, although the oppositions to this sacred truth, this fundamental article of the church and the Christian religion — concerning his divine person, its constitution, and use, as the human nature conjoined substantially to it, and subsisting in it — are in this last age increased; although they are managed under so great a variety of forms, as that they are not reducible to any heads of order; although they are promoted with more subtlety and specious pretences than in former ages; yet, if we are not wanting to our duty, with the aids of grace proposed to us, we shall finally triumph in this cause, and transmit this sacred truth inviolate to them that succeed us in the profession of it.

CHAPTER THREE

This person of Christ, which is the foundation whereon the church is built, whereunto all sorts of oppositions are endeavoured and designed, is the most ineffable effect of divine goodness and wisdom — whereof we treat in the next place. But herein, when I speak of the constitution of the person of Christ, I intend not his person absolutely, as he is the eternal Son of God. He was truly, really, completely, a divine person from eternity, which is included in the notion of his being the Son, and so distinct from the Father, which is his complete personality. His being so was not a voluntary contrivance or effect of divine wisdom and goodness, his eternal generation being a necessary internal act of the divine nature in the person of the Father.

Of the eternal generation of the divine person of the Son, the sober writers of the ancient church did constantly affirm that it was firmly to be believed, but as to the manner of it not to be inquired into. 'Scrutator majestatis absorbetur a gloria,' was their rule; and the curious disputes of Alexander and Arius about it, gave occasion to that many-headed monster of the Arian heresy which afterwards ensued. For when once men of subtile heads and unsanctified hearts gave themselves up to inquire into things infinitely above their understanding and capacity—being vainly puffed up in their fleshly minds—they fell into endless divisions among themselves, agreeing only in an opposition to the truth. But those who contented themselves to be wise to sobriety, repressed this impious boldness. To this purpose speaks Lactantius (lib. iv., *De Verâ Sapient*): 'Quomodo igitur procreavit? Nec sciri a quoquam possunt, nec narrari, opera divina; sed tamen sacræ literæ docent illum Dei filium, Dei esse sermonem.'—'How, therefore, did the Father beget the Son? These divine works can be known of none, declared by none; but the holy writings' (wherein it is determined) 'teach that he is the Son of God, that he is the Word of God.' And Ambrose (*De Fide, ad Gratianum*):

Quæro abs te, quando aut quomodo putes filium esse generatum? Mihi enim impossibile est scire generationis secretum. Mens deficit, vox silet, non mea tantum, sed et angelorum. Supra potestates, supra angelos, supra cherubim, supra seraphim, supra omnem sensum est. Tu quoque manum ori admove; scrutari non licet superna mysteria. Licet scire quod natus sit, non licet discutere quomodo natus sit; illud negare mihi non licet, hoc quærere metus est. Nam si Paulus ea quæ audivit, raptus in tertium coelum, ineffabilia dicit, quomodo nos exprimere possumus paternæ generationis arcanum, quod nec sentire potuimus nec audire? Quid te ista questionum tormenta delectant?

I inquire of you when and how the Son was begotten? Impossible it is to me to know the mystery of this generation. My mind fails, my voice is silent—and not only mine, but of the angels; it is above principalities, above angels, above the cherubim, above the seraphim, above all understanding. Lay your hand on your mouth; it is not lawful to search into these heavenly mysteries. It is lawful to know that he was born—it is not lawful to discuss how he was born; that it is not lawful for me to deny—this I am afraid to inquire into. For if Paul, when he was taken into the third heaven, affirms that the things which he heard could not be uttered; how can we express the mystery of the divine generation, which we can neither apprehend nor hear? Why do such tormenting questions delight you?

Ephraim Syrus wrote a book to this purpose, against those who would search out the nature of the Son of God. Among many other things to the same purpose are his words (cap. 2):

> Infelix profecto, miser, atque impudentissimus est, qui scrutari cupot Opificem suum. Millia millium, et centies millies millena millia angelorum et archangelorum, cum horrore glorificant, et trementes adorant; et homines lutei, pleni peccatis, de divinitate intrepide disserunt? Non illorum exhorrescit corpus, non contremescit animus; sed securi et garruli, de Christo Dei filio, qui pro me indigno peccatore passus est, deque ipsius utraque generatione loquuntur; nec saltem quod in luce cæcutiunt, sentiunt.

> He is unhappy, miserable, and most impudent, who desires to examine or search out his Maker. Thousands of thousands, and hundreds of thousands of millions of angels and archangels, do glorify him with dread, and adore him with trembling; and shall men of clay, full of sins, dispute of the Deity without fear? Horror does not shake their bodies, their minds do not tremble, but being secure and prating, they speak of the Son of God, who suffered for me, unworthy sinner, and of both his nativities or generations; at least they are not sensible how blind they are in the light.

To the same purpose speaks Eusebius at large (*Demonstratio Evang.*, lib. 5: cap. 2).

Leo well adds hereunto the consideration of his incarnation, in these excellent words (Serm. ix., *De Nativit.*):

> Quia in Christo Jesu Filio Dei non solum ad divinam essentiam, sed etiam ad humanam spectat naturam, quo dictum est per prophetam—generationem ejus quis enarrabit?'—(utramque

enim substantiam in unam convenisse personam, nisi fides credat, sermo non explicat; et ideo materia nunquam deficit laudis; qui nunquam sufficit copia laudatoris) — gaudeamus igitur quod ad eloquendum tantum, misericordiæ sacramentum impares sumus; et cum salutis nostræ altitudinem promere non valeamus, sentiamus nobis bonum esse quod vincimur. Nemo enim ad cognitionem veritatis magis propinquat, quam qui intelligit, in rebus divinis, etiamsi multum proficiat, semper sibi superesse quod quærat. (See also Fulg., lib. 2: *ad Thrasimund*).

But I speak of the person of Christ as to the assumption of the substantial adjunct of the human nature, not to be a part whereof his person is composed, but as to its subsistence therein by virtue of a substantial union. Some of the ancients, I confess, speak freely of the composition of the person of Christ in and by the two natures, the divine and human. That the Son of God after his incarnation had one nature, composed of the Deity and humanity, was the heresy of Apollinarius, Eutyches, the Monothelites, or Monophysites, condemned by all. But that his most simple divine nature, and the human, composed properly of soul and body, did compose his one person, or that it was composed of them, they constantly affirmed. Τὸν Θεοῦ μεσίτην καὶ ἀνθρώπων, κατὰ τὰς γραφὰς συγκεῖσθαι φάμεν ἔκ τε τῆς καθ᾽ ἡμας ἀνθρωπότητος τελείως ἐχοῦσας κατὰ τὸν ἴδιον λόγον, καὶ ἐκ τοῦ πεφηνότος, ἐκ Θεοῦ κατὰ φύσιν υἱοῦ, says Cyril of Alexandria. — ʻA sanctis patribus adunatione ex divinitate et humanitate Christus Dominus noster compositus prædicatur᾽ (Pet. Diacon., Lib. De Incarnat. et Grat. Christi, ad Fulgentium). And the union which they intended by this composition they called ἕνωσιν φυσικὴν, because it was of diverse natures, and ἕνωσιν κατὰ σύνθεσιν, a union by composition.

But because there neither was nor can be any composition, properly so called, of the divine and human natures, and because the Son of God was a perfect person before his incarnation, wherein he remained what he was, and was made what he was not, the expression has been forsaken and avoided; the union being better expressed by the assumption of a substantial adjunct, or the human nature into personal subsistence with the Son of God, as shall be afterwards explained. This they constantly admire as the most ineffable effect of divine wisdom and grace: Ὁ ἄσαρκος σαρκοῦται, ὁ λόγος παχύνεται, ὁ ἀόρατος ὁρᾶται, ὁ ἀναφὴς ψηλαφᾶται, ὁ ἄχρονος ἄρχεται, ὁ υἱὸς Θεοῦ υἱὸς ἀνθρώπου γίνεται, says Gregory Nazianzen (Orat. xii.), in admiration of this mystery. Hereby God communicates all things to us from his own glorious fulness, the near approaches whereof we are not able to bear. So is it illustrated by Eusebius (Demonst. Evang., lib. 4: cap.5, &c.):

Οὕτω δὲ φωτὸς ἡλίου μία καὶ ἡ αὐτὴ προσβολὴ ὁμοῦ καὶ κατὰ τὸ αὐτὸ καταυγάζει μὲν ἀέρα, φωτίζει δὲ ὀφθαλμοὺς, ἀφὴν δὲ θερμαίνει, πιαίνει δὲ γῆν, αὔξει δὲ φυτά, κ. τ. λ. (cap. vi.) Εἰ γοῦν ὥς ἐν ὑποθέσει λόγου, καθεὶς οὐρανόθεν αὐτὸς ἑαυτὸν παμφαὴς ἥλιος σὺν ἀνθρώποις ἐπὶ γῆς πολιτευοίτο, οὐδένα τῶν ἐπὶ τῆς γῆς μεῖναι ἂν ἀδιάφορον, πάντων συλλήβδην ἐμψύχων ὁμοῦ καὶ ἀψύχων ἀθρόᾳ τῃ τοῦ φωτὸς προσβολῇ διαφθαρησομένων.

The sense of which words, with some that follow in the same place, is to this purpose: By the beams of the sunlight, and life, and heat, to the procreation, sustentation, refreshment, and cherishing of all things, are communicated. But if the sun itself should come down to the earth, nothing could bear its heat and lustre; our eyes would not be enlightened but darkened by its glory, and all things be swallowed up and consumed by its greatness; whereas, through the beams of it, every thing is enlightened and kindly refreshed. So is it with this eternal beam or brightness of the Father's glory. We cannot bear the immediate approach of the Divine Being; but through him, as incarnate, are all things communicated to us, in a way suited to our reception and comprehension.

So it is admired by Leo (Serm. iii., De Nativit.):

Natura humana in Creatoris societatem assumpta est, non ut ille habitator, et illa esset habitaculum; sed ut naturæ alteri sic misceretur altera, ut quamvis alia sit quæ suscipitur, alia vero quæ suscepit, in tantam tamen unitatem conveniret utriusque diversitas, ut unus idemque sit filius, qui se, et secundum quod verus est homo, Patre dicit minorem, et secundum quod verus est Deus Patri se profitetur æqualem.

Human nature is assumed into the society of the Creator, not that he should be the inhabitant, and that the habitation, [that is, by an inhabitation in the effects of his power and grace, for otherwise the fulness of the Godhead dwelt in him bodily], but that one nature should be so mingled [that is, conjoined] with the other, that although that be of one kind which assumes, and that of another which is assumed, yet the diversity of them both should concur in such a unity or union, as that it is one and the same Son—who, as he was a true man, said that he was less than the Father, or the Father was greater than he—so as he was true God, professes himself equal to the Father.

See also Augustinus *De Fide*, ad Pet. Diacon., cap. xvii.; Justitianus Imperator Epist. ad Hormisdam, Romæ Episcop.

And the mystery is well expressed by Maxentius (Biblioth. Patr. pars prima):

Non confundimus naturarum diversitatem; veruntamen Christum non ut tu asseris Deum factum, sed Deum factum Christum confitemur. Quia non cum pauper esset, dives factus est, sed cum dives esset, pauper factus est, ut nos divites faceret; neque enim cum esset in formâ servi, formam Dei accepit; sed cum esset in formâ Dei, formam servi accepit; similiter etiam nec, cum esset caro, verbum est factum; sed cum esset verbum, caro factum est.

We do not confound the diversity of the natures, howbeit we believe not what you affirm, that Christ was made God; but we believe that God was made Christ. For he was not made rich when he was poor; but being rich, he was made poor, that he might make us rich. He did not take the form of God when he was in the form of a servant; but being in the form of God, he took on him the form of a servant. In like manner, he was not made the Word when he was flesh; but being the Word, he was made flesh.

And Jerome, speaking of the effects of this mystery (Comment. in Ezekiel, cap. 46):

> Ne miretur lector si idem et Princeps est et Sacerdos, et Vitulus, et Aries, et Agnus; cum in Scripturis sanctis pro varietate causarum legamus eum Dominum, et Deum, et Hominem, et Prophetam, et Virgam, et Radicem, et Florem, et Principem, et Regem justum, et Justitiam, Apostolum, et Episcopum, Brachium, Servum, Angelum, Pastorem, Filium, et Unigenitum, et Promogenitum, Ostium, Viam, Sagittam, Sapientiam, et multa alia.

> Let not the reader wonder if he find one and the same to be the Prince and Priest, the Bullock, Ram, and Lamb; for in the Scripture, on variety of causes, we find him called Lord, God, and Man, the Prophet, a Rod, and the Root, the Flower, Prince, Judge, and Righteous King; Righteousness, the Apostle and Bishop, the Arm and Servant of God, the Angel, the Shepherd, the Son, the Only-begotten, the First-begotten, the Door, the Way, the Arrow, Wisdom, and sundry other things.

And Ennodius has, as it were, turned this passage of Jerome into verse:

> Corda domat, qui cuncta videt,
>   quem cuncta tremiscunt;
> Fons, via, dextra, lapis, vitulus,
>   leo, lucifer, agnus;
> Janua, spes, virtus, verbum, sapientia, vates.
> Ostia, virgultum, pastor, mons, rete, columba,
> Flama, gigas, aquila, sponsus, patientia, nervus,
> Filius, excelsus, Dominus, Deus;
>   omnia Christus.
>   (*In natalem Papæ Epiphanii.*)

'Quod homo est esse Christus voluit; ut et homo possit esse quod Christus est,' says Cyprian (*De Idolorum Vanitate*, cap. 3). And,

'Quod est Christus erimus Christiani, si Christum fuerimus imitati' (Ibid.). And he explains his mind in this expression by way of admiration (*Lib. de Eleemosyn*): 'Christus hominis filius fieri voluit, ut nos Dei filios faceret; humiliavit se, ut populum qui prius jacebat, erigeret; vulneratus est, ut vulnera nostra curaret.'

Chapter Four

That he was the foundation of all the holy counsels of God, with respect to the vocation, sanctification, justification, and eternal salvation of the church, is, in the next place, at large declared. And he was so on a threefold account.

1. Of the ineffable mutual delight of the Father and the Son in those counsels from all eternity.
2. As the only way and means of the accomplishment of all those counsels, and the communication of their effects, to the eternal glory of God.
3. As he was in his own person, as incarnate, the idea and exemplar in the mind of God of all that grace and glory in the church which was designed to it in those eternal counsels.

As the cause of all good to us, he is on this account acknowledged by the ancients. Οὗτος γοῦν ὁ λόγος, ὁ Χριστὸς καὶ τοῦ εἶναι πάλαι ἡμᾶς, ἦν γὰρ ἐν Θεῷ, καὶ τοῦ εὖ εἶναι αἴτιος. Νῦν δὲ ἐτεφάνη ἀνθρώποις, αὐτὸς οὗτος ὁ λόγος, ὁ μόνος ἄμφω Θεός τε καὶ ἄνθρωπος, ἁπάντων ἡμῖν αἴτιος ἀγαθῶν, says Clemens, Adhort. ad Gentes. —'He, therefore, is the Word, the Christ, and the cause of old of our being; for he was in God, and the cause of our wellbeing. But now he has appeared to men, the same eternal Word, who alone is both God and man, and to us the cause of all that is good.' As he was in God the cause of our being and wellbeing from eternity, he was the foundation of the divine counsels in the way explained; and in his incarnation, the execution of them all was committed to him, that through him all actual good, all the fruits of those counsels, might be communicated to us.

Chapter Five

He is also declared in the next place, as he is the image and great representative of God, even the Father, to the church. On what various accounts he is so called, is fully declared in the discourse itself. In his divine person, as he was the only begotten of the Father from eternity, he is the essential image of the Father, by the generation of his person, and the communication of the divine nature to him therein. As he is incarnate, he is both in his own entire person God and man, and in the administration of his office, the image or representative of the nature and will of God to us, as is fully proved. So speaks Clem. Alexandrin., *Adhort. ad Gentes*: Ἡ μεν γὰρ τοῦ Θεοῦ εἰκὼν ὁ λόγος αὐτοῦ, καὶ υἱὸς τοῦ νοῦ γνήσιος, ὁ θεῖος λόγος, φωτὸς ἀρχέτυπον φῶς, εἰκὼν δὲ τοῦ λόγου ὁ ἄνθπώπος. —'The image of God is his own Word, the natural Son of the (eternal) Mind, the divine Word, the original Light of Light; and the image of the Word is man.' And the same author again, in his *Pædagogus*: Πρόσωπον τοῦ Θεοῦ ὁ λόγος ᾧ φωτίζεται ὁ Θεὸς καὶ γνωρίζεται. —'The Word is the face, the countenance, the representation of God, in whom he is brought to light and made known.' As he is in his divine person his eternal, essential image; so, in his incarnation, as the teacher of men, he is the representative image of God to the church, as is afterwards declared.

So also Jerome expresses his mind herein (Comment. in Ps. 66): 'Illuminet vultum suum super nos; Dei facies quæ est? utique imago ejus. Dicit enim apostolus imaginem Patris esse filium; ergo imagine sua nos illuminet; hoc est, imaginem suam filium illuminet super nos; ut ipse nos illuminet; lux enim Patris lux filii est.'—'Let him cause his face to shine upon us; or lift up the light of his countenance upon us. What is the face of God? Even his image. For the apostle says, that the Son is the image of the Father. Wherefore, let him shine on us with his image; that is, cause his Son, which is his image, to shine upon us, that he may illuminate us; for the light of the Father and of the Son are the same.' Christ being the image of God, the face of God, in him is God represented to us, and through him are all saving benefits communicated to them that believe.

Eusebius also speaks often to this purpose, as (Demonstratio Evangelica, lib. 4: cap. 2): Ὅθεν εἰκότως οἱ χρησμοὶ θεολογοῦντες, Θεὸν γενετὸν αὐτὸν ἀποφαίνουσιν, ὡς ἂν τῆς ἀνεκφράστου καὶ ἀπερινοήτου θεότητος μόνον ἐν αὐτῷ φέροντα τὴν εἰκόνα, δι᾽ ἥν καὶ Θεὸν εἶναί τε αὐτὸν καὶ λέγεσθαι τῆς πρὸς τὸ πρῶτον ἐξομοιώσεως χάριν. — 'Wherefore, the holy oracles, speaking theologically, or teaching divine things, do rightly call him God begotten,' (of the Father), 'as he who alone bears in himself the image of the ineffable and inconceivable Deity. Wherefore, he both is, and is called God, because of his being the character, similitude, or image of him who is the first.' The divine personality of Christ consists in this, that the whole divine nature being communicated to him by eternal generation, he is the image of God, even the Father, who by him is represented to us. See the same book (ch. 7) to the same purpose; also, *De Ecclesiast. Theol. contra Marcell.*, lib. 2: cap. 17.

Clemens abounds much in the affirmation of this truth concerning the person of Christ, and we may yet add, from a multitude to the same purpose, one or more testimonies from him. Treating of Christ as the teacher of all men, his παιδαγωγὸς, he affirms that he is Θεὸς ἐν ἀνθρώπου σχήματι, 'God in the figure or form of man;' ἄχραντος, πατρικῷ θελήματι διάκονος, λόγος, Θεὸς, ὁ ἐν πατρὶ ὁ ἐκ δεξιῶν τοῦ πατρὸς, σὺν καὶ τῷ σχήματι Θεοῦ, 'impolluted, serving the will of the Father, the Word, God, who is in the Father, on the right hand of the Father, and in or with the form of God.' Οὗτος ἡμῖν εἰκὼν ἡ ἀκηλίδωτος, τούτῳ παντὶ σθένει πειρατέον ἐξομοιοῦν τὴν ψυχήν. — 'He is the image (of God) to us, wherein there is no blemish; and with all our strength are we to endeavour to render ourselves like to him.' This is the great end of his being the representative image of God to us. And (Stromat., lib. 4): Ὁ μὲν οὖν Θεὸς ἀναπόδεικτος ὤν, οὐκ ἔστιν ἐπιστημονικός. Ὁ δὲ υἱὸς σοφία τε ἐστὶ καὶ ἐπιστήμη, καὶ ἀλήθεια, καὶ, ὅσα ἄλλα τούτῳ συγγενῆ. — 'As God (absolutely) falls not under demonstration (that is, cannot perfectly be declared), so he does not (immediately) effect or teach us knowledge. But the Son is wisdom, and knowledge, and truth, to us, and every thing which is cognate hereunto.' For in and by him does God teach us, and represent himself to us.

CHAPTER SEVEN

Upon the glory of this divine person of Christ depends the efficacy of all his offices; an especial demonstration whereof is given in his prophetical office. So it is well expressed by Irenæus, 'qui nil molitur ineptè:' Lib. 1: cap. 1.

> Non enim aliter nos discere poteramus quæ sunt Dei, nisi magister noster verbum existens, homo ffactus fuisset. Neque enim alius poterat enarrare nobis quæ sunt Patris, nisi proprium ipsius verbum. Quis enim alius cognovit sensum Domini? aut quis alius ejus consiliarius factus est? Neque rursus nos aliter discere poteramus, nisi Magistrum nostrum videntes, et per auditum nostrum vocem ejus percipientes, uti imitatores quidem operum, factores autem sermonum ejus facti, communionem habeamus cum ipso.

> We could not otherwise have learned the things of God, unless our Master, being and continuing the [eternal] Word, had been made man. For no other could declare to us the things of God, but his own proper Word. For who else has known the mind of the Lord? or who else has been his counsellor? Neither, on the other side, could we otherwise have learned, unless we had seen our Master, and heard his voice [in his incarnation and ministry] whereby, following his works, and yielding obedience to his doctrine, we may have communion with himself.

I do perceive that if I should proceed with the same kind of attestations to the doctrine of all the chapters in the ensuing discourse, this preface would be drawn forth to a greater length than was ever designed to it, or is convenient for it. I shall therefore choose out one or two instances more, to give a specimen of the concurrence of the ancient church in the doctrine declared in them, and so put a close to it.

CHAPTER NINE

In the ninth chapter and those following, we treat of the divine
honour that is due to the person of Christ, expressed in adoration,
invocation, and obedience, proceeding from faith and love. And
the foundation of the whole is laid in the discovery of the true
nature and causes of that honour; and three things are designed
to confirmation herein.

1. That the divine nature, which is individually the same in each
   person of the holy Trinity, is the proper formal object of all
   divine worship, in adoration and invocation; wherefore, no
   one person is or can be worshipped, but in the same individual
   act of worship each person is equally worshipped and adored.
2. That it is lawful to direct divine honour, worship, and
   invocation to any person, in the use of his peculiar name—the
   Father, Son, or Spirit—or to them altogether; but to make any
   request to one person, and immediately the same to another,
   is not exemplified in the Scripture, nor among the ancient
   writers of the church.
3. That the person of Christ, as God-man, is the proper object
   of all divine honour and worship, on the account of his divine
   nature; and all that he did in his human nature are motives
   thereunto.

The first of these is the constant doctrine of the whole ancient
church, viz, that whether (for instance), in our solemn prayers
and invocations, we call expressly on the name of the Father, or
of the Son, or of the Holy Spirit; whether we do it absolutely or
relatively, that is, with respect to the relation of one person to the
other—as calling on God as the Father of our Lord Jesus Christ, on
Christ as the Son of his love, on the Holy Spirit as proceeding from
them both—we do formally invocate and call on the divine nature,
and consequently the whole Trinity, and each person therein. This
truth they principally confirmed with the form of our initiation
into Christ at baptism: 'I baptize you in the name of the Father,

and of the Son, and of the Holy Ghost.' For as there is contained therein the sum of all divine honour, so it is directed to the same name (not the names), of the Father, Son, and Spirit, which is the same Deity or divine nature alone.

So speak the Fathers of the second General Council in their letters to the bishops of the west; as they are expressed in Theodoret, (lib. 5: cap. 9). This form of baptism teaches us, say they,

> Πιστεύειν εἰς τὸ ὄνομα τοῦ πατρὸς, καὶ τοῦ υἱοῦ, καὶ τοῦ ἁγίου πνεύματος, δηλαδὴ, θεότητός τε καὶ δυνάμεως καὶ οὐσίας μιᾶς τοῦ πατρὸς, καὶ τοῦ υἱοῦ, καὶ τοῦ ἁγίου πνεύματος πιστευομένης, ὁμοτίμου τῆς ἀξίας, καὶ συναϊδίου τῆς βασιλείας, ἐν τρισὶ τελείαις ὑποστάσεσι.

> To believe in the name of the Father, and of the Son, and of the Holy Ghost; seeing that the Deity, substance, and power of the Father, Son, and Holy Spirit, is one and the same; their dignity equal; their kingdom co-eternal, in three perfect persons.

'In nomine dixit, non nominibus, ergo non aliud nomen Patris est,' &c., 'quia unus Deus' (Ambrose, *De Spirit. Sanct.*, lib. 1: cap. 14). Ὄνομα δὲ κοινὸν τῶν τριῶν ἕν, ἡ θεότης.—'The one name common to the three is the Deity' (Gregor. Nazianzen, *Orat.* 40). Hence Augustine gives it as a rule, in speaking of the Holy Trinity: 'Quando unus trium in aliquo opere nominatur, universa operari trinitas intelligitur' (*Enchirid.*, cap. 38): 'When one person of the three is named in any work, the whole Trinity is to be understood to effect it.' 'There is one Lord, one faith, one baptism,' according to the Scriptures. Wherefore, as there is one faith in Christ, and one baptism of truth, although we are baptized and believe in the Father, Son, and Spirit, κατὰ τὸν αὐτὸν, οἶμαι, τρόπον καὶ λόγον, μία προσκύνησις ἡ πατρὸς, καὶ ἐνανθρωπήσαντος υἱοῦ, καὶ ἁγίου πνεύματος;—'so plainly, in my judgment, there is one and the same adoration, of the Father, the Son incarnate, and the Holy Spirit' (Cyril. Alex. *De Recta Fide*, cap. 32).

And this they professed themselves to hold and believe, in that ancient doxology which was first invented to decry the Arian heresy: 'Glory be to the Father, and to the Son, and to the Holy Ghost.' The same glory, in every individual act of its assignation or ascription, is directed to each person jointly and distinctly, on the account of the same divine nature in each of them. I need not produce any testimonies in the farther confirmation hereof; for, in all their writings against the Arians, they expressly and constantly contend that the holy Trinity (that is, the divine nature in three persons) is the individual object of all divine adoration, invocation, and all religious worship; and that by whatever personal name—as the Father, Son, or Spirit—we call on God, it is God absolutely who is adored, and each person participant of the same nature. (See August. *Lib. con. Serm. Arian.* cap. 35., and *Epist.* 66. ad Maximum).

For the second thing, or the invocation of God by any personal name, or by the conjunction of the distinct names of the Father, Son, and Holy Spirit together, nothing occurs more frequently among them. Yea, it is common to find in their writings, prayers begun to one person, and ended in the name of another; yea, begun to Christ, and closed in the name of His only-begotten Son; it being one and the same divine nature that is called on. Yea, the schoolmen do generally deny that the persons of the holy Trinity, under the consideration of the formal reason which is constitutive of their personality, are the formal object and term of divine worship; but in the worship of one, they are all worshipped as one God over all, blessed for ever. (See Aquin. 22. q. 81, a. 3, ad prim., and q. 84, a. 1, ad tertium; Alexand. Alens.p. 3, q. 30, m. 1, a. 3).

But yet, although we may call on God in and by the name of any divine person, or enumerate at once each person (ὦ τριὰς ἁγία ἀριθμουμένη, τριὰς ἐν ἑνὶ ὀνόματι ἀριθμουμένη, Epiphan. Ancorat., 8:22), it does not follow that we may make a request in our prayers to one person, and then immediately repeat it to another; for it would thence follow, that the person to whom we make that request in the second place, was not invocated, not called on, not equally adored with him who was so called on in the first place, although the divine nature is the object of all religious invocation, which is the same in each person. Wherefore, in our divine invocation, we may name and fix our thoughts distinctly on any person, according as our souls are affected with the distinct operations of each person in grace towards us.

For what concerns, in the third place, the ascription of divine honour, in adoration and invocation, to the person of Christ; it is that which they principally contended for, and argued from, in all their writings against the Arians.

Evidences of infinite wisdom in the constitution of the person of Christ, and rational discoveries of the condecencies therein, to the exaltation of all the other glorious properties of the divine nature, are also treated of. Herein we consider the incarnation of the Son of God, with respect to the recovery and salvation of the church alone. Some have contended that he should have been incarnate, had man never fallen or sinned. Of these are Rupertus, lib. iii., *De Gloriâ et Honore Filii Hominis*; Albertus Magnus, in 3. distinct. 10, a 4; Petrus Galatinus, lib. 3. cap. 4; as are Scotus, Halensis, and others, whom Osiander followed. The same is affirmed by Socinus concerning the birth of that man, which alone he fancied him to be, as I have elsewhere declared. But I have disproved this figment at large. Many of the ancients have laboured in this argument, of the necessity of the incarnation of the eternal Word, and the condecencies to divine wisdom therein. See Irenæus, lib iii., cap. 20, 21; Eusebius, *Demonst. Evangel.*, lib 4. cap. 1–4, &c.; Cyril Alexand., lib. 5. cap. 7, lib 1. *De Fide ad Regin.*; Chrysostom, *Homil.* 10. in Johan., et in cap. 8, ad Rom. Serm. 18; Augustine, *De Trinit.*, lib. 13. cap. 13–20; Leo, Epist. 13, 18, Sermo. de Nativit. 1, 4, 10; Basil, in Psal. 58; Albinus, lib 1. in Johan. cap. 2; Damascen., lib. iii., *De Fide*, cap. 15, 19; Anselm, *quod Deus Homo*, lib. duo. Guil. Parisiensis, lib. *Cur Deus Homo*. Some especial testimonies we may produce in confirmation of what we have discoursed, in the places directed to. There is one of them, one of the most ancient, the most learned, and most holy of them, who has so fully delivered his thoughts concerning this mystery, as that I shall principally make use of his testimony herein.

It belonged to the wisdom and righteousness of God, that Satan should be conquered and subdued in and by the same nature which he had prevailed against, by his suggestion and temptation. To this purpose that holy writer speaks (lib. 3. cap. 20), which, because his words are cited by Theodoret (Dial. ii.), I shall transcribe them from thence, as free from the injuries of his barbarous translator:

Ἥνωσεν οὖν καθὼς προέφαμεν τὸν ἄνθρωπον τῷ Θεῷ, εἰ γὰρ μὴ ἄνθρωπος ἐνίκησεν τὸν ἀντίπαλον τοῦ ἀνθρώπου, οὐκ ἂν δικαίως ἐνικήθη ὁ ἐχθρός, πάλιν τε, εἰ μὴ ὁ Θεὸς ἐδωρήσατο τὴν σωτηρίαν, οὐκ ἂν βεβαίως ἔχοιμεν αὐτὴν, καὶ ἐι μὴ συνηνώθη ὁ ἄνθρωπος τῷ Θεῷ οὔκ ἄν ἠδυνήθη μετασχεῖν τῆς ἀφθαρσίας. Ἔδει γὰρ τὸν μεσίτην τοῦ Θεοῦ τε καὶ ἀνθρώπων, διὰ τῆς ἰδίας πρὸς ἑκατέρους οἰκειότητος εἰς φιλίαν καὶ ὁμόνοιαν τοῦς ἀνφοτέρους συναγαγεῖν.

Words plainly divine; an illustrious testimony of the faith of the ancient church, and expressive of the principal mystery of the gospel!

> Wherefore, as we said before, he united man to God. For if man had not overcome the adversary of men, the enemy had not been justly conquered; and, on the other hand, if God had not given and granted salvation, we could never have a firm, indefeasible possession of it; and if man had not been united to God, he could not have been partaker of immortality. It behoved, therefore, the Mediator between God and man, by his own participation of the nature of each of them, to bring them both into friendship and agreement with each other.

And to the same purpose, speaking of the wisdom of God in our redemption by Christ, with respect to the conquest of the devil (lib 5. cap. 1):

> Potens in omnibus Dei Verbum, et non deficiens in suâ justitiâ, juste etiam adversus ipsam conversus est apostasiam, ea quæ sunt sua redimens, ab eo, non cum vi, quemadmodum ille initio dominabatur nostri, ea quæ non erant sua insatiabiliter rapiens.... Suo igitur sanguine redimente nos Domino, et dante animam suam pro anima nostra, et carnem suam pro carnibus nostris,' &c.

Again divinely: 'The all-powerful Word of God, no way defective in righteousness, set himself against the apostasy justly also; redeeming from him [Satan, the head of the apostasy] the things which were his own—not with force, as he bare rule over us, insatiably making rapine of what was not his own—but he, the Lord, redeeming us with his own blood, giving his soul for our soul, and his flesh for ours, wrought out our deliverance.'

These things are at large insisted on in the ending discourse.

It belongs to this great mystery, and is a fruit of divine wisdom, that our deliverance should be wrought in and by the same nature wherein and whereby we were ruined. The reasons hereof, and the glory of God therein, are at large discoursed in the ensuing treatise. To the same purpose speaks the same holy writer (lib 5. cap. 14):

Non in semetipso recapitulasset hæc Dominus, nisi ipse caro et sanguis secundum principalem plasmationem factus fuisset; salvans in semetipso in fine illud quod perierat in principio in Adam. Si autem ob aliam quandam dispositionem Dominus incarnatus est, et ex alterâ substantiâ carnem attulit, non ergo in semetipso recapitulatus est hominem, adhuc etiam nec caro quidem dici potest.... Habuit ergo et ipse carnem et sanguinem, non alteram quandam, sed ipsam principalem Patris plasmationem in se recapitulans, exquirens id quod perierat.

And to the same purpose (lib. 5. cap. 1): 'Neque enim vere esset sanguinem et carnem habens, per quam nos redemit, nisi antiquam plasmationem Adæ in seipsum recapitulasset.' That which these passages give testimony to, is what we have discoursed concerning the necessity of our redemption in and by the nature that sinned; and yet withal, that it should be free from all that contagion which invaded our nature by the fall. And these things are divinely expressed. 'Our Lord,' says he, 'had not gathered up these things in himself, had not he been made flesh and blood, according to its original creation.' (The reader may observe, that none of the ancient writers do so frequently express the fall of Adam by our apostasy from God, and our recovery by a recapitulation in Christ, as

Irenæus—his recapitulation being nothing but the ἀνακεφαλαίωσις mentioned by the apostle (Eph. 1:10)—and he here affirms, that, to this end, the Lord was made flesh; 'secundum principalem plasmationem,' as his words are rendered; that is plainly, the original creation of our nature in innocence, uprightness, purity, and righteousness.) 'So he saved in himself in the end, what perished in Adam at the beginning.' (The same nature, in and by the same nature.) 'For if the Lord had been incarnate for any other disposition,' (i.e., cause, reason, or end), 'and had brought flesh from any other substance,' (i.e., celestial or ethereal, as the Gnostics imagined), 'he had not recovered men, brought our nature to a head in himself, nor could he have been said to be flesh. He therefore himself had flesh and blood not of any other kind; but he took to himself that which was originally created of the Father, seeking that which was lost.' The same is observed by Augustine (Lib. de Fide, ad Petrum Diaconum):

> Sic igitur Christum Dei Filium, id est, unam ex Trinitate personam, Deum verum crede, ut divinitatem ejus de naturâ Patris natam esse non dubites; et sic eum verum hominem crede, et ejus carnem, non coelestis, non aeriæ, non alterius cujusquam putes esse naturæ, sed ejus cujus est omnium caro; id est, quam ipse Deus, homini primo de terra plasmavit, et cæteris hominibus plasmat.

> So believe Christ the Son of God, that is, one person of the Trinity, to be the true God, that you doubt not but that his divinity was born [by eternal generation] of the nature of the Father; and so believe him to be a true man, that you suppose not his flesh to be aerial, or heavenly, or of any other nature, but of that which is the flesh of men; that is, which God himself formed in the first man of the earth, and which he forms in all other men.

That which he speaks of one person of the Trinity, has respect to the heretical opinion of Hormisdas, the bishop of Rome, who contended that it was unlawful to say that one person of the Trinity was incarnate, and persecuted some Scythian monks, men not unlearned about it, who were strenuously defended by Maxentius, one of them.

It carries in it a great condecency to divine wisdom, that man should be restored to the image of God by him who was the essential image of the Father; (as is declared in our discourse;) and that he was made like to us, that we might be made like to him, and to God through him. So speaks the same Irenæus (lib. 5. *Præfat*): 'Verbum Dei Jesus Christus, qui propter immensam suam dilectionem, factus est quod sumus nos, ut nos perficeret quod est ipse.'—'Jesus Christ, the Word of God, who, from his own infinite love, was made what we are, that he might make us what he is;' that is, by the restoration of the image of God in us. And again (lib. 3. cap. 20):

Filius Dei existens semper apud Patrem, et homo factus, longam hominum expositionem in seipso recapitulavit; in compendio nobis salutem præstans, ut quod perdideramus in Adam, id est, secundum imaginem et similitudinem esse Dei, hoc in Christo Jesus reciperemus. Quia enim non erat possibile, eum hominem, qui semel victus fuerat et elisus per inobedientiam, replasmare et obtinere brabium (βραβεῖον) victoriæ; iterum autem impossibile erat ut salutem perciperet, qui sub peccato ceciderat. Utraque operatus est filius Verbum Dei existens, a Patre descendens et incarnatus, et usque ad mortem descendens, et dispensationem consummans salutis nostræ.

Being the Son of God always with the Father, and being made man, he reconciled or gathered up in himself the long-continued exposing of men, [unto sin and judgment] bringing in salvation in this compendious way [in this summary of it], that what we had lost in Adam—that is, our being in the image and likeness of God—we should recover in Christ. For it was not possible that man that had been once conquered and broken by disobedience, should by himself be reformed, and obtain the crown of victory; nor, again, was it possible that he should recover salvation who had fallen under sin. Both were wrought by the Son, the Word of God, who, descending from the Father, and being incarnate, submitted himself to death, perfecting the dispensation of our salvation.

And Clemens Alexandrinus to the same purpose (*Adhort. ad Gentes.*) Ναί φήμι ὁ λόγος ὁ τοῦ Θεοῦ ἄνθρωπος γενομένος, ἵνα δὲ καὶ σὺ παρὰ ἀνθρώπου μάθης, τῆ ποτε ἄρα ἄνθρωπος γένεται Θεός. —'The Word of God was made man, that you mightest learn of a man how man may become [as] God.' And Ambrose, in Ps. 118. Octonar. decim.:

> Imago [id est, Verbum Dei] ad eum qui est ad imaginem [hoc est, hominem] venit, et quærit imago eum qui est ad similitudinem sui, ut iterum signet, ut iterum confirmet, quia amiseras quod accepisti.

> The image of God, that is, the Word of God, came to him who was after the image of God, that is man. And this image of God seeks him who was after the image of God, that he might seal him with it again, and confirm him, because you hadst lost that which you hadst received.

And Augustine in one instance gives a rational account why it was condecent to divine wisdom that the Son, and not the Father or the Holy Spirit, should be incarnate—which we also inquire into (*Lib. de Definitionibus Orthodoxæ Fidei sive de Ecclesiastica Dogmatibus*, cap. 2):

> Non Pater carnem assumpsit, neque Spiritus Sanctus, set Filius tantum; ut qui erat in divinitate Dei Patris Filius, ipse fieret in homine hominis matris Filius; ne Filii nomen ad alterum transiret, qui non esset æternâ nativitate filius.

> The Father did not assume flesh, nor the Holy Spirit, but the Son only; that he who in the Deity was the Son of the Father, should be made the Son of man, in his mother of human race; that the name of the Son should not pass to any other, who was not the Son by an eternal nativity.

I shall close with one meditation of the same author, concerning the wisdom and righteousness of God in this mystery (*Enchirid. ad Laurent.*, cap. 99.):

Vide—universum genus humanum tam justo judicio Divino in apostaticâ radice damnatum, ut etiam si nullus inde liberaretur, nemo recte possit Dei vituperare justitiam; et qui liberantur, sic oportuisse liberari, ut ex pluribus non liberatis, atque in damnatione justissimâ derelictis, ostenderetur, quod meruisset universa conspersio, et quò etiam istos debitum judicium Dei duceret, nisi ejus indebita misericordia subveniret.'

Behold, the whole race of mankind, by the just judgment of God, so condemned in the apostatical root, that if no one were thence delivered, yet no man could rightly complain of the justice of God; and that those who are freed, ought so to be freed, that, from the greater number who are not freed, but left under most righteous condemnation, it might be manifest what the whole mass had deserved, and whither the judgment of God due to them would lead them, if his mercy, which was not due, did not relieve them.

The reader may see what is discoursed to these purposes: and because the great end of the description given of the person of Christ, is that we may love him, and thereby be transformed into his image, I shall close this preface with the words of Jerome, concerning that divine love to Christ which is at large declared.

Sive legas,' says he, 'sive scribas, sive vigiles, sive dormias, amor tibi semper buccina in auribus sonet, hic lituus excitet animam tuam, hoc amore furibundus; quære in lectulo tuo, quem desiderat anima tua (Epist. 66. ad Pammach., cap. 10).

Whether you read or write, whether you watch or sleep, let the voice of love (to Christ) sound in your ears; let this trumpet stir up your soul: being overpowered (brought into an ecstasy) with this love, seek Him on your bed whom your soul desires and longs for.

1

'YOU ARE THE CHRIST'

Our blessed Saviour, inquiring of his disciples their apprehensions concerning his person, and their faith in him, Simon Peter—as he was usually the forwardest on all such occasions, through his peculiar endowments of faith and zeal—returns an answer in the name of them all (Matt. 16:16): 'And Simon Peter answered and said, You are the Christ, the Son of the living God.'

Baronius, and sundry others of the Roman Church, do all affirm that the Lord Christ did herein prescribe the form of a general council. 'For here,' say they, 'the principal article of our Christian faith was declared and determined by Peter, whereunto all the rest of the apostles, as in duty they were obliged, did give their consent and suffrage.' This was done, as they suppose, that a rule and law might be given to future ages, how to enact and determine articles of faith. For it is to be done by the successors of Peter presiding in councils, as it was now done by Peter in this assembly of Christ and his apostles.

But they seem to forget that Christ himself was now present, and therefore could have no vicar, seeing he presided in his own person. All the claim they lay to the necessity of such a visible head of the church on the earth, as may determine articles of faith, is from the absence of Christ since his ascension into heaven. But that he should also have a substitute whilst he was present, is somewhat uncouth; and whilst they live, they shall never make the pope president where Christ is present. The truth is, he does not propose to his disciples the framing of an article of truth, but inquires after their own faith, which they expressed in this confession. Such things as these will prejudice, carnal interest, and the prepossession of the minds of men with corrupt imaginations, cause them to adventure on, to the scandal, yea, ruin of religion!

This short but illustrious confession of Peter, comprises eminently the whole truth concerning the person and office of Christ—of his person, in that although he was the Son of man (under which appellation he made his inquiry, 'Whom do men say that I, the Son of man, am?') yet was he not only so, but the eternal Son of the living God—of his office, that he was the Christ, he whom God had anointed to be the Saviour of the church, in the discharge of his kingly, priestly, and prophetic power. Instances of the like brief confessions we have elsewhere in the Scripture: 'If you shall confess with your mouth the Lord Jesus, and shall believe in your heart that God has raised him from the dead, you shall be saved' (Rom. 10:9). 'Every spirit that confesses that Jesus Christ is come in the flesh is of God: and every spirit that confesses not that Jesus Christ is come in the flesh is not of God' (1 John 4:2–3). And it is manifest, that all divine truths have such a concatenation among themselves, and do all of them so centre in the person of Christ—as vested with his offices towards the church—that they are all virtually comprised in this confession, and they will be so as counted by all who destroy them not by contrary errors and imaginations inconsistent with them, though it be the duty of all men to obtain the express knowledge of them in particular, according to the means thereof which they do enjoy. The danger of men's souls lies not in a disability to attain a comprehension of longer or more subtile confessions of faith, but in embracing things contrary to, or inconsistent with, this foundation thereof. Whatever it be whereby men cease to hold the Head, how small soever it seem, that alone is pernicious (Col. 2:18–19).

'Blessed Are You'

This confession, therefore—as containing the sum and substance of that faith which they were called to give testimony to, and concerning which their trial was approaching—is approved by our Saviour. And not only so, but eminent privileges are granted to him that made it, and in him to the whole church, that should live in the same faith and confession: 'And Jesus answered and said to him, Blessed are you, Simon Bar-jona: for flesh and blood has not revealed it to you, but my Father which is in heaven. And I say also to you, that you are Peter, and upon this rock I will build my church; and the gates of hell shall not prevail against it' (v. 17–18).

Two things our Saviour considers in the answer returned to his inquiry: 1. The faith of Peter in this confession—the faith of him that made it; 2. The nature and truth of the confession: both which are required in all the disciples of Christ—'For with the heart man believes to righteousness; and with the mouth confession is made to salvation' (Rom. 10:10).

Peter's Faith

The first thing which he speaks to is the faith of Peter, who made this confession. Without this no outward confession is of any use or advantage. For even the devils knew him to be the Holy One of God (Luke 4:34); yet would he not permit them to speak it (Mark 1:34). That which gives glory to God in any confession, and which gives us an interest in the truth confessed, is the believing of the heart, which is to righteousness. With respect hereunto the Lord Christ speaks: 'And Jesus answered and said to him, Blessed art you, Simon Bar-jona: for flesh and blood has not revealed it to you, but my Father which is in heaven' (v. 17).

He commends and sets forth the faith of Peter—(1.) From its effect; (2.) From its cause.

Its effect was, that it made him blessed in whom it was. For it is not only a blessed thing to believe and know Jesus Christ, as it is called life eternal (John 17:3); but it is that which gives an immediate interest in the blessed state of adoption, justification, and acceptance with God (John 1:12).

The immediate cause of this faith is divine revelation. It is not the effect or product of our own abilities, the best of which are but flesh and blood. That faith which renders them blessed in whom it is, is wrought in them by the power of God revealing Christ to their souls. Those who have more abilities of their own to this end than Peter had, we are not concerned in.

Peter Is not the Rock

He speaks to the confession itself, acquainting his disciples with the nature and use of it, which, from the beginning, he principally designed: 'And I say also to you, that you are Peter, and upon this rock I will build my church; and the gates of hell shall not prevail against it' (v. 18).

From the speaking of these words to Peter, there is a controversy raised in the world, whether the Lord Christ himself, or the pope of Rome, be the rock whereon the church is built. And to that state are things come in religion, among them that are called Christians, that the greatest number are for the pope and against Christ in this matter. And they have good reason for their choice. For if Christ be the rock whereon the church is built, whereas he is a living stone, those that are laid and built on him must be lively stones also, as this apostle assures us (1 Pet. 2:4–5), they must be like to Christ himself, partaking of his nature, quickened by his Spirit, so, as it were, to be bone of his bones, and flesh of his flesh (Eph. 5:30). Nor can any be built on him but by a living faith, effectual in universal obedience. These things the

...the fabric of the living temple on this foundation is usually but small, seldom conspicuous or outwardly glorious.

generality of men like not at all; and, therefore, the fabric of the living temple on this foundation is usually but small, seldom conspicuous or outwardly glorious. But if the pope be this rock, all the Papists in the world, or all that have a mind so to be—be they ever so wicked and ungodly—may be built upon him, and be made partakers of all that deliverance from the powers of hell which that rock can afford them. And all this may be obtained at a very easy rate; for the acknowledgment of the pope's sovereign authority in the church is all that is required thereunto. How they bring in the claim of their pope by Peter, his being at Rome, being bishop of Rome, dying at Rome, fixing his chair at Rome, devoting and transmitting all his right, title, power, and authority, every thing but his faith, holiness, and labour in the ministry, to the pope, I shall not here inquire; I have done it elsewhere. Here is fixed the root of the tree, which is grown great, like that in Nebuchadnezzar's dream, until it is become a receptacle for the beasts of the field and fowls of the air—sensual men and unclean spirits. I shall, therefore, briefly lay an axe to the root of it, by evidencing that it is not the person of Peter who confessed Christ, but the person of Christ whom Peter confessed, that is the rock on which the church is built.

Christ's Language

The variation of the expressions proves undeniably that our Saviour intended we should not understand the person of Peter to be the rock. He takes occasion from his name to declare what he designed, but no more: 'And I say also to you, You are Peter.' He had given him this name before, at his first calling (John 1:42). Now he gives the reason of his so doing; viz., because of the illustrious confession that he should make of the rock of the church; as the name of God under the Old Testament was called on persons, and things, and places, because of some especial relation to him. Wherefore, the expression is varied on purpose to declare, that whatever be the signification of the name Peter, yet the person so called was not the rock intended. The words are, Σὺ εἶ Πέτρος, καὶ ἐπὶ ταύτῃ τῇ πέτρᾳ. Had he intended the person of Peter, he would have expressed it plainly, Σὺ εἶ πέτρος, καὶ ἐπὶ σοὶ, κ. τ. λ.—'You are a rock, and on you will I build.' At least the gender had not been altered, but he would have said, Ἐπὶ τούτῳ τῷ πέτρῳ, which would have given some colour to this imagination. The exception which they lay hereunto, from the use of Cephas in the Syriac, which was the name of Peter, and signified a rock or a stone, lies not only against the authentic authority of the Greek original, but of their own translation of it, which reads the words, 'Tu es Petrus, et super hanc petram.'

Peter Died

If the church was built on the person of Peter, then when he died the church must utterly fail. For no building can possibly abide when its foundation is removed and taken away. Wherefore they tell us they do not intend by the person of Peter, that singular and individual person alone to be this rock; but that he and his successors the bishops of Rome are so. But this story of his successors at Rome is a shameful fable. If the pope of Rome be a true believer, he succeeds, in common with all other believers, to the privileges which belong to this confession; if he be not, he has neither lot nor portion in this matter. But the pretence is utterly vain on another account also. The apostle, showing the insufficiency of the Aaronical priesthood—wherein there was a succession of God's own appointment—affirms, that it could not bring the church to a perfect state, because the high priests died one after another, and so were many (Heb. 7:8, 23–4). And thereon he shows that the church cannot be consummated or perfected, unless it rest wholly in and on him who lives forever, and was made a priest 'after the power of an endless life.' And if the Holy Ghost judged the state of the Jewish Church to be weak and imperfect—because it rested on high priests that died one after another, although their succession was expressly ordained of God himself—shall we suppose that the Lord Christ, who came to consummate the church, and to bring it to the most perfect estate whereof in this world it is capable, should build it on a succession of dying men, concerning which succession there is not the least intimation that it is appointed of God? And as to the matter of fact, we know both what interruptions it has received, and what monsters it has produced—both sufficiently manifesting that it is not of God.

One Rock and One Foundation

There is but one rock, but one foundation. There is no mention in the Scripture of two rocks of the church. In what others invent to this purpose we are not concerned. And the rock and the foundation are the same; for the rock is that whereon the church is built, that is the foundation. But that the Lord Christ is this single rock and foundation of the church, we shall prove immediately. Wherefore, neither Peter himself, nor his pretended successors, can be this rock. As for any other rock, it belongs not to our religion; they that have framed it may use it as they please. For they that make such things are like to the things they make; so is every one that trusts in them (Ps. 115:8). 'But their rock is not as our rock, themselves being judges;' unless they will absolutely equal the pope to Jesus Christ.

Christ's Death Laid the Foundation

Immediately after this declaration of our Saviour's purpose to build his church on the rock, he reveals to his disciples the way and manner how he would lay its foundation, viz., in his death and sufferings (v. 21). And thereon this supposed rock, being a little left to his own stability, showed himself to be but a 'reed shaken with the wind.' For he is so far from putting himself under the weight of the building, that he attempts an obstruction of its foundation. He began to rebuke Christ himself for mentioning his sufferings, wherein alone the foundation of the gospel church was to be laid (v. 22). And hereon he received the severest rebuke that ever the Lord Jesus gave to any of his disciples (v. 23). And so it is known that afterward—through surprisal and temptation—he did what lay in him to recall that confession which here he made, and whereon the church was to be built. For, that no flesh might glory in itself, he that was singular in this confession of Christ, was so also in the denial of him. And if he in his own person manifested how unmeet he was to be the foundation of the church, they must be strangely infatuated who can suppose his pretended successors so to be. But some men will rather have the church to be utterly without any foundation, than that it should not be the pope.

The vanity of this pretence being removed, the substance of the great mystery contained in the attestation given by our Saviour to the confession of Peter, and the promise whereunto annexed, may be comprised in the ensuing assertions:

1. The person of Christ, the Son of the living God, as vested with his offices, whereunto he was called and anointed, is the foundation of the church, the rock whereon it is built.
2. The power and policy of hell will be always engaged in opposition to the relation of the church to this foundation, or the building of it on this rock.
3. The church that is built on this rock shall never be disjoined from it, or prevailed against by the opposition of the gates of hell.

The two former of these I shall speak briefly to, my principal design being the demonstration of a truth that arises from the consideration of them all.

A Twofold Foundation

The foundation of the church is twofold (1.) Real; (2.) Doctrinal. And in both ways, Christ alone is the foundation. The real foundation of the church he is, by virtue of the mystical union of it to him, with all the benefits whereof, from thence and thereby, it is made partaker. For thence alone has it spiritual life, grace, mercy, perfection, and glory (Eph. 4:15–16; Col. 2:19). And he is the doctrinal foundation of it, in that the faith or doctrine concerning him and his offices is that divine truth which in a peculiar manner animates and constitutes the church of the New Testament (Eph. 2:19–22). Without the faith and confession hereof, no one person belongs to that church. I know not what is now believed, but I judge it will not yet be denied, that the external formal cause of the Church of the New Testament, is the confession of the faith concerning the person, offices, and grace of Christ, with what is of us required thereon. In what sense we assert these things will be afterwards fully cleared.

That the Lord Christ is thus the foundation of the church, is testified to: 'Thus says the Lord God, Behold, I lay in Zion for a foundation a stone, a tried stone, a precious cornerstone, a sure foundation: he that believes shall not make haste' (Isa. 28:16). It is among the bold inroads that in this late age have been made on the vitals of religion, that some, in compliance with the Jews, have attempted the application of this promise to Hezekiah. The violence they have offered herein to the mind of the Holy Ghost, might be evidenced from every word of the context. But the interpretation and application of the last words of this promise by the apostles, leaves no pretence to this insinuation. 'He that believes on him shall not be ashamed' or 'confounded' (Rom. 9:33; 10:11; 1 Pet. 2:6); that is, he shall be eternally saved—which it is the highest blasphemy to apply to any other but Jesus Christ alone. He, therefore, is alone that foundation which God has laid in and of the church (See Ps. 118:22; Matt. 21:42; Mark 12:10; Luke 20:17; Acts 4:11; 1 Pet. 2:4; Eph. 2:20–22; Zech. 3:9). But this fundamental truth—of Christ being the only foundation of the church—is so expressly determined by the apostle Paul, as not to need any farther confirmation: 'For other foundation can no man lay than that is laid, which is Jesus Christ' (1 Cor. 3:11).

2

THE GATES OF HELL

There are in the words of our Saviour to Peter concerning the foundation of the church, a promise of its preservation, and a prediction of the opposition that should be made thereunto. And, accordingly, all things are come to pass, and carrying on towards a complete accomplishment. For (that we may begin with the opposition foretold) the power and policy of hell ever were, and ever will be, engaged in opposition to the church built on this foundation—that is, the faith of it concerning his person, office, and grace, whereby it is built on him. This, as to what is past, concerns matter of fact, whereof, therefore, I must give a brief account; and then we shall examine what evidences we have of the same endeavour at present.

The gates of hell, as all agree, are the power and policy of it, or the actings of Satan, both as a lion and as a serpent, by rage and by subtlety. But whereas in these things he acts not visibly in his own person, but by his agents, he has always had two sorts of them employed in his service. By the one he executes his rage, and by the other his craft; he animates the one as a lion, the other as a serpent. In the one he acts as the dragon, in the other as the beast that had two horns like the lamb, but spake like the dragon. The first is the unbelieving world; the other, apostates and seducers of all sorts. Wherefore, this work in this kind is of a double nature—the one, an effect of his power and rage, acted by the world in persecution—the other, of his policy and craft, acted by heretics in seduction. In both he designs to separate the church from its foundation.

POWER AND RAGE

The opposition of the first sort he began against the person of Christ immediately in his human nature. Fraud first he once attempted in his temptation (Matt. 4), but quickly found that that way he could make no approach to him. The prince of this world came, but had nothing in him. Wherefore he betook himself to open force, and, by all means possible, sought his destruction. So also the more at any time the church is by faith and watchfulness secured against seduction, the more he rages against it in open persecution. And (for the example and comfort of the church in its conformity to Christ) no means were left unattempted that might instigate and prepare the world for his ruin. Reproaches, contempt, scorn, false and lying accusations—by his suggestions—were heaped on him on every hand. Hereby, in the whole course of his ministry, he 'endured the contradiction of sinners against himself' (Heb. 12:3). And there is herein blessed provision made of inestimable consolation, for all those who are 'predestinated to be conformed to his image,' when God shall help them by faith to make use of his example. He calls them to take up his cross and follow him; and he has showed them what is in it, by his own bearing of it. Contempt, reproach, despiteful usage, calumnies, false accusations, wrestings of his words, blaspheming of his doctrine, reviling of his person, all that he said and did as to his principles about human government and moral conversation, encompassed him all his days. And he has assured his followers, that such, and no other (at least for the most part), shall be their lot in this world.

And some in all ages have an experience of it in an eminent manner. But have they any reason to complain? Why should the servant look for better measure than the Master met withal? To be made like to him in the worst of evils, for his sake, is the best and most honourable condition in this world. God help some to believe it! Hereby was way made for his death. But, in the whole, it was manifested how infinitely, in all his subtlety and malice, Satan falls short of the contrivances of divine wisdom and power. For all that he attained by effecting his death, in the hour of darkness, was but the breaking of his own head, the destruction of his works, with the ruin of his kingdom; and what yet remains to consummate his eternal misery, he shall himself work out in his opposition to the church. His restless malice and darkness will not suffer him to give over the pursuit of his rage, until nothing remains to give him a full entrance into endless torments—which he hastens every day. For when he shall have filled up the measure of his sins, and of the sins of the world in being instrumental to his rage, eternal judgment shall put all things to their issue. Through that shall he, with the world, enter into everlasting flames—and the whole church, built on the rock, into rest and glory.

No sooner did the Church of the New Testament begin to arise on this foundation, but the whole world of Jews and Gentiles set themselves with open force to destroy it. And all that they contended with the church about, was their faith and confession of it, that 'Jesus was the Christ, the Son of the living God.' This foundation they would cast it from, or exterminate it out of the earth. What were the endeavours of the gates of hell in this kind—with what height of rage, with what bloody and inhuman cruelties they were exercised and executed—we have some obscure remembrance, in the stories that remain from the martyrdom of Stephen to the days of Constantine. But although there be enough remaining on record, to give us a view of the insatiable malice of the old murderer, and an astonishing representation of human nature degenerating into his image in the perpetration of all horrid, inhuman cruelties—yet is it all as nothing in comparison of that prospect which the last day will give of them, when the earth shall disclose all the blood that it has received, and the righteous Judge shall lay open all the contrivances for its effusion, with the rage and malice wherewith they were attended. The same rage continues yet unallayed in its principles. And although God in many places restrain and shut it up in his providence, by the circumstances of human affairs, yet—as it has the least advantage, as it finds any door open to it—it endeavours to act itself in lesser or higher degrees. But whatever dismal appearance of things there may be in the world, we need not fear the ruin of the church by the most bloody oppositions. Former experiences will give security against future events. It is built on the rock, and those gates of hell shall not prevail against it.

Policy and Craft

The second way whereby Satan attempted the same end, and yet continues so to do, was by pernicious errors and heresies. For all the heresies wherewith the church was assaulted and pestered for some centuries of years, were oppositions to their faith in the person of Christ. I shall briefly reflect on the heads of this opposition, because they are now, after a revolution of so many ages, lifting up themselves again, though under new vizards and pretences. And they were of three sorts.

Substitutes for Christ

That which introduced other doctrines and notions of divine things, absolutely exclusive of the person and mediation of Christ. Such was that of the Gnostic, begun as it is supposed by Simon the magician. A sort of people they were, with whom the first churches, after the decease of the apostles, were exceedingly pestered, and the faith of many was overthrown. For instead of Christ and God in him reconciling the world to himself, and the obedience of faith thereon according to the gospel, they introduced endless fables, genealogies, and conjugations of deities, or divine powers; which practically issued in this, that Christ was such an emanation of light and knowledge in them as made them perfect—that is, it took away all differences of good and evil, and gave them liberty to do what they pleased, without sense of sin, or danger of punishment. This was the first way that Satan attempted the faith of the church, viz., by substituting a perfecting light and knowledge in the room of the person of Christ. And, for aught I know, it may be one of the last ways whereby he will endeavour the accomplishment of the same design. Nor had I made mention of these pernicious imaginations which have lain rotting in oblivion for so many generations, but that some again endeavour to revive them, at least so far as they were advanced and directed against the faith and knowledge of the person of Christ.

Denials of Christ's Deity

Satan attempted the same work by them who denied his divine nature—that is, in effect, denied him to be the Son of the living God, on the faith whereof the church is built. And these were of two sorts.

Openly

Such as plainly and openly denied him to have any pre-existence to his conception and birth of the holy Virgin. Such were the Ebionites, Samosatanians, and Photinians. For they all affirmed him to be a mere man, and no more, though miraculously conceived and born of the Virgin, as some of them granted; (though denied, as it is said, by the Ebionites;) on which account he was called the Son of God. This attempt lay directly against the everlasting rock, and would have substituted sand in the room of it. For no better is the best of human nature to make a foundation for the church, if not united to the divine. Many in those days followed those pernicious ways; yet the foundation of God stood sure, nor was the church moved from it. But yet, after a revolution of so many ages, is the same endeavour again engaged in. The old enemy, taking advantage of the prevalence of Atheism and profaneness among those that are called Christians, does again employ the same engine to overthrow the faith of the church—and that with more subtlety than formerly—in the Socinians. For their faith, or rather unbelief, concerning the person of Christ, is the same with those before mentioned. And what a vain, wanton generation admire and applaud in their sophistical reasonings, is no more but what the primitive church triumphed over through faith, in the most subtle management of the Samosatanians, Photinians, and others. An evidence it is that Satan is not unknowing to the workings of that vanity and darkness, of those corrupt affections in the minds of men, whereby they are disposed to a contempt of the mystery of the gospel. Who would have thought that the old exploded pernicious errors of the Samosatanians, Photinians, and Pelagians, against the power and grace of Christ, should enter on the world again with so much ostentation and triumph as they do at this day? But many men, so far as I can observe, are fallen into such a dislike of the Christ of God, that every thing concerning his person, Spirit, and grace, is an abomination to them. It is not want of understanding to comprehend doctrines, but hatred to the things themselves, whereby such persons are seduced. And there is nothing of this nature whereunto nature, as corrupted, does not contribute its utmost assistance.

> *...what a vain, wanton generation admire and applaud in their sophistical reasonings, is no more but what the primitive church triumphed over through faith*

Subtly

There were such as opposed his divine nature, under pretence of declaring it another way than the faith of the church did rest in. So was it with the Arians, in whom the gates of hell seemed once to be near a prevalency. For the whole professing world almost was once surprised into that heresy. In words they acknowledged his divine person; but added, as a limitation of that acknowledgment, that the divine nature which he had was originally created of God, and produced out of nothing; with a double blasphemy, denying him to be the true God, and making a god of a mere creature. But in all these attempts, the opposition of the gates of hell to the church respected faith in the person of Christ as the Son of the living God.

DENIALS OF HIS HUMAN NATURE

By some his human nature was opposed—for no stone did Satan leave unturned in the pursuit of his great design. And that which in all these things he aimed at, was the substitution of a false Christ in the room of Him who, in one person, was both the Son of man and the Son of the living God. And herein he infected the minds of men with endless imaginations. Some denied him to have any real human nature, but to have been a phantasm, an appearance, a dispensation, a mere cloud acted by divine power; some, that he was made of heavenly flesh, brought from above, and which (as some also affirmed) was a parcel of the divine nature. Some affirmed that his body was not animated, as ours are, by a rational soul, but was immediately acted by the power of the Divine Being, which was to it in the room of a living soul; some, that his body was of an ethereal nature, and was at length turned into the sun; with many such diabolical delusions. And there yet want not attempts, in these days, of various sorts, to destroy the verity of his human nature; and I know not what some late fantastical opinions about the nature of glorified bodies may tend to. The design of Satan, in all these pernicious imaginations, is to break the cognation and alliance between Christ in his human nature and the church, whereon the salvation of it absolutely depends.

OPPOSITION TO THE HYPOSTATIC UNION

He raised a vehement opposition against the hypostatic union, or the union of these two natures in one person. This he did in the Nestorian heresy, which greatly, and for a long time, pestered the church. The authors and promoters of this opinion granted the Lord Christ to have a divine nature, to be the Son of the living God.

They also acknowledged the truth of his human nature, that he was truly a man, even as we are. But the personal union between these two natures they denied. A union, they said, there was between them, but such as consisted only in love, power, and care. God did, as they imagined, eminently and powerfully manifest himself in the man Christ Jesus—had him in an especial regard and love, and did act in him more than in any other. But that the Son of God assumed our nature into personal subsistence with himself—whereby [the] whole Christ was one person, and all his mediatory acts were the acts of that one person, of him who was both God and man—this they would not acknowledge. And this pernicious imagination, though it seem to make great concessions of truth, does no less effectually evert the foundation of the church than the former. For, if the divine and human nature of Christ do not constitute one individual person, all that he did for us was only as a man—which would have been altogether insufficient for the salvation of the church, nor had God redeemed it with his own blood. This seems to be the opinion of some amongst us, at this day, about the person of Christ. They acknowledge the being of the eternal Word, the Son of God; and they allow in the like manner the verity of his human nature, or own that man Christ Jesus. Only they say, that the eternal Word was in him and with him, in the same kind as it is with other believers, but in a supreme degree of manifestation and power. But, though in these things there is a great endeavour to put a new colour and appearance on old imaginations, the design of Satan is one and the same in them all, viz., to oppose the building of the church upon its proper, sole foundation. And these things shall be afterwards expressly spoken to.

I intend no more in these instances but briefly to demonstrate, that the principal opposition of the gates of hell to the church lay always to the building of it, by faith, on the person of Christ.

It were easy also to demonstrate that Mohammedanism, which has been so sore a stroke to the Christian profession, is nothing but a concurrence and combination of these two ways, of force and fraud, in opposition to the person of Christ.

It is true that Satan, after all this, by another way, attempted the doctrine of the offices and grace of Christ, with the worship of God in him. And this he has carried so far, as that it issued in a fatal antichristian apostasy; which is not of my present consideration.

But we may proceed to what is of our own immediate concern. And the one work with that before described is still carried on. The person of Christ, the faith of the church concerning it, the relation of the church to it, the building of the church on it, the life and preservation of the church thereby, are the things that the gates of hell are engaged in opposition to.

Socinians

It is known with what subtlety and urgency his divine nature and person are opposed by the Socinians. What an accession is made daily to their incredulity, what inclination of mind multitudes do manifest towards their pernicious ways, are also evident to all who have any concern in or for religion. But this argument I have laboured in on other occasions.

Natural Religion

Many, who expressly deny not his divine person, yet seem to grow weary of any concern therein. A natural religion, or none at all, pleases them better than faith in God by Jesus Christ. That any thing more is necessary in religion, but what natural light will discover and conduct us in, with the moral duties of righteousness and honesty which it directs to, there are too many that will not acknowledge. What is beyond the line of nature and reason is rejected as unintelligible mysteries or follies. The person and grace of Christ are supposed to breed all the disturbance in religion. Without them, the common notions of the Divine Being and goodness will guide men sufficiently to eternal blessedness. They did so before the coming of Christ in the flesh, and may do so now he is gone to heaven.

Objective Religion

There are some who have so ordered the frame of objective religion, as that it is very uncertain whether they leave any place for the person of Christ in it or no. For, besides their denial of the hypostatic union of his natures, they ascribe all that to a light within them which God will effect only by Christ as a mediator. What are the internal actings of their minds, as to faith and trust towards him, I know not; but, from their outward profession, he seems to be almost excluded.

Inadequate Regard for Christ

There are not a few who pretend high to religion and devotion, who declare no erroneous conceptions about the doctrine of the person of Christ, who yet manifest themselves not to have that regard to him which the gospel prescribes and requires. Hence have we so many discourses published about religion, the practical holiness and duties of obedience, written with great elegance of style, and seriousness in argument, wherein we can meet with little or nothing wherein Jesus Christ, his office, or his grace, are concerned. Yea, it is odds, but in them all, we shall meet with some reflections on those who judge them to be the life and centre of our religion. The things of Christ, beyond the example of his conversation on the earth, are of no use with such persons, to the promotion of piety and gospel obedience. Concerning many books of this nature, we may say what a learned person did of one of old: 'There were in it many things laudable and delectable, *sed nomen Jesu non erat ibi.*'

Five Marks of Contempt for Christ-Centred Religion

Suited to these manifest inclinations of the minds of men to a neglect of Christ, in the religion they frame to themselves—dangerous and noxious insinuations concerning what our thoughts ought to be of him, are made and tendered.

1. It is scandalously proposed and answered, 'Of what use is the consideration of the person of Christ in our religion?' Such are the novel inquiries of men who suppose there is any thing in Christian religion wherein the person of Christ is of no consideration—as though it were not the life and soul that animates the whole of it, that which gives it its especial form as Christian—as though by virtue of our religion we received any thing from God, any benefit in mercy, grace, privilege, or glory, and not through the person of Christ—as though any one duty or act of religion towards God could be acceptably performed by us, without a respect to, or a consideration of, the person of Christ—or that there were any lines of truth in religion as it is Christian, that did not relate thereunto. Such bold inquiries, with futilous answers annexed to them, sufficiently manifest what acquaintance their authors have either with Christ himself, which in others they despise, or with his gospel, which they pretend to embrace.

2. A mock scheme of religion is framed, to represent the folly of them who design to learn the mind and will of God in and by him.

3. Reproachful reflections are made on such as plead the necessity of acquaintance with him, or the knowledge of him, as though thereby they rejected the use of the gospel.

4. Professed love to the person of Christ is traduced, as a mere fancy and vapour of distempered minds or weak imaginations.

5. The union of the Lord Christ and his church is asserted to be political only, with respect to laws and rules of government. And many other things of an alike nature are asserted, derogatory to his glory, and repugnant to the faith of the church; such as, from the foundation of Christian religion, were never vented by any persons before, who did not openly avow some impious heresy concerning his person. And I no way doubt but that men may, with less guilt and scandal, fall under sundry doctrinal misapprehensions concerning it—than, by crying hail thereunto, to despoil it of all its glory, as to our concern therein, in our practical obedience to God. Such things have we deserved to see and hear.

Contempt for Preaching Christ

The very name or expression of 'preaching Christ' is become a term of reproach and contempt; nor can some, as they say, understand what is meant thereby, unless it be an engine to drive all rational preaching, and so all morality and honesty, out of the world.

Neglect of Gospel Duties

That which all these things tend to and centre in, is that horrible profaneness of life—that neglect of all gospel duties—that contempt of all spiritual graces and their effects, which the generality of them that are called Christians, in many places, are given up to. I know not whether it were not more for the honour of Christ, that such persons would publicly renounce the profession of his name, rather than practically manifest their inward disregard to him.

That by these and the like means Satan does yet attempt the ruin of the church, as to its building on the everlasting rock, falls under the observation of all who are concerned in its welfare. And (whatever others may apprehend concerning this state of things in the world) how any that love the Lord Jesus in sincerity—especially such as are called to declare and represent him to men in the office of the ministry—can acquit themselves to be faithful to him, without giving their testimony against, and endeavouring to stop what lies in them, the progress of this prevailing declension from the only foundation of the church, I know not; nor will it be easy for themselves to declare. And in that variety of conceptions which are about him, and the opposition that is made to him, there is nothing more necessary than that we should renew and attest our confession of him—as the Son of the living God—the only rock whereon the church of them that shall be saved is founded and built.

'Pauca ideo de Christo,' as Tertullian speaks; some few things concerning the person of Christ, with respect to the confession of Peter, and the promise thereunto annexed—wherein he is declared the sole foundation of the church—will be comprised in the ensuing discourse. And He who has ordained strength out of the mouths of babes and sucklings, as he has given ability to express these poor, mean contemplations of his glory, can raise by them a revenue of honour to himself in the hearts of them that do believe. And some few things I must premise, in general, to what I do design.

1. The instances which I shall give concerning the use and consideration of the person of Christ in Christian religion, or of him as he is the foundation whereon the church is built, are but few—and those perhaps not the most signal or eminent which the greater spiritual wisdom and understanding of others might propose. And, indeed, who shall undertake to declare what are the chief instances of this incomprehensible effect of divine wisdom? 'What is his name, and what is his son's name, if you can tell?' (Prov. 30:4. See Isa. 9:6). It is enough for us to stand in a holy admiration, at the shore of this unsearchable ocean, and to gather up some parcels of that divine treasure wherewith the Scripture of truth is enriched.

2. I make no pretence of searching into the bottom or depths of any part of this 'great mystery of godliness, God manifest in the flesh.' They are altogether unsearchable, to the line of the most enlightened minds, in this life. What we shall farther comprehend of them in the other world, God only knows. We cannot in these things, by our utmost diligent search, 'find out the Almighty to perfection.' The prophets could not do so of old, nor can the angels themselves at present, who 'desire to look into these things' (1 Pet. 1:10–12). Only I shall endeavour to represent to the faith of them that do believe, somewhat of what the Scripture does plainly reveal—evidencing in what sense the person of Christ is the sole foundation of the church.

3. I shall not, herein, respect them immediately by whom the divine person of Christ is denied and opposed. I have formerly treated thereof, beyond their contradiction in way of reply. But it is their conviction which I shall respect herein, who, under an outward confession of the truth, do—either notionally or practically, either ignorantly or designedly, God knows, I know

not—endeavour to weaken the faith of the church in its adherence to this foundation. Howbeit, neither the one sort nor the other has any place in my thoughts, in comparison of the instruction and edification of others, who love the Lord Jesus Christ in sincerity.

THE MOST GLORIOUS EFFECT OF DIVINE WISDOM

The person of Christ is the most glorious and ineffable effect of divine wisdom, grace, and power; and therefore is the next foundation of all acceptable religion and worship. The divine being itself is the first formal reason, foundation, and object of all religion. It all depends on taking God to be our God; which is the first of his commands. For religion, and the worship performed in it, is nothing but the due respect of rational creatures to the divine nature, and its infinite excellencies. It is the glorifying of God as God; the way of expressing that respect being regulated by the revelation of his will. Yet the divine essence is not, in itself, the next and immediate cause of religious worship. But it is the manifestation of this being and its excellencies, wherewith the mind of rational creatures is immediately affected, and whereby it is obliged to give that religious honour and worship which is due to that being, and necessary from our relation thereunto. Upon this manifestation, all creatures capable by an intelligent nature of a sense thereof, are indispensably obliged to give all divine honour and glory to God.

The way alone whereby this manifestation may be made, is by outward acts and effects. For, in itself, the divine nature is hid from all living, and dwells in that light whereunto no creature can approach. This, therefore, God first made, by the creation of all things out of nothing. The creation of man himself—with the principles of a rational, intelligent nature, a conscience attesting his subordination to God—and the creation of all other things, declaring the glory of his wisdom, goodness, and power, was the immediate ground of all natural religion, and yet continues so to be. And the glory of it answers the means and ways of the manifestation of the divine being, existence, excellencies, and properties. And where this manifestation is despised or neglected, there God himself is so; as the apostle discourses at large (Rom. 1:18–22).

THE MYSTERY OF GODLINESS

But of all the effects of the divine excellencies, the constitution of the person of Christ as the foundation of the new creation, as 'the mystery of godliness,' was the most ineffable and glorious. I speak not of his divine person absolutely; for his distinct personality and subsistence was by an internal and eternal act of the divine being in the person of the Father, or eternal generation—which is essential to the divine essence—whereby nothing anew was outwardly wrought or did exist. He was not, he is not, in that sense, the effect of the divine wisdom and power of God, but the essential wisdom and power of God himself. But we speak of him only as incarnate, as he assumed our nature into personal subsistence with himself. His conception in the womb of the virgin, as to the integrity of human nature, was a miraculous operation of the divine power. But the prevention of that nature from any subsistence of its own—by its assumption into personal union with the Son of God, in the first instance of its conception—is that which is above all miracles, nor can be designed by that name. A mystery it is, so far above the order of all creating or providential operations, that it wholly transcends the sphere of them that are most miraculous. Herein did God glorify all the properties of the divine nature, acting in a way of infinite wisdom, grace, and condescension. The depths of the mystery hereof are open only to him whose understanding is infinite, which no created understanding can comprehend. All other things were produced and effected by an outward emanation of power from God. He said, 'Let there be light, and there was light.' But this assumption of our nature into hypostatic union with the Son of God, this constitution of one and the same individual person in two natures so infinitely distinct as those of God and man—whereby the eternal was made in time, the infinite became finite, the immortal mortal, yet continuing eternal, infinite, immortal—is that singular expression of divine wisdom, goodness, and power, wherein God will be admired and glorified to all eternity. Herein was that change introduced into the whole first creation, whereby the blessed angels were exalted, Satan and his works ruined, mankind recovered from a dismal apostasy, all things made new, all things in heaven and earth reconciled and gathered into one head, and a revenue of eternal glory raised to God, incomparably above what the first constitution of all things in the order of nature could yield to him.

In the expression of this mystery, the Scripture does sometimes draw the veil over it, as that which we cannot look into. So, in his conception of the virgin, with respect to this union which accompanied it, it was told her, that 'the power of the Highest should overshadow her' (Luke 1:35). A work it was of the power of the Most High, but hid from the eyes of men in the nature of it; and, therefore, that holy thing which had no subsistence of its own, which should be born of her, should 'be called the Son of God,' becoming one person with him. Sometimes it expresses the greatness of the mystery, and leaves it as an object of our admiration: 'without controversy, great is the mystery of godliness: God was manifest in the flesh' (1 Tim. 3:16). A mystery it is, and that of those dimensions as no creature can comprehend. Sometimes it puts things together, as that the distance of the two natures illustrate the glory of the one person: 'The Word was made flesh, and dwelt among us' (John 1:14). But what Word was this? That which was in the beginning, which was with God, which was God, by whom all things were made, and without whom was not any thing made that was made; who was light and life. This Word was made flesh, not by any change of his own nature or essence, not by a transubstantiation of the divine nature into the human, not by ceasing to be what he was, but by becoming what he was not, in taking our nature to his own, to be his own, whereby he dwelt among us. This glorious Word, which is God, and described by his eternity and omnipotence in works of creation and providence, 'was made flesh'—which expresses the lowest state and condition of human nature. Without controversy, great is this mystery of godliness! And in that state wherein he visibly appeared as so made flesh, those who had eyes given them from above, saw 'his glory, the glory as of the only-begotten of the Father.' The eternal Word being made flesh, and manifested therein, they saw his glory, the glory of the only-begotten of the Father. What heart can conceive, what tongue can express, the least part of the glory of this divine wisdom and grace? So also is it proposed to us, 'Unto us a child is born, to us a son is given: and the government shall be upon his shoulders: and his name shall be called Wonderful, Counsellor, the mighty God, the everlasting Father, the Prince of Peace' (Isa. 9:6). He is called, in the first place, Wonderful. And that deservedly (Prov. 30:4). That the mighty God should be a child born, and the everlasting Father a son given to us, may well entitle him to the name of Wonderful.

Some amongst us say, that if there were no other way for the redemption and salvation of the church, but this only of the incarnation and mediation of the Son of God, there was no wisdom in the contrivance of it. Vain man indeed would be wise, but is like the wild ass's colt. Was there no wisdom in the contrivance of that which, when it is effected, leaves nothing but admiration to the utmost of all created wisdom? Who has known the mind of the Lord in this thing, or who has been his counsellor in this work, wherein the mighty God became a child born to us, a son given to us? Let all vain imaginations cease: there is nothing left to the sons of men, but either to reject the divine person of Christ—as many do to their own destruction—or humbly to adore the mystery of infinite wisdom and grace therein. And it will require a condescending charity, to judge that those do really believe the incarnation of the Son of God, who live not in the admiration of it, as the most adorable effect of divine wisdom.

The glory of the same mystery is elsewhere testified to: 'God has spoken to us by his Son, by whom also he made the worlds; who, being the brightness of his glory, and the express image of his person, upholding all things by the word of his power, by himself purged our sin' (Heb. 1:1–3). That he purged our sins by his death, and the oblation of himself therein to God, is acknowledged. That this should be done by him by whom the worlds were made, who is the essential brightness of the divine glory, and the express image of the person of the Father therein who upholds, rules, sustains all things by the word of his power, whereby God purchased his church with his own blood (Acts 20:28), is that wherein he will be admired to eternity (see Phil. 2:6–9).

In Isaiah 6 there is a representation made of him as on a throne, filling the temple with the train of his glory. The Son of God it was who was so represented, and that as he was to fill the temple of his human nature with divine glory, when the fulness of the godhead dwelt in him bodily. And herein the seraphim, which administered to him, had six wings, with two whereof they covered their faces, as not being able to behold or look into the glorious mystery of his incarnation (vv. 2–3; John 12:39–41; 2:19; Col. 2:9). But when the same ministering spirits, under the name of cherubim, attended the throne of God, in the administration of his providence as to the disposal and government of the world, they had four wings only, and covered not their faces, but steadily beheld the glory of it (Ezek. 1:6; 10:2–3).

The Foundation of the Christian Religion

This is the glory of the Christian religion—the basis and foundation that bears the whole superstructure—the root whereon it grows. This is its life and soul, that wherein it differs from, and inconceivably excels, whatever was in true religion before, or whatever any false religion pretended to. Religion, in its first constitution, in the estate of pure, uncorrupted nature, was orderly, beautiful and glorious. Man being made in the image of God, was fit and able to glorify him as God. But whereas, whatever perfection God had communicated to our nature, he had not united it to himself in a personal union, the fabric of it quickly fell to the ground. Want of this foundation made it obnoxious to ruin. God manifested herein, that no gracious relation between him and our nature could be stable and permanent, unless our nature was assumed into personal union and subsistence with himself. This is the only rock and assured foundation of the relation of the church to God, which, now, can never utterly fail. Our nature is eternally secured in that union, and we ourselves (as we shall see) thereby. 'In him all things consist' (Col. 1:17–18); wherefore, whatever beauty and glory there was in the relation that was between God and man, and the relation of all things to God by man—in the preservation whereof natural religion did consist—it had no beauty nor glory in comparison of this which does excel, or the manifestation of God in the flesh—the appearance and subsistence of the divine and human natures in the same single individual person. And whereas God in that state had given man dominion 'over the fish of the sea, and over the fowl of the air, and over the cattle, and over all the earth' (Gen. 1:26), it was all but an obscure representation of the exaltation of our nature in Christ—as the apostle declares (Heb. 2:6–9).

There was true religion in the world after the fall, both before and after the giving of the law; a religion built upon and resolved into divine revelation. And as for the outward glory of it—the administration that it was brought into under the tabernacle and temple—it was beyond what is represented in the institutions of the gospel. Yet is Christian religion, our evangelic profession, and the state of the church thereon, far more glorious, beautiful, and perfect, than that state of religion was capable of, or could attain. And as this is evident from hence, because God in his wisdom, grace, and love to the church, has removed that state, and introduced this in the room thereof; so the apostle proves it—in all considerable instances—in his Epistle to the Hebrews, written to that purpose. There were two things, before, in religion—the promise, which was the life of it; and the institutions of worship under the law, which were the outward glory and beauty of it. And both these were nothing, or had nothing in them, but only what they before proposed and represented of Christ, God manifested in the flesh. The promise was concerning him, and the institutions of worship did only represent him. So the apostle declares it (Col. 2:17). Wherefore, as all the religion that was in the world after the fact was built on the promise of this work of God, in due time to be accomplished; so it is the actual performance of it which is the foundation of the Christian religion, and which gives it the pre-eminence above all that went before it. So the apostle expresses it (Heb. 1:1–3):

> God, who at sundry times, and in divers manners, spake in time past to the fathers by the prophets, has in these last days spoken to us by his Son, whom he has appointed heir of all things, by whom also he made the worlds; who, being the brightness of his glory, and the express image of his person, and upholding all things by the word of his power, when he had by himself purged our sins, sat down on the right hand of the Majesty on high.

All false religion pretended always to things that were mysterious. And the more men could invent, or the devil suggest, that had an appearance of that nature, as sundry things were so introduced horrid and dreadful, the more reverence and esteem were reconciled to it. But the whole compass of the craft of Satan and the imaginations of men could never extend itself to the least resemblance of this mystery. And it is not amiss conjectured, that the apostle, in his description of it (1 Tim. 3:16), did reflect upon and condemn the vanity of the Eleusinian mysteries, which were of the greatest vogue and reputation among the gentiles.

Take away the consideration hereof, and we despoil the Christian religion of all its glory, debasing it to what Mohammedanism pretends to, and to what in Judaism was really enjoyed.

FAITH RESTS IN THE INCOMPREHENSIBLE

The faith of this mystery enables the mind wherein it is—rendering it spiritual and heavenly, transforming it into the image of God. Herein consists the excellency of faith above all other powers and acts of the soul—that it receives, assents to, and rests in, things in their own nature absolutely incomprehensible. It is ἔλεγχος οὐ βλεπομένων (Heb. 11:1)—'The evidence of things not seen'—that which makes evident, as by demonstration, those things which are no way objected to sense, and which reason cannot comprehend. The more sublime and glorious—the more inaccessible to sense and reason—the things are which we believe; the more are we changed into the image of God, in the exercise of faith upon them. Hence we find this most glorious effect of faith, or the transformation of the mind into the likeness of God, no less real, evident, and eminent in many, whose rationally comprehensive abilities are weak and contemptible, in the eye of that wisdom which is of this world, than in those of the highest natural sagacity, enjoying the best improvements of reason. For 'God has chosen the poor of this world rich in faith, and heirs of the kingdom' (James 2:5). However they may be poor, and, as another apostle speaks, 'foolish, weak, base, and despised' (1 Cor. 1:27–8); yet that faith which enables them to assent to and embrace divine mysteries, renders them rich in the sight of God, in that it makes them like to him.

Some would have all things that we are to believe to be levelled absolutely to our reason and comprehension—a principle which, at this day, shakes the very foundations of the Christian religion. It is not sufficient, they say, to determine that the faith or knowledge of any thing is necessary to our obedience and salvation, that it seems to be fully and perspicuously revealed in the Scripture—unless the things so revealed be obvious and comprehensible to our reason; an apprehension which, as it arises from the pride which naturally ensues on the ignorance of God and ourselves, so it is not only an invention suited to debase religion, but an engine to evert the faith of the church in all the principal mysteries of the gospel—especially of the Trinity and the incarnation of the Son of God. But faith which is truly divine, is never more in its proper exercise—does never more elevate the soul into conformity to God—than when it acts in the contemplation and admiration of the most incomprehensible mysteries which are proposed to it by divine revelation.

Hence things philosophical, and of a deep rational indagation, find great acceptance in the world—as, in their proper place, they do deserve. Men are furnished with proper measures of them, and they find them proportionate to the principles of their own understandings. But as for spiritual and heavenly mysteries, the thoughts of men for the most part recoil, upon their first proposal, nor will be encouraged to engage in a diligent inquiry into them— yea, commonly reject them as foolish, or at least that wherein they are not concerned. The reason is that given in another case by the apostle: 'All men have not faith' (2 Thess. 3:2), which makes them absurd and unreasonable in the consideration of the proper objects of it. But where this faith is, the greatness of the mysteries which it embraces heightens its efficacy, in all its blessed effects, upon the soul. Such is this constitution of the person of Christ, wherein the glory of all the holy properties and perfections of the divine nature is manifested, and shines forth. So speaks the apostle: 'Beholding as in a glass the glory of the Lord, we are changed into the same image, from glory to glory' (2 Cor. 3:18). This glory which we behold, is the glory of the face of God in Jesus Christ (ch. 4:6), or the glorious representation which is made of him in the person of Christ, whereof we shall treat afterwards. The glass wherein this glory is represented to us—proposed to our view and contemplation—is divine revelation in the gospel. Herein we behold it, by faith alone. And those whose view is steadfast, who most abound in that contemplation by the exercise of faith, are thereby 'changed into the same image, from glory to glory'—or are more and more renewed and transformed into the likeness of God, so represented to them.

Faith and Sight Have the Same Object

That which shall, at last, perfectly effect our utmost conformity to God, and, therein, our eternal blessedness—is vision, or sight.

'We shall be like him, for we shall see him as he is' (1 John 3:2). Here faith begins what sight shall perfect hereafter. But yet 'we walk by faith, and not by sight' (2 Cor. 5:7). And although the life of faith and vision differ in degrees—or, as some think, in kind— yet have they both the same object, and the same operations, and there is a great cognation between them. The object of vision is the whole mystery of the divine existence and will; and its operation is a perfect conformity to God—a likeness to him— wherein our blessedness shall consist. Faith has the same object, and the same operations in its degree and measure. The great and incomprehensible mysteries of the divine being—of the will and wisdom of God—are its proper objects; and its operation, with respect to us, is conformity and likeness to him. And this it does, in a peculiar manner, in the contemplation of the glory of God in the face of Jesus Christ; and herein we have our nearest approaches to the life of vision, and the effects of it. For therein, 'beholding the glory of God in the face of Jesus Christ, we are changed into the same image, from glory to glory;' which, perfectly to consummate, is the effect of sight in glory. The exercise of faith herein does more raise and perfect the mind—more dispose it to holy, heavenly frames and affections—than any other duty whatever.

To be nigh to God, and to be like to him, are the same. To be always with him, and perfectly like him, according to the capacity of our nature, is to be eternally blessed. To live by faith in the contemplation of the glory of God in Christ, is that initiation into both, whereof we are capable in this world. The endeavours of some to contemplate and report the glory of God in nature—in the works of creation and providence—in the things of the greater and the lesser world—do deserve their just commendation; and it is that which the Scripture in sundry places calls us to. But for any there to abide, there to bound their designs—when they have a much more noble and glorious object for their meditations, viz., the glory of God in Christ—is both to despise the wisdom of God in that revelation of himself, and to come short of that transforming efficacy of faith in the contemplation hereof, whereby we are made like to God. For hereunto alone does it belong, and not to any natural knowledge, nor to any knowledge of the most secret recesses of nature.

I shall only say, that those who are inconversant with these objects of faith—whose minds are not delighted in the admiration of, and acquiescence in, things incomprehensible, such as is this constitution of the person of Christ—who would reduce all things to the measure of their own understandings, or else wilfully live in the neglect of what they cannot comprehend—do not much prepare themselves for that vision of these things in glory, wherein our blessedness consists.

How Faith Finds Rest and Peace

Moreover, this constitution of the person of Christ being the most admirable and ineffable effect of divine wisdom, grace, and power, it is that alone which can bear the weight of the whole superstructure of the mystery of godliness—that whereinto the whole sanctification and salvation of the church is resolved—wherein alone faith can find rest and peace. 'Other foundation can no man lay than that is laid, which is Jesus Christ' (1 Cor. 3:11). Rest and peace with God is that which we seek after. 'What shall we do to be saved?' In this inquiry, the acts of the mediatory office of Christ are, in the gospel, first presented to us—especially his oblation and intercession. Through them is he able to save to the uttermost those that come to God by him. But there were oblations for sin, and intercessions for sinners, under the Old Testament; yet of them all does the apostle affirm, that they could not make them perfect that came to God by them, not take away conscience condemning for sin (Heb. 10:1–4). Wherefore, it is not these things in themselves that can give us rest and peace, but their relation to the person of Christ. The oblation and intercession of any other would not have saved us. Hence, for the security of our faith, we are minded that 'God redeemed the church with his own blood' (Acts 20:28). He did so who was God, as he was manifested in the flesh. His blood alone could purge our consciences from dead works, who did offer himself to God, through the eternal Spirit (Heb. 9:14). And when the apostle—for our relief against the guilt of sin—calls us to the consideration of intercession and propitiation, he minds us peculiarly of his person by whom they are performed: 'If any man sin, we have an advocate with the Father, Jesus Christ the righteous: and he is the propitiation for our sins' (1 John 2:1–2). And we may briefly consider the order of these things.

1. We suppose, in this case, conscience to be awakened to a sense of sin, and of apostasy from God thereby. These things are now generally looked on as of no great concern to us—by some made a mock of—and, by the most, thought easy to be dealt withal—at time convenient. But when God fixes an apprehension of his displeasure for them on the soul—if it be not before it be too late—it will cause men to look out for relief.

2. This relief is proposed in the gospel. And it is the death and mediation of Christ alone. By them peace with God must be obtained, or it will cease for ever.

3. But, when any person comes practically to know how great a thing it is for an apostate sinner to obtain the remission of sins, and an inheritance among them that are sanctified, endless objections through the power of unbelief will arise to his disquiet.

4. Wherefore, that which is principally suited to give him rest, peace, and satisfaction—and without which nothing else can so do—is the due consideration of, and the acting of faith upon, this infinite effect of divine wisdom and goodness, in the constitution of the person of Christ. This at first view will reduce the mind to that conclusion, 'If you can believe, all things are possible.' For what end cannot be effected hereby? What end cannot be accomplished that was designed in it? Is any thing too hard for God? Did God ever do any thing like this, or make use of any such means for any other end whatever? Against this no objection can arise. On this consideration of him, faith apprehends Christ to be—as he is indeed—the power of God, and the wisdom of God, to the salvation of them that do believe; and therein does it find rest with peace.

4

THE FOUNDATION OF ALL THE COUNSELS OF GOD

Secondly, the person of Christ is the foundation of all the counsels of God, as to his own eternal glory in the vocation, sanctification, and salvation of the church. That which I intend is what the apostle expresses (Eph. 1:9–10): 'Having made known to us the mystery of his will, according to his good pleasure, which he has purposed in himself: that in the dispensation of the fulness of times, he might gather together in one all things in Christ, both which are in heaven, and which are on earth; even in him.' The 'mysteries of the will of God, according to his good pleasure which he purposed in himself'—are his counsels concerning his own eternal glory, in the sanctification and salvation of the church here below, to be united to that above. The absolute original hereof was in his own good pleasure, or the sovereign acting of his wisdom and will. But it was all to be effected in Christ—which the apostle twice repeats: he would gather 'all things into a head in Christ, even in him'—that is, in him alone.

THE SON — 'SET UP FROM EVERLASTING'

Thus it is said of him, with respect to his future incarnation and work of mediation, that the Lord possessed him in the beginning of his way, before his works of old; that he was set up from everlasting, from the beginning, or ever the earth was (Prov. 8:22–3). The eternal personal existence of the Son of God is supposed in these expressions, as I have elsewhere proved. Without it, none of these things could be affirmed of him. But there is a regard in them, both to his future incarnation, and the accomplishment of the counsels of God thereby. With respect thereunto, God 'possessed him in the beginning of his way, and set him up from everlasting.' God possessed him eternally as his essential wisdom—as he was always, and is always, in the bosom of the Father, in the mutual ineffable love of the Father and Son, in the eternal bond of the Spirit. But he signally possessed him 'in the beginning of his way'—as his wisdom, acting in the production of all the ways and works that are outwardly of him. The 'beginning of God's ways,' before his works, are his counsels concerning them—even as our counsels are the beginning of our ways, with respect to future works. And he 'set him up from everlasting,' as the foundation of all the counsels of his will, in and by whom they were to be executed and accomplished.

So it is expressed: 'I was by him, as one brought up with him; and I was daily his delight, rejoicing always before him; rejoicing in the habitable part of his earth; and my delights were with the sons of men' (vv. 30–31). And it is added, that thus it was before the foundation of the world was laid, or the chiefest part of the dust of the earth was made—that is, man was created. Not only was the delight of the Father in him, but his delight was in the habitable part of the earth, and among the sons of men—before the creation of the world. Wherefore, the eternal prospect of the work he had to do for the children of men is intended herein. In and with him, God laid the foundation of all his counsels concerning his love towards the children of men. And two things may be observed herein.

Not in His Divine Nature but in His Person

That the person of the Son 'was set up,' or exalted herein. 'I was set up,' says he, 'from everlasting.' This cannot be spoken absolutely of the person of the Son himself—the Divine nature being not capable of being so set up. But there was a peculiar glory and honour belonging to the person of the Son, as designed by the Father to the execution of all the counsels of his will. Hence was that prayer of his upon the accomplishment of them (John 17:5): 'And now, O Father, glorify me with your own self, with the glory which I had with you before the world was.' To suppose that the Lord Christ prays, in these words, for such a real communication of the properties of the divine nature to the human as should render it immense, omniscient, and unconfined to any space—is to think that he prayed for the destruction, and not the exaltation of it. For, on that supposition, it must necessarily lose all its own essential properties, and consequently its being. Nor does he seem to pray only for the manifestation of his divine nature, which was eclipsed in his exinanition or appearance in the form of a servant. There was no need to express this by—the 'glory which he had with the Father before the world was.' For he had it not, in any especial manner, before the world was; but equally from eternity, and in every moment of time. Wherefore, he had a peculiar glory of his own, with the Father, before the world was. And this was no other but that especial exaltation which he had when he was 'set up from everlasting,' as the foundation of the counsels of God, for the salvation of the church. In those eternal transactions that were between the Father and the Son, with respect to his incarnation and mediation—or his undertaking to execute and fulfill the eternal counsels of the wisdom and grace of the Father—there was an especial glory which the Son had with him—the 'glory which he had with the Father before the world was.' For the manifestation hereof he now prays and that the glory of his goodness, grace, and love—in his peculiar undertaking of the execution of the counsels of God—might be made to appear. And this is the principal design of the gospel. It is the declaration, as of the grace of God the Father, so of the love, grace, goodness, and compassion of the Son, in undertaking from everlasting the accomplishment of God's counsels, in the salvation of the church. And hereby does he hold up the pillars of the earth, or support this inferior creation, which otherwise, with the inhabitants of it, would by sin have been dissolved. And those by whom the eternal, divine pre-existence, in the form of God—antecedent to his incarnation—is denied, do what lies in them expressly to despoil him of all that glory which he had with the Father before the world was. So we have herein the whole of our design. 'In the beginning of God's ways, before his works of old' that is, in his eternal counsels with respect to the children of men, or the sanctification and salvation of the church— the Lord possessed, enjoyed the Son, as his eternal wisdom—in and with whom they were laid, in and by whom they were to be accomplished, wherein his delights were with the sons of men.

The Eternal Delight of the Father and the Son

That there was an ineffable delight between the Father and the Son in this his setting up or exaltation. 'I was,' says he, 'daily his delight, rejoicing always before him.' It is not absolutely the mutual, eternal delight of the Father and the Son—arising from the perfection of the same divine excellencies in each person—that is intended. But respect is plainly had to the counsels of God concerning the salvation of mankind by him who is his power and wisdom to that end. This counsel of peace was originally between Jehovah and the Branch (Zech. 6:13), or the Father and the Son—as he was to be incarnate. For therein was he 'fore-ordained before the foundation of the world;' (1 Pet. 1:20), viz., to be a Saviour and a deliverer, by whom all the counsels of God were to be accomplished; and this by his own will, and concurrence in counsel with the Father. And such a foundation was laid of the salvation of the church in these counsels of God—as transacted between the Father and the Son—

that it is said, that 'eternal life was promised before the world began' (Tit. 1:2). For, although the first formal promise was given after the fall, yet was there such a preparation of grace and eternal life in these counsels of God, with his unchangeable purpose to communicate them to us, that all the faithfulness of God was engaged in them. 'God, that cannot lie, promised before the world began.' There was eternal life with the Father—that is, in his counsel treasured up in Christ, and in him afterwards manifested to us (1 John 1:2). And, to show the stability of this purpose and counsel of God, with the infallible consequence of his actual promise, and efficacious accomplishment thereof, 'grace' is said to be 'given us in Christ Jesus before the world began' (2 Tim. 1:9).

In these counsels did God delight—or in the person of Christ, as his eternal wisdom in their contrivance, and as the means of their accomplishment in his future incarnation. Hence he so testifies of him: 'Behold my servant, whom I uphold; my elect, in whom my soul delights' (Isa. 42:1); as he also proclaims the same delight in him, from heaven, in the days of his flesh (Matt. 3:17; 17:5). He was the delight of God, as he in whom all his counsel for his own glory, in the redemption and salvation of the church were laid and founded: 'My servant, in whom I will be glorified' (Isa. 49:3); that is, 'by raising the tribes of Jacob, restoring the preserved of Israel, in being a light to the Gentiles, and the salvation of God to the ends of the earth' (v. 6).

We conceive not aright of the counsels of God, when we think of nothing but the effect of them, and the glory that arises from their accomplishment. It is certainly true that they shall all issue in his glory, and the demonstration of it shall fill up eternity. The manifestative glory of God to eternity, consists in the effects and accomplishment of his holy counsels. Heaven is the state of the actual accomplishment of all the counsels of God, in the sanctification and salvation of the church. But it is not with God as it is with men. Let men's counsels be ever so wise, it must needs abate of their satisfaction in them, because their conjectures (and more they have not) of their effects and events are altogether uncertain. But all the counsels of God having their entire accomplishment through revolutions perplexing and surpassing all created understandings, enclosed in them infallibly and immutably, the great satisfaction, complacency, and delight of the divine being is in these counsels themselves.

God delights in the actual accomplishment of his works. He made not this world, nor any thing in it, for its own sake. Much less did he make this earth to be a theatre for men to act their lusts upon—the use which it is now put to, and groans under. But he made 'all things for himself' (Prov. 16:4); he 'made them for his pleasure' (Rev. 4:11); that is, not only by an act of sovereignty, but to his own delight and satisfaction. And a double testimony did he give hereunto, with respect to the works of creation.

1. In the approbation which he gave of the whole upon its survey: and 'God saw all that he had made, and, behold, it was very good' (Gen. 1:31). There was that impression of his divine wisdom, power, and goodness upon the whole, as manifested his glory; wherein he was well pleased. For immediately thereon, all creatures capable of the conception and apprehension of his glory, 'sang forth his praise' (Job 38:6–7).
2. In that he rested from his works or in them, when they were finished (Gen. 2:2). It was not a rest of weariness from the labour of his work—but a rest of complacency and delight in what he had wrought—that God entered into.

But the principal delight and complacency of God, is in his eternal counsels. For all his delight in his works is but in the effects of those divine properties whose primitive and principal exercise is in the counsels themselves, from whence they proceed. Especially is it so as to these counsels of the Father and the Son, as to the redemption and salvation of the church, wherein they delight, and mutually rejoice in each other on their account. They are all eternal acts of God's infinite wisdom, goodness, and love—a delight and complacency wherein is no small part of the divine blessedness. These things are absolutely inconceivable to us, and ineffable by us; we cannot find the Almighty out to perfection. However, certain it is, from the notions we have of the divine being and excellencies, and from the revelation he has made of himself, that there is an infinite delight in God—in the eternal acting of his wisdom, goodness, and love—wherein, according to our weak and dark apprehensions of things, we may safely place no small portion of divine blessedness. Self-existence in its own immense being—thence self-sufficiency to itself in all things—and thereon self-satisfaction—is the principal notion we have of divine blessedness.

Acts of Infinite Wisdom

God delights in these his eternal counsels in Christ, as they are acts of infinite wisdom, as they are the highest instance wherein it will exert itself. Hence, in the accomplishment of them, Christ is emphatically said to be the 'Wisdom of God' (1 Cor. 1:24), he in whom the counsels of his wisdom were to be fulfilled. And in him is the manifold wisdom of God made known (Eph. 3:10). Infinite wisdom being that property of the divine nature whereby all the actings of it are disposed and regulated, suitably to his own glory, in all his divine excellencies—he cannot but delight in all the acts of it. Even amongst men—whose wisdom compared with that of God is folly itself—yet is there nothing wherein they have a real rational complacency, suitable to the principles of their nature, but in such actings of that wisdom which they have (and such as it is) towards the proper ends of their being and duty. How much more does God delight himself in the infinite perfection of his own wisdom, and its eternal acting for the representation of all the glorious excellencies of his nature! Such are his counsels concerning the salvation of the church by Jesus Christ; and because they were all laid in him and with him, therefore is he said to be his 'delight continually before the world was.' This is that which is proposed as the object of our admiration (Rom. 11:33–6).

Acts of Infinite Goodness

They are acts of infinite goodness, whereon the divine nature cannot but be infinitely delighted in them. As wisdom is the directive principle of all divine operations, so goodness is the communicative principle that is effectual in them. He is good, and he does good—yea, he does good because he is good, and for no other reason—not by the necessity of nature, but by the intervention of a free act of his will. His goodness is absolutely infinite, essentially perfect in itself; which it could not be if it belonged to it, naturally and necessarily, to act and communicate itself to any thing without God himself. The divine nature is eternally satisfied in and with its own goodness; but it is that principle which is the immediate fountain of all the communications of good to others, by a free act of the will of God. So when Moses desired to see his glory, he tells him that 'he will cause all his goodness to pass before him, and would be gracious to whom he would be gracious' (Exod. 33:19). All divine operations—in the gracious communication of God himself—are from his goodness, by the intervention of a free act of his will. And the greatest exercise and emanation of divine goodness, was in these holy counsels of God for the salvation of the church by Jesus Christ. For whereas in all other effects of his goodness he gives of his own, herein he gave himself, in taking our nature upon him. And thence, as he expresses the design of man in his fall, as upbraiding him with folly and ingratitude, 'Behold, the man is become as one of us' (Gen. 3:22), we may, with all humble thankfulness, express the means of our recovery, 'Behold, God is become like one of us,' as the apostle declares it at large (Phil. 2:6–8). It is the nature of sincere goodness—even in its lowest degree—above all other habits or principles of nature, to give a delight and complacency to the mind in the exercise of itself, and communication of its effects. A good man both delights in doing good, and has an abundant reward for the doing it, in the doing of it. And what shall we conceive concerning eternal, absolute, infinite, perfect, immixed goodness, acting itself in the highest instance (in an effect cognate and like to it) that it can extend to! So was it in the counsels of

God, concerning the incarnation of his Son and the salvation of the church thereby. No heart can conceive, no tongue can express, the least portion of that ineffable delight of the holy, blessed God, in these counsels, wherein he acted and expressed to the utmost his own essential goodness. Shall a liberal man devise liberal things, because they are suited to his inclination? Shall a good man find a secret refreshment and satisfaction in the exercise of that low, weak, imperfect, minced goodness, that his nature is inlaid withal? And shall not he whose goodness is essential to him—whose being it is, and in whom it is the immediate principle of communicating himself to others—be infinitely delighted in the highest exercise of it which divine wisdom did direct?

The effect of these eternal counsels of God in future glory is reserved for them that do believe; and therein will there be the nearest manifestation of the glory of God himself to them, when he 'shall be glorified in his saints,' and eternally 'admired in all that believe.' But the blessed delight and satisfaction of God, was, and is, in those counsels themselves, as they were acts of his infinite wisdom and goodness. Herein was the Lord Christ his 'delight continually before the foundation of the world,'—in that in him were all these counsels laid, and through him were they all to be accomplished. The constitution of his person was the only way whereby divine wisdom and goodness would act and communicate of themselves to mankind—in which actings are the eternal delight and complacency of the Divine Being.

Love and Grace

Love and grace have the same influence into the counsels of God, as wisdom and goodness have. And, in the Scripture notion of these things, they superadd to goodness this consideration—that their object is sinners, and those that are unworthy. God does universally communicate of his goodness to all his creatures, though there be an especial exercise of it towards them that believe. But as to his love and grace, as they are peculiar to his elect—the church chosen in Christ before the foundation of the world—so they respect them primarily in a lost, undone condition by sin. 'God commends his love towards us, in that, while we were yet sinners, Christ died for us' (Rom 5:8). 'God is love,' says the apostle. His nature is essentially so. And the best conception of the natural internal acting of the holy persons, is love; and all the acts of it are full of delight. This is, as it were, the womb of all the eternal counsels of God, which renders his complacency in them ineffable. Hence does he so wonderfully express his delight and complacency in the acting of his love towards the church: 'The Lord your God in the midst of you is mighty; he will save, he will rejoice over you with joy; he will rest in his love; he will joy over you with singing' (Zeph. 3:17). The reason why, in the salvation of the church, he rejoices with joy and joys with singing—the highest expression of divine complacency—is because he rests in his love, and so is pleased in the exercise of its effects.

How Divine Counsels Were Manifest in Christ

But we must return to manifest in particular how all these counsels of God were laid in the person of Christ—to which end the things ensuing may be distinctly considered.

God Made All Things Good

God made all things, in the beginning, good, exceeding good. The whole of his work was disposed into a perfect harmony, beauty, and order, suited to that manifestation of his own glory which he designed therein. And as all things had their own individual existence, and operations suited to their being, and capable of an end, a rest, or a blessedness, congruous to their natures and operations—so, in the various respects which they had each to other, in their mutual supplies, assistances, and co-operation, they all tended to that ultimate end—his eternal glory. For as, in their beings and existence, they were effects of infinite power—so were their mutual respects and ends disposed in infinite wisdom. Thereon were the eternal power and wisdom of God glorified in them; the one in their production, the other in their disposal into their order and harmony. Man was a creature that God made, that by him he might receive the glory that he aimed at in and by the whole inanimate creation—both that below, which was for his use, and that above, which was for his contemplation. This was the end of our nature in its original constitution. Whereunto are we again restored in Christ (James 1:18; Ps. 104:24; 136:5; Rom. 1:20).

GOD PERMITTED THE ENTRANCE OF SIN

God was pleased to permit the entrance of sin, both in heaven above and in earth beneath, whereby this whole order and harmony was disturbed. There are yet characters of divine power, wisdom, and goodness, remaining on the works of creation, and inseparable from their beings. But the primitive glory that was to redound to God by them—especially as to all things here below—was from the obedience of man, to whom they were put in subjection. Their good estate depended on their subordination to him in a way of natural use, as his did on God in the way of moral obedience (Gen. 1:26, 28; Ps. 8:6–8). Man, as was said, is a creature which God made, that by him he might receive the glory that he aimed at in and by the whole inanimate creation. This was the end of our nature in its original constitution. Whereunto are we again restored in Christ (James 1:18). But the entrance of sin cast all this order into confusion, and brought the curse on all things here below. Hereby were they deprived of that estate wherein they were declared exceeding good, and cast into that of vanity— under the burden whereof they groan, and will do so to the end (Gen. 3:17–18; Rom. 8:20–21). And these things we must again consider afterwards.

DIVINE WISDOM WAS NOT SURPRISED

Divine wisdom was no way surprised with this disaster. God had, from all eternity, laid in provisions of counsels for the recovery of all things into a better and more permanent estate than what was lost by sin. This is the ἀνάψυξις, the ἀποκατάστασις πάντων, the revivification, the restitution of all things (Acts 3:19, 21); the ἀνακεφαλαίωσις, or the gathering all things in heaven and earth into a new head in Christ Jesus (Eph. 1:10). For although, it may be, there is more of curiosity than of edification in a scrupulous inquiry into the method or order of God's eternal decrees or counsels, and the disposal of them into a subserviency one to another; yet this is necessary from the infinite wisdom, prescience, and immutability of God—that he is surprised with nothing, that he is put to no new counsels, by any events in the works of creation. All things were disposed by him into those ways and methods—and that from eternity—which conduce to, and certainly issue in, that glory which is ultimately intended. For as we are careful to state the eternal decrees of God, and the actual operations of his providence, so as that the liberty of the will of man, as the next cause of all his moral actions, be not infringed thereby—so ought we to be careful not to ascribe such a sacrilegious liberty to the wills of any creatures, as that God should be surprised, imposed on, or changed by any of their acting whatever. For 'known to him are all his works from the foundation of the world,' and with him there is neither 'variableness nor shadow of turning.'

A NEW ORDER

There were, therefore, eternal counsels of God, whereby he disposed all things into a new order, to his own glory, in the sanctification and salvation of the church. And of them two things may be considered: Their original; the design of their accomplishment.

(1.) Their first spring or original was in the divine will and wisdom alone, without respect to any external moving cause. No reason can be given, no cause be assigned, of these counsels, but the will of God alone. Hence are they called or described, by—the 'good pleasure which he purposed in himself' (Eph. 1:9), 'the purpose of him who works all things according to the counsel of his own will' (v. 11). 'Who has known the mind of the Lord? Or who has been his counsellor? Or who has first given to him, and it shall be recompensed to him again? For of him, and through him, and to him, are all things' (Rom. 11:34–6). The incarnation of Christ, and his mediation thereon, were not the procuring cause of these eternal counsels of God, but the effects of them, as the Scripture constantly declares. But (2.) The design of their accomplishment was laid in the person of the Son alone. As he was the essential wisdom of God, all things were at first created by him. But upon a prospect of the ruin of all by sin, God would in and by him—as he was fore-ordained to be incarnate—restore all things. The whole counsel of God to this end centred in him alone. Hence their foundation is rightly said to be laid in him, and is declared so to be by the apostle (Eph. 1:4). For the spring of the sanctification and salvation of the church lies in election, the decree whereof comprises the counsels of God concerning them. Herein, God from the beginning 'chooses us to salvation through sanctification of the Spirit' (2 Thess. 2:13); the one being the end he designs, the other the means and way thereof. But this he did in Christ; 'he chooses us in him before the foundation of the world, that we should be holy and without blame before him in love;' that is, 'unto salvation through sanctification of the Spirit.' In him we were not actually, nor by faith, before the foundation of the world; yet were we then chosen in him, as the only foundation of the execution of all the counsels of God concerning our sanctification and salvation.

Thus as all things were originally made and created by him, as he was the essential wisdom of God—so all things are renewed and recovered by him, as he is the provisional wisdom of God, in and by his incarnation. Therefore are these things put together and compared to his glory. He 'is the image of the invisible God, the first born of every creature: for by him were all things created that are in heaven, and that are in earth, visible and invisible; ... all things were created by him and for him: and he is before all things, and by him all things consist: and he is the head of the body, the church; who is the beginning, the firstborn from the dead; that in all things he might have the pre-eminence' (Col. 1:15–18).

A Twofold Foundation

Two things, as the foundation of what is ascribed to the Lord Christ in the ensuing discourse, are asserted (v. 15).—(1.) That he is 'the image of the invisible God.' (2.) That he is 'the firstborn of every creature;' things seeming very distant in themselves, but gloriously united and centring in his person.

The Image of the Invisible God

He is 'the image of the invisible God;' or, as it is elsewhere expressed, he is 'in the form of God'—his essential form, for other form there is none in the divine nature—the 'brightness of the glory, and the express image of the Father's person.' And he is called here the 'invisible God,' not absolutely with respect to his essence, though it be most true—the divine essence being absolutely invisible, and that equally, whether considered as in the Father or in the Son—but he is called so with respect to his counsels, his will, his love, and his grace. For so none has seen him at any time; but the only-begotten, which is in the bosom of the Father, he declares him (John 1:18). As he is thus the essential, the eternal image of the invisible God, his wisdom and power—the efficiency of the first creation, and its consistence being created, is ascribed to him: 'By him were all things created, that are in heaven, and that are in earth, visible and invisible' (Col. 1:17). And because of the great notions and apprehensions that were then in the world—especially among the Jews, to whom the apostle had respect in this epistle—of the greatness and glory of the invisible part of the creation in heaven above, he mentions them in particular, under the most glorious titles that any could, or then did, ascribe to them—'Whether they be thrones, or dominions, or principalities, or powers; all things were created by him, and for him'—the same expression that is used of God absolutely (Rom. 11:36; Rev. 4:11). Add hereunto those other places to this purpose (John 1:1–3; Heb. 1:1–3); and those that are not under the efficacy of spiritual infatuations, cannot but admire at the power of unbelief, the blindness of the minds of men, and the craft of Satan, in them who deny the divine nature of Jesus Christ. For whereas the apostle plainly affirms, that the works of the creation do demonstrate the eternal power and Godhead of him by whom they were created (Rom. 1:19–20), and not only so, but it is uncontrollably evident in the light of nature: it being so directly, expressly, frequently affirmed, that all things whatever, absolutely, and in their distributions into heaven and earth, with the things contained respectively in them, were made and created by Christ—is the highest rebellion against the light and teachings of God, to disbelieve his divine existence and power.

The Firstborn of Every Creature

Again it is added, that he is 'the firstborn of every creature;' which principally respects the new creation, as it is declared (v. 18) 'He is the head of the body, the church; who is the beginning, the first born from the dead; that in all things he might have the pre-eminence.' For in him were all the counsels of God laid for the recovery of all things to himself—as he was to be incarnate. And the accomplishment of these counsels of God by him the apostle declares at large in the ensuing verses. And these things are both conjoined and composed in this place. As God the Father did nothing in the first Creation but by him—as his eternal wisdom (John 1:3; Heb. 1:2; Prov. 8) so he designed nothing in the new creation, or restoration of all things to his glory, but in him—as he was to be incarnate. Wherefore in his person were laid all the foundation of the counsels of God for the sanctification and salvation of the church. Herein he is glorified, and that in a way unspeakably exceeding all that glory which would have accrued to him from the first creation, had all things abode in their primitive constitution.

His person, therefore, is the foundation of the church—the great mystery of godliness, or the religion we profess—the entire life and soul of all spiritual truth—in that all the counsels of the wisdom, grace, and goodness of God, for the redemption, vocation, sanctification, and salvation of the church, were all laid in him, and by him were all to be accomplished.

5

THE GREAT REPRESENTATIVE
OF GOD AND HIS WILL

What may be known of God, is—his nature and existence, with the holy counsels of his will. A representation of them to us is the foundation of all religion, and the means of our conformity to him—wherein our present duty and future blessedness do consist. For to know God, so as thereby to be made like to him, is the chief end of man. This is done perfectly only in the person of Christ, all other means of it being subordinate thereunto, and none of them of the same nature therewithal. The end of the Word itself, is to instruct us in the knowledge of God in Christ. That, therefore, which I shall now demonstrate, is, that in the person and mediation of Christ (which are inseparable, in all the respects of faith to him) there is made to us a blessed representation of the glorious properties of the divine nature, and of the holy counsels of the will of God. The first of these I shall speak to in this chapter—the other, in that which ensues; wherein we shall manifest how all divine truths do centre in the person of Christ and the consideration of sundry things is necessary to the explication hereof.

GOD IS ABSOLUTELY INCOMPREHENSIBLE

God, in his own essence, being, and existence, is absolutely incomprehensible. His nature being immense, and all his holy properties essentially infinite, no creature can directly or perfectly comprehend them, or any of them. He must be infinite that can perfectly comprehend that which is infinite; wherefore God is perfectly known to himself only—but as for us, how little a portion is heard of him! Hence he is called 'The invisible God,' and said to dwell in 'light inaccessible.' The subsistence of his most single and simple nature in three distinct persons, though it raises and ennobles faith in its revelation, yet it amazes reason which would trust to itself in the contemplation of it—whence men grow giddy who will own no other guide, and are carried out of the way of truth. 'No man has seen God at any time; the only-begotten Son, who is in the bosom of the Father, he has declared him' (John 1:18; 1 Tim. 6:16).

NO DIRECT APPREHENSION OF THE DIVINE ESSENCE

Therefore, we can have no direct intuitive notions or apprehensions of the divine essence, or its properties. Such knowledge is too wonderful for us. Whatever is pleaded for an intellectual vision of the essence of God in the light of glory, yet none pretend to a possibility of an immediate, full comprehension of it. But, in our present state, God is to us, as he was to Moses under all the external manifestations of his glory, 'in thick darkness' (Exod. 20:21). All the rational conceptions of the minds of men are swallowed up and lost, when they would exercise themselves directly on that which is absolutely immense, eternal, infinite. When we say it is so, we know not what we say, but only that it is not otherwise. What we deny of God, we know in some measure—but what we affirm we know not; only we declare what we believe and adore. 'Neque sensus

est ejus, neque phantsia, neque opinio, nec ratio, nec scientia,' says
Dionys (*De Divin. Nomine*, 1). We have no means—no corporeal,
no intellectual instrument or power—for the comprehension of
him; nor has any other creature: Ἐπεὶ αὐτὸ ὅπέρ ἐστιν ὁ Θεὸς, οὐ
μόνον προφῆται, ἀλλ᾽ οὐδὲ ἄγγελοι εἶδον, οὔτε ἀρχάγγελοι· αλλ᾽ ἐὰν
ἐρωτήσῃς αὐτοὺς, ἀκούσῃ περὶ μὲν τῆς οὐσίας οὐδὲν ἀποκρινομένους·
δόξα δὲ ἐν ὑψίστοις μόνον ᾄδόντας τω Θεῷ· κἂν παρὰ τῶν Χερουβὶμ
ἢ τῶν Σεραφὶμ ἐπιθυμήσῃς τι μαθεῖν, τὸ μυστικὸν τοῦ ἁγιασμοῦ
μέλος ἀκούσῃ, καὶ ὅτι πλήρης ὁ οὐρανὸς καὶ ἡ γῆ τῆς δόξης αὐτοῦ.
—'For that which is God' (the essence of God) 'not only have not
the prophets seen, but neither the angels nor the archangels. If
you will inquire of them, you shall hear nothing of the substance
of God, but only hear them say, Glory to God in the highest.' If
you ask the cherubim and seraphim, you shall only hear the praise
of holiness, The whole earth is full of his glory,' says Chrysostom,
on John 1:18. That God is in himself absolutely incomprehensible
to us, is a necessary effect of our infinite distance from him. But
as he externally represents himself to us, and by the notions which
are ingenerated in us by the effects of his properties, are our
conceptions of him (Ps. 19:1; Rom. 1:20). This is declared in the
answer given to that request of Moses: 'I beseech you, show me
your glory' (Exod. 33:18). Moses had heard a voice speaking to him,
but he that spoke was 'in thick darkness'—he saw him not. Glorious
evidences he gave of his majestatic presence, but no appearance
was made of his essence or person. Hereon Moses desires, for the
full satisfaction of his soul (as the nearer any one is to God the
more earnest will be his desire after the full fruition of him), that
he might have a sight of his glory—not of that created glory in
the tokens of his presence and power which he had beheld, but of
the glory of his essence and being. Through a transport of love to
God, he would have been in heaven while he was on the earth; yea,
desired more than heaven itself will afford, if he would have seen
the essence of God with his corporeal eyes. In answer hereunto
God tells him, that he cannot see his face and live; none can have
either bodily sight or direct mental intuition of the divine being.
But this I will do, says God, 'I will make my glory pass before you,

and you shall see my back parts' (Exod. 33:18–23). This is all that God would grant, viz., such external representations of himself, in the proclamation of his name, and created appearances of his glory, as we have of a man whose back parts only we behold as he passes by us. But as to the being of God, and his subsistence in the Trinity of persons, we have no direct intuition into them, much less comprehension of them.

We Cannot Even Comprehend Angels

It is evident, therefore, that our conceptions of God, and of the glorious properties of his nature, are both ingenerated in us and regulated, under the conduct of divine revelation, by reflections of his glory on other things, and representations of his divine excellencies in the effects of them. So the invisible things of God, even his eternal power and Godhead, are clearly seen, being manifested and understood by the things that are made (Rom. 1:20). Yet must it be granted that no mere creature, not the angels above, not the heaven of heavens, are meet or able to receive upon them such characters of the divine excellencies, as to be a complete, satisfactory representation of the being and properties of God to us. They are all finite and limited and so cannot properly represent that which is infinite and immense. And this is the true reason why all worship or religious adoration of them is idolatry. Yet are there such effects of God's glory in them, such impressions of divine excellencies upon them, as we cannot comprehend nor search out to perfection. How little do we conceive of the nature, glory, and power of angels! So remote are we from an immediate comprehension of the uncreated glory of God, as that we cannot fully apprehend nor conceive aright the reflection of it on creatures in themselves finite and limited. Hence, they thought of old, when they had seen an angel, that so much of the divine perfections had been manifested to them that thereon they must die (Judges 13:21–2). Howbeit, they come infinitely short of making any complete representation of God; nor is it otherwise with any creature whatever.

Men Desire a Fuller Representation of God

Mankind seem to have always had a common apprehension that there was need of a nearer and more full representation of God to them than was made in any of the works of creation or providence. The heavens indeed declared his glory, and the firmament always showed his handy-work—the invisible things of his eternal power and Godhead were continually made known by the things that are made; but men generally miscarried and missed it in the contemplation of them, as the apostle declares (Rom 1): For still they were influenced by a common presumption, that there must be a nearer and more evident manifestation of God—that made by the works of creation and providence being not sufficient to guide them to him. But in the pursuit hereof they utterly ruined themselves; they would do what God had not done. By common consent they framed representations of God to themselves; and were so besotted therein, that they utterly lost the benefit which they might have received by the manifestation of him in the works of the creation, and took up with most foolish imaginations. For whereas they might have learned from thence the being of God, his infinite wisdom, power, and goodness—viz., in the impressions and characters of them on the things that were made—in their own representations of him, they 'changed the glory of the invisible God into an image made like to corruptible man, and to birds, and four-footed beasts, and creeping things' (Rom. 1:23). Wherefore this common presumption—that there was no way to attain a due sense of the divine being but by some representation of it—though true in itself, yet, by the craft of Satan, and foolish superstitions of the minds of men, became the occasion of all idolatry and flagitious wickedness in the world. Hence were all those ἐπιφάνειαι, or supposed 'illustrious appearances' of their gods, which Satan deluded the Gentiles by; and hence were all the ways which they devised to bring God into human nature, or the likeness of it. Wherefore, in all the revelations that ever God made of himself, his mind and will, he always laid this practice of making representations of him under the most severe interdict and prohibition. And this he did evidently for these two reasons:

IMAGES OFFEND AGAINST GOD'S WISDOM AND SOVEREIGNTY

Because it was a bold and foolish entrenching upon his provisional wisdom in the case. He had taken care that there should be a glorious image and representation of himself, infinitely above what any created wisdom could find out. But as, when Moses went into the mount, the Israelites would not wait for his return, but made a calf in his stead; so mankind—refusing to wait for the actual exhibition of that glorious image of himself which God had provided—broke in upon his wisdom and sovereignty, to make some of their own. For this cause was God so provoked, that he gave them up to such stupid blindness, that in those things wherein they thought to show themselves wise, and to bring God nearer to them, they became contemptibly foolish—abased their nature, and all the noble faculties of their minds to hell, and departed to the utmost distance from God, whom they sought to bring near to them.

IMAGES ARE FALSE REPRESENTATIVES

Because nothing that can fall into the invention or imagination of men could make any other but false representations of him, and so substitute an idol in his place. His own immediate works have great characters of his divine excellencies upon them, though to us obscure and not clearly legible without the light of revelation. Somewhat he did, of old, represent of his glorious presence—though not of his being—in the visible institutions of his worship. But all men's inventions to this end, which are neither divine works of nature, nor divine institutions of worship, are all but false representations of God, and therefore accursed by him.

Wherefore it is granted, that God has placed many characters of his divine excellencies upon his works of creation and providence—many of his glorious presence upon the tabernacle and temple of old—but none of these things ever did or could give such a representation of him as wherein the souls of men might fully acquiesce, or obtain such conceptions of him as might enable them to worship and honour him in a due manner. They cannot, I say—by all that may be seen in them, and learned from them—represent God as the complete object of all our affections, of all the actings of our souls in faith, trust, love, fear, obedience, in that way whereby he may be glorified, and we may be brought to the everlasting fruition of him. This, therefore, is yet to be inquired after.

Doctrinal Revelation Insufficient

Wherefore, a mere external doctrinal revelation of the divine nature and properties, without any exemplification or real representation of them, was not sufficient to the end of God in the manifestation of himself. This is done in the Scripture. But the whole Scripture is built on this foundation, or proceeds on this supposition—that there is a real representation of the divine nature to us, which it declares and describes. And as there was such a notion on the minds of all men, that some representation of God, wherein he might be near to them, was necessary—which arose from the consideration of the infinite distance between the divine nature and their own, which allowed of no measures between them—so, as to the event, God himself has declared that, in his own way, such a representation was needful—unto that end of the manifestation of himself which he designed.

Only the Person of Christ Is Sufficient

For all this is done in the person of Christ. He is the complete image and perfect representation of the Divine Being and excellencies. I do not speak of it absolutely, but as God proposes himself as the object of our faith, trust, and obedience. Hence it is God, as the Father, who is so peculiarly represented in him and by him; as he says: 'He that has seen me has seen the Father' (John 14:9).

Unto such a representation two things are required—

1. That all the properties of the divine nature—the knowledge whereof is necessary to our present obedience and future blessedness—be expressed in it, and manifested to us.
2. That there be, therein, the nearest approach of the divine nature made to us, whereof it is capable, and which we can receive. And both these are found in the person of Christ, and therein alone.

In the person of Christ we consider both the constitution of it in the union of his natures, and the respect of it to his work of mediation, which was the end of that constitution.

His Person Shows All the Holy Properties of God

Therein, as so considered, is there a blessed representation made to us of all the holy properties of the nature of God—of his wisdom, his power, his goodness, grace, and love, his righteousness, truth, and holiness, his mercy and patience. As this is affirmed concerning them all in general, or the glory of God in them, which is seen and known only in the face of Christ, so it were easy to manifest the same concerning every one of them in particular, by express testimonies of Scripture. But I shall at present confine myself to the proofs of the whole assertion which do ensue.

The Nearest Approach of the Divine Nature

There is, therein, the most incomprehensible approach of the divine nature made to ours, such as all the imaginations of men did ever infinitely fall short of—as has been before declared. In the assumption of our nature into personal union with himself, and our cognition to God thereby, with the union which believers obtain with him thereon—being one in the Father and the Son, as the Father is in the Son, and the Son in the Father (John 17:20–21)—there is the nearest approach of the divine being to us that the nature of things is capable of. Both these ends were designed in those representations of God which were of human invention; but in both of them they utterly failed. For, instead of representing any of the glorious properties of the nature of God, they debased it, dishonoured it, and filled the minds of men with vile conceptions of it; and instead of bringing God nearer to them, they put themselves at an infinite moral distance from him. But my design is the confirmation of our assertions from the Scripture.

The Image of the Invisible God

'He is the image of the invisible God' (Col. 1:15). This title or property of 'invisible,' the apostle here gives to God, to show what need there was of an image or representation of him to us, as well as of one in whom he would declare the counsels of his will. For he intends not only the absolute invisibility of his essence, but his being unknown to us in himself. Wherefore (as was before observed), mankind was generally prone to make visible representations of this invisible God, that, in them, they might contemplate on him and have him present with them, as they foolishly imagined. To the craft of Satan abusing this inclination of mankind, idolatry owes its original and progress in the world: howbeit, necessary it was that this invisible God should be so represented to us by some image of him, as that we might know him, and that therein he might be worshipped according to his own mind and will. But this must be of his own contrivance—an effect of his own infinite wisdom. Hence, as he absolutely rejects all images and representations of him of men's devisings (for the reasons before mentioned), and declares that the honour that any should think would thereby redound to him was not given to him, but to the devil; so that which he has provided himself, to his own holy ends and purposes, is every way approved of him. For he will have 'all men honour the Son, even as they honour the Father;' and so as that 'he who honours not the Son, honours not the Father' (John 5:23).

This image, therefore, is the person of Christ; 'he is the image of the invisible God.' This, in the first place, respects the divine person absolutely, as he is the essential image of the Father: which must briefly be declared.

IN THE FATHER

The Son is sometimes said to be ἐν Πατρὶ, 'in the Father,' and the Father in the Son: 'Do you not believe that I am in the Father, and the Father in me?' (John 14:10). This is from the unity or sameness of their nature—for he and the Father are one (John 10:30). Thence all things that the Father has are his (John 16:15), because their nature is one and the same. With respect to the divine essence absolutely considered, wherein the Father is in the Son, and the Son in the Father, the one cannot be said to be the image of the other. For he and the Father are one; and one and the same thing cannot be the image of itself, in that wherein it is one.

WITH THE FATHER

The Son is said not only to be ἐν Πατρὶ, 'in the Father,' in the unity of the same essence; but also πρὸς τὸν Πατέρα or Θεὸν, 'with the Father,' or 'with God,' in the distinction of his person: 'The Word was with God, and the Word was God' (John 1:1). 'The Word was God,' in the unity of the divine essence—and 'the Word was with God,' in its distinct personal subsistence. 'The Word'—that is, the person of the Son, as distinct from the Father—'was with God,' or the Father. And in this respect he is the essential image of the Father, as he is called in this place, and Hebrews 1:3; and that because he partakes of all the same divine properties with the Father.

But although the Father, on the other side, be partaker of all the essential divine properties of the Son, yet is not he said to be the image of the Son. For this property of an image respects not the things themselves, but the manner of the participation of them. Now the Son receives all from the Father, and the Father nothing from the Son. Whatever belongs to the person of the Son, as the person of the Son, he receives it all from the Father by eternal generation: 'For as the Father has life in himself, so has he given to the Son to have life in himself' (John 5:26). He is therefore the essential image of the Father, because all the properties of the divine nature are communicated to him together with personality—from the Father.

In His Incarnation

In his incarnation, the Son was made the representative image of God to us—as he was, in his person, the essential image of the Father, by eternal generation. The invisible God—whose nature and divine excellencies our understandings can make no approach to—does in him represent, exhibit, or make present to our faith and spiritual sense, both himself and all the glorious excellencies of his nature.

Wherefore our Lord Jesus Christ, the Son of God, may be considered three ways.

1. Merely with respect to his divine nature. This is one and the same with that of the Father. In this respect the one is not the image of the other, for both are the same.
2. With respect to his divine person as the Son of the Father, the only-begotten, the eternal Son of God. Thus he receives, as his personality, so all divine excellencies, from the Father; so he is the essential image of the Father's person.
3. As he took our nature upon him, or in the assumption of our nature into personal union with himself, in order to the work of his mediation. So is he the only representative image of God to us—in whom alone we see, know, and learn all the divine excellencies—so as to live to God, and be directed to the enjoyment of him. All this himself instructs us in.

He reflects it on the Pharisees, as an effect of their blindness and ignorance, that they had neither heard the voice of God at any time, nor seen his shape (John 5:37). And in opposition hereunto he tells his disciples, that they had known the Father, and seen him (John 14:7). And the reason he gives thereof is, because they that knew him, knew the Father also. And when one of his disciples, not yet sufficiently instructed in this mystery, replied, 'Lord, show us the Father, and it suffices us' (John 14:8), his answer is, 'Have I been so long time with you, and yet have you not known me? he that has seen me has seen the Father' (John 14:9).

Three things are required to the justification of this assertion.

1. That the Father and he be of the same nature, have the same essence and being. For otherwise it would not follow that he who had seen him had seen the Father also. This ground of it he declares in the next verse: 'The Father is in me, and I am in the Father' namely, because they were one in nature and essence. For the divine nature being simply the same in them all, the divine persons are in each other, by virtue of the oneness of that nature.

2. That he be distinct from him. For otherwise there cannot be a seeing of the Father by the seeing of him. He is seen in the Son as represented by him—as his image—the Word—the Son of the Father, as he was with God. The unity of nature and the distinction of persons is the ground of that assertion of our Saviour: 'He that has seen me, has seen the Father also.'

3. But, moreover, the Lord Christ has a respect herein to himself, in his entire person as he was incarnate, and therein to the discharge of his mediatory work. 'Have I been so long time with you, and have you not known me?' Whilst he was with them, dwelt among them, conversed with them, he was the great representative of the glory of God to them. And, notwithstanding this particular mistake, they did then see his glory, 'the glory of the only-begotten of the Father' (John 1:14). And in him was manifested the glory of the Father. He 'is the image of the invisible God.' In him God was, in him he dwelt, in him is he known, in him is he worshipped according to his own will, in him is there a nearer approach made to us by the divine nature than ever could enter into the heart of man to conceive. In the constitution of his person—of two natures, so infinitely distinct and separate in themselves—and in the work it was designed to, the wisdom, power, goodness, love, grace, mercy, holiness, and faithfulness of God, are manifested to us. This is the

one blessed 'image of the invisible God,' wherein we may learn, wherein we may contemplate and adore, all his divine perfections.

The same truth is testified to (Heb. 1:3). God spoke to us in the Son, who is 'the brightness of his glory, and the express image of his person.' His divine nature is here included, as that without which he could not have made a perfect representation of God to us. For the apostle speaks of him, as of him 'by whom the worlds were made,' and who 'upholds all things by the word of his power.' Yet does he not speak of him absolutely as he was God, but also as he who 'in himself purged our sins, and sat down at the right hand of the majesty on high;' that is, in his whole person. Herein he is ἀπαύγασμα τῆς δόξης, the effulgency, the resplendency of divine glory, that wherein the divine glory shines forth in an evident manifestation of itself to us. And as a farther explication of the same mystery, it is added, that he is the character or 'express image' of the person of the Father. Such an impression of all the glorious properties of God is on him, as that thereby they become legible to all them that believe.

So the same apostle affirms again that he is the 'image of God' (2 Cor. 4:4); in what sense, and to what end, he declares (v. 6): 'We have the knowledge of the glory of God in the face of Jesus Christ.' Still it is supposed that the glory of God, as essentially in him, is invisible to us, and incomprehensible by us. Yet is there a knowledge of it necessary to us, that we may live to him, and come to the enjoyment of him. This we obtain only in the face or person of Christ—ἐν προσώπῳ τοῦ Χριστοῦ; for in him that glory is represented to us.

This was the testimony which the apostles gave concerning him, when he dwelt among them in the days of his flesh. They saw 'his glory, the glory as of the only-begotten of the Father, full of grace and truth' (John 1:14). The divine glory was manifest in him, and in him they saw the glory of the Father. So the same apostle witnesses again, who recorded this testimony: 'For the life was manifested, and we have seen it, and bear witness, and show to you that eternal life which was with the Father, and was manifested to us' (1 John 1:2). In the Son incarnate, that eternal life which was originally in and with the Father was manifest to us.

It may be said, that the Scripture itself is sufficient for this end of the declaration of God to us, so that there is no need of any other representation of him; and these things serve only to turn the minds of men from learning the mind and will of God therein, to seek for all in the person of Christ. But the true end of proposing these things is, to draw men to the diligent study of the Scripture, wherein alone they are revealed and declared. And in its proper use, and to its proper end, it is perfect and most sufficient. It is λόγος τοῦ Θεοῦ —'the word of God;' howbeit it is not λόγος οὐσιώδης, the internal, essential Word of God—but λόγος προφορικὸς, the external word spoken by him. It is not, therefore, nor can be, the image of God, either essential or representative; but is the revelation and declaration of it to us, without which we can know nothing of it.

Christ is the image of the invisible God, the express image of the person of the Father; and the principal end of the whole Scripture, especially of the gospel, is to declare him so to be, and how he is so. What God promised by his prophets in the holy Scriptures concerning his Son, Jesus Christ, that is fully declared in the gospel (Rom. 1:1–4). The gospel is the declaration of Christ as 'the power of God, and the wisdom of God' (1 Cor. 1:23–4); or an evident representation of God in his person and mediation to us (Gal. 3:1). Wherefore three things are herein to be considered.

1. *'Objectum reale et formale fidei'*—the real, formal object of our faith in this matter. This is the person of Christ, the Son of God incarnate, the representative image of the glory of God to us; as in the testimonies insisted on.

2. *'Medium revelans'*, or *'lumen deferens'*—the means of its revelation, or the objective light whereby the perception and knowledge of it is conveyed to our minds. This is the gospel; compared to a glass because of the prospect which we have of the image of God therein (2 Cor. 3:18). But without it—by any other means, and not by it—we can behold nothing of this image of God.

3. *'Lumen præparans, elevans, disponens subjectum'*—the internal light of the mind in the saving illumination of the Holy Spirit, enabling us—by that means, and in the use of it—spiritually to behold and discern the glory of God in the face of Christ (2 Cor. 4:6).

CONTEMPLATING CHRIST

Through both these, in their several ways of operation, there proceeds—from the real object of our faith, Christ, as the image of God—a transforming power, whereby the soul is changed into the same image, or is made conformable to Christ; which is that whereunto we are predestinated. But we may yet a little farther contemplate on these things, in some instances wherein the glory of God and our own duty are concerned.

GOD'S WISDOM EXALTED; HUMAN PRIDE DEBASED

The glory of God's wisdom is exalted, and the pride of the imaginations of men is proportionally debased. And in these two consists the real foundation of all religion in our souls. This God designed in the dispensation of himself and his will (1 Cor. 1:29, 31); this he calls us to (Isa. 2:22; Zech. 2:13). As this frame of heart is prevalent in us, so do all other graces shine and flourish. And it is that which influences all our duties, so far as they are acceptable to God. And there is no truth more instructive to it than that before us. It is taken for granted—and the event has demonstrated it to be so—that some express representation should be made of God to us, wherein we might contemplate the glorious excellencies of his nature, and he might draw nigh to us, and be present with us. This, therefore, men attempted to effect and accomplish; and this God alone has performed, and could so do. And their several ways for this end are herein manifest. As the way whereby God has done it is the principal exaltation of his infinite wisdom and goodness (as shall be immediately more fully declared), so the way whereby men attempted it was the highest instance of wickedness and folly.

It is, as we have declared, in Christ alone that God has done it. And that therein he has exalted and manifested the riches, the treasures of his infinite wisdom and goodness, is that which the gospel, the Spirit, and the church, do give testimony to. A more glorious effect of divine wisdom and goodness, a more illustrious manifestation of them, there never was, nor ever shall be, than in the finding out and constitution of this way of the representation of God to us. The ways of men, for the same end, were so far from giving a right representation of the perfections of the divine nature, that they were all of them below, beneath, and unworthy of our own. For in nothing did the blindness, darkness, and folly of our nature, in its depraved condition, ever so exert and evidence themselves, as in contriving ways for the representation of God to us—that is, in idolatry, the worst and vilest of evils (so Ps. 115:4–8; Isa. 44; Rev. 9:19–20). This pride and folly of men was that which lost all knowledge of God in the world, and all obedience to him. The Ten Commandments are but a transcript of the light and law of nature. The first of these required that God—the only true God—the creator and governor of all—should be acknowledged, worshipped, believed in, and obeyed. And the second was, that we should not make to ourselves any image or representation of him. Whatever he would do himself, yet he strictly forbade that we should make any such to ourselves. And here began the apostasy of the world from God. They did not absolutely reject him, and so cast off the first fundamental precept of the law of nature—but they submitted not to his wisdom and authority in the next, which was evidently educed from it. They would make images and representations of him to themselves; and by this invention of their own, they first dishonoured him, and then forsook him, giving themselves up to the rule and service of the devil. Wherefore, as the way that God in infinite wisdom found out for the representation of himself to us, was the only means of recovery from the first apostasy—the way found out by men, to the same end, was the great means of casting the generality of mankind to the farthest degree of a new apostasy from God whereof our nature is capable. And of the same kind will all our contrivances be found to be—in what belongs to his worship and glory—though, to us, they may appear both pious and necessary. This, therefore, should lead us into a continual admiration of the wisdom and grace of God, with a due sense of our own vileness and baseness by nature. For we are in nothing better or wiser than they who fell into the utmost folly and wickedness, in their designs for the highest end, or the representation of God to us. The more we dwell on such considerations, the more fear and reverence of God, with faith, trust, and delight in him, will be increased—as also humility in ourselves, with a sense of divine grace and love.

Christ Gives Us the Clearest Knowledge of God

There is a peculiar ground of the spiritual efficacy of this representation of God. The revelations that he has made of himself, and of the glorious properties of his nature, in the works of creation and providence, are, in themselves, clear, plain, and manifest (Ps. 19:1–2; Rom. 1:19–20). Those which are made in Christ are sublime and mysterious. Howbeit, the knowledge we have of him as he is represented to us in Christ is far more clear, certain, steady, effectual and operative, than any we can attain in and by all other ways of revelation. The reason hereof is, not only because there is a more full and extensive revelation made of God, his counsels and his will, in Christ and the gospel, than in all the works of creation and providence; but because this revelation and representation of God is received by faith alone, the other by reason only: and it is faith that is the principle of spiritual light and life in us. What is received thereby is operative and effectual, to all the ends of the life of God. For we live by faith here, as we shall by sight hereafter. Reason alone—especially as it is corrupted and depraved—can discern no glory in the representation of God by Christ; yea, all that is spoken thereof, or declared in the gospel, is foolishness to it. Hence many live in a profession of the faith of the letter of the gospel, yet—having no light, guide, nor conduct, but that of reason—they do not, they cannot, really behold the glory of God in the face of Jesus Christ; nor has the revelation of it any efficacy upon their souls. The manifestation of him in the light of nature, by the works of creation and providence, is suited to their reason, and does affect it: for that which is made in Christ, they say of it, as the Israelites did of manna, that came down from heaven, 'What is it?' we know not the meaning of it. For it is made to faith alone, and all men have not faith. And where God shines into the heart, by that faith which is of divine operation—there, with 'open face, we behold the glory of God, as in a glass;' or have the knowledge of the glory of God in the face of Jesus Christ. There is not the meanest believer, but—in the real exercise of faith in Christ—has more glorious apprehensions of God, his wisdom, goodness, and grace, of all his glorious excellencies, than the most learned and wise in the world can attain to, in the exercise of reason on the proper objects of it. So are these things opposed by the apostle (1 Cor. 1). Wherefore, faith in Christ is the only means of the true knowledge of God; and the discoveries which are made of him and his excellencies thereby are those alone which are effectual to conform us to his image and likeness. And this is the reason why some men are so little affected with the gospel—notwithstanding the continual preaching of it to them, and their outward profession of it. It does not inwardly affect them, it produces no blessed effects in them. Some sense they have of the power of God in the works of creation and providence, in his rule and government, and in the workings of natural conscience. Beyond these, they have no real sense of him. The reason is, because they have not faith—whereby alone the representation that is made of God in Christ, and declared in the gospel, is made effectual to the souls of men.

Natural Understanding of God Never Satisfies

Wherefore it is the highest degeneracy from the mystery of the Christian religion, for men to satisfy themselves in natural discoveries of the divine being and excellencies, without an acquaintance with that perfect declaration and representation of them which is made in the person of Christ, as he is revealed and declared in the gospel. It is confessed that there may be good use made of the evidence which reason gives or takes from its own innate principles—with the consideration of the external works of divine wisdom and power—concerning the being and rule of God. But to rest herein—to esteem it the best and most perfective knowledge of God that we can attain—not to rise up to the more full, perfect, and evident manifestation of himself that he has made in Christ—is a declaration of our unbelief, and a virtual renunciation of the gospel. This is the spring of that declension to a mere natural religion which discovers itself in many, and usually ends in the express denial of the divine person of Christ. For when the proper use of it is despised, on what grounds can the notion of it be long retained? But a supposition of his divine person is the foundation of this discourse. Were he not the essential image of the Father in his own divine person, he could not be the representative image of God to us as he is incarnate. For if he were a man only—however miraculously produced and gloriously exalted, yet the angels above, the glorious heavens, the seat and throne of God, with other effects of creating power and wisdom, would no less represent his glory than it could be done in him. Yet are they nowhere, jointly nor separately, styled 'the image of the invisible God'—'the brightness of his glory, and the express image of his person;' nor does God shine into our hearts to give us the knowledge of his glory in the face of them. And it argues the woeful enmity of the carnal mind against God and all the effects of his wisdom, that, whereas he has granted us such a glorious image and representation of himself, we like it not, we delight not in the contemplation of it, but either despise it or neglect it, and please ourselves in that which is incomparably beneath it.

Barren and Fruitless Knowledge

Because God is not thus known it is—that the knowledge of him is so barren and fruitless in the world, as it manifests itself to be. It were easy to produce, yea, endless to number the testimonies that might be produced out of heathen writers, given to the being and existence of God, his authority, monarchy, and rule; yet what were the effects of that knowledge which they had? Besides that wretched idolatry wherein they were all immersed, as the apostle declares (Rom. 1), it rescued them from no kind of wickedness and villany; as he there also manifests. And the virtues which were found among them were evidently derived from other causes, and not from the knowledge they had of God. The Jews have the knowledge of God by the letter of the Old Testament; but they—not knowing him in Christ, and having lost all sense and apprehension of those representations which were made of his being in him, in the law— they continue universally a people carnal, obstinate, and wicked. They have neither the virtues of the heathens among them, nor the power of the truth of religion. As it was with them of old, so it, yet continues to be; 'they profess that they know God, but in works they deny him, being abominable and disobedient, and to every good work reprobate' (Tit. 1:16). So is it among many that are called Christians at this day in the world: great pretence there is to the knowledge of God—yet did flagitious sins and wickedness scarce ever more abound among the heathens themselves. It is the knowledge of 'God in Christ' alone that is effectually powerful to work the souls of men into a conformity to him. Those alone who behold the glory of God in the face of Jesus Christ are changed into the same image, from glory to glory.

6

THE REPOSITORY OF SACRED TRUTH

Divine supernatural truth is called by the apostle, 'The truth which is after godliness' (Tit. 1:1). Whereas, therefore, the person of Christ is the great mystery of godliness, we must, in the next place, inquire—What is the relation of spiritual supernatural truth thereunto? And this I shall do, in pursuit of what was proposed in the foregoing chapter, viz., that he is the great representative to the church, of God, his holy properties, and the counsels of his will.

All divine truth may be referred to two heads. First, that which is essentially so; and then that which is so declaratively. The first is God himself, the other is the counsel of his will.

First, God himself is the first and only essential truth, in whose being and nature the springs of all truth do lie. Whatever is truth—so far as it is so, derives from him, is an emanation from that eternal fountain of it. Being, truth, and goodness, is the principal notion of God; and in him they are all the same. How this is represented in Christ—as in himself he is the essential image of the Father, and as incarnate the representative image of him to us—has been declared.

Secondly, the counsels of God are the next spring and cause—as also the subject-matter or substance—of all truth that is so declaratively. Divine truth is 'the declaration of the counsel of God' (Acts 20:27). Of them all the person of Christ is the sacred repository and treasury—in him are they to be learned. All their efficacy and use depend on their relation to him. He is the centre and circumference of all the lines of truth—that is, which is divine, spiritual, and supernatural. And the beauty of it is presented to us only in his face or person. We see it not, we know it not, but as God shines into our hearts to give us the knowledge of it therein (2 Cor. 4:6).

So he testifies of himself, 'I am the truth' (John 14:6). He is so essentially—as he is one with the Father, the God of truth (Deut. 32:4). He is so efficiently—as by him alone it is fully and effectually declared; for 'no man has seen God at any time; the only-begotten Son, who is in the bosom of the Father, he has declared him' (John 1:18). He is so substantially—in opposition to the types and shadows of the Old Testament; for in him dwelt 'the fulness of the godhead bodily' (Col. 2:9). 'The body is of Christ' (v. 17). He is so subjectively—for all divine truth, relating to the saving knowledge of God, is treasured up in him. 'In him are hid all the treasures of wisdom and knowledge' (v. 3) . That is, the wisdom and knowledge of God—in his counsels concerning the vocation, sanctification, and salvation, of the church—concerning which the apostle falls into that holy admiration, 'O the depth of the riches both of the wisdom and knowledge of God!' (Rom. 11:33). And they are called 'treasures' on a twofold account, both mentioned together by the Psalmist. 'How precious are your thoughts to me, O Lord; how great is the sum of them!' They are treasures, because precious and invaluable—and are therefore usually preferred above all earthly treasures which men most highly esteem (Prov. 3:14–15). And they are so, because of the greatness of the sum of them; and therefore also called 'unsearchable riches' (Eph. 3:8). These precious, unsearchable treasures of the wisdom and knowledge of God—that is, all divine supernatural truths—are hid, or safely deposited, in Christ—in and from whom alone they are to be learned and received.

So we are said to learn the truth as it is in Jesus (Eph. 4:21). And the knowledge of all evangelic sacred truth is, in the Scripture, most frequently expressed by the knowledge of Him (John 8:19; 17:3; 2 Cor. 2:14; 4:5–6; Eph. 1:17; Phil. 3:8, 10; 1 John 1:1–2; 2:4, 13–14; 5:20; 2 Pet. 2:20).

Setting aside what we have discoursed and proved before—concerning the laying of the foundation of all the counsels of God in the person of Christ, and the representation of them in the ineffable constitution thereof—I shall give some few instances of this relation of all supernatural truths to him—manifesting that we cannot learn them, nor know them, but with a due respect thereunto.

The Glory of Truth

There are two things wherein the glory of truth consists. (1.) Its light. (2) Its efficacy or power. And both these do all supernatural truths derive from this relation to Christ.

Light

No truth whatever brings any spiritual light to the mind, but by virtue thereof. 'In him is life, and the life is the light of men' (John 1:4). He is 'the true Light, which lights every man that comes into the world' (v. 9). Wherefore, as truth is the only means of illumination, so it cannot communicate any light to the mind, but only as it is a beam from him, as it is an organ to convey it from that fountain. Separated from him and its relation to him, it will not retain, it cannot communicate, any real spiritual light or understanding to the souls of men. How should it, if all light be originally in him—as the Scripture testifies? Then alone is the mind irradiated with heavenly truth, when it is received as proceeding from, and leading to, the Sun of Righteousness—the blessed spring of all spiritual light—which is Christ himself. Whatever notional knowledge men may have of divine truths, as they are doctrinally proposed in the Scripture, yet—if they know them not in their respect to the person of Christ as the foundation of the counsels of God—if they discern not how they proceed from him, and centre in him—they will bring no spiritual, saving light to their understanding. For all spiritual life and light is in him, and from him alone. An instance hereof we have in the Jews. They have the Scriptures of the Old Testament, wherein the substance of all divine truth is revealed and expressed; and they are diligent in the study of them; howbeit their minds are not at all illuminated nor irradiated by the truths contained in them, but they live and walk in horrible darkness. And the only reason hereof is, because they know not, because they reject, the relation of them to Christ—without which they are deprived of all enlightening power.

POWER

Efficacy or power is the second property of divine truth. And the end of this efficacy is to make us like to God (Eph. 4:20–24). The mortification of sin, the renovation of our natures, the sanctification of our minds, hearts, and affections, the consolation of our souls, with their edification in all the parts of the life of God, and the like, are the things that God has designed to effect by his truth (John 17:17) whence it is able to 'build us up, and give us an inheritance among all them that are sanctified' (Acts 20:32). But it is from their relation to the person of Christ that they have any thing of this power and efficacy. For they have it no otherwise but as they are conveyances of his grace to the souls of men (so 1 John 1:1–2).

Wherefore, as professors of the truth, if separated from Christ as to real union, are withering branches—so truths professed, if doctrinally separated from him, or their respect to him, have no living power or efficacy in the souls of men. When Christ is formed in the heart by them, when he dwells plentifully in the soul through their operation, then, and not else, do they put forth their proper power and efficacy. Otherwise, they are as waters separated from the fountain—they quickly dry up or become a noisome puddle; or as a beam interrupted from its continuity to the sun—it is immediately deprived of light.

ALL DIVINE TRUTHS DECLARE GRACE OR GRATITUDE

All divine spiritual truths are declarative, either of the grace and love of God to us, or our duty, obedience, and gratitude to him. But, as to these things, Christ is all and in all; we can have no due apprehensions of the love and grace of God, no understanding of the divine truths of the Word—wherein they are revealed, and whereby they are exhibited to them that believe—but in the exercise of faith on Christ himself. For in, by, and from him alone, it is that they are proposed to us, that we are made partakers of them. It is from his fulness that all grace is received. No truth concerning them can, by any imagination, be separated from him. He is the life and soul of all such truths—without which, they, as they are written in the Word, are but a dead letter, and that of such a character as is illegible to us, as to any real discovery of the grace and love of God. And as to those of the other sort, which are instructive to us in our duty, obedience, and gratitude—we cannot come to a practical compliance with any one of them, but by the aids of grace received from him. For without him we can do nothing (John 15:5) and he alone understands divine truth who does it (John 7:17). There is not, therefore, any one text of Scripture which presses our duty to God, that we can so understand as to perform that duty in an acceptable manner, without an actual regard to Christ, from whom alone we receive ability for the performance of it, and in or through whom alone it is accepted with God.

ALL TRUTH'S BENEFITS DEPEND ON CHRIST

All the evidence of divine spiritual truth, and all the foundation of our real interest in the things whereof it is a declaration—as to benefit, advantage, and comfort—depend on their relation to Christ. We may take an instance in one article of divine truth, which seems to be most disengaged from any such relation, namely, the resurrection of the dead. But there is no man who rightly believes or comprehends this truth, who does it not upon the evidence given to it, and example of it, in the person of Christ rising from the dead. Nor can any man have a comfortable expectation or faith of an especial interest in a blessed resurrection (which is our whole concern in that truth (Phil. 3:11), but by virtue of a mystical union to him, as the head of the church that shall be raised to glory. Both these the apostle insists upon at large (1 Cor. 15). So is it with all other truths whatever.

Wherefore, all divine supernatural truths revealed in the Scripture, being nothing but the declaration of these counsels of God, whose foundation was laid in the person of Christ; and whereas they are all of them expressive of the love, wisdom, goodness, and grace of God to us, or instructive in our obedience and duty to him—all the actings of God towards us, and all ours towards him, being in and through him alone; and whereas all the life and power of these truths, all their beauty, symmetry, and harmony in their union and conjunction, which is expressive of divine wisdom, is all from him, who, as a living spirit diffused through the whole system, both acts and animates it—all the treasures of truth, wisdom, and knowledge, may be well said to be hid in him. And we may consider some things that ensue hereon.

THOSE WHO REJECT CHRIST CORRUPT ALL SPIRITUAL TRUTH

Hence it is, that those who reject the divine person of Christ—who believe it not, who discern not the wisdom, grace, love, and power of God therein—do constantly reject or corrupt all other spiritual truths of divine revelation. Nor can it otherwise be. For they have a consistency only in their relation to the mystery of godliness—'God manifest in the flesh'—and from thence derive their sense and meaning. This being removed—the truth, in all other articles of religion, immediately falls to the ground. An instance hereof we have in the Socinians. For, although they retain the common notions of the unity and existence of the divine nature, which are indelibly fixed on the minds of men, yet is there no one truth that belongs peculiarly to the Christian religion, but they either deny it or horribly deprave it. Many things concerning God and his essential properties—as his immutability, immensity, prescience—they have greatly perverted. So is that fulfilled in them which was spoken by Jude the apostle (v. 10). They 'speak evil of those things which they know not: and what they know naturally, as brute beasts, in those things they corrupt themselves.' So they do in the things mentioned, whereof there are natural notions in the minds of men; but of evangelic truths—which they know not—they speak evil, and deride them. The holy Trinity they blaspheme—the incarnation of the Son of God they scorn—the work of his mediation in his oblation and intercession, with the satisfaction and merit of his obedience and suffering, they reject. So do they whatever we are taught of the depravation of our natures by the fall, of the renovation of them by the Holy Ghost; and to all other articles of our faith do they offer violence, to corrupt them. The beginning of their transgression or apostasy, is in a disbelief of the divine person of Christ. That being rejected, all other sacred truths are removed from their basis and centre, that which gives them their unity and harmony. Hereon they fluctuate up and down in the minds of men, and, appearing to them under various deceiving colours, are easily misapprehended or disbelieved. Yea, there can no direct, proper representation be made of them to the understandings of men. Dissolve the knot, centre, and harmony in the most beautiful composition or structure—and every part will contribute as much to the deformity and ruin of the whole, as it did before to its beauty and consistency. So is it with every doctrine—so is it with the whole system of evangelic truths. Take the person of Christ out of them, dissolve their harmony in relation thereunto—whereby we no longer hold the Head in the faith and profession of them—and the minds of men cannot deliver them from an irreconcilable difference among themselves. Hereon some of them are immediately rejected, and some of them corrupted; for they lose their native light and beauty. They will neither agree nor consist any where but in Christ. Hence it is that no instance can be given of any, who, from the original of the Christian religion, rejected the divine person of Christ, and preserved any one evangelic truth besides, pure and uncorrupted. And I do freely confess, that all which we believe concerning the holy Trinity, the eternal counsels of God, the efficacy of the mediation of Christ, his satisfaction and merit, the way which we own of the sanctification, justification, and salvation of the church—are to be esteemed fables, as the Socinians contend, if what we believe concerning the person of Christ be so also.

TRUTH IS FRUITLESS APART FROM CHRIST

Hence it is that the knowledge and profession of the truth, with many, is so fruitless, inefficacious, and useless. It is not known, it is not understood nor believed—in its relation to Christ; on which account alone it conveys either light or power to the soul. Men profess they know the truth; but they know it not in its proper order, in its harmony and use. It leads them not to Christ, it brings not Christ to them; and so is lifeless and useless. Hence, ofttimes, none are more estranged from the life of God than such as have much notional knowledge of the doctrines of the Scripture. For they are all of them useless, and subject to be abused, if they are not improved to form Christ in the soul, and transform the whole person into his likeness and image. This they will not effect where their relation to him is not understood—where they are not received and learned as a revelation of him, with the mystery of the will and wisdom of God in him. For whereas he is our life, and in our living to God we do not so much live as he lives in us, and the life which we lead in the flesh is by the faith of him—so that we have neither principle nor power of spiritual life, but in, by, and from him—whatever knowledge we have of the truth, if it do not effect a union between him and our souls, it will be lifeless in us, and unprofitable to us. It is learning the truth as it is in Jesus, which alone renews the image of God in us (Eph. 4:21–4). Where it is otherwise—where men have notions of evangelic truths, but know not Christ in them—whatever they profess, when they come really to examine themselves, they will find them of no use to them, but that all things between God and their souls are stated on natural light and common presumptions.

7

POWER TRANSFUSED
INTO CHRIST'S OFFICES FROM HIS PERSON

It is by the exercise and discharge of the office of Christ—as the king, priest, and prophet of the church—that we are redeemed, sanctified, and saved. Thereby does he immediately communicate all gospel benefits to us—give us an access to God here by grace, and in glory hereafter; for he saves us, as he is the mediator between God and man. But hereon an inquiry may be made—whence it is that the acts and duties of this office of Christ, in their exercise and discharge, should have such a power and efficacy, with respect to their supernatural and eternal ends; for the things which depend upon them, which are effected by them, are all the principal means of the glory of God, and the only concerns of the souls of men. And this, I say, is his holy, mysterious person; from thence alone all power and efficacy is derived, and transfused into his offices, and into all that is due in the discharge of them.

A truth this is, of that importance, that the declaration and demonstration of it is the principal design of one entire book of the holy Scriptures, viz., of the Epistle of Paul the Apostle to the Hebrews. That the glorious excellency of the person of Christ enables him, in the discharge of his offices, to accomplish those ends—which none other, though vested with the same offices, could, in the exercise of them, attain to—is the sum and substance of the doctrinal part of that discourse. Here, therefore, we must a little fix our meditations—and our interest calls us thereunto. For if it be so, it is evident that we can receive no good, no benefit, by virtue of any office of Christ, nor any fruits of their exercise, without an actual respect of faith to his person, whence all their life and power is derived.

God gave of old both kings, priests, and prophets, to the church. He both anointed them to their offices, directed them in their discharge, was present with them in their work, and accepted of their duties; yet by none of them, nor by all of them together, was the church supernaturally enlightened, internally ruled, or eternally saved: nor could it so be. Some of them—as Moses in particular—had as much power, and as great a presence of God with him, as any mere man could be made partaker of; yet was he not, in his ministry, the saviour of the church—nor could he be so any otherwise than typically and temporally. The ministry of them all was subservient to that end which, by its own power, it could not attain.

It is evident, therefore, that the redemption and salvation of the church do not depend merely on this—that God has given one to be the king, priest, and prophet of the church, by the actings of which offices it is redeemed and saved; but on the person of him who was so given to us: as is fully attested (Isa. 9:6–7).

This must be declared.

Two things were required, in general, to the person of Christ, that his offices might be effectual to the salvation of the church, and without which they could not so have been. And they are such, as that their contrivance in the constitution of one and the same person, no created wisdom could reach to. Wherefore the infinite wisdom of God is most gloriously manifested therein.

CHRIST REQUIRED ANOTHER NATURE

The first of these is, that he should have a nature provided for him, which originally was not his own. For in his divine nature, singly considered, he had no such relation to them for whom he was to discharge his offices, as was necessary to communicate the benefit of them, nor could he discharge their principal duties. God could not die, nor rise again, nor be exalted to be a prince and a saviour, in his divine nature. Nor was there that especial alliance between it and ours, as should give us an especial interest in what was done thereby.

It was mankind in whose behalf he was to exercise these offices. He was not to bear them with respect immediately to the angels; and, therefore, he took not their nature on him. Οὐ γὰρ δήπου ἀγγέλων ἐπιλαμβάνεται—'He took not the nature of angels to him' (Heb. 2:16); because he was not to be a mediator for them, a saviour to them. Those of them who had sinned were left to everlasting ruin; and those who retained their original righteousness needed no redemption. But God prepared a body for him—that is, a human nature (Heb. 10:5). The promise hereof—viz., that he should be of the seed of the woman—was the foundation of the church; that is, he was made so to the church in and by that promise (Gen. 3:15). In the accomplishment thereof he was 'made of a woman,' that so he might be 'made under the law' (Gal. 4:4); and 'took upon him the seed of Abraham'. For because the children were partakers of flesh and blood, 'he also himself took part of the same' (Heb. 2:14). For 'in all things it behoved him to be made like to his brethren, that he might be a merciful and faithful high priest in things pertaining to God' (v. 17). And this was absolutely necessary to the discharge of his offices, on the twofold account before mentioned.

TO FULFILL HIS OFFICES

Those acts of his offices, whereon the sanctification and salvation of the church do principally depend, could not be performed but in and by that nature. Therein alone could he yield obedience to the law, that it might be fulfilled in us—without which we could not stand in judgment before God (see Rom. 8:3; 10:3–4). Therein alone could he undergo the curse of the law, or be made a curse for us, that the blessing might come upon us (Gal. 3:13–14). It was necessary that, as a priest, he should have something of his own to offer to God, to make atonement for sin (Heb. 8:3). The like may be said of his whole ministry on the earth—of all the effects of his incarnation.

To Share the Benefits of His Mediation

Herein that cognation and alliance between him and the church, which were necessary to entitle it to a participation of the benefits of his mediation, do depend. For hereby he became our *göel*—the next of kin—unto whom belonged the right of redemption and from whom alone we could claim relief and succour in our lost condition. This is divinely and at large declared by the apostle (Heb. 2:10–18). Having at large explained this context in our exposition of that chapter, and therein declared both the necessity and benefit of the cognation between the church and its High Priest, I shall not here farther insist upon it. See to the same purpose, Ephesians 5:25–7. Wherefore, had he not been partaker of our nature, we could have received no benefit—not that without which we must eternally perish—by any office that he could have undertaken. This, therefore, was necessary to the constitution of his person, with respect to his offices.

Christ Had to Be More than a Man

There was yet more required thereunto, or to render his offices effectual to their proper ends. Not one of them could have been so, had he been no more than a man—had he had no nature but ours. This I shall particularly demonstrate, considering them in their usual distribution—unto the glory of his divine person, and our own edification in believing.

AS A PROPHET

He could not have been the great and singular prophet of the church, had he been a man only, though ever so excellent and glorious; and that for these three reasons:

He Had to Be a Prophet of the Whole Catholic Church

He was to be the prophet of the whole catholic church; that is, of all the elect of God, of all that shall be saved in all ages and places, from the beginning of the world to the end thereof. He had a personal ministry for the instruction of the church, whilst he was on the earth; but his prophetic office was not confined thereunto. For that was limited to one nation (Matt. 15:24; Rom. 15:8), and was for a short season only. But the church was never without a prophet—that is, one on whom it was incumbent to reveal to it, and instruct it in, the will of God—nor can be so to the consummation of all things. This is Christ alone.

FROM THE BEGINNING. I take it for granted that, from the beginning, from the giving of the first promise, the Son of God did, in an especial manner, undertake the care of the church—as to all the ends of the wisdom, will, and grace of God; and I take it for granted here, because I have proved it at large elsewhere. It evidently follows on the eternal compact between the Father and him to this end. In the work which belonged hereunto—that which concerned its instruction in the will of God, its saving illumination and spiritual wisdom, is of such importance, as that, without it, none can be partaker of any other blessings whatever. In this instruction and illumination consists the discharge of the prophetic office of Christ.

WHEN HE TOOK OFFICE. Upon the account of his susception of his office even before his incarnation, considered as God; he is said to act in it so as to be sent of God to his work, 'The Ruler of Israel, whose goings forth have been from of old, from everlasting'

(Micah 5:2). His goings forth are not his eternal generation, which consists in one individual eternal act of the Father; but it is the egress, the exercise of his power and care for the church, that is so expressed. These were from the beginning the first foundation of the church, in answer to his everlasting counsels, 'Thus says the Lord of hosts, After the glory has he sent me to the nations which spoiled you;' and 'I will shake mine hand upon them, and they shall be a spoil to their servants: and ye shall know that the Lord of hosts has sent me' (Zech 2:8–9). He who is sent calls himself 'The Lord of hosts,' and affirms that he will destroy the nations by the shaking of his hand; who can be no other but God himself. That is, it was the Son of God, who was to be incarnate, as is declared in the next words: 'Sing and rejoice, O daughter of Zion: for, lo, I come, and I will dwell in the midst of you, says the Lord. And many nations shall be joined to the Lord in that day, and shall be my people: and I will dwell in the midst of you; and you shall know that the Lord of hosts has sent me to you' (v. 10–11). He promises that he will dwell in the midst of the people; which was accomplished when 'the Word was made flesh, and dwelt among us' (John 1:14); which was the time of the calling of the Gentiles, when many nations were to be joined to the Lord; and those that were so called were to be his people: 'They shall be my people.' And yet in all this he was sent by the Lord of hosts: 'You shall know that the Lord of hosts has sent me to you.' Wherefore, with respect to his susception of his offices towards the church, the Lord of hosts in the person of the Son is said to be sent by the Lord of hosts; that is, in the person of the Father. So was he the prophet of the church even before his incarnation, sent or designed by the Father to instruct it—to communicate spiritual and saving light to it. So he testified concerning himself to the Jews, 'Before Abraham was, I am' (John 8:58). Which, as it invincibly proves his eternal pre-existence to his incarnation, so it is not only intended. He was so before Abraham, as that the care of the church was then and always from the beginning on him. And he discharged this office four ways:

1. By personal appearances in the likeness of human nature, in the shape of a man, as an indication of his future incarnation; and under those appearances instructing the church. So he appeared to Abraham, to Jacob, to Moses, to Joshua, as I have proved elsewhere. And those peculiar appearances of the person of the Son for the instruction of believers, are a full demonstration that the care and work of it were committed to him in a peculiar manner. And I am not without thoughts, although I see some difficulty in it, that the whole Old Testament, wherein God perpetually treats with men by an assumption of human affections to himself, so to draw us with the cords of a man, proceeded from the person of the Son, in a preparation for, and prospect of, his future incarnation.

2. By the ministry of angels upon his undertaking to be the mediator for the church with God, the angels were in a peculiar manner put into dependence on him, even as he became a new and immediate head to the whole creation. This belonged to that especial glory which he had with the Father 'before the world was,' whereof we have treated before. All things were to be anew gathered into a head in him, 'both which are in heaven, and which are on earth' (Eph. 1:10). And he became 'the firstborn of every creature' (Col. 1:15), the Lord and proprietor of them. Hence the whole ministry of angels was subordinate to him; and whatever instruction was thereby given to the church in the mind and will of God, it was immediately from him, as the great prophet of the church.

3. By sending his Holy Spirit to inspire, act, and guide the prophets, by whom God would reveal himself. God spoke to them by the 'mouth of his holy prophets, which have been since the world began' (Luke 1:70). But it was the Spirit of Christ that was in them that spoke by them, that revealed the things which concerned the redemption and salvation of the church (1 Pet. 1:11–12). And by this Spirit he himself preached to those that were disobedient in the days of Noah, who are now in prison for their disobedience (1 Pet. 3:19–20). For he

was so the prophet of the church always as to tender manifold instructions to the perishing, unbelieving world. Hence is he said to lighten 'every man that comes into the world' (John 1:9), by one way or other communicating to them some notices of God and his will; for his light shines in, or irradiates darkness itself—that darkness which is come on the minds of men by sin—though the 'darkness comprehend it not' (v. 5).

4. By the ministry of holy men, acted and moved by his Spirit. So he gave forth the word that was written for an everlasting rule of faith and obedience to the church.

Thus were the office and work of instructing and illuminating of the church on his hand alone from the beginning, and thus were they by him discharged. This was not a work for him who was no more but a man. His human nature had no existence until the fulness of time, the latter days, and therefore could effect or operate nothing before. And whereas the apostle distinguishes between the speaking of God in the Son and his speaking in the prophets, opposing the one to the other (Heb. 1:1–2), he does it with respect to his personal ministry to the Church of the Jews, and not with respect to his being the peculiar fountain of life and light to the whole church in all ages.

It is true, we have under the gospel many unspeakable advantages from the prophetic office of Christ, above what they enjoyed under the Old Testament; but he was the prophet of the church equally in all ages. Only he has given out the knowledge of the mind of God in different degrees and measures; that which was most perfect being for many reasons reserved to the times of the gospel; the sum whereof is, that God designed him to a pre-eminence above all in his own personal ministry.

If any shall now inquire how the Lord Christ could be the prophet of the church before he took our nature on him and dwelt among us; I shall also ask how they suppose him to be the prophet of the church now he has left the world and is gone to heaven, so as that we neither see him nor hear him anymore? If they shall say that he is so by his Spirit, his Word, and the ministry which he has ordained; I say, so was he the prophet of the church before his incarnation also. To confine the offices of Christ, as to their virtue, power and efficacy, to the times of the gospel only, is utterly to evacuate the first promise, with the covenant of grace founded thereon. And their minds are secretly influenced by a disbelief of his divine person, who suppose that the respect of the church to Christ, in faith, love, trust, and instruction, commences from the date of his incarnation.

A Creature's Mind Is too Small

The full comprehension of the mind and will of God, of the whole divine counsel concerning his glory in the sanctification and salvation of the church, could not at once reside in the mind of any mere creature. Yet was this necessary to him who was to be the prophet of the church; that is, the fountain of truth, life, and knowledge to it. Hence is his name 'Wonderful, Counsellor,' as he who was participant of all the eternal counsels of God; whereon in him as incarnate all the treasures of divine wisdom and knowledge were hid (Col. 2:3). In him this could be alone, in whom was life, and 'the life was the light of men' (John 1:4). God did reveal his mind and will by angels and men. But as he did it at sundry times, so he did it by several parts, or various parcels—not only as the church was fit to receive it, but as they were able to communicate it. The whole of the divine counsels could not be comprehended, and so not declared, by any of them. Hence the angels themselves—notwithstanding their residence in the presence of God, beholding his face, and all the glorious messages wherein they were employed—learned more of his mind after the personal ministry of Christ, and the revelation of the mysteries of his counsel therein, than ever they knew before (Eph. 3:8–9, 11; 1 Pet. 1:12). And on the account of their imperfection in the comprehension of his counsels, it is said that 'he charged his angels with folly' (Job 4:18). And the best of the prophets not only received divine truth by parcel, but comprehended not the depths of the revelations made to them (1 Pet. 1:11–12).

To this purpose is that divine testimony, 'No man has seen God at any time; the only-begotten Son, who is in the bosom of the Father, he has declared him' (John 1:18). It is of all the prophets concerning whom it is affirmed, that no man has seen God at any time. So is it evident in the antithesis between Moses the principal of them, and the Lord Christ, in the verse foregoing: 'For the law was given by Moses, but grace and truth came by Jesus Christ.' Wherefore no man, no other man or prophet whatever has seen God at any time; that is, had a perfect comprehension of his counsels, his mind and will, as they were to be declared to the church. This is the privilege of the only-begotten Son, who is in the bosom of the Father; not only as being his eternal delight and love, but also as one acquainted with all his secret counsels—as his fellow and participant of all his bosom thoughts.

He says that 'all that ever came before him were thieves and robbers, but the sheep did not hear them' (John 10:8). This some of old impiously applied to the prophets of the Old Testament; whereas he intended it only of those false prophets who pretended of themselves that they, any of them, were the Messiah, the great Shepherd of the sheep, whom his elect sheep would not attend to. But it is true that all who went before him, neither separately nor jointly, had the knowledge of God, so as to declare him fully to the church.

It is the most fond and wicked imagination of the Socinians, invented to countenance their disbelief and hatred of his divine person, that during the time of his flesh he was taken up into heaven, and there taught the doctrine of the gospel, as Mohammed feigned concerning himself and his Alkoran. The reason and foundation of his perfect knowledge of God was, his being the only-begotten Son in the bosom of the Father, and not a fictitious rapture of his human nature.

To this purpose have we his own testimony (John 3:13), 'And no man has ascended up to heaven, but he that came down from heaven, even the Son of man which is in heaven.' The matter whereof he treats is the revelation of heavenly things. For, finding Nicodemus slow in the understanding of the doctrine and necessity of regeneration, which yet was plain and evident in comparison of some other heavenly mysteries, he asks of him, 'If I have told you earthly things, and you do not believe,' (things wrought in the earth and in your own breasts), 'how shall you believe if I tell you of heavenly things?' if I declare to you the deep counsels of the will of God above (v. 12). But hereon a question might arise, how he should himself come to the knowledge of these heavenly things whereof they had never heard before, and which no other man could tell them of, especially considering what he had said before, 'We speak that we do know, and testify that we have seen' (v. 11). Hereof he gives an account in these words. Wherefore the ascending into heaven, which he denies to all men whatever—'No man has ascended up to heaven'—is an entrance into all the divine, heavenly counsels of God; no man either has or ever had a full comprehension of these heavenly things but he himself alone. And to him it is ascribed on a double account: first, That he came down from heaven; secondly, that when he did so, he yet still continued in heaven: which two properties give us such a description of the person of Christ as declare him a full possessor of all the counsels of God. He descended from heaven in his incarnation, whereby he became the Son of man; and he is and was then in heaven in the essence and glory of his divine nature. This is the full of what we assert. In the knowledge and revelation of heavenly mysteries, to the calling, sanctification, and salvation of the church, does the prophetical office of Christ consist. This he positively affirms could not otherwise be, but that he who came down from heaven was also at the same instant in heaven. This is that glorious person whereof we speak. He who, being always in heaven in the glory and essence of his divine nature, came down from heaven, not locally, by a mutation of his residence, but by dispensation in the assumption of our nature into personal union with himself—he alone is meet and able to be the prophet of the church in the revelation of the heavenly mysteries of the counsels of the will of God. In him alone were 'hid all the treasures of wisdom and knowledge' (Col. 2:3), because in him alone 'dwelt the fulness of the Godhead bodily' (v. 9).

I do not hereby ascribe the infusion of omniscience, of infinite understanding, wisdom, and knowledge, into the human nature of Christ. It was and is a creature, finite and limited, nor is a capable subject of properties absolutely infinite and immense. Filled it was with light and wisdom to the utmost capacity of a creature; but it was so, not by being changed into a divine nature or essence, but by the communication of the Spirit to it without measure. The Spirit of the Lord did rest upon him, the spirit of wisdom and understanding, the spirit of counsel and might, the spirit of knowledge and of the fear of the Lord, and made him of quick understanding in the fear of the Lord (Isa. 11:2–3).

His Unique Understanding

The Spirit of God dwelling in him, in all the fullness of his graces and gifts, gave him an understanding peculiar to himself; as above that of all creatures, so beneath the essential omniscience of the divine nature. Hence some things, as he was a man, he knew not (Mark 13:32), but as they were given him by revelation (Rev. 1:1). But he is the prophet of the church in his whole entire person, and revealed the counsel of God, as he was in heaven in the bosom of the Father. Cursed be he that trusts in man, that makes flesh his arm, as to the revelations of the counsels of God. Here lies the safety, the security, the glory of the church. How deplorable is the darkness of mankind, in their ignorance of God and heavenly things! In what ways of vanity and misery have the generality of them wandered ever since our first apostasy from God! Nothing but hell is more full of horror and confusion than the minds and ways of men destitute of heavenly light. How miserably did those among them who boasted themselves to be wise, wax foolish in their imaginations! How woefully did all their inquiries after the nature and will of God, their own state, duty, and happiness, issue in curiosity, uncertainty, vanity, and falsehood! He who is infinitely good and compassionate, did from the beginning give some relief in this woeful state, by such parcels of divine revelations as he thought meet to communicate to them by the prophets of old—such as they were able to receive. By them he set up a light shining in a dark place, as the light of stars in the night. But it was the rising of the Sun of Righteousness alone that dispelled the darkness that was on the earth, the thick darkness that was on the people, bringing life and immortality to light by the gospel. The divine person of the Son of God, in whom were hid all the treasures of wisdom and knowledge, who is in the bosom of the Father, has now made known all things to the church, giving us the perfect idea and certainty of all sacred truth, and the full assurance of things invisible and eternal.

Three things are necessary, that we may have the benefit and comfort of divine light or truth:

1. The fulness of its revelation;
2. The infallibility of it; and,
3. The authority from whence it proceeds.

If either of these be wanting, we cannot attain to stability and assurance in the faith of it, or obedience to it.

FULL REVELATION. Full it must be, to free us from all attempt of fear that any thing is detained or hidden from us that were needful for us to know. Without this the mind of man can never come to rest in the knowledge of truth. All that he knows may be useless to him, for the want of that which he neither does nor can know, because not revealed.

INFALLIBLE REVELATION. And it must be infallible also. For this divine truth whereof we treat, being concerning things unseen—heavenly, eternal mysteries, transcending the reach of human reason—nothing but the absolute infallibility of the revealer can bring the mind of man to assurance and acquiescence. And whereas the same truth enjoins to us duties, many of them contrary to our inclinations and cross to our several interests—the great guides of corrupted nature—the revelation of it must proceed from sovereign authority, that the will may comply with the mind in the embracement of it. All these are absolutely secured in the divine person of the great prophet of the church. His infinite wisdom, his infinite goodness, his essential veracity, his sovereign authority over all, give the highest assurance whereof a created understanding is capable, that nothing is detained from us—that there is no possibility of error or mistake in what is declared to us, nor any pretence left of declining obedience to the commands of the truth that we do receive. This gives the soul assured rest and peace in the belief of things which 'eye has not seen, nor ear heard, nor can enter into the heart of man to conceive.' Upon the assurance of this truth alone can it with joy prefer things invisible and eternal above all present satisfactions and desires. In the persuasion hereof can it forego the best of present enjoyments, and undergo the worst of present evils; namely, in the experience of its present efficacy, and choice of that future recompense which it secures. And he believes not the gospel to his own advantage, or the glory of God, whose faith rests not in the divine person of Jesus Christ, the great prophet of the church. And he who there finds rest to his soul, dares not admit of any copartners with him as to instruction in the mind of God.

AUTHORITATIVE REVELATION. It was requisite to the office of this great prophet of the church, and the discharge thereof, that he should have power and authority to send the Holy Spirit to make his revelations of divine truth effectual to the minds of men. For the church which he was to instruct, was not only in darkness, by reason of ignorance and want of objective light or divine revelations, but was incapacitated to receive spiritual things in a due manner when revealed. Wherefore, it was the work of this prophet, not only to make known and declare the doctrines of truth, which are our external directive light, but also to irradiate and illuminate our minds, so that we might savingly apprehend them. And it is no wonder if those who are otherwise minded, who suppose themselves able to receive spiritual things, the things of God, in a due manner, upon their external proposal to them, are regardless of the divine person of Christ as the prophet of the church. But hereon they will never have experience of the life and power of the doctrine of the gospel, if the apostle is to be believed (1 Cor. 2:9–12). Now, this internal illumination of the minds of men to the acknowledgment of the truth can be wrought in them only by the Holy Spirit of God (Eph. 1:17–19; 2 Cor. 3:18). None, therefore, could be the prophet of the church, but he who had the power to send the Holy Spirit to enable it to receive his doctrine by the saving illumination of the minds of men. And this alone he could do, whose Spirit he is, proceeding from him; whom he therefore frequently promised so to send.

Without a respect to these things, we cannot really be made partakers of the saving benefits and fruits of the prophetic office of Christ. And this we can have only in the exercise of faith on his divine person, which is the eternal spring from whence this office derives all life and efficacy.

The command of God, in respect to him as the prophet of the church, is, 'This is my beloved Son, in whom I am well pleased; hear him.' Unless we actually regard him by faith as the only begotten Son of God, we can perform no duty aright in the hearing of him, nor shall we learn the truth as we ought. Hence it is that those who deny his divine person, though they pretend to attend to him as the teacher of the church, do yet learn no truth from him, but embrace pernicious errors in the stead thereof. So it is with the Socinians, and all that follow them. For whereas they scarcely own any other office of Christ but his prophetic—looking on him as a man sent to teach the mind of God, and to confirm his doctrine by his sufferings, whereon he was afterward highly exalted of God—they learn nothing from him in a due manner.

But this respect to the person of Christ is that which will ingenerate in us all those holy qualifications that are necessary to enable us to know the mind and will of God. For hence do reverence, humility, faith, delight, and assurance, arise and flow; without whose continual exercise, in vain shall men hope to learn the will of God by the utmost of their endeavours. And the want of these things is the cause of much of that lifeless, unsanctified knowledge of the doctrine of the gospel which is amongst many.

They learn not the truth from Christ, so as to expect all teachings from his divine power. Hence they never come to know it, either in its native beauty drawing the soul into the love and delight of what they know, or in its transforming efficacy changing the mind into its own image and likeness.

AS A KING

The same also is the state of things with respect to his kingly office and power. But this I have at large treated on elsewhere, and that much to the same purpose; namely, in the exposition of the third verse of the first chapter of the Epistle to the Hebrews. Wherefore I shall not here enlarge upon it.

Some seem to imagine, that the kingly power of Christ towards the church consists only in external rule by the gospel and the laws thereof, requiring obedience to the officers and rulers that he has appointed therein. It is true, that this also belongs to his kingly power and rule; but to suppose that it consists solely therein, is an ebullition from the poisonous fountain of the denial of his divine person. For if he be not God over all, whatever in words may be pretended or ascribed to him, he is capable of no other rule or power. But indeed no one act of his kingly office can be aright conceived or acknowledged, without a respect had to his divine person. I shall instance only to this purpose in two things in general.

OVER ALL CREATION

The extent of his power and rule gives evidence hereunto. It is over the whole creation of God. 'All power is given him in heaven and earth' (Matt. 28:18). 'All things are put under his feet, he only excepted who put all things under him' (1 Cor. 15:27); and he is made 'head over all things to the church' (Eph. 1:22). Not only those who are above the rule of external law, as the holy angels; and those who have cast off all such rule, as the devils themselves; but all things that in their own nature are not capable of obedience to an external law or rule, as the whole inanimate creation, heaven, and earth, and the sea, with all things in them and under them (Phil. 2:10), with the dead bodies of men, which he shall raise at the last day.

For this power over the whole creation is not only a moral right to rule and govern it; but it is also accompanied with virtue, force, or almighty power, to act, order, and dispose of it at his pleasure. So is it described by the apostle from the psalmist, 'You, Lord, in the beginning have laid the foundation of the earth; and the heavens are the works of your hands: they shall perish, but you remain; and they all shall wax old as does a garment; and as a vesture shall you fold them up, and they shall be changed: but you are the same, and your years shall not fail' (Heb. 1:10–12). That power is required to his kingly office whereby he created all things in the beginning, and shall change them all, as a man folds up a vesture, in the end. Omnipotence, accompanied with eternity and immutability, are required hereunto.

It is a vain imagination, to suppose that this power can reside in a mere creature, however glorified and exalted. All essential divine properties are concurrent with it, and inseparable from it. And where are the properties of God, there is the nature of God; for his being and his properties are one and the same.

If the Lord Christ, as king of the church, be only a mere man, and be as such only to be considered, however he may be exalted and glorified—however he may be endowed with honour, dignity, and authority—yet he cannot put forth or act any real physical power immediately and directly, but where he is present. But this is in heaven only; for the heaven must receive him 'until the times of the restitution of all things' (Acts 3:21). And hereon his rule and power would be the greatest disadvantage to the church that could befall it. For suppose it immediately under the rule of God, even the Father; his omnipotence and omnipresence, his omniscience and infinite wisdom—whereby he could be always present with every one of them, know all their wants, and give immediate relief according to the counsel of his will—were a stable foundation for faith to rest upon, and an everlasting spring of consolation. But now, whereas all power, all judgment, all rule, is committed to the Son, and the Father does nothing towards the church but in and by him, if he have not the same divine power and properties with him, the foundation of the church's faith is cast down, and the spring of its consolation utterly stopped up.

I cannot believe in him as my heavenly king, who is not able by himself, and by the virtue of his presence with me, to make what changes and alterations he pleases in the minds of men, and in the whole creation of God, to relieve, preserve, and deliver me, and to raise my body at the last day.

To suppose that the Lord Christ, as the king and head of the church, has not an infinite, divine power, whereby he is able always to relieve, succour, save, and deliver it—if it were to be done by the alteration of the whole or any part of God's creation, so as that the fire should not burn, nor the water overwhelm them, nor men be able to retain their thoughts or ability one moment to afflict them; and that their distresses are not always effects of his wisdom, and never from the defect of his power—is utterly to overthrow all faith, hope, and the whole of religion itself.

Ascribe therefore to the Lord Christ, in the exercise of his kingly office, only a moral power, operative by rules and laws, with the help of external instruments—deprive him of omnipresence and omniscience, with infinite, divine power and virtue, to be acted at his pleasure in and over the whole creation—and you rase the foundation of all Christian faith and hope to the ground.

There are no true believers who will part with their faith herein for the whole world; namely, that the Lord Jesus Christ is able, by his divine power and presence, immediately to aid, assist, relieve, and deliver them in every moment of their surprisals, fears, and dangers, in every trial or duty they may be called to, in every difficulty they have to conflict withal. And to expect these things any otherwise but by virtue of his divine nature, is woefully to deceive our own souls. For this is the work of God.

Spiritual Rule

The rule of Christ, as king of the church, is internal and spiritual, over the minds, souls, and consciences of all that do believe. There is no one gracious acting of soul in any one believer, at any time in the whole world, either in opposition to sin or the performance of duty, but it is influenced and under the guidance of the kingly power of Christ. I suppose we have herein not only the common faith, but also the common spiritual sense and experience, of them all. They know that in their spiritual life it is he that lives in them as the efficient cause of all its acts and that without him they can do nothing. To him they have respect in every the most secret and retired acting of grace, not only performed as under his eye, but by his assistance; on every occasion do they immediately, in the internal acting of their minds, look to him, as one more present with their souls than they are with themselves; and have no thoughts of the least distance of his knowledge or power. And two things are required hereto.

HE KNOWS OUR HEARTS. That he be καρδιογνώστης—that he have an actual inspection into all the frames, dispositions, thoughts, and internal actings, of all believers in the whole world, at all times, and every moment. Without this, he cannot bear that rule in their souls and consciences which we have described, nor can they act faith in him, as their occasions do require. No man can live by faith on Christ, no man can depend on his sovereign power, who is not persuaded that all the frames of his heart, all the secret groans and sighs of his spirit, all the inward labourings of his soul against sin, and after conformity to himself, are continually under his eye and cognizance. Wherefore it is said, that all things are naked and opened to his eyes (Heb. 4:13). And he says of himself, that he 'searches' (that is, knows) 'the hearts and reins of men' (Rev. 2:23). And if these things are not the peculiar properties of the divine nature, I know nothing that may be so esteemed.

HE EXERCISES POWER IN OUR HEARTS. There is required hereunto an influence of power into all the acting of the souls of believers—all intimate, efficacious operation with them in every duty, and under every temptation. These all of them do look for, expect, and receive from him, as the king and head of the church. This also is an effect of divine and infinite power. And to deny these things to the Lord Christ, is to rase the foundation of Christian religion. Neither faith in, nor love to him, nor dependence on him, nor obedience to his authority, can be preserved one moment, without a persuasion of his immediate intuition and inspection into the hearts, minds, and thoughts of all men, with a real influence into all the acting of the life of God in all them that believe. And the want of the faith hereof is that which has disjoined the minds of many from adherence to him, and has produced a lifeless carcass of the Christian religion, instead of the saving power thereof.

AS A PRIEST

The same may be said concerning his sacerdotal office, and all the acts of it. It was in and by the human nature that he offered himself a sacrifice for us. He had somewhat of his own to offer (Heb. 8:3;) and to this end a body was prepared for him (Heb. 10:5). But it was not the work of a man, by one offering, and that of himself, to expiate the sins of the whole church, and forever to perfect them that are sanctified, which he did (Heb. 10:14). God was to purchase his church 'with his own blood' (Acts 20:28). But this also I have spoken to at large elsewhere.

This is the sum of what we plead for: We can have no due consideration of the offices of Christ, can receive no benefit by them, nor perform any act of duty with respect to them, or any of them, unless faith in his divine person be actually exercised as the foundation of the whole. For that is it whence all their glory, power, and efficacy are derived. Whatever, therefore, we do with respect to his rule, whatever we receive by the communication of his Spirit and grace, whatever we learn from his Word by the teachings of his Spirit, whatever benefit we believe, expect, and receive, by his sacrifice and intercession on our behalf; our faith in them all, and concerning them all, is terminated on his divine person. The church is saved by his offices, because they are his. This is the substance of the testimony given concerning him, by God, even the Father. 'This is the record' that God has testified concerning his Son, 'that God has given to us eternal life, and this life is in his Son' (1 John 5:10–11). Eternal life is given to us, as it was wrought out and procured by the mediation of Christ on our behalf. But yet in him it was originally, and from him do we receive it in the discharge of his office; for this life is in the Son of God.

Hence it is that all those by whom the divine person of Christ is denied, are forced to give such a description of his offices, as that it is utterly impossible that the church should be saved by the discharge of them.

8

THE FAITH OF THE OLD TESTAMENT CHURCH
IN THE PERSON OF CHRIST

A brief view of the faith of the church under the Old Testament concerning the divine person of Christ, shall close these discourses, and make way for those that ensue, wherein our own duty with respect whereunto shall be declared.

That the faith of all believers, from the foundation of the world, had a respect to him, I shall afterwards demonstrate; and to deny it, is to renounce both the Old Testament and the New. But that this faith of theirs did principally respect his person, is what shall here be declared. Therein they knew was laid the foundation of the counsels of God for their deliverance, sanctification, and salvation. Otherwise it was but little they clearly understood of his office, or the way whereby he would redeem the church.

The apostle Peter, in the confession he made of him (Matt. 16:16), exceeded the faith of the Old Testament in this, that he applied the promise concerning the Messiah to that individual person: 'You are the Christ, the Son of the living God'—he that was to be the

Redeemer and Saviour of the church. Howbeit Peter then knew little of the way and manner whereby he was principally so to be. And therefore, when he began to declare them to his disciples—namely, that they should be by his death and sufferings—he in particular was not able to comply with it, but, says he, 'Master, that be far from you' (v. 22). As 'flesh and blood'—that is, his own reason and understanding—did not reveal or declare Him to Peter to be the Christ, the Son of the living God, but the Father which is in heaven; so he stood in need of fresh assistance from the same almighty hand to believe that He should redeem and save his church by his death. And therefore he did refuse the external revelation and proposition of it, though made by Christ himself, until he received internal aid from above. And to suppose that we have faith now in Christ or his death on any other terms, is an evidence that we have no faith at all.

Wherefore, the faith of the saints under the Old Testament did principally respect the person of Christ—both what it was, and what it was to be in the fulness of time, when he was to become the seed of the woman. What his especial work was to be, and the mystery of the redemption of the church thereby, they referred to his own wisdom and grace—only, they believed that by him they should be saved from the hand of all their enemies, or all the evil that befell them on the account of the first sin and apostasy from God.

God gave them, indeed, representations and prefigurations of his office and work also. He did so by the high priest of the law, the tabernacle, with all the services and services thereunto belonging. All that Moses did, as a faithful servant in the house of God, was but a 'testimony of those things which were to be spoken after' (Heb. 3:5). Howbeit the apostle tells us that all those things had but a 'shadow of good things to come, and not the very image of the things themselves' (Heb. 10:1). And although they are now to us full of light and instruction, evidently expressing the principal works of Christ's mediation, yet were they not so to them. For the veil is now taken off from them in their accomplishment, and a declaration is made of the counsels of God in them by the gospel. The meanest believer may now find out more of the work of Christ in the types of the Old Testament, than any prophets or wise men could have done of old. Therefore they always earnestly longed for their accomplishment—that the day might break, and the shadows fly away by the rising of the Sun of Righteousness with healing in his wings. But as to his person, they had glorious revelations concerning it; and their faith in him was the life of all their obedience.

The first promise, which established a new intercourse between God and man, was concerning his incarnation—that he should be the seed of the woman (Gen. 3:15); that is, that the Son of God should be 'made of a woman, made under the law' (Gal. 4:4). From the giving of that promise the faith of the whole church was fixed on him whom God would send in our nature, to redeem and save them. Other way of acceptance with him there was none provided, none declared, but only by faith in this promise. The design of God in this promise—which was to reveal and propose the only way which in his wisdom and grace he had prepared for the deliverance of mankind from the state of sin and apostasy whereinto they were cast, with the nature of the faith and obedience of the church—will not admit of any other way of salvation, but only faith in him who was thus promised to be a saviour. To suppose that men might fall off from faith in God by the revelation of himself in this promise, and yet be saved by attending to instructions given by the works of creation and providence, is an imagination that will no longer possess the minds of men than whilst they are ignorant of, or do forget, what it is to believe and to be saved.

The great promise made to Abraham was, that He should take his seed upon him, in whom all the nations of the earth should be blessed (Gen. 12:3; 15:18; 22:18); which promise is explained by the apostle, and applied to Christ (Gal. 3:8). Hereon 'Abraham believed on the Lord, and it was counted to him for righteousness' (Gen. 15:6); for he saw the day of Christ, and rejoiced (John 8:56).

The faith that Jacob instructed his sons in was—that the Shiloh should come, and to him should be the gathering of the nations (Gen. 49:10). Job's faith was—that his Redeemer was the Living One, and that he should stand on the earth in the latter day (Job 19:25).

The revelations made to David principally concerned His person, and the glory thereof (see Ps. 2, 45, 68, 110, 118, especially 45 and 72 compared), which give an account of their apprehensions concerning him.

The faith of Daniel was, that God would show mercy, for the Lord's sake (Dan. 9:17); and of all the prophets that the 'Redeemer should come to Zion, and to them that turn from transgression in Jacob' (Isa. 59:20).

Of the same nature were all his personal appearances under the Old Testament, especially that most illustrious representation made of him to the prophet Isaiah (ch. 6), and the glorious revelation of his name (ch. 9:6).

It is true that both these and other prophets had revelations concerning his sufferings also. For 'the Spirit of Christ that was in them testified beforehand of his sufferings, and the glory that should follow' (1 Pet. 1:11) — an illustrious testimony whereunto we have given us (Ps. 22, Isa. 53). Nevertheless their conceptions concerning them were dark and obscure. It was his person that their faith principally regarded. Thence were they filled with desires and expectations of his coming, or his exhibition and appearance in the flesh. With the renewed promises hereof did God continually refresh the church in its straits and difficulties. And hereby did God call off the body of the people from trust in themselves, or boasting in their present privileges, which they were exceedingly prone to.

In process of time this faith, which wrought effectually in the Church of Israel, degenerated into a lifeless opinion, that proved the ruin of it. Whilst they really lived in the faith of him as the Saviour and Redeemer of the church from all its spiritual adversaries, as he who was to make 'an end of sin, and bring in everlasting righteousness,' to whom all their present ordinances were subservient and directive; all grace, love, zeal, and patient waiting for the accomplishment of the promise, flourished among them. But in process of time, growing carnal, trusting in their own righteousness, and the privileges which they had by the law, their faith concerning the person of Christ degenerated into a corrupt, obstinate opinion, that he should be only a temporal king and deliverer; but as to righteousness and salvation they were to trust to themselves and the law. And this prejudicate opinion, being indeed a renunciation of all the grace of the promises of God, proved their utter ruin. For when he came in the flesh, after so many ages, filled up with continued expectations, they rejected and despised him as one that had neither form nor comeliness for which he should be desired. So does it fall out in other churches. That which was faith truly spiritual and evangelic in their first planting, becomes a lifeless opinion in succeeding ages. The same truths are still professed, but that profession springs not from the same causes, nor does it produce the same effects in the hearts and lives of men. Hence, in process of time, some churches continue to have an appearance of the same body which they were at first, but—being examined—are like a lifeless, breathless carcass, wherein the animating Spirit of grace does not dwell. And then is any church, as it was with that of the Jews, nigh to destruction, when it corrupts formerly professed truths, to accommodate them to the present lusts and inclinations of men.

9

HOW WE HONOUR THE PERSON OF CHRIST

Many other considerations of the same nature with those foregoing, relating to the glory and honour of the person of Christ, may be taken from all the fundamental principles of religion. And our duty it is in them all, to 'consider the Apostle and High Priest of our profession'—'the Author and Finisher of our faith'. I shall not insist on more, but proceed to those principles of truth which are immediately directive of our duty towards him; without diligent attendance whereunto, we do but in vain bear the name of Christians. And the substance of what is designed may be included in the following assertion:

'The glory, life, and power of Christian religion, as Christian religion, and as seated in the souls of men, with all the acts and duties which properly belong thereunto, and are, therefore, peculiarly Christian, and all the benefits and privileges we receive by it, or by virtue of it, with the whole of the honour and glory that arise to God thereby, have all of them their formal nature and reason from their respect and relation to the person of Christ; nor is he a Christian who is otherwise minded.'

In the confirmation hereof it will appear what judgment ought to be passed on that inquiry—which, after the uninterrupted profession of the catholic church for so many ages of a faith to the contrary, is begun to be made by some amongst us—namely, of what use is the person of Christ in religion? For it proceeds on this supposition, and is determined accordingly—that there is something in religion wherein the person of Christ is of no use at all—a vain imagination, and such as is destructive to the whole real intercourse between God and man, by the one and only Mediator!

The respect which we have in all acts of religion to the person of Christ may be reduced to these four heads:

1. Honour [ch. 9–10].
2. Obedience [ch. 11–14].
3. Conformity [ch. 15].
4. The use we make of him, for the attaining and receiving of all gospel privileges—all grace and glory.

And hereunto the whole of our religion, as it is Christian or evangelic, may be reduced.

The person of Christ is the object of divine honour and worship. The formal object and reason hereof is the divine nature, and its essential infinite excellencies. For they are nothing but that respect to the Divine Being which is due to it from all rational creatures, regulated by revelation, and enforced by divine operations. Wherefore the person of Christ is primarily the object of divine honour and worship, upon the account of his divine nature and excellencies. And those who, denying that nature in him, do yet pretend to worship him with divine and religious adoration, do but worship a golden calf of their own setting up; for a Christ who is not over all, God blessed forever, is not better. And it implies a contradiction, that any creature should, on any accounts be the immediate, proper object of divine worship; unless the divine essential excellencies be communicated to it, or transfused into it, whereby it would cease to be a creature. For that worship is nothing but the ascription of divine excellencies to what is so worshipped.

But we now consider the Lord Christ in his whole entire person, the Son of God incarnate, 'God manifest in the flesh.' His infinite condescension, in the assumption of our nature, did no way divest him of his divine essential excellencies. For a time, they were shadowed and veiled thereby from the eyes of men; when 'he made himself of no reputation, and took on him the form of a servant.' But he eternally and unchangeably continued 'in the form of God,' and 'thought it not robbery to be equal with God' (Phil. 2:6–7). He can no more really and essentially, by any act of condescension or humiliation, cease to be God, than God can cease to be.

> *He can no more really and essentially, by any act of condescension or humiliation, cease to be God, than God can cease to be.*

Wherefore, his being clothed with our nature derogates nothing from the true reason of divine worship due to him, but adds an effectual motive to it. He is, therefore, the immediate object of all duties of religion, internal and external; and in the dispensation of God towards us, none of them can be performed in a due manner without a respect to him.

This, then, in the first place, is to be confirmed; namely, that all divine honour is due to the Son of God incarnate—that is, the person of Christ.

It is the will of the Father, 'That all men should honour the Son, even as they honour the Father. He that honours not the Son, honours not the Father which has sent him' (John 5:23). Some considerations on this divine testimony will confirm our position. It is of the Son incarnate that the words are spoken—as all judgment was committed to him by the Father, as he was 'sent' by him (v. 22)—that is, of the whole person of Christ in the exercise of his mediatory office. And with respect hereunto it is that the mind of God is peculiarly revealed. The way whereby God manifests his will, that all men should thus honour the Son, as they honour the Father, is by committing all power, authority, and judgment to him, 'For the Father loves the Son, and shows him all things that himself does: and he will show him greater works than these, that ye may marvel. For as the Father raises up the dead, and quickens them;

even so the Son quickens whom he will. For the Father judges no man, but has committed all judgment to the Son' (vv. 20–22). Not that these things are the formal reason and cause of the divine honour which is to be given him; but they are reasons of it, and motives to it, in that they are evidences of his being the Son of God.

But it may be said, what need is there that the Father should so interpose an act of his will and sovereign pleasure as to this honouring of the Son, seeing the sole cause and reason of this divine honour is the divine nature, which the Son is no less partaker of than the Father? I answer:

1. He does not in this command intend the honour and worship of Christ absolutely as God, but distinctly as the Son; which peculiar worship was not known under the Old Testament, but was now declared necessary in the committing all power, authority, and judgment to him. This is the honour whereof we speak.

2. He does it, lest any should conceive that 'as he was now sent of the Father,' and that in the 'form of a servant,' this honour should not be due to him. And the world was then far from thinking that it was so; and many, I fear, are yet of the same mind.

He is, therefore, to be honoured by us, according to the will of God, καθὼς, 'in like manner,' as we honour the Father.

1. With the same honour; that is, divine, sacred, religious, and supreme. To honour the Father with other honour, is to dishonour him. When men design to give glory and honour to God which is not truly divine, it is idolatry; for this honour, in truth, is nothing but the ascription of all infinite, divine excellencies to him. Whereon, when men ascribe to him that which is not so, they fall into idolatry, by the worship of their own imaginations. So was it with the Israelites, when they thought to have given glory to God by making a golden calf, whereon they proclaimed a feast to Jehovah (Exod. 32:5). And

so was it with the heathen in all their images of God, and the glory which they designed to give him thereby, as the apostle declares (Rom. 1:23–5). This is one kind of idolatry—as the other is—the ascribing to creatures anything that is proper and peculiar to God, any divine excellency. And we do not honour God the Father with one kind of honour, and the Son with another. That were not to honour the Son καθὼς, 'as' we honour the Father, but in a way infinitely different from it.

2. In the same manner, with the same faith, love, reverence, and obedience, always, in all things, in all acts and duties of religion whatever.

This distinct honour is to be given to the person of the Son by virtue of this command of the Father, though originally on the account of his oneness in nature with the Father. And our duty herein is pressed with the highest enforcement; he that honours not the Son, honours not the Father. He who denies the Son (herein) 'has not the Father; but he that acknowledges the Son, has the Father also' (1 John 2:23). 'And this is the record, that God has given to us eternal life; and this life is in his Son. He that has the Son, has life; and he that has not the Son of God has not life' (1 John 5:11–12) . If we are wanting herein, whatever we pretend, we do not worship nor honour God at all.

And there is reason to give this caution—reason to fear that this great fundamental principle of our religion is, if not disbelieved, yet not much attended to in the world. Many, who profess a respect to the Divine Being and the worship thereof, seem to have little regard to the person of the Son in all their religion; for although they may admit of a customary interposition of his name in their religious worship, yet the same distinct veneration of him as of the Father, they seem not to understand, or to be exercised in. Howbeit, all the acceptance of our persons and duties with God depends on this one condition—'That we honour the Son, even as we honour the Father.' To honour the Son as we ought to honour the Father, is that which makes us Christians, and which nothing else will so do.

This honour of the person of Christ may be considered—in the

175

duties of it [this chapter], wherein it consists; and in the principle, life, or spring, of those duties [next chapter].

The duties whereby we ascribe and express divine honour to Christ may be reduced to two heads, first, adoration; secondly, invocation.

ADORATION

Adoration is the prostration of soul before him as God, in the acknowledgment of his divine excellencies and the ascription of them to him. It is expressed in the Old Testament by השתחוה; that is, humbly to bow down ourselves or our souls to God. The LXX render it constantly by προσκυνέω; which is the word used in the New Testament to the same purpose. The Latins expressed it usually by *adoro*. And these words, though of other derivations, are of the same signification with that in the Hebrew; and they do all of them include some external sign of inward reverence, or a readiness thereunto. Hence is that expression, 'He bowed down his head and worshipped' (Gen. 24:26; see Ps. 95:6). And these external signs are of two sorts. First, such as are natural and occasional; secondly, such as are solemn, stated, or instituted. Of the first sort are the lifting up of our eyes and hands towards heaven upon our thoughts of him, and sometimes the casting down of our whole persons before him; which deep thoughts with reverence will produce. Outward instituted signs of this internal adoration are all the ordinances of evangelic worship. In and by them do we solemnly profess and express our inward veneration of him. Other ways may be invented to the same purpose, but the Scripture knows them not, yea, condemns them. Such are the veneration and adoration of the pretended images of him, and of the Host, as they call it, among the Papists.

This adoration is due continually to the person of Christ, and that—as in the exercise of the office of mediation. It is due to him from the whole rational creation of God. So is it given in charge to the angels above. For when he brought the first-begotten into the world, he said, Προσκυνησάτωσαν αὐτῷ πάντες ἄγγελοι Θεοῦ; that is, הִשְׁתַּחֲווּ־לוֹ כָּל־אֱלֹהִים, 'Worship him, all ye gods' (Ps. 97:7). 'Let all the angels of God worship him,' adore him, bow down before him (Heb. 1:6). See our exposition of that place—the design of the whole chapter being to express the divine honour that is due to the person of Christ, with the grounds thereof. This is the command given also to the church, 'He is your Lord, and worship him' (Ps. 45:11).

A glorious representation hereof—whether in the church above, or in that militant here on the earth—is given us (Rev. 5:6–14):

> And I beheld, and, lo, in the midst of the throne and of the four beasts, and in the midst of the elders, stood a Lamb as it had been slain, having seven horns and seven eyes, which are the seven Spirits of God sent forth into all the earth. And he came and took the book out of the right hand of him that sat upon the throne. And when he had taken the book, the four beasts and four and twenty elders fell down before the Lamb, having every one of them harps, and golden vials full of odours, which are the prayers of saints. And they sung a new song, saying, 'You are worthy to take the book, and to open the seals thereof: for you were slain, and have redeemed us to God by your blood, out of every kindred, and tongue, and people, and nation; and has made us to our God kings and priests: and we shall reign on the earth.'

> And I beheld, and I heard the voice of many angels round about the throne, and the beasts, and the elders: and the number of them was ten thousand times ten thousand, and thousands of thousands; saying with a loud voice, 'Worthy is the Lamb that was slain to receive power, and riches, and wisdom, and strength, and honour, and glory, and blessing.'

> And every creature which is in heaven, and on the earth, and under the earth, and such as are in the sea, and all that are in them, heard I saying, 'Blessing, and honour, and glory, and power, be to him that sits upon the throne, and to the Lamb, for ever and ever.'

> And the four beasts said, 'Amen.' And the four and twenty elders fell down and worshipped him that lives for ever and ever.

The especial object of divine adoration, the motives to it, and the nature of it, or what it consists in, are here declared.

The object of it is Christ, not separately, but distinctly from the Father, and jointly with him. And he is proposed, first, as having fulfilled the work of his mediation in his incarnation and oblation—as a Lamb slain. Secondly, in his glorious exaltation—'in the midst of the throne of God.' The principal thing that the heathen of old observed concerning the Christian religion, was, that in it 'praises were sung to Christ as to God.'

The motives to this adoration are the unspeakable benefits which we receive by his mediation, 'You are worthy, for you were slain, and have redeemed us to God.'

Hereon the same glory, the same honour, is ascribed to him as to God the Father: 'Blessing, and honour, and glory, and power, be to him that sits upon the throne, and to the Lamb, for ever and ever.'

The nature of this adoration is described to consist in three things:

1. Solemn prostration: 'And the four living creatures said, Amen. And the four and twenty elders fell down and worshipped him that lives for ever and ever' (So also is it described Rev. 4:10–11).
2. In the ascription of all divine honour and glory, as is at large expressed (Rev. 5:11–13).
3. In the way of expressing the design of their souls in this adoration, which is by the praises: 'They sung a new song'—that is, of praise; for so are all those psalms which have that title of a new song.

And in these things—namely, solemn prostration of soul in the acknowledgment of divine excellencies, ascriptions of glory and honour with praise—does religious adoration consist. And they belong not to the great holy society of them who worship above and here below—whose hearts are not always ready to this solemn adoration of the Lamb, and who are not on all occasions exercised therein.

And this adoration of Christ differs from the adoration of God, absolutely considered, and of God as the Father, not in its nature, but merely on the account of its especial motives. The principal motive to the adoration of God, absolutely considered, is the work of creation—the manifestation of his glory therein—with all the effects of his power and goodness thereon ensuing. So it is declared, 'You are worthy, O Lord, to receive glory, and honour, and power: for you have created all things, and for your pleasure they are and were created' (Rev. 4:11). And the principal motive to the adoration and worship of God as the Father, is that eternal love, grace, and goodness, which he is the fountain of in a peculiar manner (Eph. 1:4–5). But the great motive to the adoration of Christ is the work of redemption, 'Worthy is the Lamb that was slain to receive power, and riches, and wisdom, and strength, and honour, and glory, and blessing' (Rev. 5:12). The reason whereof is given, 'For you were slain, and have redeemed us to God by your blood; and made us to our God kings and priests' (Rev. 5:9–10). The adoration is the same, 'Blessing, and honour, and glory, and power, be to him that sits upon the throne, and to the Lamb, for ever and ever' (Rev. 5:13). But the immediate motives of it are different, as its objects are distinct.

Herein no small part of the life of the Christian religion consists. The humbling of our souls before the Lord Christ, from an apprehension of his divine excellencies—the ascription of glory, honour, praise, with thanksgiving to him, on the great motive of the work of redemption with the blessed effects thereof—are things wherein the life of faith is continually exercised; nor can we have any evidence of an interest in that blessedness which consists in the eternal assignation of all glory and praise to him in heaven, if we are not exercised to this worship of him here on earth.

Invocation

Invocation is the second general branch of divine honour—of that honour which is due and paid to the Son, as to the Father. This is the first exercise of divine faith—the breath of the spiritual life.

And it consists in two things, or has two parts. First, an ascription of all divine properties and excellencies to him whom we invocate. This is essential to prayer, which without it is but vain babbling. Whoever comes to God hereby, 'must believe that he is, and that he is the rewarder of them that diligently seek him.' Secondly, there is in it also a representation of our wills, affections, and desires of our souls, to him on whom we call, with an expectation of being heard and relieved, by virtue of his infinitely divine excellencies. This is the proper acting of faith with respect to ourselves; and hereby it is our duty to give honour to the person of Christ.

When he himself died in the flesh, he committed his departing soul by solemn invocation into the hands of his Father, 'Father, into your hands I commit my spirit' (Ps. 31:5; Luke 23:46). And to evidence that it is the will of God that we should honour the Son, as we honour the Father, even as the Son himself in his human nature, who is our example, honoured the Father—he who first died in the faith of the gospel, bequeathed his departing soul into the hands of Jesus Christ by solemn invocation, 'They stoned Stephen, ἐπικαλούμενον, solemnly invocating, and saying, Lord Jesus, receive my spirit' (Acts 7:59). And having by faith and prayer left his own soul safe in the hands of the Lord Jesus, he adds one petition more to him, wherewith he died: 'Lord, lay not this sin to their charge' (Acts 7:60). Herein did he give divine honour to Christ in the especial invocation of his name, in the highest instances that can be conceived. In his first request, wherein he committed his departing soul into his hands, he ascribed to him divine omniscience, omnipresence, love, and power; and in the latter, for his enemies, divine authority and mercy, to be exercised in the pardon of sin. In his example is the rule established for the especial invocation of Christ for the effects of divine power and mercy.

Hence the apostle describes the church, or believers, and distinguishes it, or them, from all others, by the charge of this duty, 'With all that call on the name of our Lord Jesus Christ, both their Lord and ours' (1 Cor. 1:2). To call on the name of the Lord Jesus expresses solemn invocation in the way of religious worship. The Jews did call on the name of God. All others in their way called on the names of their gods. This is that whereby the church is distinguished from them all—it calls on the name of our Lord Jesus Christ.

He requires that, as we believe on God, that is, the Father, so we should believe on him also; and therein honour the Son, as we honour the Father (John 14:1). The nature of this faith, and the manner how it is exercised on Christ, we shall declare afterwards. But the apostle, treating of the nature and efficacy of this invocation, affirms, that we cannot call on him in whom we have not believed (Rom. 10:14). Whence it follows, on the contrary, that he on whom we are bound to believe, on him it is our duty to call. So the whole Scripture is closed with a prayer of the church to the Lord Christ, expressing their faith in him: 'Even so, come, Lord Jesus' (Rev. 22:20).

The Object of Prayer

There is not any one reason of prayer—not any one motive to it—not any consideration of its use or efficacy—but renders this peculiar invocation of Christ a necessary duty. Two things in general are required to render the duty of invocation lawful and useful. First, that it have a proper object. Secondly, that it have prevalent motives and encouragements to it. These in concurrence are the formal reason and ground of all religious worship in general, and of prayer in particular. So are they laid down as the foundation of all religion, 'I am the Lord your God'—that is, the proper object of all religious worship—'which brought you out of the land of Egypt, out of the house of bondage' (Exod. 20:2–3); which being summarily and typically representative of all divine benefits, temporal, spiritual, and eternal, is the great motive thereunto. The want of both these in all mere creatures, saints and angels, makes the invocation of them, not only useless, but idolatrous. But they both eminently concur in the person of Christ, and his acting towards us. All the perfections of the divine nature are in him; whence he is the proper object of religious invocation. On this account when he acted in and towards the church as the great angel of the covenant, God instructed the people to all religious observance of him, and obedience to him, 'Beware of him, and obey his voice, provoke him not; for he will not pardon your transgressions; for my name is in him' (Exod. 23:21). Because the name of God was in him—that is, the divine nature, with sovereign authority to punish or pardon sin—therefore was all religious obedience due to him. And no motives are wanting hereunto. All that the Lord Christ has done for us, and all the principles of love, grace, compassion, and power, from whence what he has so done did proceed, are all of this nature; and they are accompanied with the encouragement of his relation to us, and charge concerning us. Take away this duty, and the peculiar advantage of the Christian religion is destroyed.

We have lived to see the utmost extremes that the Christian religion can divert into. Some, with all earnestness, do press the formal invocation of saints and angels as our duty; and some will not grant that it is lawful for us so to call on Christ himself.

The Socinians grant generally that it is lawful for us to call on Christ; but they deny that it is our duty at any time so to do. But as they own that it is not our duty, so on their principles it cannot be lawful. Denying his divine person, they leave him not the proper object of prayer. For prayer without an ascription of divine excellencies—as omniscience, omnipresence, and almighty power—unto him whom we invocate, is but vain babbling, that has nothing of the nature of true prayer in it; and to make such ascriptions to him who by nature is not God, is idolatrous.

The solemn ordinary worship of the church, and so of private believers in their families and closets, is under an especial directory and guidance. For the person of the Father—as the eternal fountain of power, grace, and mercy—is the formal object of our prayers, to whom our supplications are directed. The divine nature, also lately considered, is the object of natural worship and invocation; but it is the same divine nature, in the person of the Father, that is the proper object of evangelic worship and invocation. So our Saviour has taught us to call on God under the name and notion of a father (Matt. 6:9); that is, his God and our God, his Father and our Father (John 20:17). And this invocation is to be by and in the name of the Son, Jesus Christ, through the aid of the Holy Ghost. He is herein considered as the mediator between God and man—as the Holy Ghost is he by whom supplies of grace, enabling us to the acceptable performance of our duties are actually communicated to us. This is the way whereby God will be glorified. This is the mystery of our religion, that we worship God according to the economy of his wisdom and grace, wherein he dispenses of himself to us, in the persons of the Father, Son, and Spirit. Otherwise he will not be honoured or worshipped by us. And those who in their worship or invocation do attempt an approach to the divine nature as absolutely considered, without respect to the dispensation of God in the distinct persons of the holy Trinity, do reject the mystery of the gospel, and all the benefit of it. So is it with many. And not a few, who pretend a great devotion to God, do supply other things into the room of Christ, as saints and angels—rejecting also the aids of the Spirit to comply with imaginations of their own, whose assistance herein they more approve of.

But this is the nature and method of ordinary solemn evangelic invocation. So it is declared, 'Through him we have access by one Spirit to the Father' (Eph. 2:18). It is the Father to whom we have our access, whom we peculiarly invocate; as it is expressed, 'For this cause I bow my knees to the Father of our Lord Jesus Christ, of whom the whole family in heaven and earth is named, that he would grant you...' (Eph. 3:14–16). But it is through him—that is, by Christ in the exercise of his mediatory office—that we have this access to the Father; we ask in his name, and for his sake (John 14:13–14; 16:23–4). They did so of old, though not in that express exercise of faith which we now attain to. 'Hear, O Lord, and have mercy, for the Lord's sake' (Dan. 9:17). All this are we enabled to by one Spirit—through the aids and assistance of the Spirit of grace and supplication (Rom. 8:26–7). So that prayer is our crying—'Abba, Father,' by the Spirit of the Son (Gal. 4:6). This is farther declared (Heb. 4:15–16; 10:19–22). Herein is the Lord Christ considered, not absolutely with respect to his divine person, but with respect to his office, that through 'him our faith and hope might be in God' (1 Pet. 1:21).

Motives to Pray

Wherefore, it being our duty, as has been proved, to invocate the name of Christ in a particular manner, and this being the ordinary solemn way of the worship of the church—we may consider on what occasions, and in what seasons, this peculiar invocation of Christ, who in his divine person is both our God and our advocate, is necessary for us, and most acceptable to him.

Temptations & Desertions

Times of great distresses in conscience through temptations and desertions, are seasons requiring an application to Christ by especial invocation. Persons in such conditions, when their souls, as the Psalmist speaks, are overwhelmed in them, are continually solicitous about compassion and deliverance. Some relief, some refreshment, they often find in pity and compassion from them who either have been in the same condition themselves, or by Scripture light do know the terror of the Lord in these things. When their complaints are despised, and their troubles ascribed to other causes than what they are really sensible of, and feel within themselves—as is commonly done by physicians of no value—it is an aggravation of their distress and sorrow. And they greatly value every sincere endeavour for relief, either by counsel or prayer. In this state and condition the Lord Christ in the gospel is proposed as full of tender compassion—as he alone who is able to relieve them. In that himself has suffered, being tempted, he is touched with a feeling of our infirmities, and knows how to have compassion on them that are out of the way (Heb. 2:18; 4:15; 5:2). So is he also, as he alone who is able to succour, to relieve, and to deliver them. 'He is able to succour them that are tempted' (Heb. 2:18). Hereon are they drawn, constrained, encouraged to make applications to him by prayer, that he would deal with them according to his compassion and power. This is a season rendering the discharge of this duty necessary. And hereby have innumerable souls found consolation, refreshment, and deliverance. A time of trouble is a time of the especial exercise of faith in Christ. So himself gives direction, 'Let not your heart be troubled: you believe in God, believe also in me' (John 14:1). Distinct acting of faith on Christ are the great means of support and relief in trouble. And it is by especial invocation, whereby they put forth and exert themselves.

An instance hereof, as to temptation, and the distress wherewith it is attended, we have in the apostle Paul. He had 'a thorn in the flesh,' 'a messenger of Satan to buffet' him. Both expressions declare the deep sense he had of his temptation, and the perplexity wherewith it was accompanied. 'For this cause he besought the Lord thrice, that it might depart from him' (2 Cor. 12:7–8). He applied himself solemnly to prayer for its removal, and that frequently. And it was the Lord—that is, the Lord Jesus Christ—to whom he made his application. For so the name Lord is to be interpreted—if there be nothing contrary in the context—as the name of God is of the Father, by virtue of that rule, 'To us there is one God, the Father; and one Lord Jesus Christ' (1 Cor. 8:6). And it is evident also in the context. The answer he received to his prayer was, 'My grace is sufficient for you; for my power is made perfect in weakness'. And whose power that was, who gave him that answer, he declares in the next words, 'Most gladly therefore will I glory in my infirmities, that the power of Christ may rest upon me,' that is, the power of him on whom he called, who gave him that answer, 'My power is made perfect in weakness.'

Discoveries of Christ's Glory & Love

Times of gracious discoveries either of the glory of Christ in himself, or of his love to us, are seasons that call for this duty. The glory of Christ in his person and offices is always the same, and the revelation that is made of it in the Scripture varies not; but—as to our perception and apprehension of it, whereby our hearts and minds are affected with it in an especial manner—there are apparent seasons of it which no believers are unacquainted withal. Sometimes such a sense of it is attained under the dispensation of the Word; wherein as Christ on the one hand is set forth evidently crucified before our eyes, so on the other he is gloriously exalted. Sometimes it is so in prayer, in meditation, in contemplation on him. As an ability was given to the bodily sight of Stephen, to see, upon the opening of the heavens, 'the glory of God, and Jesus standing at his right hand' (Acts 7:55–6) — so he opens the veil sometimes, and gives a clear, affecting discovery of his glory to the minds and souls of believers; and in such seasons are they drawn forth and excited to invocation and praise. So Thomas — being surprised with an apprehension and evidence of his divine glory and power after his resurrection, wherein he was declared to be the Son of God with power (Rom. 1:4) — cried to him, 'My Lord and my God' (John 20:28). There was in his words both a profession of his own faith and a solemn invocation of Christ. When, therefore, we have real discoveries of the glory of Christ, we cannot but speak to him, or of him. 'These things said Isaiah, when he saw his glory, and spake of him' (John 12:41). And Stephen, upon a view of it in the midst of his enraged enemies, testified immediately, 'I see the heavens opened, and the Son of man standing on the right hand of God.' And thereby was he prepared for that solemn invocation of his name which he used presently after, 'Lord Jesus, receive my spirit' (Acts 7:56, 59). And so, also, upon his appearance as the Lamb, to open the book of prophecies; wherein there was an eminent manifestation of his glory — seeing none else could be found in heaven, or earth, or under the earth, that was able to open the book, or so much as to look thereon' (Rev. 5:3). 'The four and twenty elders fell down before him,' and presenting all the prayers of the saints, 'sang a new song' of praise to him (Rev. 5:8–10). This is our duty, this will be our wisdom, upon affecting discoveries of the glory of Christ; namely, to apply ourselves to him by invocation or praise; and thereby will the refreshment and advantage of them abide upon our minds.

So is it also as to his love. The love of Christ is always the same and equal to the church. Howbeit there are peculiar seasons of the manifestation and application of a sense of it to the souls of believers. So it is when it is witnessed to them, or shed abroad in their hearts by the Holy Ghost. Then is it accompanied with a constraining power, to oblige us to live to him who died for us and rose again (2 Cor. 5:14–15). And of our spiritual life to Christ, invocation of him is no small portion and this sense of his love we might enjoy more frequently than for the most part we do, were we not so much wanting to ourselves and our own concerns. For although it be an act of sovereign grace in God to grant it to us, and affect us with it, as it seems good to him, yet is our duty required to dispose our hearts to its reception. Were we diligent in casting out all that 'filthiness and superfluity of naughtiness' which corrupts our affections, and disposes the mind to abound in vain imaginations; were our hearts more taken off from the love of the world, which is exclusive of a sense of divine love; did we more meditate on Christ and his glory—we should more frequently enjoy these constraining visits of his love than now we do. So himself expresses it, 'Behold, I stand at the door, and knock: if any man hear my voice, and open the door, I will come in to him, and will sup with him, and he with me' (Rev. 3:20). He makes intimation of his love and kindness to us. But ofttimes we neither hear his voice when he speaks, nor do open our hearts to him. So do we lose that gracious, refreshing sense of his love, which he expresses in that promise, 'I will sup with him, and he shall sup with me.' No tongue can express that heavenly communion and blessed intercourse which is intimated in this promise. The expression is metaphorical, but the grace expressed is real, and more valued than the whole world by all that have experience of it. This sense of the love of Christ and the effect of it in communion with him, by prayer and praises, is divinely set forth in the Book of Canticles. The church therein is represented as the spouse of Christ; and, as a faithful spouse, she is always either solicitous about his love, or rejoicing in it. And when she has attained a sense of it, she abounds in invocation admiration and praise. So does the church of the New Testament, upon an apprehension of his love, and the unspeakable fruits of it: 'Unto him that loved us, and washed us from our sins in his own blood, and has made us kings and priests to God and his Father; to him be glory and dominion for ever and ever, Amen' (Rev. 1:5–6). This, therefore, is another season that calls for this duty.

Times of Persecution

Times of persecution for his Name's sake, and for the profession of the gospel, are another season rendering this peculiar invocation of Christ both comely and necessary. Two things will befall the minds of believers in such a season.

First, that their thoughts will be neatly exercised about him, and conversant with him. They cannot but continually think and meditate on him for whom they suffer. None ever suffered persecution on just grounds, with sincere ends, and in a due manner, but it was so with them. The invincible reasons they have to suffer for him—taken from his person love, grace, and authority—from what he is in himself, what he has done for them, and what account of all things is to be given to him—do continually present themselves to their minds. Wildernesses, prisons, and dungeons, have been filled with thoughts of Christ and his love. And many in former and latter ages have given an account of their communion and holy intercourse with the Lord Christ under their restraints and sufferings. And those who at any time have made an entrance into such a condition, will all of them give in the testimony of their own experience in this matter.

Secondly, such persons have deep and fixed apprehensions of the especial concern which the Lord Christ has in them as to their present condition—as also of his power to support them, or to work out their deliverance. They know and consider—that 'in all their afflictions he is afflicted'—suffers in all their sufferings—is persecuted in all their persecutions; that in them all he is full of love, pity, and unspeakable compassion towards them; that his grace is sufficient for them—that his power shall be perfected in their weakness, to carry them through all their sufferings, to his and their own glory. In these circumstances, it is impossible for them who are under the conduct of his Spirit, not to make especial applications continually to him for those aids of grace—for those pledges of love and mercy—for those supplies of consolation and spiritual refreshments, which their condition calls for. Wherefore, in this state, the invocation of Christ is the refuge and sheet-anchor of the souls of them who truly believe in him. So it was to all the holy martyrs of old, and in latter ages.

This doctrine and duty is not for them who are at ease. The afflicted, the tempted, the persecuted, the spiritually disconsolate, will prize it, and be found in the practice of it. And all those holy souls who, in most ages, on the account of the profession of the gospel, have been reduced to outwardly unbelievable distresses, have, as was said, left their testimony to this duty, and the benefits of it. The refreshment which they found therein was a sufficient balance against the weight of all outward calamities, enabling them to rejoice under them with 'joy unspeakable and full of glory.' This is the church's reserve against all the trials it may be exercised withal, and all the dangers whereunto it is exposed. Whilst believers have liberty of access to him in their supplications, who has all power in his hand, who is full of ineffable love and compassion towards them, especially as suffering for his sake—they are more than conquerors in all their tribulations.

A Deep Sense of Need

When we have a due apprehension of the eminent acting of any grace in Christ Jesus, and withal a deep and abiding sense of our own want of the same grace, it is a season of especial application to him by prayer for the increase of it. All graces as to their habit were equal in Christ—they were all in him in the highest degree of perfection; and every one of them did he exercise in its due manner and measure on all just occasions. But outward causes and circumstances gave opportunity to the exercise of some of them in a way more eminent and conspicuous than others were exercised in. For instance, such were his unspeakable condescension, self-denial, and patience in sufferings; which the apostle to this purpose insists upon (Phil. 2:5–8). Now the great design of all believers is to be like Jesus Christ, in all grace, and all the exercise of it. He is in all things their pattern and example. Wherefore, when they have a view of the glory of any grace as it was exercised in Christ, and withal a sense of their own defect and want therein—conformity to him being their design—they cannot but apply themselves to him in solemn invocation, for a farther communication of that grace to them, from his stores and fulness. And these things mutually promote one another in us, if duly attended to. A due sense of our own defect in any grace will farther us in the prospect of the glory of that grace in Christ. And a view, a due contemplation, of the glorious exercise of any grace in him, will give us light to discover our own great defect therein, and want thereof. Under a sense of both, an immediate application to Christ by prayer would be all unspeakable furtherance of our growth in grace and conformity to him. Nor can there be any more effectual way or means to draw supplies of grace from him, to draw water from the wells of salvation. When, in a holy admiration of, and fervent love to, any grace as eminently exercised in and by him, with a sense of our own want of the same grace, we ask it of him in faith—he will not deny it to us. So the disciples, upon the prescription of a difficult duty, to whose due performance a good measure of faith was required—out of a sense of the all-fulness of him, and their own defect in that grace which was necessary to the peculiar duty there prescribed—immediately pray to him, saying, 'Lord, increase our faith' (Luke 17:5). The same is the case with respect to any temptation that may befall us, wherewith he was exercised, and over which he prevailed.

The Time of Death

The time of death, whether natural, or violent for his sake, is a season of the same nature. So Stephen recommended his departing soul into his hands with solemn prayer. 'Lord Jesus,' said he, 'receive my spirit.' To the same purpose have been the prayers of many of his faithful martyrs in the flames, and under the sword. In the same manner does the faith of innumerable holy souls work in the midst of their deathbed groans. And the more we have been in the exercise of faith on him in our lives, the more ready will it be in the approaches of death, to make its resort to him in a peculiar manner.

And it may be other instances of an alike nature may be given to the same purpose.

Should We Ask Christ to Intercede for Us?

An answer to an inquiry which may possibly arise from what we have insisted on, shall close this discourse. For whereas the Lord Jesus Christ, as Mediator, intercedes with the Father for us, it may be inquired, Whether we may pray to him, that he would so intercede on our behalf; whether this be comprised in the duty of invocation or prayer to him?

No Precedent

There is no precedent nor example of any such thing, of any such prayer, in the Scripture; and it is not safe for us to venture on duties not exemplified therein. Nor can any instance of a necessary duty be given, of whose performance we have not an example in the Scripture.

His Person Is the Object of Our Faith

In the invocation of Christ, we 'honour the Son, even as we honour the Father.' Wherefore his divine person is therein the formal object of our faith. We consider him not therein as acting in his mediatory office towards God for us, but as he who has the absolute power and disposal of all the good things we pray for. And in our invocation of him, our faith is fixed on, and terminated on his person. But—as he is in the discharge of his mediatory office—through him 'our faith and hope are in God' (1 Pet. 1:21). He who is the Mediator, or Jesus Christ the Mediator—as God and man in one person—is the object of all divine honour and worship. His person, and both his natures in that person, is so the object of religious worship. This is that which we are in the proof and demonstration of. Howbeit it is his divine nature, and not his discharge of the office of mediation, that is the formal reason and object of divine worship. For it consists in an ascription of infinitely divine excellencies and properties to him whom we so worship. And to do this on any account but of the divine nature, is in itself a contradiction, and in them that do it idolatry. Had the Son of God never been incarnate, he had been the object of all divine worship. And could there have been a mediator between God and us who was not God also, he could never have been the object of any divine worship or invocation. Wherefore Christ the Mediator, God and man in one person, is in all things to be honoured, even as we honour the Father; but it is as he is God, equal with the Father, and not as Mediator—in which respect he is inferior to him. With respect to his divine person, we ask immediately of himself in our supplications—as he is Mediator—we ask of the Father in his name. The different actings of faith on him, under the same distinction shall be declared in the next chapter.

10

WHY WE HONOUR THE PERSON OF CHRIST

The principle and spring of this assignation of divine honour to Christ, in both the branches of it, is faith in him. And this has been the foundation of all acceptable religion in the world since the entrance of sin.

FAITH—FROM THE BEGINNING

There are some who deny that faith in Christ was required from the beginning, or was necessary to the worship of God, or the justification and salvation of them that did obey him. For, whereas it must be granted that 'without faith it is impossible to please God,' which the apostle proves by instances from the foundation of the world (Heb. 11)—they suppose it is faith in God under the general notion of it, without any respect to Christ, that is intended. It is not my design to contend with any, nor expressly to confute such ungrateful opinions—such pernicious errors. Such this is, which—being pursued in its proper tendency—strikes at the very foundation of Christian religion; for it at once deprives us of all contribution of light and truth from the Old Testament.

Somewhat I have spoken before of the faith of the saints of old concerning him. I shall now, therefore, only confirm the truth, by some principles which are fundamental in the faith of the gospel.

The First Promise

The first promise (Gen. 3:15)—truly called Proteuangelion—was revealed, proposed, and given, as containing and expressing the only means of delivery from that apostasy from God, with all the effects of it, under which our first parents and all their posterity were cast by sin. The destruction of Satan and his work in his introduction of the state of sin, by a Saviour and Deliverer, was prepared and provided for in it. This is the very foundation of the faith of the church; and if it be denied, nothing of the economy or dispensation of God towards it from the beginning can be understood. The whole doctrine and story of the Old Testament must be rejected as useless, and no foundation be left in the truth of God for the introduction of the New.

Christ—'The Seed of the Woman'

It was the person of Christ, his incarnation and mediation, that were promised under the name of the 'seed of the woman,' and the work he should do in breaking the head of the serpent, with the way whereby he should do it in suffering, by his power. The accomplishment hereof was in God's sending his Son in the likeness of sinful flesh, in the fulness of time, made under the law, or by his manifestation in the flesh, to destroy the works of the devil. So is this promise interpreted (Gal. 3:13; 4:4; Heb. 2:14–16; 1 John 3:8). This cannot be denied but upon one of these two grounds:

First, that nothing is intended in that divine revelation but only a natural enmity that is between mankind and serpents. But this is so foolish an imagination, that the Jews themselves, who constantly refer this place to the Messiah, are not guilty of. All the whole truth concerning God's displeasure on the sin of our first parents, with what concerns the nature and consequence of that sin, is everted hereby. And whereas the foundation of all God's future dealing with them and their posterity is plainly expressed herein, it is turned into that which is ludicrous, and of very little concern in human life. For such is the enmity between mankind and serpents—which not one in a million knows any thing of or is troubled with. This is but to lay the axe of atheism to all religion built on divine revelation. Besides, on this supposition, there is in the words not the least intimation of any relief that God tendered to our parents for their delivery from the state and condition whereinto they had cast themselves by their sin and apostasy. Wherefore they must be esteemed to be left absolutely under the curse, as the angels were that fell—which is to root all religion out of the world. For amongst them who are absolutely under the curse, without any remedy, there can be no more than is in hell.

Or, second, it must be, because some other way of deliverance and salvation, and not that by Christ, is here proposed and promised. But, whereas they were to be wrought by the 'seed of the woman'—if this were not that Christ in whom we do believe, there was another promised, and he is to be rejected. And this is fairly at once to blot out the whole Scripture as a fable; for there is not a line of doctrinal truth in it but what depends on the traduction of Christ from this first promise.

SACRIFICES CONFIRM THE PROMISE

This promise was confirmed, and the way of the deliverance of the church by virtue of it declared, in the institution of expiatory sacrifices. God in them and by them declared from the beginning, that 'without shedding of blood there was no remission;' that atonement for sin was to be made by substitution and satisfaction. With respect to them, the Lord Christ was called 'The Lamb of God,' even as he took away the sins of the world by the sacrifice of himself (John 1:29). For we 'were redeemed with the precious blood of Christ, as of a lamb without blemish and without spot' (1 Pet. 1:19). Wherein the Holy Spirit refers to the institution and nature of sacrifices from the beginning. And he is thence represented in heaven as a 'Lamb that had been slain' (Rev. 5:6)—the glory of heaven arising from the fruits and effects of his sacrifice. And because of the representation thereof in all the former sacrifices, is he said to be a 'Lamb slain from the foundation of the world' (Rev. 13:8). And it is strange to me that any who deny not the expiatory sacrifice of Christ, should doubt whether the original of these sacrifices were of divine institution or the invention of men. And it is so, amongst others, for the reasons ensuing:

First, on the supposition that they were of men's finding out and voluntary observation, without any previous divine revelation, it must be granted that the foundation of all acceptable religion in the world was laid in, and resolved into, the wisdom and wills of men, and not into the wisdom, authority, and will of God. For that the great solemnity of religion, which was as the centre and testimony of all its other duties, did consist in these sacrifices even before the giving of the law, will not be denied. And in the giving of the law, God did not, on this supposition, confirm and establish his own institutions with additions to them of the same kind, but set his seal and approbation to the inventions of men. But this is contrary to natural light, and the whole current of Scripture revelations.

Second, all expiatory sacrifices were, from the beginning, types and representations of the sacrifice of Christ; whereon all their use, efficacy, and benefit among men—all their acceptance with God—did depend. Remove this consideration from them, and they were as irrational a service, as unbecoming the divine nature, as any thing that reasonable creatures could fix upon. They are to this day as reasonable a service as ever they were, but that only their respect to the sacrifice of Christ is taken from them. And what person of any ordinary understanding could now suppose them a meet service whereby to glorify the divine nature? Besides, all expiatory sacrifices were of the same nature, and of the same use, both before and after the giving of the law. But that all those afterwards were typical of the sacrifice of Christ, the apostle demonstrates at large in his Epistle to the Hebrews. The inquiry, therefore, is, whether this blessed prefiguration of the Lord Christ and his sacrifice, as he was the Lamb of God taking away the sin of the world, was an effect of the wisdom, goodness, and will of God, or of the wills and inventions of men. And let it be considered, also, that these men, who are supposed to be the authors of this wonderful representation of the Lord Christ and his sacrifice, did indeed know little of them—or, as the assertors of this opinion imagine, nothing at all. To suppose that those who knew no more of Christ than they could learn from the first promise—which, as some think, was nothing at all—should of their own heads find out and appoint this divine service, which consisted only in the prefiguration of him and his sacrifice; and that God should not only approve of it, but allow it as the principal means for the establishment and exercise of the faith of all believers for four thousand years; is to indulge to thoughts deviating from all rules of sobriety. He that sees not a divine wisdom in this institution, has scarce seriously exercised his thoughts about it. But I have elsewhere considered the causes and original of these sacrifices, and shall not therefore farther insist upon them.

Our First Parents Believed the Promise

Our first parents and all their holy posterity did believe this promise, or did embrace it as the only way and means of their deliverance from the curse and state of sin; and were thereon justified before God. I confess we have not infallible assurance of any who did so in particular, but those who are mentioned by name in Scripture, as Abel, Enoch, Noah, and some others; but to question it concerning others also, as of our first parents themselves, is foolish and impious. This is done by the Socinians to promote another design, namely, that none were justified before God on the belief of the first promise, but on their walking according to the light of nature, and their obedience to some especial revelations about temporal things—the vanity whereof has been before discovered. Wherefore, our first parents and their posterity did so believe the first promise, or they must be supposed either to have been kept under the curse, or else to have had, and to make use of, some other way of deliverance from it. To imagine the first is impious—for the apostle affirms that they had this testimony, that they pleased God (Heb. 11:5); which under the curse none can do—for that is God's displeasure. And in the same place he confirms their faith, and justification thereon, with a 'cloud of witnesses' (Heb. 12:1). To affirm the latter is groundless; and it includes a supposal of the relinquishment of the wisdom, grace, and authority of God in that divine revelation, for men to betake themselves to none knows what. For that there was in this promise the way expressed which God in his wisdom and grace had provided for their deliverance, we have proved before. To forsake this way, and to betake themselves to any other, whereof he had made no mention or revelation to them, was to reject his authority and grace.

As for those who are otherwise minded, it is incumbent on them directly to prove these three things:

First, that there is another way—that there are other means for the justification and salvation of sinners—than that revealed, declared, and proposed in that first promise. And when this is done, they must show to what end—on that supposition—the promise itself was given, seeing the end of it is evacuated.

Second, that upon a supposition that God had revealed in the promise the way and means of our deliverance from the cures and state of sin, it was lawful to men to forsake it, and to betake themselves to another way, without any supernatural revelation for their guidance. For if it was not, their relinquishment of the promise was no less apostasy from God in the revelation of himself in a way of grace, than the first sin was as to the revelation of himself in the works of nature: only, the one revelation was by inbred principles, the other by external declaration; nor could it otherwise be.

Or, third, that there was some other way of the participation of the benefit of this promise, besides faith in it, or in him who was promised therein; seeing the apostle has declared that no promise will profit them by whom it is not mixed with faith (Heb. 4:2). Unless these things are plainly proved—which they will never be—whatever men declaim about universal objective grace in the documents of nature, it is but a vain imagination.

SAINTS AND PROPHETS DECLARED THE PROMISE

The declaration of this promise, before the giving of the law, with the nature and ends of it, as also the use of sacrifices, whereby it was confirmed, was committed to the ordinary ministry of our first parents and their godly posterity, and the extraordinary ministry of the prophets which God raised up among them. For God spake of our redemption by Christ by the mouth of his holy prophets from the beginning of the world (Luke 1:70). No greater duty could be incumbent on them, by the light of nature and the express revelation of the will of God, than that they should, in their several capacities, communicate the knowledge of this promise to all in whom they were concerned. To suppose that our first parents, who received this promise, and those to whom they first declared it, looking on it as the only foundation of their acceptance with God and deliverance from the curse, were negligent in the declaration and preaching of it, is to render them brutish, and guilty of a second apostasy from God. And to this principle—which is founded in the light of nature—there is countenance given by revelation also. For Enoch did prophesy of the things which were to accompany the accomplishment of this promise (Jude 14); and Noah was a preacher of the righteousness to be brought in by it (2 Pet. 2:5)—as he was an heir of the righteousness which is by faith, in himself (Heb. 11:7).

COVENANTS AND PROMISES CONFIRMED THE PROMISE

All the promises that God gave afterwards to the church under the Old Testament, before and after giving the law—all the covenants that he entered into with particular persons, or the whole congregation of believers—were all of them declarations and confirmations of the first promise, or the way of salvation by the mediation of his Son, becoming the seed of the woman, to break the head of the serpent, and to work out the deliverance of mankind. As most of these promises were expressly concerning him, so all of them in the counsel of God were confirmed in him (2 Cor. 1:20). And as there are depths in the Scripture of the Old

Testament concerning him which we cannot fathom, and things innumerable spoken of him or in his person which we conceive not, so the principal design of the whole is the declaration of him and his grace. And it is unprofitable to them who are otherwise minded. Sundry promises concerning temporal things were, on various occasions, superadded to this great spiritual promise of life and grace. And the enemies of the person and mediation of Christ do contend that men are justified by their faith and obedience with respect to those particular revelations, which were only concerning temporal things. But to suppose that all those revelations and promises were not built upon and resolved into, did not include in them, the grace and mercy of this first promise—is to make them curses instead of blessings, and deprivations of that grace which was infinitely better than what, on this supposition, was contained in them. The truth is, they were all additions to it, and confirmations of it; nor had any thing of spiritual good in them, but upon a supposition of it. In some of them there was an ampliation of grace in the more full declaration of the nature of this promise, as well as an application to their persons to whom they were made. Such was the promise made to Abraham, which had a direct respect to Christ, as the apostle proves (Gal. 3–4).

THOSE WHO FELL AWAY FOUND NO OTHER WAY

Those who voluntarily, through the contempt of God and divine grace, fell off from the knowledge and faith of this promise, whether at once and by choice, or gradually through the love of sin, were in no better condition than those have been, or would be, who have so fallen off or should so apostatize from Christian religion after its revelation and profession. And although this proved, in process of time, both before and after the flood, to be the condition of the generality of mankind, yet is it in vain to seek after the means of salvation among them who had voluntarily rejected the only way which God had revealed and provided for that end. God thereon 'suffered all nations to walk in their own ways' (Acts 14:16)—'winking at the times of their ignorance'—not calling them to repentance (Acts. 17:30); yea, he 'gave them up to their own hearts lust, and they walked in their own counsels' (Ps. 81:12). And nothing can be more derogatory to the wisdom and holiness of God, than to imagine that he would grant other ways of salvation to them who had rejected that only one which he had provided; which was by faith in Christ, as revealed in that first promise.

Salvation by Faith in Christ from the Beginning

From these considerations, which are all of them unquestionable principles of truth, two things are evident.

First, that there was no way of the justification and salvation of sinners revealed and proposed from the foundation of the world, but only by Jesus Christ, as declared in the first promise.

Second, that there was no way for the participation of the benefits of that promise, or of his work of mediation, but by faith in him as so promised. There was, therefore, faith in him required from the foundation of the world; that is, from the entrance of sin. And how this faith respected his person has been before declared. Now, faith in him as promised for the works and ends of his mediation, and faith in him as actually exhibited and as having accomplished his work, are essentially the same, and differ only with respect to the economy of times, which God disposed at his pleasure. Hence the efficacy of his mediation was the same to them who then so believed, as it is now to us after his actual exhibition in the flesh.

But yet it is acknowledged, that—as to the clearness and fulness of the revelation of the mystery of the wisdom and grace of God in him—as to the constitution of his person in his incarnation, and therein the determination of the individual person promised from the beginning, through the actual accomplishment of the work which he was promised for—faith in him, as the foundation of that divine honour which it is our duty to give to him, is far more evidently and manifestly revealed and required in the gospel, or under the New Testament, than it was under the Old (see Eph. 3:8–11). The respect of faith now to Christ is that which renders it truly evangelic. To believe in him, to believe on his name, is that signal especial duty which is now required of us.

FAITH—IN HIS PERSON

Wherefore the ground of the actual assignation of divine honour to the person of Christ, in both branches of it, adoration and invocation, is faith in him. So he said to the blind man whose eyes he opened, 'Do you believe on the Son of God?' (John 9:35). And he said, 'Lord, I believe; and he worshipped him' (John 9:38). All divine worship or adoration is a consequent effect and fruit of faith. So also is invocation; for 'How shall they call on him in whom they have not believed?' (Rom. 10:14). Him in whom we believe, we ought to adore and invocate. For these are the principal ways whereby divine faith acts itself. And so to adore or invocate any in whom we ought not to believe, is idolatry.

This faith, therefore, on the person of Christ is our duty; yea, such a duty it is, as that our eternal condition does more peculiarly depend on the performance or nonperformance of it than on any other duty whatever. For constantly under those terms is it prescribed to us. 'He that believes on the Son has everlasting life: and he that believes not the Son shall not see life; but the wrath of God abides on him' (John 3:36). Wherefore the nature and exercise of this faith must be inquired into.

NOT JUST THE MESSAGE

There is a faith which is exercised towards those by whom the mind and will of God is revealed. So it is said of the Israelites, 'They believed the Lord and Moses' (Exod. 14:31); that is, that he was sent of God, was no deceiver—that it was the word and will of God which he revealed to them. So 2 Chronicles 20:20, 'Believe in the Lord your God, so you shall be established; believe his prophets, so you shall prosper.' It was not the persons of the prophets, but their message, that was the object of the faith required. It was to believe what they said, as from God—not to believe in them as if they were God. So it is explained by the apostle, 'King Agrippa, do you believe the prophets? I know that you believe' (Acts 26:27). He believed that they were sent of God, and that the word they spake was from him; otherwise there was no believing of them who were dead so many ages before.

And this is all the faith in Christ himself which some will allow. To believe in Christ, they say, is only to believe the doctrine of the gospel revealed by him. Hence they deny that any could believe in him before his coming into the world, and the declaration of the mind of God in the gospel made by him. An assent to the truth of the gospel, as revealed by Christ, is with them the whole of that faith in Christ Jesus which is required of us.

Of all that poison which at this day is diffused in the minds of men, corrupting them from the mystery of the gospel, there is no part that is more pernicious than this one perverse imagination, that to believe in Christ is nothing at all but to believe the doctrine of the gospel; which yet, we grant, is included therein. For as it allows the consideration of no office in him but that of a prophet, and that not as vested and exercised in his divine person, so it utterly overthrows the whole foundation of the relation of the church to him, and salvation by him.

That which suits my present design, is to evince that it is the person of Christ which is the first and principal object of that faith wherewith we are required to believe in him; and that so to do, is not only to assent to the truth of the doctrine revealed by him, but also to place our trust and confidence in him for mercy, relief, and protection—for righteousness, life, and salvation—for a blessed resurrection and eternal reward. This I shall first manifest from some few of those multiplied testimonies wherein this truth is declared, and whereby it is confirmed as also with some arguments taken from them; and then proceed to declare the ground, nature, and exercise of this faith itself.

As to the testimonies confirming this truth, it must be observed of them all in general, that wherever faith is required towards our Lord Jesus Christ, it is still called believing 'in him,' or 'on his name,' according as faith in God absolutely is every where expressed. If no more be intended but only the belief of the doctrine revealed by him, then whose doctrine soever we are obliged to believe, we may be rightly said to believe in them, or to believe on their name. For instance, we are obliged to believe the doctrine of Paul the apostle, the revelations made by him, and that on the hazard of our eternal welfare by the unbelieving of them; yet that we should be said to believe in Paul, is that which he did utterly detest (1 Cor. 1:13, 15).

For the places themselves the reader may consult, among others (John 1:12; 3:16, 18, 36; 6:29, 35, 41; 7:38, 39; Acts 14:23; 16:31; 19:4; 24:24; 26:18; Rom. 3:26; 9:33; 10:11; 1 Pet. 2:6; 1 John 5:10, 13). There is not one of these but sufficiently confirms the truth. Some few others not named may be briefly insisted on.

John 14:1, 'You believe in God, believe also in me.' The distinction made between God and him limits the name of God to the person of the Father. Faith is required in them both, and that distinctly: 'You believe in God, believe also in me.' And it is the same faith, of the same kind, to be exercised in the same way and manner, that is required; as is plain in the words. They will not admit of a double faith, of one faith in God, and of another in Christ, or of a distinct way of their exercise.

Wherefore, as faith divine is fixed on, and terminated in, the person of the Father; so is it likewise distinctly in and on the person of the Son: and it was to evidence his divine nature to them—which is the ground and reason of their faith—that he gave his command to his disciples. This he farther testifies (vv. 9–11). And as to the exercise of this faith, it respected the relief of their souls, under troubles, fears, and disconsolations: 'Let not your heart be troubled: ye believe in God, believe also in me.' To believe in him to the relief of our souls against troubles, is not to assent merely to the doctrine of the gospel, but also to place our trust and confidence in him, for such supplies of grace, for such an exercise of the acts of divine power, as whereby we may be supported and delivered. And we have herein the whole of what we plead. Divine faith acted distinctly in, and terminated on, the person of Christ—and that with respect to supplies of grace and mercy from him in a way of divine power.

So he speaks to Martha, 'He that believes in me, though he were dead, yet shall he live: and whosoever lives, and believes in me, shall never die. Do you Believe this?' (John 11:25–7). Whereunto she answers 'Yes, Lord; I believe that you are the Christ, the Son of God.' His person was the object of her faith; and her belief in him comprised a trust for all spiritual and eternal mercies.

I shall add one more, wherein not only the thing itself, but the especial ground and reason of it, is declared—'The life which I now live in the flesh, I live by the faith of the Son of God, who loved me, and gave himself for me' (Gal. 2:20). That faith he asserts which is the cause of our spiritual life—that life to God which we lead in the flesh, or whilst we are in the body, not yet admitted to sight and enjoyment. Of this faith the Son of God is both the author and the object; the latter whereof is here principally intended. And this is evident from the reason and motive of it, which are expressed. This faith I live by, am in the continual exercise of, because he 'loved me, and gave himself for me.' For this is that which powerfully influences our hearts to fix our faith in him and on him. And that person who so loved us is the same in whom we do believe. If his person was the seat of his own love, it is the object of our faith And this faith is not only our duty, but our life. He that has it not, is dead in the sight of God.

But I hope it is not yet necessary to multiply testimonies to prove it our duty to believe in Jesus Christ—that is, to believe in the person of the Son of God, for other faith in Christ there is none; yet I shall add one or two considerations in the confirmation of it.

It Is Our Duty to Call on Him

There is no more necessary hereunto—namely, to prove the person of Christ the Son of God to be the proper and distinct object of faith divine—than what we have already demonstrated concerning the solemn invocation of him. For, says the apostle, 'How can they call on him in whom they have not believed?' (Rom. 10:14). It holds on either side. We cannot, we ought not, to call on him in whom we do not, we ought not to believe. And in whom we do believe, on him we ought to call. Wherefore, if it be our duty to call on the name of Christ, it is our duty to believe in the person of Christ. And if to believe in Christ be no more but to believe the doctrine of the gospel which he has revealed, then every one whose doctrine we are obliged to believe, on them we ought to call also. And on this ground, we may call on the names of the prophets and apostles, as well as on the name of Jesus Christ, and be saved thereby. But whereas invocation or prayer proceeds from faith, and that prayer is for mercy, grace, life, and eternal salvation; faith must be fixed on the person so called on, as able to give them all to us, or that prayer is in vain.

We Are Baptized into His Name

Again, that we are baptized into the name of Jesus Christ, and that distinctly with the Father, is a sufficient evidence of the necessity of faith in his person; for we are therein given up to universal spiritual subjection of soul to him, and dependence on him. Not to believe in him, on his name—that is, his person—when we are so given up to him, or baptized into him, is virtually to renounce him. But to put a present close to this contest: Faith in Christ is that grace whereby the church is united to him—incorporated into one mystical body with him. It is thereby that he dwells in them, and they in him. By this alone are all supplies of grace derived from him to the whole body. Deny his person to be the proper and immediate object of this faith, and all these things are utterly overthrown—that is, the whole spiritual life and eternal salvation of the church.

This faith in the person of Christ, which is the foundation of all that divine honour in sacred adoration and invocation which is assigned to him, may be considered two ways. First, as it respects his person absolutely. Secondly, as he is considered in the discharge of the office of mediation.

FAITH IN HIS PERSON ABSOLUTELY

In the first sense, faith is placed absolutely and ultimately on the person of Christ, even as on the person of the Father. He counts it no robbery herein to be equal with the Father. And the reason hereof is, because the divine nature itself is the proper and immediate object of this faith, and all the acts of it. This being one and the same in the person of the Father and of the Son, as also of the Holy Spirit, two things do follow thereon. First, that each person is equally the object of our faith, because equally participant of that nature which is the formal reason and object of it. Second, it follows also, that in acting faith on, and ascribing therewithal divine honour to, any one person, the others are not excluded; yea, they are included therein. For by reason of the mutual inbeing of the Divine persons in the unity of the same nature, the object of all spiritual worship is undivided. Hence are those expressions of the Scriptures, 'He that has seen the Son, has seen the Father; he that honours the Son, honours the Father, for he and the Father are one.'

The Divine Nature Is the Ground of Faith

And to clear our present design, three things may be observed from hence; namely, that the divine nature, with all its essential properties, is the formal reason and only ground of divine faith.

CHRIST—PARTAKER OF THE DIVINE NATURE. That the Lord Christ is not the absolute and ultimate object of our faith, any otherwise but under this consideration, of his being partaker of the nature of God—of his being in the form of God, and equal to him. Without this, to place our faith in him would be robbery and sacrilege; as is all the pretended faith of them who believe not his divine person.

ALL PERSONS OF THE TRINITY EQUALLY HONOURED. There is no derogation from the honour and glory of the Father—not the least diversion of any one single act of duty from him, nor from the Holy Spirit—by the especial acting of faith on the person of Christ; for all divine honour is given solely to the divine nature: and this being absolutely the same in each person, in the honouring of one, they are all equally honoured. He that honours the Son, he therein honours the Father also.

FAITH IN THE THE PERSON OF CHRIST INDISPENSABLE. Hence it appears what is that especial acting of faith on the person of Christ which we intend, and which in the Scripture is given in charge to us, as indispensably necessary to our salvation. And there are three things to be considered in it.

1. That his divine nature is the proper formal object of this faith, on the consideration whereof alone it is fixed on him. If you ask a reason why I believe on the Son of God—if you intend what cause I have for it, what motives to it—I shall answer, it is because of what he has done for me, whereof afterwards. So does the apostle (Gal. 2:20). But if you intend, what is the formal reason, ground, and warranty whereon I thus believe in him, or place my trust and confidence in him, I say it is only this, that he is 'over all, God blessed for ever;' and were he not so, I could not believe in him. For to believe in any, is to expect from him that to be done for me which none but God can do.

2. That the entire person of Christ, as God and man, is the immediate object of our faith herein. The divine nature is the reason of it; but his divine person is the object of it. In placing our faith on him, we consider him as God and man in one and the same person. We believe in him because he is God; but we believe in him as he is God and man in one person.

   And this consideration of the person of Christ—namely, as he is God and man—in our acting of faith on him, is that which renders it peculiar, and limits or determines it to his person, because he only is so—the Father is not, nor the Holy Spirit. That faith which has the person of God and man for its object, is peculiarly and distinctly placed on Christ.

3. The motives to this distinct acting of faith on his person are always to be considered as those also which render this faith peculiar. For the things which Christ has done for us, which are the motives of our faith in him, were peculiar to him alone; as in the place before quoted (Gal. 2:20). Such are all the works of his mediation, with all the fruits of them, whereof

we are made partakers. So God, in the first command, wherein he requires all faith, love, and obedience from the church, enforced it with the consideration of a signal benefit which it had received, and therein a type of all spiritual and eternal mercies (Exod. 20:2–3). Hence two things are evident, which clearly state this matter.

First, that faith which we place upon and the honour which we give thereby to the person of Christ, is equally placed on and honour equally given thereby to the other persons of the Father and the Holy Spirit, with respect to that nature which is the formal reason and cause of it. But it is peculiarly fixed on Christ, with respect to his person as God and man, and the motives to it, in the acts and benefits of his mediation.

Second, all of Christ is considered and glorified in this acting of faith on him—his divine nature, as the formal cause of it; his divine entire person, God and man, as its proper object; and the benefits of his mediation, as the especial motives thereunto.

This faith in the person of Christ is the spring and fountain of our spiritual life. We live by the faith of the Son of God. In and by the actings hereof is it preserved, increased, and strengthened. 'For he is our life' (Col. 3:4); and all supplies of it are derived from him, by the acting of faith in him. We receive the forgiveness of sins, and an inheritance among them that are sanctified, 'by the faith that is in him' (Acts 26:18). Hereby do we abide in him; without which we can do nothing (John 15:5). Hereby is our peace with God maintained—'For he is our peace' (Eph. 2:14); and in him we have peace, according to his promise (John 16:33). All strength for the mortification of sin, for the conquest of temptations—all our increase and growth in grace—depend on the constant actings of this faith in him.

The way and method of this faith is that which we have described. A due apprehension of the love of Christ, with the effects of it in his whole mediatory work on our behalf—especially in his giving himself for us, and our redemption by his blood—is the great motive thereunto. They whose hearts are not deeply affected herewith, can never believe in him in a due manner. 'I live,' says the apostle, 'by the faith of the Son of God, who loved me, and gave himself for me.' Unless a sense hereof be firmly implanted in our souls, unless we are deeply affected with it, our faith in him would be weak and wavering, or rather none at all. The due remembrance of what the blessed Lord Jesus has done for us, of the ineffable love which was the spring, cause, and fountain of what he so did—thoughts of the mercy, grace, peace, and glory which he has procured thereby—are the great and unconquerable motives to fix our faith, hope, trust, and confidence in him.

His divine nature is the ground and warranty for our so doing. This is that from whence he is the due and proper object of all divine faith and worship. From the power and virtue thereof do we expect and receive all those things which in our believing on him we seek after; for none but God can bestow them on us, or work them in us. There is in all the acting of our faith on him, the voice of the confession of Thomas, 'My Lord and my God.'

His divine person, wherein he is God and man, wherein he has that nature which is the formal object of divine worship, and wherein he wrought all those things which are the motives thereunto, is the object of this faith; which gives its difference and distinction from faith in God in general, and faith in the person of the Father, as the fountain of grace, love, and power.

FAITH IN THE MEDIATOR

Faith is acted on Christ under the formal notion of mediator between God and man. So it is expressed, 'Who by him do believe in God, that raised him up from the dead, and gave him glory; that your faith and hope might be in God' (1 Pet. 1:21). And this acting of faith towards Christ is not contrary to that before described, nor inconsistent with it, though it be distinct from it. To deny the person of Christ to fall under this double consideration—of a divine person absolutely, wherein he is 'over all, God blessed for ever,' and, as manifested in the flesh, exercising the office of mediator between

God and man—is to renounce the gospel. And according to the variety of these respects, so are the acting of faith various; some on him absolutely, on the motives of his mediation; some on him as mediator only. And how necessary this variety is to the life, support, and comfort of believers, they all know in some measure who are so (see our exposition on Heb. 1:1–3). Sometimes faith considers him as on the throne; sometimes as standing at the right hand of God; sometimes as the mediator between God and man, the man Christ Jesus. Sometimes his glorious power, sometimes his infinite condescension, is their relief.

Wherefore, in the sense now intended, he is considered as the ordinance, as the servant of God, 'who raised him up from the dead, and gave him glory.' So our faith respects not only his person, but all the acts of his office. It is faith in his blood (Rom. 3:25). It is the will of God, that we should place our faith and trust in him and them, as the only means of our acceptance with him—of all grace and glory from him. This is the proper notion of a mediator. So is he not the ultimate object of our faith, wherein it rests, but God through him. 'Through him have we access by one Spirit to the Father' (Eph. 2:18). So he is the way whereby we go to God (John 14:6; see Heb. 10:19–22). And this so is faith in him; because he is the immediate, though not the ultimate, object of it (Acts 26:18).

This is that which renders our faith in God evangelic. The especial nature of it arises from our respect to God in Christ, and through him. And herein faith principally regards Christ in the discharge of his sacerdotal office. For although it is also the principle of all obedience to him in his other offices, yet as to fixing our faith in God through him, it is his sacerdotal office and the effects of it that we rest upon and trust to. It is through him as the high priest over the house of God, as he who has made for us a new and living way into the holy place, that we draw nigh to God (Heb. 4:14–16; 10:19–22; 1 John 1:3).

No comfortable, refreshing thoughts of God, no warrantable or acceptable boldness in an approach and access to him, can any one entertain or receive, but in this exercise of faith on Christ as the mediator between God and man. And if, in the practice of religion, this regard of faith to him—this acting of faith on God through him—be not the principle whereby the whole is animated and guided, Christianity is renounced, and the vain cloud of natural religion embraced in the room of it. Not a verbal mention of Him, but the real intention of heart to come to God by him, is required of us; and thereinto all expectation of acceptance with God, as to our persons or duties, is resolved.

We have had great endeavours of late, by the Socinians, to set forth and adorn a natural religion; as if it were sufficient to all ends of our living to God. But as most of its pretended ornaments are stolen from the gospel, or are framed in an emanation of light from it, such as nature of itself could not rise to; so the whole proceeds from a dislike of the mediation of Christ, and even weariness of the profession of faith in him. So is it with the minds of men who were never affected with supernatural revelations, with the mystery of the gospel, beyond the owning of some notions of truth—who never had experience of its power in the life of God.

But here lies the trial of faith truly evangelic. Its steady beholding of the Sun of Righteousness proves it genuine and from above. And let them take heed who find their heart remiss or cold in this exercise of it. When men begin to satisfy themselves with general hopes of mercy in God, without a continual respect to the interposition and mediation of Christ, whereinto their hope and trust is resolved, there is a decay in their faith, and proportionally in all other evangelic graces also. Herein lies the mystery of Christian religion, which the world seems to be almost weary of.

11

OBEDIENCE TO CHRIST

All holy obedience, both internal and external is that which we proposed as the second part of our religious regard to the person of Christ. His great injunction to his disciples is, 'That they keep his commandments'—without which, none are so.

Some say the Lord Christ is to be considered as a lawgiver, and the gospel as a new law given by him, whereby our obedience to him is to be regulated. Some absolutely deny it, and will not grant the gospel in any sense to be a new law. And many dispute about these things, whilst obedience itself is on all hands generally neglected. But this is that wherein our principal concern lies. I shall not, therefore, at present, immix myself in any needless disputations. Those things wherein the nature and necessity of our obedience to him is concerned, shall be briefly declared.

THE LAW

The law under the Old Testament, taken generally, had two parts—first, the moral preceptive part of it; and, secondly, the institutions of worship appointed for that season. These are jointly and distinctly called the law.

CHRIST DID NOT ABROGATE THE MORAL LAW

In respect to the first of these, the Lord Christ gave no new law, nor was the old abrogated by him—which it must be if another were given in the room of it, to the same ends. For the introduction of a new law in the place of and to the end of a former, is an actual abrogation of it. Neither did he add any new precepts to it, nor give any counsels for the performance of duties in matter or manner beyond what it prescribed. Any such supposition is contrary to the wisdom and holiness of God in giving the law, and inconsistent with the nature of the law itself. For God never required less of us in the law than all that was due to him; and his prescription of it included all circumstances and causes that might render any duty at any time necessary in the nature or degree of it. Whatever at any time may become the duty of any person towards God, in the substance or degrees of it, it is made so by the law. All is included in that summary of it, 'You shall love the Lord your God with all your heart, and your neighbour as thyself.' Nothing can be the duty of men but what and when it is required by the love of God or our neighbour. Wherefore, no additions were made to the preceptive part of the law by our Saviour, nor counsels given by him for the performance of more than it did require.

In this regard the gospel is no new law—only the duties of the moral and eternal law are plainly declared in the doctrine of it, enforced in its motives, and directed as to their manner and end. Nor in this sense did the Lord Christ ever declare himself to be a new lawgiver; yea, he declares the contrary—that he came to confirm the old (Matt. 5:17).

CHRIST GAVE A NEW LAW OF WORSHIP

Secondly, the law may be considered as containing the institutions of worship which were given in Horeb by Moses, with other statutes and judgments. It was in this sense abolished by Christ. For the things themselves were appointed but to the time of reformation. And thereon, as the supreme Lord and lawgiver of the gospel church, he gave a new law of worship, consisting in several institutions and ordinances of worship thereunto belonging. See Hebrews 3:3–6, and our explanation of that place.

OBEDIENCE TO CHRIST AND THE LAW

Obedience to the Lord Christ may be considered with respect to both these—the moral law which he confirmed, and the law of evangelic worship which he gave and appointed. And some few things may be added to clear the nature of it.

NOT JUST DOING WHAT HE REQUIRES

Obedience to Christ does not consist merely in doing the things which he requires. So far the church under the Old Testament was obliged to yield obedience to Moses; and we are yet so to the prophets and apostles. This is done, or may be so, with respect to any subordinate directive cause of our obedience, when it is not formally so denominated from his authority. All obedience to Christ proceeds from an express subjection of our souls and consciences to him.

DEPENDS ON HIS DIVINE NATURE

No religious obedience could be due to the Lord Christ directly, by the rule and command of the moral law, were he not God by nature also. The reason and foundation of all the obedience required therein is, 'I am the Lord your God; you shall have no other gods before me.' This contains the formal reason of our religious obedience. The Socinians pretend highly to obedience to the precepts of Christ; but all obedience to Christ himself they utterly overthrow. The obedience they pretend to him, is but obeying God the Father according to his commands; but they take away the foundation of all obedience to his person, by denying his divine nature. And all religious obedience to any who is not God by nature, is idolatry. Wherefore, all obedience to God, due by the moral law, has respect to the person of Christ, as one God with the Father and Holy Spirit, blessed for ever.

AS MEDIATOR

There is a peculiar respect to him in all moral obedience as Mediator.

Christ Confirmed All the Commands of the Moral Law

In that by the supreme authority over the church wherewith he was vested, he has confirmed all the commands of the moral law, giving them new enforcements; whence he calls them his commands. 'This,' says he, 'is my commandment, That you love one another;' which yet was the old commandment of the moral law, 'You shall love your neighbour as yourself.' Hence the apostle calls it an old and new commandment (1 John 2:7–8).

This law was given to the church under the Old Testament in the hand of a mediator; that is, of Moses (Gal. 3:19). It had an original power of obliging all mankind to obedience, from its first institution or prescription in our creation; which it never lost nor abated in. Howbeit the church was obliged to have a respect to it, as it was given to them, 'ordained by angels in the hand of a mediator' (see Mal. 4:4). Hereon many things hard and difficult did ensue, which we are now freed from. We are not obliged to the observance of the moral law itself, as given in the hand of that mediator, which gave it the formal reason of a covenant to that people, and had other statutes and judgments inseparable from it. But the same law continues still in its original authority and power, which it had from the beginning, to oblige all indispensably to obedience.

Howbeit, as the Church of Israel, as such, was not obliged to obedience to the moral law absolutely considered, but as it was given to them peculiarly in the hand of a mediator—that is, of Moses; no more is the Evangelic Church, as such, obliged by the original authority of that law, but as it is confirmed to us in the hand of our Mediator. This renders all our moral obedience evangelic. For there is no duty of it, but we are obliged to perform it in faith through Christ, on the motives of the love of God in him, of the benefits of his mediation, and the grace we receive by him: whatever is otherwise done by us is not acceptable to God.

They do, therefore, for the most part, but deceive themselves and others, who talk so loudly about moral duties. I know of none that are acceptable to God, which are not only materially, but formally so, and no more.

If the obligation they own to them be only the original power of the moral law, or the law of our creation, and they are performed in the strength of that law to the end of it, they are no way accepted of God. But if they intend the duties which the moral law requires, proceeding from, and performed by, faith in Christ, upon the grounds of the love of God in him, and grace received from him—then are they duties purely evangelic. And although the law has never lost, nor ever can lose, its original power of obliging us to universal obedience, as we are reasonable creatures; yet is our obedience to it as Christians, as believers, immediately influenced by its confirmation to the Evangelic Church in the hand of our Mediator.

Christ Requires Evangelic Obedience

God has given to the Lord Christ all power in his name, to require this obedience from all that receive the gospel. Others are left under the original authority of the law, either as implanted in our natures at their first creation, as are the Gentiles; or as delivered by Moses, and written in tables of stone, as it was with the Jews (Rom. 2:12–15). But as to them that are called to the faith of the gospel, the authority of Christ does immediately affect their minds and consciences. 'He feeds' or rules his people 'in the strength of the Lord, in the majesty of the name of the Lord his God' (Micah 5:4). All the authority and majesty of God is in him and with him—so of old, as the great Angel of God's presence, he was in the church in the wilderness with a delegated power, 'Behold, I send an Angel before you, to keep you in the way, and to bring you into the place which I have prepared: beware of him, and obey his voice, provoke him not; for he will not pardon your transgressions: for my name is in him. But if you shall indeed obey his voice, and do all that I speak' (Exod. 23:20–22). The name of God the Father is so in him—that is, he is so partaker of the same nature with him—that his voice is the voice of the Father: 'If you obey his voice, and do all that I speak.' Nevertheless, he acts herein as the Angel of God, with power and authority delegated from him. So is he still immediately present with the church, requiring obedience in the name and majesty of God.

Christ Is the Judge of Our Obedience

All judgment upon and concerning this obedience is committed to him by the Father: 'For the Father judges no man' (that is, immediately as the Father), 'but has committed all judgment to the Son' (John 5:22); He 'has given him authority to execute judgment, because he is the Son of man' (v. 27). And his judgment is the judgment of God; for the Father, who judges none immediately in his own person, judges all in him: 'If ye call on the Father, who without respect of persons judges according to every man's work' (1 Pet. 1:17). He does so in and by the Son, to whom all judgment is committed. And to him are we to have regard in all our obedience, to whom we must give our account concerning it, and by whom we are and must be finally judged upon it. To this purpose speaks the apostle, 'We shall all stand before the judgment-seat of Christ. For it is written, as I live, says the Lord, every knee shall bow to me, and every tongue shall confess to God. So then every one of us shall give account of himself to God' (Rom. 14:10–12). He proves that we shall all stand before the judgment-seat of Christ, or be judged by him, by a testimony of Scripture that we shall be also judged by God himself, and give an account of ourselves to him. And as this does undeniably prove and confirm the divine nature of Christ, without the faith whereof there is neither cogency in the apostle's testimony nor force in his arguing; so he declares that God judges us only in and by him. In this regard of our moral obedience to Christ lies the way whereby God will be gloried.

Christ Appointed the Way We Are to Worship

Secondly, all things are yet more plain with respect to institutions of divine worship. The appointment of all divine ordinances under the New Testament was his especial province and work, as the Son and Lord over his own house; and obedience to him in the observance of them is that which he gives in especial charge to all his disciples (Matt. 28:18–20). And it is nothing but a loss of that subjection of soul and conscience to him which is indispensably required of all believers, that has set the minds of so many at liberty to do and observe in divine worship what they please, without any regard to his institutions. It is otherwise with respect to moral duties; for the things of the moral law have an obligation on our consciences antecedent to the enforcement of them by the authority of Christ, and there hold us fast. But as to things of the latter sort, our consciences can no way be affected with a sense of them, or a necessity of obedience in them, but by the sole and immediate authority of Christ himself. If a sense hereof be lost in our minds, we shall not abide in the observance of his commands.

> *…it is nothing but a loss of that subjection of soul and conscience to him which is indispensably required of all believers, that has set the minds of so many at liberty to do and observe in divine worship what they please…*

12

LOVE—THE PRINCIPLE OF OBEDIENCE

That which enlivens and animates the obedience whereof we have discoursed, is love. This himself makes the foundation of all that is acceptable to him. 'If,' says he, 'you love me, keep my commandments' (John 14:15). As he distinguishes between love and obedience, so he asserts the former as the foundation of the latter. He accepts of no obedience to his commands that does not proceed from love to his person. That is no love which is not fruitful in obedience; and that is no obedience which proceeds not from love. So he expresses on both sides: 'If a man love me, he will keep my words;' and, 'He that loves me not keeps not my sayings' (vv. 23–4).

In the Old Testament the love of God was the life and substance of all obedience. 'You shall love the Lord your God with all your heart, with all your soul, your mind and strength,' was the sum of the law. This includes in it all obedience, and, where it is genuine, will produce all the fruits of it; and where it was not, no multiplication of duties was accepted with him. But this in general we do not now treat of.

That the person of Christ is the especial object of this divine love, which is the fire that kindles the sacrifice of our obedience to him—this is that alone which at present I design to demonstrate.

The apostle has recorded a very severe denunciation of divine wrath against all that love him not: 'If any man love not the Lord Jesus Christ, let him be Anathema Maranatha' (1 Cor. 16:22). And what was added to the curse of the law we may add to this of the gospel: 'And all the people shall say, Amen' (Deut. 27:26). And, on the other hand, he prays for grace on all that 'love him in sincerity' (Eph. 6:24). Wherefore, none who desire to retain the name of Christian, can deny, in words at least, but that we ought, with all our hearts, to love the Lord Jesus Christ.

I do not so distinguish love from obedience as though it were not itself a part, yea, the chiefest part, of our obedience. So is faith also; yet is it constantly distinguished from obedience, properly so called. This alone is that which I shall demonstrate—namely, that there is, and ought to be, in all believers, a divine, gracious love to the person of Christ, immediately fixed on him, whereby they are excited to, and acted in, all their obedience to his authority.

False Love

Had it been only pleaded, that many who pretend love to Christ do yet evidence that they love him not, it is that which the Scripture testifies, and continual experience proclaims. If an application of this charge had been made to them whose sincerity in their profession of love to him can be no way evidenced, it ought to be borne with patience, amongst other reproaches of the same kind that are cast upon them. And some things are to be premised to the confirmation of our assertion.

In Hypocrites

It is granted that there may be a false pretence of love to Christ; and as this pretence is ruinous to the souls of them in whom it is, so it ofttimes renders them prejudicial and troublesome to others. There ever were, and probably ever will be, hypocrites in the church and a false pretence of love is of the essential form of hypocrisy. The first great act of hypocrisy, with respect to Christ, was treachery, veiled with a double pretence of love. He cried, 'Hail, Master! and kissed him,' who betrayed him. His words and actions proclaimed love, but deceit and treachery were in his heart. Hence the apostle prays for grace on them who love the Lord Jesus ἐν ἀφθαρσίᾳ—without dissimulation or doubling, without pretences and aims at other ends, without a mixture of corrupt affections; that is, in sincerity (Eph. 6:24). It was prophesied of him, that many who were strangers to his grace should lie to him, בְּנֵי־נֵכָר יְכַחֲשׁוּ־לִי (Ps. 18:44)—feignedly submit, or yield feigned obedience to him. So is it with them who profess love to him, yet are enemies of his cross, 'whose end is destruction, whose god is their belly, and whose glory is in their shame, who mind earthly things' (Phil. 3:18–19). All that are called Christians in the world, do, by owning that denomination, profess a love to Jesus Christ; but greater enemies, greater haters of him, he has not among the children of men, than many of them are. This falsely pretended love is worse than avowed hatred; neither will the pretence of it stand men in stead at the last day. No other answer will be given to the plea of it, be it in whom it will, but 'Depart from me, I never knew you, ye workers of iniquity.' Whereas, therefore, he himself has prescribed this rule to all who would be esteemed his disciples, 'If you love me, keep my commandments,' we may safely conclude, all who live in a neglect of his commands, whatever they pretend or profess, they love him not. And the satisfaction which men, through much darkness, and many corrupt prejudices, have attained to in the profession of Christian religion, without an internal, sincere love to Christ himself, is that which ruins religion and their own souls.

IN THE SELF-DECEIVED

As there is a false pretence of love to Christ, so there is, or may be, a false love to him also. The persons in whom it is may in some measure be sincere, and yet their love to Christ may not be pure, nor sincere—such as answers the principles and rules of the gospel; and as many deceive others, so some deceive themselves in this matter. They may think that they love Christ, but indeed do not so; and this I shall manifest in some few instances.

Love without Faith

That love is not sincere and incorrupt which proceeds not from—which is not a fruit of faith. Those who do not first really believe on Christ, can never sincerely love him. It is faith alone that works by love towards Christ and all his saints. If, therefore, any do not believe with that faith which unites them to Christ, which within purifies the heart, and is outwardly effectual in duties of obedience, whatever they may persuade themselves concerning love to Christ, it is but a vain delusion. Where the faith of men is dead, their love will not be living and sincere.

Love for a False Christ

That love is not so which arises from false ideas and representations that men make of Christ, or have made of him in their minds. Men may draw images in their minds of what they most fancy, and then dote upon them. So some think of Christ only as a glorious person exalted in heaven at the right hand of God, without farther apprehensions of his natures and offices. So the Roman missionaries represented him to some of the Indians—concealing from them his cross and sufferings. But every false notion concerning his person or his grace—what he is, has done, or does—corrupts the love that is pretended to him. Shall we think that they love Christ by whom his divine nature is denied or that those do so who disbelieve the reality of his human nature? Or those by whom the union of both in the same person is rejected? There cannot be true evangelic love to a false Christ, such as these imaginations do fancy.

Love Unregulated by Scripture

So is that love which is not in all things—as to causes, motives, measures, and ends—regulated by the Scripture. This alone gives us the nature, rules, and bounds of sincere spiritual love. We are no more to love Christ, than to fear and worship him, according to our own imaginations. From the Scripture are we to derive all the principles and motives of our love. If either the acts or effects of it will not endure a trial thereby, they are false and counterfeit; and many such have been pretended to, as we shall see immediately.

Love Focussed on Objects and Images

That is so, unquestionably, which fixes itself on undue objects, which, whatever is pretended, are neither Christ nor means of conveying our love to him. Such is all that love which the Romanists express in their devotion to images, as they fancy, of Christ; crucifixes, pretended relics of his cross, and the nails that pierced him, with the like superstitious representations of him, and what they suppose he is concerned in. For although they express their devotion with great appearance of ardent affections, under all outward signs of them—in adorations, kissings, prostrations, with sighs and tears; yet all this while it is not Christ which they thus cleave to, but a cloud of their own imaginations, wherewith their carnal minds are pleased and affected. That is no god which a man hews out of a tree, though he form it for that end, though he falls down to it and worships it, and prays to it, and says, 'Deliver me, for you are my god' (Isa. 44:17). The authors of this superstition, whereby the love of innumerable poor souls is depraved and abused, do first frame in their minds what they suppose may solicit or draw out the natural and carnal affections of men to it, and then outwardly represent it as an object for them. Wherefore some of their representations of him are glorious, and some of them dolorous, according as they aim to excite affections in carnal minds. But, as I said, these things are not Christ, nor is he any way concerned in them.

Love Defined as Ecstatic Experiences

I acknowledge there have been great pretences of such a love to Christ as cannot be justified. Such is that which some of the devotionists of the Roman Church have endeavoured rather to express out of their fancy than declare out of their experience. Raptures, ecstasies, self-annihilations, immediate adhesions and enjoyments, without any act of the understanding, and with a multitude of other swelling words of vanity, they labour to set off what they fancy to be divine love. But there wants not evidences of truth sufficient to defeat these pretences, be they ever so specious or glorious.

EXCEEDS ALL SCRIPTURE PRECEDENTS. As it is by them described, it exceeds all Scripture precedents. For men to assume to themselves an apprehension that they love Christ in another manner and kind, in a higher degree at least, and thence to enjoy more intimacy with him, more love from him, than did any of the apostles—John, or Paul, or Peter, or any other of those holy ones whose love to him is recorded in the Scripture—is intolerable vanity and presumption. But no such things as these devotees pretend to are mentioned, or in the least intimated concerning them, and their love to their Lord and Master. No man will pretend to more love than they had, but such as have none at all.

WITHOUT PRECEDENT OR PRECEPT. It is no way directed, warranted, approved, by any command, promise, or rule of the Scripture. As it is without precedent, so it is without precept. And hereby, whether we will or no, all our graces and duties must be tried, as to any acceptation with God. Whatever pretends to exceed the direction of the Word may safely be rejected—cannot safely be admitted. Whatever enthusiasms or pretended inspirations may be pleaded for the singular practice of what is prescribed in the Scripture, yet none can be allowed for an approved principle of what is not so prescribed. Whatever exceeds the bounds thereof is resolved into the testimony of every distempered imagination. Nor will it avail that these things amongst them are submitted to the judgment of the church. For the church has no rule to judge by but the Scripture; and it can pass but one judgment of what is not warranted thereby—namely, that it is to be rejected.

IRRATIONAL. As it is described by those who applaud it, it is not suited to the sober, sedate actings of the rational faculties of our souls. For whereas all that God requires of us, is that we love him with all our souls and all our minds, these men cry up a divine love by an immediate adhesion of the will and the affections to God, without any actings of the mind and understanding at all. Love, indeed, is the regular acting of our whole souls, by all their faculties and rational powers, in an adherence to God. But these men have fancied a divine love for them whom they would admire and extol, which disturbs all their regular acting, and renders them of little or no use in that which, without their due exercise, is nothing but fancy. And hence it is that, under pretence of this love, sundry persons among them—yea, all that have pretended to it—have fallen into such ridiculous excesses and open delusions as sufficiently discover the vanity of the love itself pretended by them.

Wherefore we plead for no other love to the person of Christ but what the Scripture warrants as to its nature; what the gospel requires of us as our duty; what the natural faculties of our minds are suited to and given us for; what they are enabled to by grace; and without which in some degree of sincerity, no man can yield acceptable obedience to him.

True Love

These things being premised, that which we assert is, that there is, and ought to be, in all believers, a religious, gracious love to the person of Christ, distinct from, and the reason of, their obedience to his commands; — that is, it is distinct from all other commands; but is also itself commanded and required of us in a way of duty.

That there is in the church such a love to the person of Christ, the Scripture testifies, both in the precepts it gives for it and the examples of it. And all those who truly believe cannot apprehend that they understand any thing of faith, or love of Christ, or themselves, by whom it is called in question. If, therefore, I should enlarge on this subject, a great part of the doctrine of the Scripture from first to last must be represented and a transcript of the hearts of believers, wherein this love is seated and prevalent, be made, according to our ability. And there is no subject that I could more willingly enlarge upon. But I must at present contract myself, in compliance with my design. Two things only I shall demonstrate:

1. That the person of Christ is the object of divine love.
2. What is the nature of that love in us; what are the grounds of it, and the motives to it, in them that do believe.

In reference to the first of these, the ensuing position shall be the subject of the remainder of this chapter [point 2, chapter 13].

The person of Christ is the principal object of the love of God, and of the whole creation participant of his image. The reason why I thus extend the assertion will appear in the declaration of it.

THE FATHER LOVES THE SON

No small part of the eternal blessedness of the holy God consists in the mutual love of the Father and the Son, by the Spirit. As he is the only-begotten of the Father, he is the first, necessary, adequate, complete object of the whole love of the Father. Hence he says of himself, that from eternity he was 'by him, as one brought up with him: and was daily his delight, rejoicing always before him' (Prov. 8:30) — which place was opened before. In him was the ineffable, eternal, unchangeable delight and complacency of the Father, as the full object of his love. The same is expressed in that description of him, 'The only-begotten Son, who is in the bosom of the Father' (John 1:18). His being the only-begotten Son declares his eternal relation to the person of the Father, of whom he was begotten in the entire communication of the whole divine nature. Hereon he is in the bosom of the Father—in the eternal embraces of his love, as his only-begotten Son. The Father loves, and cannot but love, his own nature and essential image in him.

Herein originally is God love: 'For God is love' (1 John 4:8). This is the fountain and prototype of all love, as being eternal and necessary. All other acts of love are in God but emanations from hence, and effects of it. As he does good because he is good, so he loves because he is love. He is love eternally and necessarily in this love of the Son; and all other workings of love are but acts of his will, whereby somewhat of it is outwardly expressed. And all love in the creation was introduced from this fountain, to give a shadow and resemblance of it.

Love is that which contemplative men have always almost adored. Many things have they spoken to evince it to be the light, life, lustre and glory of the whole creation. But the original and pattern of it was always hid from the wisest philosophers of old. Something they reached after about God's love to himself, with rest and complacency in his own infinite excellencies; but of this ineffable mutual love of the Father and the Son, both in and by that Spirit which proceeds from them both, they had neither apprehension nor conjecture. Yet, as herein does the principal part (if we may so speak) of the blessedness of the holy God consist, so is it the only fountain and prototype of all that is truly called love—a blessing and glory which the creation had never been made partaker of, but only to express, according to the capacity of their several natures, this infinite and eternal love of God! For God's love of himself—which is natural and necessary to the divine being—consists in the mutual complacency of the Father and the Son by the Spirit. And it was to express himself, that God made any thing without himself. He made the heavens and the earth to express his being, goodness, and power. He created man 'in his own image,' to express his holiness and righteousness; and he implanted love in our natures to express this eternal mutual love of the holy persons of the Trinity. But we must leave it under the veil of infinite incomprehensibleness; though admiration and adoration of it be not without the highest spiritual satisfaction.

Again, he is the peculiar object of the love of the Father, of the love of God, as he is incarnate—as he has taken on him, and has now discharged, the work of mediation, or continues in the discharge of it; that is, the person of Christ, as God-man, is the peculiar object of the divine love of the Father. The person of Christ in his divine nature is the adequate object of that love of the Father which is 'ad intra'—a natural necessary act of the divine essence in its distinct personal existence; and the person of Christ as incarnate, as clothed with human nature, is the first and full object of the love of the Father in those acts of it which are 'ad extra', or are towards anything without himself. So he declares himself in the prospect of his future incarnation and work, 'Behold my servant, whom I uphold; mine elect, in whom my soul delights' (Isa. 42:1). The delight of the soul of God, his rest and complacency—which are the great effects of love—are in the Lord Christ, as his elect and servant in the work of mediation. And the testimony hereof he renewed twice from heaven afterwards, 'Lo, a voice from heaven, saying, This is my beloved Son, in whom I am well pleased' (Matt. 3:17); as it is again repeated (Matt. 17:5). All things are disposed to give a due sense to us of this love of God to him. The testimony concerning it is twice repeated in the same words from heaven. And the words of it are emphatical to the utmost of our comprehension: 'My Son, my servant, mine elect, my beloved Son, in whom I rest, in whom I delight, and am well pleased.' It is the will of God to leave upon our hearts a sense of this love to Christ; for his voice came from heaven, not for his sake, who was always filled with a sense of this divine love, but for ours, that we might believe it.

This he pleaded as the foundation of all the trust reposed in him, and all the power committed to him. 'The Father loves the Son, and has given all things into his hand' (John 3:35). 'The Father loves the Son, and shows him all things that himself does' (John 5:20). And the sense or due apprehension of it is the foundation of Christian religion. Hence he prays that we may know that God has loved him (John 17:23, 26).

In this sense, the person of Christ is the πρῶτον δεκτικὸν—the first recipient subject of all that divine love which extends itself to the church. It is all, the whole of it, in the first place fixed upon him, and by and through him is communicated to the church. Whatever it receives in grace and glory, it is but the streams of this fountain—love to himself. So he prays for all his disciples, 'that the love,' says he, 'wherewith you have loved me may be in them, and I in them' (John 17:26). They can be partakers of no other love, neither in itself nor in its fruits, but that alone wherewith the Father first loved him. He loves him for us all, and us no otherwise but as in him. He makes us 'accepted in the Beloved' (Eph. 1:6). He is the Beloved of the Father κατ' ἐξοχὴν; as in all things he was to have the pre-eminence (Col. 1:18). The love of the body is derived to it from the love to the Head; and in the love of him God loves the whole church, and no otherwise. He loves none but as united to him, and participant of his nature.

Wherefore the love of the Father to the Son, as the only begotten, and the essential image of his person, wherein the ineffable delight of the divine nature consists, was the fountain and cause of all love in the creation, by an act of the will of God for its representation. And the love of God the Father to the person of Christ as incarnate, being the first adequate object of divine love wherein there is anything 'ad extra,' is the fountain and especial cause of all gracious love towards us and in us. And our love to Christ being the only outward expression and representation of this love of the Father to him, therein consists the principal part of our

> *Nothing renders us so like to God as our love to Jesus Christ, for he is the principal object of his love…*

renovation into his image. Nothing renders us so like to God as our love to Jesus Christ, for he is the principal object of his love—in him his soul rests—in him is he always well pleased. Wherever this is wanting, whatever there may be besides, there is nothing of the image of God. He that loves not Jesus Christ, let him be Anathema Maranatha; for he is unlike to God—his carnal mind is enmity against God.

The Angels Love the Person of Christ

Among those who are in the image of God, the angels above are of the first consideration. We are, indeed, as yet much in the dark to the things that are 'within the veil.' They are above us as to our present capacity, and hid from us as to our present state; but there is enough in the Scripture to manifest the adhesion of angels to the person of Christ by divine love. For love proceeding from sight is the life of the church above; as love proceeding from faith is the life of the church below. And this life the angels themselves do live.

As Members of God's Family

They were all, to their inexpressible present advantage and security for the future, brought into that recovery and recapitulation of all things which God has made in him. He has 'gathered together in one all things in Christ, both which are in heaven, and which are on earth, even in him' (Eph. 1:10). The things in heaven, and things on earth—angels above, and men below—were originally united in the love of God. God's love to them, whence springs their mutual love between themselves, was a bond of union between them, rendering them one complete family of God in heaven and earth, as it is called (Eph. 3:15). On the entrance of sin, whereby mankind forfeited their interest in the love of God, and lost all love to him, or anything for him, this union was utterly dissolved, and mutual enmity came into the place of its principle in love. God is pleased to gather up these divided parts of his family into one—in one head, which is Christ Jesus. And as there is hereby a union established again between angels and the church in love, so their adherence to the head, the centre, life, and spring of this union, is by love, and no otherwise. It is not faith, but love, that is the bond of this union between Christ and them; and herein no small part of their blessedness and glory in heaven consists.

In Worship and Service

That worship, adoration, service, and obedience, which they yield to him, are all in like manner animated with love and delight. In love they cleave to him, in love they worship and serve him. They had a command to worship him on his nativity (Heb. 1:6); and they did it with joy, exultation, and praises—all effects of love and delight (Luke 2:13–14). And as they continue about the throne of God, they say, with a loud voice, 'Worthy is the Lamb that was slain to receive power, and riches, and wisdom, and strength, and honour, and glory, and blessing' (Rev. 5:12). Their continual ascription of glory and praise to him is an effect of reverential love and delight; and from thence also is their concern in his gospel and grace (Eph. 3:9–10; 1 Pet. 1:12). Nor without this love in the highest degree can it be conceived how they should be blessed and happy in their continual employment. For they are 'all ministering spirits, sent forth to minister for the heirs of salvation' (Heb. 1:14). Were they not acted herein by their fervent love to Christ, they could have no delight in their own ministry.

We have not, we cannot have, in this world, a full comprehension of the nature of angelic love. Our notions are but dark and uncertain, in things whereof we can have no experience. Wherefore, we cannot have here a clear intuition into the nature of the love of spirits, whilst our own is mixed with what derives from the acting of the animal spirits of our bodies also. But the blessedness of angels does not consist in the endowments of their nature—that they are great in power, light, knowledge, and wisdom; for, notwithstanding these things, many of them became devils. But the excellency and blessedness of the angelic state consist in these two things: First, that they are disposed, and able constantly, inseparably, universally, uninterruptedly, to cleave to God in love. And as they do so to God, so they do to the person of Christ; and through him, as their head, to God, even the Father. Secondly, add hereunto that gracious reflex sense which they have of the glory, dignity, eternal sweetness, and satisfaction, which arise from hence, and we have the sum of angelic blessedness.

THE CHURCH LOVES CHRIST

The church of mankind is the other part of the rational creation whereon the image of God is renewed. Love to the person of Christ, proceeding from faith, is their life, their joy, and glory.

It was so to the church under the Old Testament. The whole Book of Canticles is designed to no other purpose, but variously to shadow forth, to insinuate and represent, the mutual love of Christ and the church. Blessed is he who understands the sayings of that book, and has the experience of them in his heart. Psalm 45 among others, is designed to the same purpose. All the glorious descriptions which are given of his person in the residue of the prophets, were only means to excite love to him, and desires after him. Hence is he called חֶמְדַּת כָּל־הַגּוֹיִם (Hag. 2:7), 'The Desire of all nations'—he alone who is desirable to, and the only beloved of the church gathered out of all nations.

The clear revelation of the person of Christ, so as to render him the direct object of our love, with the causes and reasons of it, is one of the most eminent privileges of the New Testament. And it is variously attested in precepts, promises, instances, and solemn approbations.

Wherever he supposes or requires this love in any of his disciples, it is not only as their duty, as that which they were obliged to by the precepts of the gospel, but as that without which no other duty whatever is accepted by him. 'If,' says he 'you love me, keep my commandments' (John 14:15). He so requires love to himself, as not to expect or approve of any obedience to his commands without it. It is a great and blessed duty to feed the sheep and lambs of Christ; yet will not he accept of it unless it proceeds out of love to his person. 'Simon, son of Jonas, do you love me? Feed my lambs' (John 21:15–17). Three times did he repeat the same words to him who had failed in his love towards him, by denying him thrice. Without this love to him, he requires of none to feed his sheep, nor will accept of what they pretend to do therein. It were a blessed thing, if a due apprehension hereof did always abide with them that are called to that work.

Hereunto does he annex those blessed promises which comprise the whole of our peace, safety, and consolation in this world. 'He,' says he, 'that loves me, shall be loved of my Father, and I will love him, and manifest myself to him' (John 14:21); and verse 23, 'My Father will love him, and we will come to him, and make our abode with him.' What heart can conceive, what tongue can express, the glory of these promises, or the least part of the grace that is contained in them? Who can conceive aright of the divine condescension, love, and grace that are expressed in them? How little a portion is it that we know of God in these things! But if we value them not, if we labour not for an experience of them according to our measure, we have neither lot nor portion in the gospel. The presence and abode of God with us as a Father, manifesting himself to be such to us, in the infallible pledges and assurances of our adoption—the presence of Christ with us, revealing himself to us, with all those ineffable mercies wherewith these things are accompanied—are all contained in them. And these promises are peculiarly given to them that love the person of Christ, and in the exercise of love towards him.

Hereunto are designed the gospel Gerizim and Ebal—the denunciation of blessings and curses. As blessings are declared to be their portion 'who love the Lord Jesus in sincerity' (Eph. 6:24)—so those who love him not, have the substance of all curses denounced against them, even 'Anathema Maranatha' (1 Cor. 16:22). So far shall such persons be, whatever they may profess of outward obedience to the gospel, from any blessed interest in the promises of it, as that they are justly liable to final excision from the church in this world, and eternal malediction in that which is to come.

It is evident, therefore, that the love of the church of believers to the person of Christ is not a distempered fancy, not a deluding imagination, as some have blasphemed; but that which the nature of their relation to him makes necessary—that wherein they express their renovation into the image of God—that which the Scripture indispensably requires of them, and whereon all their spiritual comfort do depend. These things being spoken in general, the particular nature, effects, operations, and motives of this divine love, must now be farther inquired into.

13

DIVINE LOVE AND THE PERSON OF CHRIST

That we may the better understand that love to the person of Christ which we plead for, some things must be premised concerning the nature of divine love in general; and thereon its application to the particular acting and exercise of it which we inquire into will be plain and easy.

Our First Love

God has endowed our nature with a faculty and ability of fixing our love upon himself. Many can understand nothing of love but the adherence of their minds and souls to things visible and sensible, capable of a present natural enjoyment. For things unseen, especially such as are eternal and infinite, they suppose they have a veneration, a religious respect, a devout adoration; but how they should love them, they cannot understand. And the apostle grants that there is a greater difficulty in loving things that cannot be seen, than in loving those which are always visibly present to us (1 John 4:20). Howbeit, this divine love has a more fixed station and prevalence in the minds of men than any other kind of love whatever.

God Made Us to Cleave to Him in Love

The principal end why God endued our natures with that great and ruling affection, that has the most eminent and peculiar power and interest in our souls, was, in the first place, that it might be fixed on himself—that it might be the instrument of our adherence to him. He did not create this affection in us, that we might be able by it to cast ourselves into the embraces of things natural and sensual. No affection has such power in the soul to cause it to cleave to its object, and to work it into a conformity to it. Most other affections are transient in their operations, and work by a transport of nature—as anger, joy, fear, and the like; but love is capable of a constant exercise, is a spring to all other affections, and unites the soul with an efficacy not easy to be expressed to its object. And shall we think that God, who made all things for himself, did create this ruling affection in and with our natures, merely that we might be able to turn from him, and cleave to other things with a power and faculty above any we have of adherence to him? Wherefore, at our first creation, and in our primitive condition, love was the very soul and quickening principle of the life of God; and on our adherence to him thereby the continuance of our relation to him did depend. The law, rule, and measure of it was, 'You shall love the Lord your God with all your heart, and all your soul.' For this end did God create this affection in us. Not only our persons in their nature and being, but in all their powers and faculties, were fitted and prepared to this end, of living to God, and coming to the enjoyment of him. And all their exercise on created objects was to be directed to this end. Wherefore, the placing of our love on anything before God, or above him is a formal expression of our apostasy from him.

Divine Excellencies

Divine excellencies are a proper, adequate object of our love. The will, indeed, can adhere to nothing in love, but what the understanding apprehends as to its truth and being; but it is not necessary that the understanding do fully comprehend the whole nature of that which the will does so adhere to. Where a discovery is made to and by the mind of real goodness and amiableness, the will there can close with its affections. And these are apprehended as absolutely the most perfect in the divine nature and holy properties of it. Whereas, therefore, not only that which is the proper object of love is in the divine excellencies, but it is there only perfectly and absolutely, without the mixture of anything that should give it an alloy, as there is in all creatures, they are the most suitable and adequate object of our love.

There is no greater discovery of the depravation of our natures by sin and degeneracy of our wills from their original rectitude, than that—whereas we are so prone to the love of other things, and therein do seek for satisfaction to our souls where it is not to be obtained—it is so hard and difficult to raise our hearts to the love of God.

Were it not for that depravation, he would always appear as the only suitable and satisfactory object to our affections.

Divine Goodness

The especial object of divine, gracious love, is the divine goodness. 'How great is his goodness, how great is his beauty!' (Zech. 9:17.) Nothing is amiable or a proper object of love, but what is good, and as it is so. Hence divine goodness, which is infinite, has an absolutely perfect amiableness accompanying it. Because his goodness is inexpressible, his beauty is so. 'How great is his goodness, how great is his beauty!' Hence are we called to give thanks to the Lord, and to rejoice in him—which are the effects of love—because he is good (Ps. 106:1; 136:1).

Neither is divine goodness the especial object of our love as absolutely considered; but we have a respect to it as comprehensive of all that mercy, grace, and bounty, which are suited to give us the best relief in our present condition and an eternal future reward. Infinite goodness, exerting itself in all that mercy, grace, faithfulness, and bounty, which are needful to our relief and blessedness in our present condition, is the proper object of our love. Whereas, therefore, this is done only in Christ, there can be no true love of the divine goodness, but in and through him alone.

The goodness of God, as a creator, preserver, and rewarder, was a sufficient, yea, the adequate object of all love antecedently to the entrance of sin and misery. In them, in God under those considerations, might the soul of man find full satisfaction as to its present and future blessedness. But since the passing of sin, misery, and death upon us, our love can find no amiableness in any goodness—no rest, complacency, and satisfaction in any—but what is effectual in that grace and mercy by Christ, which we stand in need of for our present recovery and future reward. Nor does God require of us that we should love him otherwise but as he 'is in Christ reconciling the world to himself.' So the apostle fully declares it: 'In this was manifested the love of God towards us, because that God sent his only-begotten Son into the world, that we might live through him. Herein is love, not that we loved God, but that he loved us, and sent his Son to be the propitiation for our sins. And we have known and believed the love that God has to us. God is love; and he that dwells in love dwells in God, and God in him' (1 John 4:9-10, 16). God is love, of a nature infinitely good and gracious, so as to be the only object of all divine love. But this love can no way be known, or be so manifested to us, as that we may and ought to love him, but by his love in Christ, his sending of him and loving us in him. Before this, without this, we do not, we cannot love God. For 'herein is love, not that we loved God, but that he loved us, and sent his Son to be the propitiation for our sins.' This is the cause, the spring and fountain, of all our love to him. They are but empty notions and imaginations, which some speculative persons please themselves withal, about love to the divine goodness absolutely considered. For however infinitely amiable it may be in itself, it is not so really to them, it is not suited to their state and condition, without the consideration of the communications of it to us in Christ.

The Nature of Divine Love

These things being premised, we may consider the especial nature of this divine love, although I acknowledge that the least part of what believers have an experience of in their own souls can be expressed at least by me. Some few things I shall mention, which may give us a shadow of it, but not the express image of the thing itself.

Desire to Enjoy God

Desire of union and enjoyment is the first vital act of this love. The soul, upon the discovery of the excellencies of God, earnestly desires to be united to them—to be brought near to that enjoyment of them whereof it is capable, and wherein alone it can find rest and satisfaction. This is essential to all love; it unites the mind to its object, and rests not but in enjoyment. God's love to us arises out of the overflowing of his own immense goodness, whereof he will communicate the fruits and effects to us. God is love; and herein is love, not that we loved God, but that he loved us, and sent his only-begotten Son. Yet also does this love of God tend to the bringing of us to him, not that he may enjoy us, but that he may be enjoyed by us. This answers the desire of enjoyment in us: 'You shall call me;' [that is, out of the dust at the last day] 'you will have a desire to the work of your hands' (Job 14:15). God's love will not rest, until it has brought us to himself. But our love to God arises from a sense of our own wants—our insufficiency to come to rest in ourselves, or to attain to blessedness by our own endeavours. In this state, seeing all in God, and expecting all from the suitableness of his excellencies to our rest and satisfaction, our souls cleave to him, with a desire of the nearest union whereof our natures are capable. We are made for him, and cannot rest until we come to him.

Our goodness extends not to God; we cannot profit him by any thing that we are, or can do. Wherefore, his love to us has not respect originally to any good in ourselves, but is a gracious, free act of his own. He does good for no other reason but because he is good. Nor can his infinite perfections take any cause for their original actings without himself. He wants nothing that he would supply by the enjoyment of us. But we have indigency in ourselves to cause our love to seek an object without ourselves. And so his goodness—with the mercy, grace, and bounty included therein—is the cause, reason, and object of our love. We love them for themselves; and because we are wanting and indigent, we love them with a desire of union and enjoyment—wherein we find that our satisfaction and blessedness consists. Love in general unites the mind to the object—the person loving to the thing or person beloved. So is it expressed in an instance of human, temporary, changeable love—namely, that of Jonathan to David. His soul 'was knit with the soul of David, and he loved him as his own soul' (1 Sam. 18:1). Love had so effectually united them, as that the soul of David was as his own. Hence are those expressions of this divine love, by 'cleaving to God, following hard after him, thirsting, panting after him,' with the like intimations of the most earnest endeavours of our nature after union and enjoyment.

When the soul has a view by faith (which nothing else can give it) of the goodness of God as manifested in Christ—that is of the essential excellencies of his nature as exerting themselves in him—it reaches after him with its most earnest embraces, and is restless until it comes to perfect fruition. It sees in God the fountain of life, and would drink of the 'river of his pleasures' (Ps. 36:8–9)—that in his 'presence is fulness of joy, and at his right hand are pleasures for evermore' (Ps. 16:11). It longs and pants to drink of that fountain—to bathe itself in that river of pleasures; and wherein it comes short of present enjoyment, it lives in hopes that when we 'awake, it shall be satisfied with his likeness' (Ps. 17:15). There is nothing grievous to a soul filled with this love, but what keeps it from the full enjoyment of these excellencies of God. What does so naturally and necessarily, it groans under. Such is our present state in the body, wherein, in some sense, we are 'absent from the Lord' (2 Cor. 5:4, 8–9). And what does so morally, in the deviations of its will and affections, as sin—it hates and abhors and loathes itself for. Under the conduct of this love, the whole tendency of the soul is to the enjoyment of God;—it would be lost in itself, and found in him—nothing in itself, and all in him. Absolute complacency herein—that God is what he is, that he should be what he is, and nothing else, and that as such we may be united to him, and enjoy Him according to the capacity of our natures is the life of divine love.

A DESIRE TO BE LIKE GOD

It is a love of assimilation. It contains in it a desire and intense endeavour to be like to God, according to our capacity and measure. The soul sees all goodness, and consequently all that is amiable and lovely, in God—the want of all which it finds in itself. The fruition of his goodness is that which it longs for as its utmost end, and conformity to it as the means thereof. There is no man who loves not God sincerely, but indeed he would have him to be somewhat that he is not, that he might be the more like to him. This such persons are pleased withal whilst they can fancy it in any thing (Ps. 50:21). They that love him, would have him be all that he is—as he is, and nothing else; and would be themselves like to him. And as love has this tendency, and is that which gives disquiet to the soul when and wherein we are unlike to God, so it stirs up constant endeavours after assimilation to him, and has a principal efficacy to that end. Love is the principle that actually assimilates and conforms us to God, as faith is the principle which originally disposes thereunto. In our renovation into the image of God, the transforming power is radically seated in faith, but acts itself by love. Love proceeding from faith gradually changes the soul into the likeness of God; and the more it is in exercise, the more is that change effected.

To labour after conformity to God by outward actions only, is to make an image of the living God, hewed out of the stock of a dead tree. It is from this vital principle of love that we are not forced into it as by engines, but naturally grow up into the likeness and image of God. For when it is duly affected with the excellencies of God in Christ, it fills the mind with thoughts and contemplations on them, and excites all the affections to a delight in them. And where the soul acts itself constantly in the mind's contemplation, and the delight of the affections, it will produce assimilation to the object of them. To love God is the only way and means to be like to him.

Resting in God

It is a love of complacency, and therein of benevolence. Upon that view which we have by spiritual light and faith of the divine goodness, exerting itself in the way before described, our souls do approve of all that is in God, applaud it, adore it, and acquiesce in it. Hence two great duties do arise, and hereon do they depend. First, joyful ascriptions of glory and honour to God. All praise and thanksgiving, all blessing, all assignation of glory to him, because of his excellencies and perfections, do arise from our satisfactory complacence in them. The righteous 'rejoice in the Lord, and give thanks at the remembrance of his holiness' (Ps. 97:12). They are so pleased and satisfied at the remembrance of God's holiness, that it fills their hearts with joy and causes them to break forth in praises. Praise is nothing but an outward expression of the inward complacency of our hearts in the divine perfections and their operations. And, secondly, love herein acts itself by benevolence, as the constant inclination of the mind to all things wherein the glory of God is concerned. It wills all the things wherein the name of God may be sanctified, his praises made glorious, and his will done on earth as it is in heaven. As God says of his own love to us, that 'he rejoices in it with singing, and rests in it' (Zeph. 3:17)—as having the greatest complacency in it, rejoicing over us with his 'whole heart and his whole soul' (Jer. 32:41);—so, according to our measure, do we by love rest in the glorious excellencies of God, rejoicing in them with our whole hearts and our whole souls.

Friendship with God

This divine love is a love of friendship. The communion which we have with God therein is so intimate, and accompanied with such spiritual boldness, as gives it that denomination. So Abraham was called 'The friend of God' (Isa. 41:8; James 2:23). And because of that mutual trust which is between friends, 'the secret of the Lord is with them that fear him, and he will show them his covenant' (Ps. 25:14). For, as our Saviour teaches us, 'servants'—that is, those who are so, and no more—'know not what their lord does;' he rules them, commands them, or requires obedience from them; but as to his secret—his design and purpose, his counsel and love—they know nothing of it. But says he to his disciples, 'I have called you friends, for all things that I have heard of my Father I have made known to you' (John 15:15). He proves them to be rightly called his friends, because of the communication of the secret of his mind to them.

This is the great difference between them who are only servants in the house of God, and those who are so servants as to be friends also. The same commands are given to all equally, and the same duties are required of all equally, inasmuch as they are equally servants; but those who are no more but so, know nothing of the secret counsel, love, and grace of God, in a due manner. For the natural man receives not the things that are of God. Hence all their obedience is servile. They know neither the principal motives to it nor the ends of it. But they who are so servants as to be friends also, they know what their Lord does; the secret of the Lord is with them, and he shows them his covenant. They are admitted into an intimate acquaintance with the mind of Christ ('we have the mind of Christ,' 1 Cor. 2:16), and are thereon encouraged to perform the obedience of servants, with the love and delight of friends.

The same love of friendship is expressed by that intimate converse with, and especial residence that is between God and believers. God dwells in them, and they dwell in God; for God is love (1 John 4:16). 'If a man,' says the Lord Christ, 'love me, he will keep my words: and my Father will love him, and we will come to him, and make our abode with him' (John 14:23); and, 'If any man hear my voice, and open the door, I will come in to him, and will sup with him, and he with me' (Rev. 3:20). These are not an empty sound of words;—there is substance under them, there is truth in them. Those whose hearts are duly exercised in and to the love of God have experience of the refreshing approaches both of the Father and of the Son to their souls, in the communications of a sense of their love, and pledges of their abode with them.

LOVING THE INCARNATE SON

These things have I briefly premised, concerning the nature of divine love, that we may the better apprehend what we understand by it, in the application of it to the person of Christ.

For the formal object of this love is the essential properties of the divine nature—its infinite goodness in particular. Wherever these are, there is the object and reason of this love. But they are all of them in the person of the Son, no less than in the person of the Father. As, therefore, we love the Father on this account, so are we to love the Son also.

But the Person of Christ is to be considered as he was incarnate, or clothed with our nature. And this takes nothing off from the formal reason of this love, but only makes an addition to the motives of it. This, indeed, for a season veiled the loveliness of his divine excellencies, and so turned aside the eyes of many from him. For when he took on him 'the form of a servant, and made himself of no reputation,' he had, to them who looked on him with carnal eyes, 'neither form nor comeliness,' that he should be desired or be loved. Howbeit, the entire person of Christ, God and man, is the object of this divine love, in all the acts of the whole exercise of it. That single effect of infinite wisdom and grace, in the union of the divine and human natures in the one person of the Son of God, renders him the object of this love in a peculiar manner. The way whereby we may attain this peculiar love, and the motives to it, shall close these considerations.

A due consideration of, and meditation on, the proposal of the person of Christ to us in the Scripture, are the proper foundation of this love. This is the formal reason of our faith in him, and love to him. He is so proposed to us in the Scripture, that we may believe in him and love him, and for that very end. And in particular with respect to our love, to ingenerate it in us, and to excite it to its due exercise, are those excellencies of his person—as the principal effect of divine wisdom and goodness, which we have before insisted on—frequently proposed to us. To this end is he represented as 'altogether lovely,' and the especial glories of his person are delineated, yea, drawn to the life, in the holy records of the Old and New Testaments. It is no work of fancy or imagination—it is not the feigning images in our minds of such things as are meet to satisfy our carnal affections, to excite and act them; but it is a due adherence to that object which is represented to faith in the proposal of the gospel. Therein, as in a glass, do we behold the glory of Christ, who is the image of the invisible God, and have our souls filled with transforming affections to him.

A Mystical Declaration

The whole Book of Canticles is nothing but a mystical declaration of the mutual love between Christ and the church. And it is expressed by all such ways and means as may represent it intense, fervent, and exceeding all other love whatever; which none, I suppose, will deny, at least on the part of Christ. And a great part of it consists in such descriptions of the person of Christ and his love as may render him amiable and desirable to our souls, even 'altogether lovely.' To what end does the Holy Spirit so graphically describe and represent to us the beauty and desirableness of his person, if it be not to ingenerate love in us to him? All want of love to him on this proposal is the effect of prevalent unbelief. It is pretended that the descriptions given of Christ in this book are allegorical, from whence nothing can be gathered or concluded. But God forbid we should so reflect on the wisdom and love of the Holy Spirit to the church—that he has proposed to the faith of the church an empty sound and noise of words, without mind or sense. The expressions he uses are figurative, and the whole nature of the discourse, as to its outward structure, is allegorical. But the things intended are real and substantial; and the metaphors used in the expression of them are suited, in a due attendance to the analogy of faith, to convey a spiritual understanding and sense of the things themselves proposed in them. The church of God will not part with the unspeakable advantage and consolation—those supports of faith and incentives of love—which it receives by that divine proposal of the person of Christ and his love which is made therein, because some men have no experience of them nor understanding in them. The faith and love of believers is not to be regulated by the ignorance and boldness of them who have neither the one nor the other. The title of the 45th Psalm is, שִׁיר יְדִידֹת, 'A song of loves—that is, of the mutual love of Christ and the church. And to this end—that our souls may be stirred up to the most ardent affection towards him—is a description given us of his person, as 'altogether lovely.' To what other end is he so evidently delineated in the whole harmony of his divine beauties by the pencil of the Holy Spirit?

Not to insist on particular testimonies, it is evident to all whose eyes are opened to discern these things, that there is no property of the divine nature which is peculiarly amiable—such as are goodness, grace, love, and bounty, with infinite power and holiness—but it is represented and proposed to us in the person of the Son of God, to this end, that we should love him above all, and cleave to him. There is nothing in the human nature, in that fulness of grace and truth which dwelt therein, in that inhabitation of the Spirit which was in him without measure, in any thing of those 'all things' wherein he has the pre-eminence—nothing in his love, condescension, grace, and mercy—nothing in the work that he fulfilled, what he did and suffered therein—nothing in the benefits we receive thereby—nothing in the power and glory that

he is exalted to at the right hand of God—but it is set forth in the
Scripture and proposed to us, that, believing in him, we may love
him with all our hearts and souls. And, besides all this, that singular,
that infinite effect of divine wisdom, whereunto there is nothing
like in all the works of God, and wherewith none of them may be
compared—namely, the constitution of his person by the union
of his natures therein, whereby he becomes to us the image of the
invisible God, and wherein all the blessed excellencies of his distinct
natures are made most illustriously conspicuous in becoming one
entire principle of all his mediatory operations on our behalf—is
proposed to us as the complete object of our faith and love. This
is that person whose loveliness and beauty all the angels of God,
all the holy ones above, do eternally admire and adore. In him are
the infinite treasures of divine wisdom and goodness continually
represented to them. This is he who is the joy, the delight, the
love, the glory of the church below. 'You whom our souls do
love,' is the title whereby they know him and converse with him
(Song 1:7; 3:1, 4). This is he who is the desire of all nations—the
beloved of God and men.

The mutual intercourse on this ground of love between Christ
and the church, is the life and soul of the whole creation; for on
the account hereof all things consist in him.

There is more glory under the eye of God, in the sighs, groans,
and mournings of poor souls filled with the love of Christ,
after the enjoyment of him according to his promises—in their
fervent prayers for his manifestation of himself to them—in the
refreshments and unspeakable joys which they have in his gracious
visits and embraces of his love—than in the thrones and diadems
of all the monarchs on the earth. Nor will they themselves part
with the ineffable satisfactions which they have in these things,
for all that this world can do for them or to them. *Mallem ruere
cum Christo, quam regnare cum Cæsare.* These things have not only
rendered prisons and dungeons more desirable to them than the
most goodly palaces, on future accounts, but have made them
really places of such refreshment and joys as men shall seek in vain
to extract out of all the comforts that this world can afford.

O curvæ in terras animæ et coelestium inanes!

Many there are who, not comprehending, not being affected with, that divine, spiritual description of the person of Christ which is given us by the Holy Ghost in the Scripture, do feign to themselves false representations of him by images and pictures, so as to excite carnal and corrupt affections in their minds. By the help of their outward senses, they reflect on their imaginations the shape of a human body, cast into postures and circumstances dolorous or triumphant; and so, by the working of their fancy, raise a commotion of mind in themselves, which they suppose to be love to Christ. But all these idols are teachers of lies. The true beauty and amiableness of the person of Christ, which is the formal object and cause of divine love, is so far from being represented herein, as that the mind is thereby wholly diverted from the contemplation of it. For no more can be so pictured to us but what may belong to a mere man, and what is arbitrarily referred to Christ, not by faith, but by corrupt imagination.

NOT BY IMAGES

The beauty of the person of Christ, as represented in the Scripture, consists in things invisible to the eyes of flesh. They are such as no hand of man can represent or shadow. It is the eye of faith alone that can see this King in his beauty. What else can contemplate on the untreated glories of his divine nature? Can the hand of man represent the union of his natures in the same person, wherein he is peculiarly amiable? What eye can discern the mutual communications of the properties of his different natures in the same person, which depends thereon, whence it is that God laid down his life for us, and purchased his church with his own blood? In these things, O vain man! does the loveliness of the person of

> *The beauty of the person of Christ, as represented in the Scripture, consists in things invisible to the eyes of flesh. They are such as no hand of man can represent or shadow. It is the eye of faith alone that can see this King in his beauty.*

Christ to the souls of believers consist, and not in those strokes of art which fancy has guided a skilful hand and pencil to. And what eye of flesh can discern the inhabitation of the Spirit in all fulness in the human nature? Can his condescension, his love, his grace, his power, his compassion, his offices, his fitness and ability to save sinners, be deciphered on a tablet, or engraven on wood or stone? However such pictures may be adorned, however beautified and enriched, they are not that Christ which the soul of the spouse does love; they are not any means of representing his love to us, or of conveying our love to him; they only divert the minds of superstitious persons from the Son of God, to the embraces of a cloud, composed of fancy and imagination.

Others there are who abhor these idols, and when they have so done, commit sacrilege. As they reject images, so they seem to do all love to the person of Christ, distinct from other acts of obedience, as a fond imagination. But the most superstitious love to Christ—that is, love acted in ways tainted with superstition—is better than none at all. But with what eyes do such persons read the Scriptures? With what hearts do they consider them? What do they conceive is the intention of the Holy Ghost in all those descriptions which he gives us of the person of Christ as amiable and desirable above all things, making wherewithal a proposal of him to our affections—inciting us to receive him by faith, and to cleave to him in love? yea, to what end is our nature endued with this affection—unto what end is the power of it renewed in us by the sanctification of the Holy Spirit—if it may not be fixed on this most proper and excellent object of it?

As Revealed in Scripture

This is the foundation of our love to Christ—namely, the revelation and proposal of him to us in the Scripture as altogether lovely. The discovery that is made therein of the glorious excellencies and endowments of his person—of his love, his goodness, and grace—of his worth and work—is that which engages the affections of believers to him. It may be said, that if there be such a proposal of him made to all promiscuously, then all would equally discern his amiableness and be affected with it, who assent equally to the truth of that revelation. But it has always fallen out otherwise. In the days of his flesh, some that looked on him could see neither 'form nor comeliness' in him wherefore he should be desired; others saw his glory—'glory as of the only-begotten of the Father, full of grace and truth.' To some he is precious; to others he is disallowed and rejected—a stone which the builders refused, when others brought it forth, crying, 'Grace, grace to it!' as the head of the corner. Some can see nothing but weakness in him; to others the wisdom and power of God do evidently shine forth in him. Wherefore it must be said, that notwithstanding that open, plain representation that is made of him in the Scripture, unless the Holy Spirit gives us eyes to discern it, and circumcise our hearts by the cutting off corrupt prejudices and all effects of unbelief, implanting in them, by the efficacy of his grace, this blessed affection of love to him, all these things will make no impression on our minds.

As it was with the people on the giving of the law, notwithstanding all the great and mighty works which God had wrought among them, yet having not given them 'a heart to perceive, and eyes to see, and ears to hear'—which he affirms that he had not done (Deut. 29:4)—they were not moved to faith or obedience by them; so is it in the preaching of the gospel. Notwithstanding all the blessed revelation that is made of the excellencies of the person of Christ therein, yet those into whose hearts God does not shine to give the knowledge of his glory in his face, can discern nothing of it, nor are their hearts affected with it.

We do not, therefore, in these things, follow 'cunningly-devised fables.' We do not indulge to our own fancies and imaginations;—they are not unaccountable raptures or ecstasies which are pretended to, nor such an artificial concatenation of thoughts as some ignorant of these things do boast that they can give an account of. Our love to Christ arises alone from the revelation that is made of him in the Scripture—is ingenerated, regulated, measured, and is to be judged thereby.

14

MOTIVES TO LOVE CHRIST

The motives to this love of Christ is the last thing, on this head of our religious respect to him, that I shall speak to.

When God required of the church the first and highest act of religion, the sole foundation of all others—namely, to take him as their God, to own, believe, and trust in him alone as such (which is wholly due to him for what he is, without any other consideration whatever)—yet he thought meet to add a motive to the performance of that duty from what he had done for them (Exod. 20:2–3). The sense of the first command is, that we should take him alone for our God; for he is so, and there is no other. But in the prescription of this duty to the church, he minds them of the benefits which they had received from him in bringing them out of the house of bondage.

God, in his wisdom and grace, orders all the causes and reasons of our duty, so as that all the rational powers and faculties of our souls may be exercised therein. Wherefore he does not only propose himself to us, nor is Christ merely proposed to us as the proper object of our affections, but he calls us also to the consideration of all those things that may satisfy our souls that it is the most just, necessary, reasonable and advantageous course for us so to fix our affections an him.

And these considerations are taken from all that he did for us, with the reasons and grounds why he did it. We love him principally and ultimately for what he is; but nextly and immediately for what he did. What he did for us is first proposed to us, and it is that which our souls are first affected withal. For they are originally acted in all things by a sense of the want which they have, and a desire of the blessedness which they have not. This directs them to what he has done for sinners; but that leads immediately to the consideration of what he is in himself. And when our love is fixed on him or his person, then all those things wherewith, from a sense of our own wants and desires, we were first affected, become motives to the confirming and increasing of that love. This is the constant method of the Scripture; it first proposes to us what the Lord Christ has done for us, especially in the discharge of his sacerdotal office, in his oblation and intercession, with the benefits which we receive thereby. Hereby it leads us to his person, and presses the consideration of all other things to engage our love to him (see Philippians 2:5–11, with chapter 3:8–11).

Motives to the love of Christ are so great, so many, so diffused through the whole dispensation of God in him to us, as that they can by no hand be fully expressed, let it be allowed ever so much to enlarge in the declaration of them; much less can they be represented in that short discourse whereof but a very small part is allotted to their consideration—such as ours is at present. The studying, the collection of them or so many of them as we are able, the meditation on them and improvement of them, are among the principal duties of our whole lives. What I shall offer is the reduction of them to these two heads:

1. The acts of Christ, which is the substance of them; and,
2. The spring and fountain of those acts, which is the life of them.

HIS MEDIATORIAL ACTS

In general they are all the acts of his mediatory office, with all the fruits of them, whereof we are made partners. There is not any thing that he did or does, in the discharge of his mediatory office, from the first susception of it in his incarnation in the womb of the blessed Virgin to his present intercession in heaven, but is an effectual motive to the love of him; and as such is proposed to us in the Scripture. Whatever he did or does with or towards us in the name of God, as the king and prophet of the church—whatever he did or does with God for us, as our high priest—it all speaks this language in the hearts of them that believe: O love the Lord Jesus in sincerity.

The consideration of what Christ thus did and does for us is inseparable from that of the benefits which we receive thereby. A due mixture of both these—of what he did for us, and what we obtain thereby—comprises the substance of these motives: 'Who loved me, and gave himself for me'—'Who loved us, and washed us in his own blood, and made us kings and priests to God'—'For you were slain, and have bought us to God with your blood.' And both these are of a transcendent nature, requiring our love to be so also. Who is able to comprehend the glory of the mediatory acting of the Son of God, in the assumption of our nature—in what he did and suffered therein? And for us, eye has not seen, nor ear heard, nor can it enter into the heart of man to conceive, what we receive thereby. The least benefit, and that obtained by the least expense of trouble or charge, deserves love, and leaves the brand of a crime where it is not so entertained. What, then, do the greatest deserve, and you procured by the greatest expense—even the price of the blood of the Son of God?

If we have any faith concerning these things, it will produce love, as that love will obedience. Whatever we profess concerning them, it springs from tradition and opinion, and not from faith, if it engage not our souls into the love of him. The frame of heart which ensues on the real faith of these things is expressed (Ps. 103:1–5):

> Bless the Lord, O my soul;
>   and all that is within me,
> bless his holy name.
> Bless the Lord, O my soul,
>   and forget not all his benefits;
> who forgives all your iniquities;
> who heals all your diseases;
> who redeems your life from destruction;
> who crowns you with lovingkindness
>   and tender mercies;
> who satisfies your mouth with good things;
> so that your youth is renewed like the eagle's.

Let men pretend what they will, there needs no greater, no other evidence, to prove that any one does not really believe the things that are reported in the gospel, concerning the mediatory acting of Christ, or that he has no experience in his own soul and conscience of the fruits and effects of them, than this—that his heart is not engaged by them to the most ardent love towards his person.

He is no Christian who lives not much in the meditation of the mediation of Christ, and the especial acts of it. Some may more abound in that work than others, as it is fixed, formed and regular; some may be more able than others to dispose their thought concerning them into method and order; some may be more diligent than others in the observation of times for the solemn performance of this duty; some may be able to rise to higher and clearer apprehensions of them than others. But as for those, the bent of whose minds does not lie towards thoughts of them—whose hearts are not on all occasions retreating to the remembrance of them—who embrace not all opportunities to call them over as they are able—on what grounds can they be esteemed Christians? How do they live by the faith of the Son of God? Are the great things of the gospel, of the mediation of Christ, proposed to us, as those which we may think of when we have nothing else to do, that we may meditate upon or neglect at our pleasure—as those wherein our concern is so small as that they must give place to all other occasions or diversions whatever? Nay; if our minds are not filled with these things—if Christ does not dwell plentifully in our hearts by faith—if our souls are not possessed with them, and in their whole inward frame and constitution so cut into this mould as to be led by a natural complacency to a converse with them—we are strangers to the life of faith. And if we are thus conversant about these things, they will engage our hearts into the love of the person of Christ. To suppose the contrary, is indeed to deny the truth and reality of them all, and to turn the gospel into a fable.

Take one instance from among the rest—namely, his death. Has he the heart of a Christian, who does not often meditate on the death of his Saviour, who does not derive his life from it? Who can look into the gospel and not fix on those lines which either immediately and directly, or through some other paths of divine grace and wisdom, do lead him thereunto? And can any have believing thoughts concerning the death of Christ, and not have his heart affected with ardent love to his person? Christ in the gospel 'is evidently set forth, crucified' before us. Can any by the eye of faith look on this bleeding, dying Redeemer, and suppose love to his person to be nothing but the work of fancy or imagination? They know the contrary, who 'always bear about in the body the dying of the Lord Jesus,' as the apostle speaks (2 Cor. 4:10). As his whole 'name,' in all that he did, is 'as ointment poured forth,' for which 'the virgins love him' (S. of S. 1:3)—so this precious perfume of his death is that wherewith their hearts are ravished in a peculiar manner.

Again: as there can be no faith in Christ where there is no love to him on the account of his mediatory acts; so, where it is not, the want of it casts persons under the highest guilt of ingratitude that our nature is liable to. The highest aggravation of the sin of angels was their ingratitude to their maker. For whereas, by his mere will and pleasure, they were stated in the highest excellency, pre-eminence, and dignity, that he thought good to communicate to any creatures—or, it may be, that any mere created nature is capable of in itself—they were unthankful for what they had so received from undeserved goodness and bounty; and so cast themselves into everlasting ruin. But yet the sin of men, in their ingratitude towards Christ on the account of what he has done for them, is attended with an aggravation above that of the angels. For although the angels were originally instated in that condition of dignity which in this world we cannot attain to, yet were they not redeemed and recovered from misery as we are.

In all the crowd of evil and wicked men that the world is pestered withal, there are none, by common consent, so stigmatised for unworthy villainy, as those who are signally ungrateful for singular benefits. If persons are unthankful to them, if they have not the highest love for them, who redeem them from ignominy and death, and instate them in a plentiful inheritance (if any such instances may be given), and that with the greatest expense of labour and charge—mankind, without any regret, does tacitly condemn them to greater miseries than those which they were delivered from. What, then, will be the condition of them whose hearts are not so affected with the mediation of Christ and the fruits of it, as to engage the best, the choicest of their affections to him! The gospel itself will be 'a savour of death' to such ungrateful wretches.

His Love to Us

That which the Scripture principally insists on as the motive of our love to Christ, is his love to us—which was the principle of all his mediatory actings in our behalf.

Love is that jewel of human nature which commands a valuation wherever it is found. Let other circumstances be what they will, whatever distances between persons may be made by them, yet real love, where it is evidenced so to be, is not despised by any but such as degenerate into profligate brutality. If it be so stated as that it can produce no outward effects advantageous to them that are beloved, yet it commands a respect, as it were, whether we will or no, and some return in its own kind. Especially it does so if it be altogether undeserved, and so evidences itself to proceed from a goodness of nature, and an inclination to the good of them on whom it is fixed. For, whereas the essential nature of love consists in willing good to them that are beloved—where the act of the will is real, sincere, and constantly exercised, without any defect of it on our part, no restraints can possibly be put upon our minds from going out in some acts of love again upon its account, unless all their faculties are utterly depraved by habits of brutish and filthy lusts. But when this love, which is thus undeserved, also abounds in effects troublesome and chargeable in them in whom it is, and highly beneficial to them on whom it is placed—if there be any such affection left in the nature of any man, it will prevail to a reciprocal love. And all these things are found in the love of Christ, to that degree and height as nothing parallel to it can be found in the whole creation. I shall briefly speak of it under two general heads.

The Only Source of His Mediatorial Acts

The sole spring of all the mediatory acting of Christ, both in the susception of our nature and in all that he did and suffered therein, was his own mere love and grace, working by pity and compassion. It is true, he undertook this work principally with respect to the glory of God, and out of love to him. But with respect to us, his only motive to it was his abundant, overflowing love. And this is especially remembered to us in that instance wherein it carried him through the greatest difficulties—namely, in his death and the oblation of himself on our behalf (Gal. 2:20; Eph. 5:2, 25–6; 1 John 3:16; Rev. 1:5–6). This alone inclined the Son of God to undertake the glorious work of our redemption, and carried him through the death and dread which he underwent in the accomplishment of it.

Should I engage into the consideration of this love of Christ, which was the great means of conveying all the effects of divine wisdom and grace to the church—that glass which God chose to represent himself and all his goodness in to believers—that spirit of life in the wheel of all the motions of the person of Christ in the redemption of the church to the eternal glory of God, his own and that of his redeemed also—that mirror wherein the holy angels and blessed saints shall for ever contemplate the divine excellencies in their suitable operations;—I must now begin a discourse much larger than that which I have passed through. But it is not suited to my present design so to do. For, considering the growing apprehensions of many about the person of Christ, which are utterly destructive of the whole nature of that love which we ascribe to him, do I know how soon a more distinct explication and defence of it may be called for. And this cause will not be forsaken.

They know nothing of the life and power of the gospel, nothing of the reality of the grace of God, nor do they believe aright one article of the Christian faith, whose hearts are not sensible of the love of Christ herein; nor is he sensible of the love of Christ, whose affections are not thereon drawn out to him. I say, they make a pageant of religion—a fable for the theatre of the world—a business of fancy and opinion—whose hearts are not really affected with the love of Christ, in the susception and discharge of the work of mediation, so as to have real and spiritually sensible affections for him. Men may babble things which they have learned by rote; they have no real acquaintance with Christianity, who imagine that the placing of the most intense affections of our souls on the person of Christ—the loving him with all our hearts because of his love—our being overcome thereby until we are sick of love—the constant motions of our souls towards him with delight and adherence—are but fancies and imaginations. I renounce that religion, be it whose it will, that teaches, insinuates, or gives countenance to, such abominations. That doctrine is as discrepant from the gospel as the Alkoran—as contrary to the experience of believers as what is acted in and by the devils which instructs men to a contempt of the most fervent love to Christ, or casts reflections upon it. I had rather choose my eternal lot and portion with the meanest believer, who, being effectually sensible of the love of Christ, spends his days in mourning that he can love him no more than he finds himself on his utmost endeavours for the discharge of his duty to do, than with the best of them, whose vain speculations and a false pretence of reason puff them up to a contempt of these things.

Absolutely Selfless

This love of Christ to the church is singular in all those qualifications which render love obliging to reciprocal affections. It is so in its reality. There can be no love amongst men, but will derive something from that disorder which is in their affections in their highest actings. But the love of Christ is pure and absolutely free from any alloy. There cannot be the least suspicion of anything of self in it. And it is absolutely undeserved. Nothing can be found amongst men that can represent or exemplify its freedom from any desert on our part. The most candid and ingenuous love amongst us is, when we love another for his worth, excellency, and usefulness, though we have no singular benefit of them ourselves; but not the least of any of these things were found in them on whom he set his love, until they were wrought in them, as effects of that love which he set upon them.

Men sometimes may rise up to such a high degree and instance in love, as that they will even die for one another; but then it must be on a superlative esteem which they have of their worth and merit. It may be, says the apostle, treating of the love of Christ, and of God in him, that 'for a good man some would even dare to die' (Rom. 5:7). It must be for a good man—one who is justly esteemed '*commune bonum*,' a public good to mankind—one whose benignity is ready to exercise loving-kindness on all occasions, which is the estate of a good man;—peradventure some would even dare to die for such a man. This is the height of what love among men can rise to; and if it has been instanced in any, it has been accompanied with an open mixture of vain-glory and desire of renown. But the Lord Christ placed his love on us, that love from whence he died for us, when we were sinners and ungodly; that is, every thing which might render us unamiable and undeserving. Though we were as deformed as sin could render us, and more deeply indebted than the whole creation could pay or answer, yet did he fix his love upon us, to free us from that condition, and to render us meet for the most intimate society with himself. Never was there love which had such effects—which cost him so dear in whom it was, and proved so advantageous to them on whom it was placed. In the pursuit of it he underwent everything that is evil in his own person, and we receive everything that is good in the favour of God and eternal blessedness.

On the account of these things, the apostle ascribes a constraining power to the love of Christ (2 Cor. 5:14). And if it constrains us to any return to him, it does so to that of love in the first place. For no suitable return can be made for love but love, at least not without it. As love cannot be purchased—'For if a man would give all the substance of his house for love, it would utterly be condemned' (Song 8:7)—so if a man would give all the world for a requital of love, without love it would be despised. To fancy that all the love of Christ to us consists in the precepts and promises of the gospel, and all our love to him in the observance of his commands, without a real love in him to our persons, like that of a 'husband to a wife' (Eph. 5:25–6), or a holy affection in our hearts and minds to his person, is to overthrow the whole power of religion—to despoil it of its life and soul, leaving nothing but the carcass of it.

This love to Christ, and to God in him, because of his love to us, is the principal instance of divine love, the touchstone of its reality and sincerity. Whatever men may boast of their affectionate endearments to the divine goodness, if it be not founded in a sense of this love of Christ, and the love of God in him, they are but empty notions they nourish withal, and their deceived hearts feed upon ashes. It is in Christ alone that God is declared to be love; without an apprehension whereof none can love him as they ought. In him alone that infinite goodness, which is the peculiar object of divine love, is truly represented to us, without any such deceiving phantasm as the workings of fancy or depravation of reason may impose upon us. And on him does the saving communication of all the effects of it depend. And an infinite condescension is it in the holy God, so to express his 'glory in the face of Jesus Christ,' or to propose himself as the object of our love in and through him. For considering our weakness as to an immediate comprehension of the infinite excellencies of the divine nature, or to bear the rays of his resplendent glory, seeing none can see his face and live, it is the most adorable effect of divine wisdom and grace, that we are admitted to the contemplation of them in the person of Jesus Christ.

There is yet farther evidence to be given of this love to the person of Christ, from all those blessed effects of it which are declared in the Scripture, and whereof believers have the experience in themselves. But something I have spoken concerning them formerly, in my discourse about communion with God; and the nature of the present design will not admit of enlargement upon them.

15

CONFORMITY TO CHRIST

The third thing proposed to declare the use of the person of Christ in religion, is that conformity which is required of us to him. This is the great design and projection of all believers. Every one of them has the idea or image of Christ in his mind, in the eye of faith, as it is represented to him in the glass of the gospel: Τὴν δόξαν Κυρίου κατοπτριζόμενοι (2 Cor. 3:18). We behold his glory 'in a glass,' which implants the image of it on our minds. And hereby the mind is transformed into the same image, made like to Christ so represented to us—which is the conformity we speak of. Hence every true believer has his heart under the conduct of an habitual inclination and desire to be like to Christ. And it were easy to demonstrate, that where this is not, there is neither faith nor love. Faith will cast the soul into the form or frame of the thing believed (Rom. 6:17). And all sincere love works an assimilation. Wherefore the best evidence of a real principle of the life of God in any soul—of the sincerity of faith, love, and obedience—is an internal cordial endeavour, operative on all occasions, after conformity to Jesus Christ.

There are two parts of the duty proposed. The first respects the internal grace and holiness of the human nature of Christ; the other, his example in duties of obedience. And both of them—both materially as to the things wherein they consist, and formally as they were his or in him—belong to the constitution of a true disciple.

INTERNAL CONFORMITY

In the first place, internal conformity to his habitual grace and holiness is the fundamental design of a Christian life. That which is the best without it is a pretended imitation of his example in outward duties of obedience. I call it pretended, because where the first design is wanting, it is no more but so; nor is it acceptable to Christ nor approved by him. And therefore an attempt to that end has often issued in formality, hypocrisy, and superstition. I shall therefore lay down the grounds of this design, the nature of it, and the means of its pursuit.

CHRIST RENEWED THE IMAGE OF GOD IN OUR NATURE

God, in the human nature of Christ, did perfectly renew that blessed image of his on our nature which we lost in Adam, with an addition of many glorious endowments which Adam was not made partaker of. God did not renew it in his nature as though that portion of it whereof he was partaker had ever been destitute or deprived of it, as it is with the same nature in all other persons. For he derived not his nature from Adam in the same way that we do; nor was he ever in Adam as the public representative of our nature, as we were. But our nature in him had the image of God implanted in it, which was lost and separated from the same nature in all other instances of its subsistence. 'It pleased the Father that in him should all fulness dwell'—that he should be 'full of grace and truth', and 'in all things have the pre-eminence.' But of these gracious endowments of the human nature of Christ I have discoursed elsewhere.

CHRIST EXEMPLIFIES WHAT GOD INTENDS FOR US

One end of God in filling the human nature of Christ with all grace, in implanting his glorious image upon it, was, that he might in him propose an example of what he would by the same grace renew us to, and what we ought in a way of duty to labour after. The fulness of grace was necessary to the human nature of Christ, from its hypostatic union with the Son of God. For whereas therein the 'fulness of the godhead dwelt in him bodily,' it became τὸ ἅγιον, a 'holy thing' (Luke 1:35). It was also necessary to him, as to his own obedience in the flesh, wherein he fulfilled all righteousness, 'did no sin, neither was guile found in his mouth' (1 Pet. 2:22). And it was so to the discharge of the office he undertook; for 'such an high priest became us, who is holy, harmless, undefiled, and separate from sinners' (Heb. 7:26). Howbeit, the infinite wisdom of God had this farther design in it also—namely, that he might be the pattern and example of the renovation of the image of God in us, and of the glory that ensues thereon. He is in the eye of God as the idea of what he intends in us, in the communication of grace and glory; and he ought to be so in ours, as to all that we aim at in a way of duty.

He has 'predestinated us to be conformed to the image of his Son, that he might be the first-born among many brethren' (Rom. 8:29). In the collation of all grace on Christ, God designed to make him 'the first born of many brethren;' that is, not only to give him the power and authority of the firstborn, with the trust of the whole inheritance to be communicated to them, but also as the example of what he would bring them to. 'For both he that sanctifies and they that are sanctified are all of one: for which cause he is not ashamed to call them brethren' (Heb. 2:11). It is Christ who sanctifies believers; yet is it from God, who first sanctified him, that he and they might be of one, and so become brethren, as bearing the image of the same Father. God designed and gave to Christ grace and glory; and he did it that he might be the prototype of what he designed to us, and would bestow upon us. Hence the apostle shows that the effect of this predestination to conformity to the image of the Son is the communication of all effectual, saving grace, with the glory that ensues thereon, 'Moreover, whom he did predestinate, them he also called; and whom he called, them he also justified; and whom he justified, them he also glorified' (Rom. 8:30).

The great design of God in his grace is, that as we have borne the 'image of the first Adam' in the depravation of our natures, so we should bear the 'image of the second' in their renovation. 'As we have borne the image of the earthy,' so 'we shall bear the image of the heavenly' (1 Cor. 15:49). And as he is the pattern of all our graces, so he is of glory also. All our glory will consist in our being 'made like to him;' which, what it is, does not as yet appear (1 John 3:2). For 'he shall change our vile body, that it may be fashioned like to his glorious body' (Phil. 3:21). Wherefore the fulness of grace was bestowed on the human nature of Christ, and the image of God gloriously implanted thereon, that it might be the prototype and example of what the church was through him to be made partaker of. That which God intends for us in the internal communication of his grace, and in the use of all the ordinances of the church, is, that we may come to the 'measure of the stature of the fulness of Christ' (Eph. 4:13). There is a fulness of all grace in Christ. Hereunto are we to be brought, according to the measure that is designed to every one of us. 'For to every one of us is given grace, according to the measure of the gift of Christ' (v. 7). He has, in his sovereign grace, assigned different measures to those on whom he bestows it. And therefore it is called 'the stature', because as we grow gradually to it, as men do to their just stature; so there is a variety in what we attain to, as there is in the statures of men, who are yet all perfect in their proportion.

THE GOSPEL PRESENTS THE IMAGE OF GOD IN CHRIST

This image of God in Christ is represented to us in the gospel. Being lost from our nature, it was utterly impossible we should have any just comprehension of it. There could be no steady notion of the image of God, until it was renewed and exemplified in the human nature of Christ. And thereon, without the knowledge of him, the wisest of men have taken those things to render men most like to God which were adverse to him. Such were the most of those things which the heathens adored as heroic virtues. But being perfectly exemplified in Christ, it is now plainly represented to us in the gospel. Therein with open face we behold, as in a glass, the glory of the Lord, and are changed into the same image (2 Cor. 3:18). The veil being taken away from divine revelations by the doctrine of the gospel and from our hearts 'by the Lord the Spirit,' we behold the image of God in Christ with open face, which is the principal means of our being transformed into it. The gospel is the declaration of Christ to us, and the glory of God in him; as to many other ends, so in especial, that we might in him behold and contemplate that image of God we are gradually to be renewed into. Hence, we are so therein to learn the truth as it is in Jesus, as to be 'renewed in the spirit of our mind,' and to 'put on the new man, which after God is created in righteousness and true holiness' (Eph. 4:20, 23–4) — that is, 'renewed after the image of him who created him' (Col. 3:10).

The Life of God in Us—Conformity to Christ

It is, therefore, evident that the life of God in us consists in conformity to Christ; nor is the Holy Spirit, as the principal and efficient cause of it, given to us for any other end but to unite us to him, and make us like him. Wherefore, the original gospel duty, which animates and rectifies all others, is a design for conformity to Christ in all the gracious principles and qualifications of his holy soul, wherein the image of God in him consists. As he is the prototype and exemplar in the eye of God for the communication of all grace to us, so he ought to be the great example in the eye of our faith in all our obedience to God, in our compliance with all that he requires of us.

God himself, or the divine nature in its holy perfections, is the ultimate object and idea of our transformation in the renewing of our minds. And, therefore, under the Old Testament, before the incarnation of the Son, he proposed his own holiness immediately as the pattern of the church: 'Be holy, for the Lord your God is holy' (Lev. 11:44; 19:2; 20:26). But the law made nothing perfect. For to complete this great injunction, there was yet wanting an express example of the holiness required; which is not given us but in him who is 'the first-born, the image of the invisible God.'

There was a notion, even among the philosophers, that the principal endeavour of a wise man was to be like to God. But in the improvement of it, the best of them fell into foolish and proud imaginations. Howbeit, the notion itself was the principal beam of our primigenial light, the best relic of our natural perfections; and those who are not some way under the power of a design to be like to God are every way like to the devil. But those persons who had nothing but the absolute essential properties of the divine nature to contemplate on in the light of reason, failed all of them, both in the notion itself of conformity to God, and especially in the practical improvement of it. Whatever men may fancy to the contrary, it is the design of the apostle, in sundry places of his writings, to prove that they did so (especially Rom. 1; 1 Cor. 1). Wherefore, it was an infinite condescension of divine wisdom and grace, gloriously to implant that image of him which we are to endeavour conformity to in the human nature of Christ, and then so fully to represent and propose it to us in the revelation of the gospel.

The infinite perfections of God, considered absolutely in themselves, are accompanied with such an incomprehensible glory as it is hard to conceive how they are the object of our imitation. But the representation that is made of them in Christ, as the image of the invisible God, is so suited to the renewed faculties of our souls, so congenial to the new creature or the gracious principle of spiritual life in us, that the mind can dwell on the contemplation of them, and be thereby transformed into the same image.

Herein lies much of the life and power of Christian religion, as it resides in the souls of men. This is the prevailing design of the minds of them that truly believe the gospel; they would in all things be like to Jesus Christ. And I shall briefly show—(1.) What is required hereunto; and (2.) What is to be done in a way of duty for the attaining that end.

Requires Spiritual Light

A spiritual light, to discern the beauty, glory, and amiableness of grace in Christ, is required hereunto. We can have no real design of conformity to him, unless we have their eyes who 'beheld his glory, the glory of the only-begotten of the Father, full of grace and truth' (John 1:14). Nor is it enough that we seem to discern the glory of his person, unless we see a beauty and excellency in every grace that is in him. 'Learn of me,' says he; 'for I am meek and lowly in heart' (Matt. 11:29). If we are not able to discern an excellency in meekness and lowliness of heart (as they are things generally despised), how shall we sincerely endeavour after conformity to Christ in them? The like may be said of all his other gracious qualifications. His zeal, his patience, his self-denial, his readiness for the cross, his love to his enemies, his benignity to all mankind, his faith and fervency in prayer, his love to God, his compassion towards the souls of men, his unweariedness in doing good, his purity, his universal holiness;—unless we have a spiritual light to discern the glory and amiableness of them all, as they were in him, we speak in vain of any design for conformity to him. And this we have not, unless God shine into our hearts to give us the light of the knowledge of his glory in the face of Jesus Christ. It is, I say, a foolish thing to talk of the imitation of Christ, whilst really, through the darkness of our minds, we discern not that there is an excellency in the things wherein we ought to be like to him.

Requires Love for the Graces that Were in Christ

Love to them so discovered in a beam of heavenly light, is required to the same end. No soul can have a design of conformity to Christ but his who so likes and loves the graces that were in him, as to esteem a participation of them in their power to be the greatest advantage, to be the most invaluable privilege, that can in this world be attained. It is the savour of his good ointments for which the virgins love him, cleave to him, and endeavour to be like him. In that whereof we now discourse—namely, of conformity to him—he is the representative of the image of God to us. And, if we do not love and prize above all things those gracious qualifications and dispositions of mind wherein it consists, whatever we may pretend of the imitation of Christ in any outward acts or duties of obedience, we have no design of conformity to him. He who sees and admires the glory of Christ as filled with these graces—as he 'was fairer than the children of men,' because 'grace was poured into his lips'—unto whom nothing is so desirable as to have the same mind, the same heart, the same spirit that was in Christ Jesus—is prepared to press after conformity to him. And to such a soul the representation of all these excellencies in the person of Christ is the great incentive, motive, and guide, in and to all internal obedience to God.

Lastly, That wherein we are to labour for this conformity may be reduced to two heads.

Demands Opposition to All Sin

An opposition to all sin, in the root, principle, and most secret springs of it, or original cleavings to our nature. He 'did no sin, neither was there any guile found in his mouth.' He 'was holy, harmless, undefiled, separate from sinners.' He was the 'Lamb of God, without spot or blemish;' like to us, yet without sin. Not the least tincture of sin did ever make an approach to his holy nature. He was absolutely free from every drop of that fomes which has invaded us in our depraved condition. Wherefore, to be freed from all sin, is the first general part of an endeavour for conformity to Christ. And although we cannot perfectly attain hereunto in this life, as we have 'not already attained, nor are already perfect,' yet he who groans not in himself after it—who does not loathe every thing that is of the remainder of sin in him and himself for it—who does not labour after its absolute and universal extirpation—has no sincere design of conformity to Christ, nor can so have. He who endeavours to be like him, must 'purify himself, even as he is pure.' Thoughts of the purity of Christ, in his absolute freedom from the least tincture of sin, will not suffer a believer to be negligent, at any time, for the endeavouring the utter ruin of that which makes him unlike to him. And it is a blessed advantage to faith, in the work of mortification of sin, that we have such a pattern continually before us.

Demands Growth in Grace

The due improvement of, and continual growth, in every grace, is the other general part of this duty. In the exercise of his own all-fulness of grace, both in moral duties of obedience and the especial duties of his office, did the glory of Christ on the earth consist. Wherefore, to abound in the exercise of every grace—to grow in the root and thrive in the fruit of them—is to be conformed to the image of the Son of God.

IN ALL DUTIES

Secondly, the following the example of Christ in all duties towards God and men, in his whole conversation on the earth, is the second part of the instance now given concerning the use of the person of Christ in religion. The field is large which here lies before us, and filled with numberless blessed instances. I cannot here enter into it; and the mistakes that have been in a pretence to it, require that it should be handled distinctly and at large by itself; which, if God will, may be done in due time. One or two general instances wherein he was most eminently our example, shall close this discourse.

MEEKNESS

His meekness, lowliness of mind, condescension to all sorts of persons—his love and kindness to mankind—his readiness to do good to all, with patience and forbearance—are continually set before us in his example. I place them all under one head, as proceeding all from the same spring of divine goodness, and having effects of the same nature. With respect to them, it is required that 'the same mind be in us that was in Christ Jesus ' (Phil. 2:5); and that we 'walk in love, as he also loved us' (Eph. 5:2).

In these things was he the great representative of the divine goodness to us. In the acting of these graces on all occasions did he declare and manifest the nature of God, from whom he came. And this was one end of his exhibition in the flesh. Sin had filled the world with a representation of the devil and his nature, in mutual hatred, strife, variance, envy, wrath, pride, fierceness, and rage, against one another; all which are of the old murderer. The instances of a cured, of a contrary frame, were obscure and weak in the best of the saints of old. But in our Lord Jesus the light of the glory of God herein first shone upon the world. In the exercise of these graces, which he most abounded in, because the sins, weaknesses and infirmities of men gave continual occasion thereunto, did he represent the divine nature as love—as infinitely good, benign, merciful, and patient—delighting in the exercise of these its holy properties. In them was the Lord Christ our example in an especial manner. And they do in vain pretend to be his disciples, to be followers of him, who endeavour not to order the whole course of their lives in conformity to him in these things.

One Christian who is meek, humble, kind, patient, and useful to all; that condescends to the ignorance, weaknesses and infirmities of others; that passes by provocations, injuries, contempt, with patience and with silence, unless where the glory and truth of God call for a just vindication; that pities all sorts of men in their failings and miscarriages, who is free from jealousies and evil surmises; that loves what is good in all men, and all men even wherein they are not good, nor do good—does more express the virtues and excellencies

For men to pretend to follow the example of Christ, and in the meantime to be proud, wrathful envious, bitterly zealous, calling for fire from heaven to destroy men, or fetching it themselves from hell, is to cry, 'Hail to him,' and to crucify him afresh to their power.

of Christ than thousands can do with the most magnificent works of piety or charity, where this frame is wanting in them. For men to pretend to follow the example of Christ, and in the meantime to be proud, wrathful envious, bitterly zealous, calling for fire from heaven to destroy men, or fetching it themselves from hell, is to cry, 'Hail to him,' and to crucify him afresh to their power.

SELF-DENIAL

Self-denial, readiness for the cross, with patience in sufferings, are the second sort of things which he calls all his disciples to follow his example in. It is the fundamental law of his gospel, that if any one will be his disciple, 'he must deny himself, take up his cross, and follow him.' These things in him, as they are all of them summarily represented (Phil. 2:5–8), by reason of the glory of his person and the nature of his sufferings, are quite of another kind than that we are called to. But his grace in them all is our only pattern in what is required of us. 'Christ also suffered for us, leaving us an example, that we should follow his steps: who, when he was reviled, reviled not again; when he suffered, he threatened not' (1 Pet. 2:21–3). Hence are we called to look to 'Jesus, the author and finisher of our faith; who, for the joy that was set before him, endured the cross, and despised the shame.' For we are to 'consider him, who endured such contradiction of sinners against himself,' that we faint not (Heb. 12:3). Blessed be God for this example—for the glory of the condescension, patience, faith, and endurance, of Jesus Christ, in the extremity of all sorts of sufferings. This has been the pole-star of the church in all its storms; the guide, the comfort, supportment and encouragement of all those holy souls, who, in their several generations, have in various degrees undergone persecution for righteousness' sake; and yet continues so to be to them who are in the same condition.

And I must say, as I have done on some other occasions in the handling of this subject, that a discourse on this one instance of the use of Christ in religion—from the consideration of the person who suffered, and set us this example; of the principle from whence, and the end for which, he did it; of the variety of evils of all sorts he had to conflict withal; of his invincible patience under them all, and immovableness of love and compassion to mankind, even his persecutors; the dolorous afflictive circumstances of his sufferings from God and men; the blessed efficacious workings of his faith and trust in God to the uttermost; with the glorious issue of the whole, and the influence of all these considerations to the consolation and support of the church—would take up more room and time than what is allotted to the whole of that whereof it is here the least part. I shall leave the whole under the shade of that blessed promise, 'If so be that we suffer with him, we may be also glorified together; for I reckon that the sufferings of this present time are not worthy to be compared with the glory which shall be revealed in us' (Rom. 8:17–18).

The last thing proposed concerning the person of Christ, was the use of it to believers, in the whole of their relation to God and duty towards him. And the things belonging thereunto may be reduced to these general heads:

1. Their sanctification, which consists in these four things:
   a. The mortification of sin;
   b. The gradual renovation of our natures;
   c. Assistances in actual obedience;
   d. The same in temptations and trials.
2. Their justification, with its concomitants and consequent; as,
   a. Adoption;
   b. Peace;
   c. Consolation and joy in life and death;
   d. Spiritual gifts, to the edification of themselves and others;
   e. A blessed resurrection;
   f. Eternal glory.

There are other things which also belong hereunto—as their guidance in the course of their conversation in this world, direction to usefulness in all states and conditions, patient waiting for the accomplishment of God's promises to the church, the communication of federal blessings to their families, and the exercise of loving-kindness towards mankind in general, with sundry other concerns of the life of faith of the like importance; but they may be all reduced to the general heads proposed.

What should have been spoken with reference to these things belongs to these three heads:

1. A declaration that all these things are wrought in and communicated to believers, according to their various natures, by an emanation of grace and power from the person of Jesus Christ, as the head of the church—as he who is exalted and made a Prince and a Saviour, to give repentance and the forgiveness of sins.
2. A declaration of the way and manner how believers do live upon Christ in the exercise of faith, whereby, according to the promise and appointment of God, they derive from him the whole grace and mercy whereof in this world they are made partakers, and are established in the expectation of what they shall receive hereafter by his power. And that two things do hence ensue. First, the necessity of universal evangelical obedience, seeing it is only in and by the duties of it that faith is, or can be, kept in a due exercise to the ends mentioned. Secondly, that believers do hereby increase continually with the increase of God, and grow up into him who is the head, until they become the fulness of him who fills all in all.
3. A conviction that a real interest in, and participation of, these things cannot be obtained any other way but by the actual exercise of faith on the person of Jesus Christ.

These things were necessary to be handled at large with reference to the end proposed. But, for sundry reasons, the whole of this labour is here declined. For some of the particulars mentioned I have already insisted on in other discourses heretofore published, and that with respect to the end here designed. And this argument cannot be handled as it deserves, to full satisfaction, without an entire discourse concerning the life of faith; which my present design will not admit of.

16

THE INFINITE WISDOM OF GOD

From the consideration of the things before insisted on, we may endeavour, according to our measure, to take a view of, and humbly adore, the infinite wisdom of God, in the holy contrivance of this great 'mystery of godliness, God manifest in the flesh.' As it is a spiritual, evangelic mystery, it is an effect of divine wisdom, in the redemption and salvation of the church, to the eternal glory of God; and as it is a 'great mystery,' so it is the mystery of the 'manifold wisdom of God' (Eph. 3:9–10) — that is, of infinite wisdom working in great variety of acting and operations, suited to, and expressive of, its own infinite fulness: for herein were 'all the treasures of wisdom and knowledge' laid up, and laid out (Col. 2:3). An argument this is, in some parts whereof divers of the ancient writers of the church have laboured, some occasionally, and some with express design. I shall insist only on those things which Scripture light leads us directly to. The depths of divine wisdom in this glorious work are hid from the eyes of all living. 'God understands the way thereof; and he knows the place thereof;' as he speaks (Job 28:21, 23). Yet is it so glorious in its effects, that 'destruction and death say, We have heard the fame thereof with our ears' (v. 22). The fame and report of this divine wisdom reach even to hell. Those who eternally perish shall hear a fame of this wisdom, in the glorious effects of it towards the blessed souls above, though some of them would not believe it here in the light of the gospel, and none of them can understand it there, in their everlasting darkness. Hence the report which they have of the wisdom is an aggravation of their misery.

These depths we may admire and adore, but we cannot comprehend: 'For who has known the mind of the Lord herein, or with whom took he counsel?' Concerning the original causes of his counsels in this great mystery we can only say, 'O the depth of the riches both of the wisdom and knowledge of God! how unsearchable are his judgements, and his ways past finding out!' This alone is left to us in the way of duty, that in the effects of them we should contemplate on their excellency, so as to give glory to God, and live in a holy admiration of his wisdom and grace. For to give glory to him, and admire him, is our present duty, until he shall come eternally 'to be glorified in his saints, and to be admired in all them that believe' (2 Thess. 1:10).

We can do no more but stand at the shore of this ocean, and adore its unsearchable depths. What is delivered from them by divine revelation we may receive as pearls of price, to enrich and adorn our souls. For 'the secret things belong to the Lord our God, but those things which are revealed belong to us,' that we may do 'the words of this law' (Deut. 29:29). We shall not, therefore, in our inquiry into this great mystery, intrude ourselves into the things which we have not seen, but only endeavour a right understanding of what is revealed concerning it. For the end of all divine revelations is our knowledge of the things revealed, with our obedience thereon; and to this end things revealed do belong to us.

Some things in general are to be premised to our present inquiry.

First, we can have no view or due prospect of the wisdom of God in any of his works, much less in this of 'sending his Son in the likeness of sinful flesh,' or the constitution of his person, and the work of redemption to be accomplished thereby, unless we consider also the interest of the other holy properties of the divine nature in them. Such are his holiness, his righteousness, his sovereign authority, his goodness, love, and grace.

There are three excellencies of the divine nature principally to be considered in all the external works of God

1. His goodness, which is the communicative property thereof. This is the eternal fountain and spring of all divine communications. Whatever is good in and to any creature, is an emanation from divine goodness. 'He is good, and he does good.' That which acts originally in the divine nature, to the communication of itself in any blessed or gracious effects to the creatures, is goodness.
2. Wisdom, which is the directive power or excellency of the divine nature. Hereby God guides, disposes, orders, and directs all things to his own glory, in and by their own immediate proper ends (Prov. 16:4; Rev. 4:11).
3. Power, which is the effective excellency of the divine nature, effecting and accomplishing what wisdom designs and order.

Whereas wisdom, therefore, is that holy excellency or power of the Divine Being, wherein God designs, and whereby he effects, the glory of all the other properties of his nature, we cannot trace the paths of it in any work of God, unless we know the interest and concern of those other properties in that work. For that which wisdom principally designs, is the glorification of them. And to this end the effective property of the divine nature, which is almighty power, always accompanies, or is subservient to, the directive or infinite wisdom, which is requisite to perfection in operation. What infinite goodness will communicate *ad extra*—what it will open the eternal fountain of the Divine Being and all sufficiency to give forth—that infinite wisdom designs, contrives, and directs to the glory of God; and what wisdom so designs, infinite power effects (see Isa. 40:13–15, 17, 28).

Second, we can have no apprehensions of the interest of the other properties of the divine nature in this great mystery of godliness, whose glory was designed in infinite wisdom, without the consideration of that state and condition of our own wherein they are so concerned. That which was designed to the eternal glory of God in this great work of the incarnation of his Son, was the redemption of mankind, or the recovery and salvation of the church. What has been disputed by some concerning it, without respect to the sin of man and the salvation of the church, is curiosity, and indeed presumptuous folly. The whole Scripture constantly assigns this sole end of that effect of divine goodness and wisdom; yea, asserts it as the only foundation of the gospel (John 3:16). Wherefore, to a due contemplation of divine wisdom in it, it is necessary we should consider what is the nature of sin, especially of that first sin, wherein our original apostasy from God did consist—what was the condition of mankind thereon—what is the concern of the holy God therein, on the account of the blessed properties of his nature—what way was suited to our recovery, that God might be glorified in them all. Without a previous consideration of these things, we can have no due conceptions of the wisdom of God in this glorious work which we inquire after. Wherefore I shall so far speak of them, that, if it be the will of God, the minds of those who read and consider them may be opened and prepared to give admittance to some rays of that divine wisdom in this glorious work, the lustre of whose full light we are not able in this world to behold.

When there was a visible pledge of the presence of God in the 'bush that burned' and was not consumed, Moses said he 'would turn aside to see that great sight' (Exod. 3:3). And this great representation of the glory of God being made and proposed to us, it is certainly our duty to divert from all other occasions to the contemplation of it. But as Moses was then commanded to put off his shoes, the place whereon he stood being holy ground, so it will be the wisdom of him that writes, and of them that read, to divest themselves of all carnal affections and imaginations, that they may draw nigh to this great object of faith with due reverence and fear.

THE NATURE OF OUR SIN AND APOSTASY

The first thing we are to consider, in order to the end proposed, is—the nature of our sin and apostasy from God. For from thence we must learn the concern of the divine excellencies of God in this work. And there are three things that were eminent therein.

Man in the Image of God

A reflection on the honour of the holiness and wisdom of God, in the rejection of his image. He had newly made man in his own image. And this work he so expresses as to intimate a peculiar effect of divine wisdom in it, whereby it was distinguished from all other external works of creation whatever (Gen. 1:26–7), 'And God said, Let us make man in our image, after our likeness. So God created man in his own image, in the image of God created he him.' Nowhere is there such an emphasis of expression concerning any work of God. And sundry things are represented as peculiar therein.

Unique Features

First, that the word of consultation and that of execution are distinct. In all other works of creation, the word of determination and execution was the same. When he created light—which seems to be the beauty and glory of the whole creation—he only said, 'Let there be light; and there was light' (Gen. 1:3). So was it with all other things. But when he comes to the creation of man, another process is proposed to our faith. These several words are distinct, not in time, but in nature. 'God said, Let us make man in our image and likeness;' and thereon it is added distinctly, as the execution of that antecedent counsel, 'So God made man in his own image.' This puts a signal eminency on this work of God.

Secondly, a distinct, peculiar concern of all the persons of the holy Trinity, in their consultation and operation, is in like manner proposed to us: 'And God said, Let us make man.' The truth hereof I have sufficiently evinced elsewhere, and discovered the vanity of all other glosses and expositions. The properties of the divine nature principally and originally considerable, in all external operations (as we have newly observed), are goodness, wisdom, and power. In this great work, divine goodness exerted itself eminently and effectually in the person of the Father—the eternal fountain and spring, as of the divine nature, so of all divine operations. Divine wisdom acted itself peculiarly in the person of the Son; this being the principal notion thereof—the eternal Wisdom of the Father. Divine power wrought effectually in the person of the Holy Spirit; who is the immediate actor of all divine operations.

Thirdly, the proposition of the effecting this work, being by way of consultation, represents it a signal effect of infinite wisdom. These expressions are used to lead us to the contemplation of that wisdom.

Thus, 'God made man in his own image;' that is, in such a rectitude of nature as represented his righteousness and holiness—in such a state and condition as had a reflection on it of his power and rule. The former was the substance of it—the latter a necessary consequent thereof. This representation, I say, of God, in power and rule, was not that image of God wherein man was created, but a consequent of it. So the words and their order declare: 'Let us make man in our image, and after our likeness; and let them have dominion over the fish of the sea.' Because he was made in the image of God, this dominion and rule were granted to him. So fond is their imagination, who would have the image of God to consist solely in these things. Wherefore, the loss of the image of God was not originally the loss of power and dominion, or a right thereunto; but man was deprived of that right, on the loss of that image which it was granted to (wherein it did consist see Eccles. 7:29; Eph. 4:24).

Three Divine Designs

Three things God designed in this communication of his image to our nature, which were his principal ends in the creation of all things here below; and therefore was divine wisdom more eminently exerted therein than in all the other works of this inferior creation.

The first was, that he might therein make a representation of his holiness and righteousness among his creatures. This was not done in any other of them. Characters they had on them of his goodness, wisdom, and power. In these things the 'heavens declare the glory of God, and the firmament shows his handy-work.' His eternal power and Godhead are manifest in the things that are made; but none of them, not the whole fabric of heaven and earth, with all their glorious ornaments and endowments, were either fit or able to receive any impressions of his holiness and righteousness—of any of the moral perfections or universal rectitude of his nature. Yet, in the demonstration and representation of these things the glory of God principally consists. Without them, he could not be known and glorified as God. Wherefore he would have an image and representation of them in the creation here below. And this he will always have, so long as he will be worshipped by any of his creatures. And therefore, when it was lost in Adam, it was renewed in Christ, as has been declared.

The second was, that it might be a means of rendering actual glory to him from all other parts of the creation. Without this, which is as the animating life and form of the whole, the other creatures are but as a dead thing. They could not any way declare the glory of God, but passively and objectively. They were as an harmonious, well-tuned instrument, which gives no sound unless there be a skilful hand to move and act it. What is light, if there be no eye to see it? or what is music, if there be no ear to hear it? How glorious and beautiful soever any of the works of creation appear to be, from impressions of divine power, wisdom, and goodness on them; yet, without this image of God in man, there was nothing here below to understand God in them—to glorify God by them. This alone is that whereby, in a way of admiration, obedience, and praise, we were enabled to render to God all the glory which he designed from those works of his power.

The third was, that it might be a means to bring man to that eternal enjoyment of himself, which he was fitted for and designed to. For this was to be done in a way of obedience;—'Do this and live,' was that rule of it which the nature of God and man, with their mutual relation to one another, did require. But we were made meet for this obedience, and enabled to it, only by virtue of this image of God implanted in our natures. It was morally a power to live to God in obedience, that we might come to the enjoyment of him in glory.

Evident it is that these were the principal ends of God in the creation of all things. Wherefore this constitution of our nature, and the furnishment of it with the image of God, was the most eminent effect of infinite wisdom in all the outward works of the divine nature.

MAN DEFACED THE IMAGE

In the entrance of sin, and by apostasy from God, man voluntarily rejected and defaced this blessed representation of the righteousness and holiness of God—this great effect of his goodness and wisdom, in its tendency to his eternal glory, and our enjoyment of him. No greater dishonour could be done to him—no endeavour could have been more pernicious in casting contempt on his counsel. For as his holiness, which was represented in that image, was despoiled, so we did what lay in us to defeat the contrivance of his wisdom. This will be evident by reflecting on the ends of it now mentioned.

Creation Left Bereft

Hereon there remained nothing, in all the creation here below, whereby any representation might be made of God's holiness and righteousness, or any of the moral perfections of his nature. How could it be done, this image being lost out of the world? The brute, inanimate part of the creation, however stupendously great in its matter and glorious in its outward form, was no way capable of it. The nature of man under the loss of this image—fallen, depraved, polluted, and corrupted—gives rather a representation and image of Satan than of God. Hence—instead of goodness, love, righteousness, holiness, peace, all virtues usefully communicative and effective of the good of the whole race of mankind, which would have been effects of this image of God, and representatives of his nature—the whole world, from and by the nature of man, is filled with envy, malice, revenge, cruelty, oppression, and all engines of promoting self, whereunto man is wholly turned, as fallen off from God. He that would learn the divine nature, from the representation that is made of it in the present acting of the nature of man, will be gradually led to the devil instead of God. Wherefore no greater indignity could be offered to divine wisdom and holiness, than there was in this rejection of the image of God wherein we were created.

The Rest of Creation Could not Glorify God

There was no way left whereby glory might redound to God from the remainder of the creation here below. For the nature of man alone was designed to be the way and means of it, by virtue of the image of God implanted on it. Wherefore man by sin did not only draw off himself from that relation to God wherein he was made, but drew off the whole creation here below with himself into a uselessness to his glory. And upon the entrance of sin, before the cure of our apostasy was actually accomplished, the generality of mankind divided the creatures into two sorts—those above, or the heavenly bodies, and those here below. Those of the first sort they worshipped as their gods; and those of the other sort they abused to their lusts. Wherefore God was every way dishonored in and by them all, nor was there any glory given him on their account. What some attempted to do of that nature, in a wisdom of their own, ended in folly and a renewed dishonour of God; as the apostle declares (Rom. 1:18–19, 21–2).

Man Lost All Power to Fulfill his Purpose

Man hereby lost all power and ability of attaining that end for which he was made—namely, the eternal enjoyment of God. Upon the matter, and as much as in us lay, the whole end of God in the creation of all things here below was utterly defeated.

But that which was the malignity and poison of this sin, was the contempt that was cast on the holiness of God, whose representation, and all its express characters, were utterly despised and rejected therein. Herein, then, lay the concern of the holiness or righteousness of God in this sin of our nature, which we are inquiring after. Unless some reparation be made for the indignity cast upon it in the rejection of the image and representation of it—unless there be some way whereby it may be more eminently exalted in the nature of man than it was debased and despised in the same nature; it was just, equal, righteous with God—that which becomes the rectitude and purity of his nature—that mankind should perish eternally in that condition whereinto it was cast by sin.

It was not, therefore, consistent with the glory of God, that mankind should be restored, that this nature of ours should be brought to the enjoyment of him, unless his holiness be more exalted, be more conspicuously represented in the same nature, than ever it was depressed or despised thereby. The demonstration of its glory in any other nature, as in that of angels, would not serve to this end; as we shall see afterward.

We must now a little return to what we before laid down. Wisdom being the directive power of all divine operations, and the end of all those operations being the glory of God himself, or the demonstration of the excellencies of the holy properties of his nature, it was incumbent thereon to provide for the honour and glory of divine holiness in an exaltation answerable to the attempt for its debasement. Without the consideration hereof, we can have no due prospect of the acting of infinite wisdom in this great work of our redemption and recovery by the incarnation of the Son of God.

SIN WROUGHT CHAOS

Sin brought disorder and disturbance into the whole rule and government of God. It was necessary, from the infinite wisdom of God, that all things should be made in perfect order and harmony—

all in a direct subordination to his glory. There could have been no original defect in the natural or moral order of things, but it must have proceeded from a defect in wisdom; for the disposal of all things into their proper order belonged to the contrivance thereof. And the harmony of all things among themselves, with all their mutual relations and aspects in a regular tendency to their proper and utmost end—whereby though every individual subsistence or being has a peculiar end of its own, yet all their actings and all their ends tend directly to one utmost common end of them all—is the principal effect of wisdom. And thus was it at the beginning, when God himself beheld the universe, and, 'lo, it was exceeding good.'

All things being thus created and stated, it belonged to the nature of God to be the rector and disposer of them all.

It was not a mere free act of his will, whereby God chose to rule and govern the creation according to the law of the nature of all things, and their relation to him; but it was necessary, from his divine being and excellences, that so he should do. Wherefore, it concerned both the wisdom and righteousness of God to take care that either all things should be preserved in the state wherein they were created, and no disorder be suffered to enter into the kingdom and rule of God, or that, in a way suited to them, his glory should be retrieved and re-established; for God is not the God of confusion—neither the author nor approver of it—neither in his works nor in his rule. But sin actually brought disorder into the kingdom and rule of God. And this it did not in any one particular instance, but that which was universal as to all things here below. For the original harmony and order of all things consisted in their subordination to the glory of God. But this they all lost, as was before declared. Hence he who looked on them in their constitution, and, to manifest his complacency in them, affirmed them to be 'exceeding good,' immediately on the entrance of sin, pronounced a curse on the whole earth, and all things contained therein.

To suffer this disorder to continue unrectified, was not consistent with the wisdom and righteousness of God. It would make the kingdom of God to be like that of Satan—full of darkness and confusion. Nothing is more necessary to the good of the universe, and without which it were better it were annihilated, than the preservation of the honour of God in his government. And this could no otherwise be done, but by the infliction of a punishment proportionable in justice to the demerit of sin. Some think this might be done by a free dismission of sin, or a passing it over without any punishment at all. But what evidence should we then have that good and evil were not alike, and almost equal to God in his rule—that he does not like sin as well as uprightness? Nor would this supposition leave any grounds of exercising justice among men. For if God, in misrule of all things, dismissed the greatest sin without any penalty inflicted, what reason have we to judge that evils among ourselves should at all be punished? That, therefore, be far from God, that the righteous should be as the wicked: 'Shall not the Judge of all the earth do right?'

Wherefore, the order of God's rule being broken, as it consisted in the regular obedience of the creature, and disorder with confusion being brought thereby into the kingdom and government of God; his righteousness, as it is the rectorial virtue and power of the divine nature, required that his glory should be restored, by reducing the sinning creature again into order by punishment. Justice, therefore, must be answered and complied withal herein, according to its eternal and unanswerable law, in a way suited to the glory of God, or the sinning creature must perish eternally.

Herein the righteousness of God, as the rectorial virtue of the divine nature, was concerned in the sin and apostasy of men. The vindication and glory of it—to provide that in nothing it were eclipsed or diminished—was incumbent on infinite wisdom, according to the rule before laid down. That must direct and dispose of all things anew to the glory of the righteousness of God, or there is no recovery of mankind. And in our inquiry after the impressions of divine wisdom on the great and glorious means of our restoration under consideration, this provision made thereby for the righteousness of God, in his rule and government of all, is greatly to be attended to.

Man Put His Faith in Satan

Man by sin put himself into the power of the devil, God's greatest adversary. The devil had newly, by rebellion and apostasy from his first condition, cast himself under the eternal displeasure and wrath of God. God had righteously purposed in himself not to spare him, nor contrive any way for his deliverance to eternity. He, on the other side, was become obdurate in his malice and hatred of God, designing his dishonour and the impeachment of his glory with the utmost of his remaining abilities. In this state of things, man voluntarily leaves the rule and conduct of God, with all his dependence upon him, and puts himself into the power of the devil; for he believed Satan above God—that is, placed his faith and confidence in him, as to the way of attaining blessedness and true happiness. And in whom we place our trust and confidence, them do we obey, whatever we profess. Herein did God's adversary seem for a season to triumph against him, as if he had defeated the great design of his goodness, wisdom, and power. So he would have continued to do, if no way had been provided for his disappointment.

This, therefore, also belonged to the care of divine wisdom—namely, that the glory of God in none of the holy properties of his nature did suffer any diminution hereby.

All this, and inconceivably more than we are able to express, being contained in the sin of our apostasy from God, it must needs follow that the condition of all mankind became thereby inexpressibly evil. As we had done all the moral evil which our nature was capable to act, so it was meet we should receive all the penal evil which our nature was capable to undergo; and it all issued in death temporal and eternal, inflicted from the wrath of God.

This is the first thing to be considered in our tracing the footsteps of divine wisdom in our deliverance by the incarnation of the Son of God. Without due conceptions of the nature of this sin and apostasy—of the provocation given to God thereby, of the injury attempted to be done to the glory of all his properties, of his concern in their reparation, with the unspeakable misery that mankind was fallen into—we cannot have the least view of the glorious acting of divine wisdom in our deliverance by Christ; and, therefore, the most of those who are insensible of these things, do wholly reject the principal instances of infinite wisdom in our redemption; as we shall yet see farther afterward. And the great reason why the glory of God in Christ so little irradiates the minds of many, that it is so much neglected and despised, is because they are not acquainted nor affected with the nature of our first sin and apostasy, neither in itself nor its woeful effects and consequents.

It Was Fitting that God Should Save

But, on the supposition of these things, a double inquiry arises with reference to the wisdom of God, and the other holy properties of his nature immediately concerned in our sin and apostasy.

Whereas man by sin had defaced the image of God, and lost it, whereby there was no representation of his holiness and righteousness left in the whole creation here below—no way of rendering any glory to him, in, for, or by, any other of his works—no means to bring man to the enjoyment of God, for which he was made—and whereas he had brought confusion and disorder into the rule and kingdom of God, which, according to the law of creation and its sanction, could not be rectified but by the eternal ruin of the sinner; and had, moreover, given up himself to the rule and conduct of Satan—whether, I say, hereon it was meet, with respect to the holy properties of the divine nature, that all mankind should be left eternally in this condition, without remedy or relief? Or whether there were not a condecency and suitableness to them, that at least our nature in some portion of it should be restored?

Upon a supposition that the granting of a recovery was suited to the holy perfections of the divine nature, acting themselves by infinite wisdom, what rays of that wisdom may we discern in the finding out and constitution of the way and means of that recovery?

The first of these I shall speak briefly to in this place, because I have treated more largely concerning it in another. For there are many things which argue a condecency to the divine perfections herein—namely, that mankind should not be left utterly remediless in that guilt of misery whereinto it was plunged. I shall at present only insist on one of them.

The Total Destruction of Humanity Could not Manifest God's Glory

God had originally created two sorts of intellectual creatures, capable of the eternal enjoyment of himself—namely, angels and men. That he would so make either sort or both, was a mere effect of his sovereign wisdom and pleasure; but on a supposition that he would so make them, they must be made for his glory. These two sorts thus created he placed in several habitations, prepared for them, suitable to their natures and the present duties required of them; the angels in heaven above, and men on earth below. Sin first invaded the nature of angels, and cast innumerable multitudes of them out of their primitive condition. Hereby they lost their capacity of, and right to, that enjoyment of God which their nature was prepared and made meet for; neither would God ever restore them thereunto. And in the instance of dealing with them, when he 'spared them not, but shut them up in chains of everlasting darkness to the judgement of the great day,' he manifested how righteous it was to leave sinning, apostate creatures in everlasting misery. If anything of relief be provided for any of them, it is a mere effect of sovereign grace and wisdom, whereunto God was no way obliged. Howbeit, the whole angelic nature, that was created in a capacity for the eternal enjoyment of God, perished not; nor does it seem consistent with the wisdom and goodness of God, that the whole entire species or kind of creatures made capable of glory in the eternal enjoyment of him, should at once immediately be excluded from it. That such a thing should fall out as it were accidentally, without divine provision and disposal, would argue a defect in wisdom, and a possibility of a surprisal into the loss of the whole glory he designed in the creation of all things; and to have it a mere effect of divine ordination and disposal, is as little consistent with his goodness. Wherefore, the same nature which sinned and perished in the angels that fell, abides in the enjoyment of God in those myriads of blessed spirits which 'left not their first habitation.'

The nature of man was in like manner made capable of the eternal enjoyment of God. This was the end for which it was created, to the glory of him by whom it was made; for it became the divine wisdom and goodness, to give to everything an operation and end suited to its capacity. And these, in this race of intellectual creatures, were to live to God, and to come to the eternal enjoyment of him. This operation and end their nature being capable of, they being suited to it, to them it was designed. But sin entered them also; we also 'sinned, and came short of the glory of God.' The inquiry hereon is, whether it became the divine goodness and wisdom that this whole nature, in all that were partakers of it, should fail and come short of that end for which alone it was made of God? For whereas the angels stood, in their primitive condition, every one in his own individual person, the sin of some did not prejudice others, who did not sin actually themselves. But the whole race of mankind stood all in one common head and state; from whom they were to be educed and derived by natural generation. The sin and apostasy of that one person was the sin and apostasy of us all. In him all sinned and died. Wherefore, unless there be a recovery made of them, or of some from among them, that whole species of intellectual nature—the whole kind of it, in all its individuals— which was made capable of doing the will of God, so as to come to the eternal fruition of him, must be eternally lost and excluded from it. This, we may say, became not the wisdom and goodness of God, no more than it would have done to have suffered the whole angelic nature, in all its individuals, to have perished for ever. No created understanding could have been able to discern the glory of God in such a dispensation, whereby it would have had no glory. That the whole nature, in all the individuals of it, which was framed by the power of God out of nothing, and made what it was for this very end, that it might glorify him, and come to the enjoyment of him, should eternally perish, if any way of relief for any portion of it were possible to infinite wisdom, does not give an amiable representation of the divine excellencies to us.

It was therefore left on the provision of infinite wisdom, that this great effect, of recovering a portion of fallen mankind out of this miserable estate, wherein there was a suitableness, a condecency to the divine excellencies, should be produced; only, it was to be done on and by a free act of the will of God; for otherwise there was no obligation on him from any of his properties so to do.

But it may be yet said, on the other side, that the nature of man was so defiled, so depraved, so corrupted, so alienated and separated from God, so obnoxious to the curse by its sin and apostasy, that it was not reparable to the glory of God; and therefore it would not argue any defect in divine power, nor any unsuitableness to divine wisdom and goodness, if it were not actually repaired and restored. I answer two things.

No Ground to Reflect on God's Goodness in the Perishing

The horrible nature of the first sin, and the heinousness of our apostasy from God therein, were such and so great, as that God thereon might righteously, and suitably to all the holy properties of his nature, leave mankind to perish eternally in that condition whereinto they had cast themselves; and if he had utterly forsaken the whole race of mankind in that condition, and left them all as remediless as the fallen angels, there could have been no reflection on his goodness, and an evident suitableness to his justice and holiness. Wherefore, wherever there is any mention in the Scripture of the redemption or restoration of mankind, it is constantly proposed as an effect of mere sovereign grace and mercy (see Eph. 1:3–11). And those who pretend a great difficulty at present, in the reconciliation of the eternal perishing of the greatest part of mankind with those notions we have of the divine goodness, seem not to have sufficiently considered what was contained in our original apostasy from God, nor the righteousness of God in dealing with the angels that sinned. For when man had voluntarily broken all the relation of love and moral good between God and him, had defaced his image—the only representation of his holiness and righteousness in this lower world—and deprived him of all his glory from the works of his hands, and had put himself into the society and under the conduct of the devil; what dishonour could it have been to God, what diminution would there have been of his glory, if he had left him to his own choice—to eat for ever of the fruit of his own ways, and to be filled with his own devices to eternity? It is only infinite wisdom that could find out a way for the salvation of any one of the whole race of mankind, so as that it might be reconciled to the glory of his holiness, righteousness, and rule. Wherefore, as we ought always to admire sovereign grace in the few that shall be saved, so we have no ground to reflect on divine goodness in the multitudes that perish, especially considering that they all voluntarily continue in their sin and apostasy.

Properties of God Were Revealed in the Reparation of Humanity

I grant the nature of man was not reparable nor recoverable by any such actings of the properties of God as he had exerted in the creation and rule of all things. Were there not other properties of the divine nature than what were discovered and revealed in the creation of all—were not some of them so declared capable of an exercise in another way or in higher degrees than what had as yet been instanced in—it must be acknowledged that the reparation of mankind could not be conceived compliant with the divine excellencies, nor to be effected by them. I shall give one instance in each sort; namely, first in properties of another kind than any which had been manifested in the works of creation, and then the acting of some of them so manifested, in another way, or farther degree than what they were before exerted in or by.

Of the first sort are love, grace, and mercy, which I refer to one head—their nature being the same, as they have respect to sinners. For although there were none of them manifested in the works of creation, yet are they no less essential properties of the divine nature than either power, goodness, or wisdom. With these it was that the reparation of our nature was compliant—unto them it had a condecency; and the glory of them infinite wisdom designed therein. That wisdom, on which it is incumbent to provide for the manifestation of all the other properties of God's nature, contrived this work to the glory of his love, mercy, and grace; as in the gospel it is everywhere declared.

Of the second sort is divine goodness. This, as the communicative property of the divine nature, had exerted itself in the creation of all things. Howbeit, it had not done so perfectly—it had not done so to the uttermost. But the nature of goodness being communicative, it belongs to its perfection to act itself to the uttermost. This it had not yet done in the creation. Therein 'God made man,' and acted his goodness in the communication of our being to us, with all its endowments. But there yet remained another effect of it; which was, that God should be made man, as the way to, and the means of, our recovery.

How Could Mankind be Restored?

These things being premised, we proceed to inquire more particularly by what way and means the recovery of mankind might be wrought, so as that God might be glorified thereby.

If fallen man be restored and reinstated in his primitive condition, or brought into a better, it must either be by himself, or by some other undertaking for him; for it must be done by some means or other. So great an alteration in the whole state of things was made by the entrance of sin, that it was not consistent with the glory of any of the divine excellencies that a restoration of all things should be made by a mere act of power, without the use of any means for the removal of the cause of that alteration. That man himself could not be this means—that is, that he could not restore himself—is openly evident. Two ways there were whereby he might attempt it, and neither jointly nor severally could he do anything in them.

Not By Obedience

He might do it by returning to obedience to God on his own accord. He fell off from God on his own accord by disobedience, through the suggestion of Satan; wherefore, a voluntary return to his former obedience would seem to reduce all things to their first estate. But this way was both impossible, and, upon a supposition of it, would have been insufficient to the end designed.

Powerless

This he could not do. He had, by his sin and fall, lost that power whereby he was able to yield any acceptable obedience to God; and a return to obedience is an act of greater power than a persistency in the way and course of it, and more is required thereunto. But all man's original power of obedience consisted in the image of God. This he had defaced in himself, and deprived himself of. Having, therefore, lost that power which should have enabled him to live to God in his primitive condition, he could not retain a greater power in the same kind to return thereunto. This, indeed, was that which Satan deceived and deluded him withal; namely, that by his disobedience he should acquire new light and power, which he had not yet received—he should be 'like to God.' But he was so far from any advantage by his apostasy, that one part of his misery consisted in the loss of all power or ability to live to God.

This is the folly of that Pelagian heresy, which is now a third time attempting to impose itself on the Christian world. It supposes that men have a power of their own to return to God, after they had lost the power they had of abiding with him. It is not, indeed, as yet, pretended by many that the first sin was a mere transient act, that no way vitiated our nature, or impaired the power, faculty, or principle of obedience in us. A wound, they say, a disease, a weakness, it brought upon us, and rendered us legally obnoxious to death temporal, which we were naturally liable to before. Wherefore, it is not said that men can return to that perfect obedience which the law required; but that they can comply with and perform that which the gospel requires in the room thereof. For they seem to suppose that the gospel is not much more but an accommodation of the rule of obedience to our present reason and abilities, with some motives to it, and an example for it in the personal obedience and suffering of Christ. For whereas man forsook the law of obedience first prescribed to him, and fell into various incapacities of observing it, God did not, as they suppose, provide, in and by the gospel, a righteousness whereby the law might be fulfilled, and effectual grace to raise up the nature of man to the performance of acceptable obedience; but only brings down the law and the rule of it into a compliance to our weakened, diseased, depraved nature—than which, if anything can be spoken more dishonourably of the gospel, I know it not. However, this pretended power of returning to some kind of obedience, but not that which was required of us in our primitive condition, is no way sufficient to our restoration; as is evident to all.

Unwilling

As man could not effect his own recovery, so he would not attempt it. For he was fallen into that condition wherein, in the principles of all his moral operations, he was at enmity against God; and whatever did befall him, he would choose to continue in his state of apostasy; for he was wholly 'alienated from the life of God.' He likes it not, as that which is incompliant with his dispositions, inclinations, and desires—as inconsistent with everything wherein he places his interest. And hence, as he cannot do what he should through impotency, he will not do even what he can through obstinacy. It may be, we know not distinctly what to ascribe to man's impotency, and what to his obstinacy; but between both, he neither can nor will return to God. And his power to good, though not sufficient to bring him again to God, yet is it not so small but that he always chooses not to make use of it to that end. In brief, there was left in man a fear of divine power—a fear of God because of his greatness—which makes him do many things which otherwise he would not do; but there is not left in him any love to divine goodness, without which he cannot choose to return to God.

Unable to Make Restitution

But let us leave these things which men will dispute about, though in express contradiction to the Scripture and the experience of them that are wrought upon to believe; and let us make an impossible supposition—that man could and would return to his primitive obedience; yet no reparation of the glory of God, suffering in the loss of the former state of all things, would thereon ensue. What satisfaction would be hereby made for the injury offered to the holiness, righteousness, and wisdom of God, whose violation in their blessed effects was the principal evil of sin? Notwithstanding such a supposition, all the disorder that was brought into the rule and government of God by sin, with the reflection of dishonour upon him, in the rejection of his image, would still continue. And such a restitution of things wherein no provision is made for the reparation of the glory of God, is not to be admitted. The notion of it may possibly please men in their apostate condition, wherein they are wholly turned off from God, and into self—not caring what becomes of his glory, so it may go well with themselves; but it is highly contradictory to all equity, justice, and the whole reason of things, wherein the glory of God is the principal and centre of all.

Practically, things are otherwise among many. The most profligate sinners in the world, that have a conviction of an eternal condition, would be saved. Tell them it is inconsistent with the glory of the holiness, righteousness, and truth of God, to save unbelieving, impenitent sinners—they are not concerned in it. Let them be saved that is—eternally delivered from the evil they fear—and let God look to his own glory; they take no care about it. A soul that is spiritually ingenuous, would not be saved in any way but that whereby God may be glorified. Indeed, to be saved, and not to the glory of God, implies a contradiction; for our salvation is eternal blessedness, in a participation of the glory of God.

Mankind Could Not Restore Glory to God

Secondly, it follows, therefore, that man must make satisfaction to the justice of God, and thereby a reparation of his glory, that he may be saved. This, added to a complete return to obedience, would effect a restitution of all things; it would do so as to what was past, though it would make no new addition of glory to God. But this became not the nature and efficacy of divine wisdom. It became it not merely to retrieve what was past, without a new manifestation and exaltation of the divine excellencies. And therefore, in our restitution by Christ, there is such a manifestation and exaltation of the divine properties as incomparably exceeds whatever could have ensued on, or been effected by, the law of creation, had man continued in his original obedience. But at present it is granted that this addition of satisfaction to a return to obedience, would restore all things to their just condition. But as that return was impossible to man, so was this satisfaction for the injury done by sin much more. For suppose a mere creature, such as man is, such as all men are, in what condition you please, and under all advantageous circumstances, yet, whatever he can do towards God is antecedently and absolutely due from him in that instant wherein he does it, and that in the manner wherein it is done. They must all say, when they have done all that they can do, 'We are unprofitable servants; we have done what was our duty.' Wherefore, it is impossible that, by anything a man can do well, he should make satisfaction for anything he has done ill. For what he so does is due in and for itself; and to suppose that satisfaction will be made for a former fault by that whose omission would have been another, had the former never been committed, is madness. An old debt cannot be discharged with ready money for new commodities; nor can past injuries be compensated by present duties, which we are anew obliged to. Wherefore—mankind being indispensably and eternally obliged to the present performance of all duties of obedience to God, according to the utmost of their capacity and ability, so as that the non-performance of them in their season, both as to their matter and manner, would be their sin—it is utterly impossible that by anything, or all that they can do, they should make the least satisfaction to God for anything they have done against him; much less for the horrible apostasy whereof we treat. And to attempt the same end by any way which God has not appointed, which he has not made their duty, is a new provocation of the highest nature (see Micah 6:6–8).

It is therefore evident, on all these considerations, that all mankind, as to any endeavours of their own, anything that can be fancied as possible for them to design or do, must be left irreparable, in a condition of eternal misery. And unless we have a full conviction hereof, we can neither admire nor entertain the mystery of the wisdom of God in our reparation. And therefore it has been the design of Satan, in all ages, to contrive presumptuous notions of men's spiritual abilities—to divert their minds from the contemplation of the glory of divine wisdom and grace, as alone exalted in our recovery.

We are proceeding on this supposition, that there was a condecency to the holy perfections of the divine nature, that mankind should be restored, or some portion of it recovered to the enjoyment of himself; so angelic nature was preserved to the same end in those that did not sin. And we have showed the general grounds whereon it is impossible that fallen man should restore or recover himself. Wherefore we must, in the next place, inquire what is necessary to such a restoration, on the account of that concern of the divine excellencies in the sin and apostasy of man which we have stated before; for hereby we may obtain light, and an insight into the glory of that wisdom whereby it was contrived and effected. And the things following, among others, may be observed under that end.

Through Obedience Bringing More Glory than Disobedience Brought Dishonour

It was required that there should be an obedience yielded to God, bringing more glory to him than dishonour did arise and accrue from the disobedience of man. This was due to the glory of divine holiness in giving of the law. Until this was done, the excellency of the law, as becoming the holiness of God, and as an effect thereof, could not be made manifest. For if it were never kept in any instance, never fulfilled by any one person in the world, how should the glory of it be declared? How should the holiness of God be represented by it? How should it be evident that the transgression of it was not rather from some defect in the law itself, than from any evil in them that should have yielded obedience to it? The obedience yielded by the angels that stood and sinned not, made it manifest that the transgression of it by them that fell and sinned was from their own wills, and not from any unsuitableness to their nature and state in the law itself. But if the law given to man should never be complied withal in perfect obedience by any one whatever, it might be thought that the law itself was unsuited to our nature, and impossible to be complied withal. Nor did it become infinite wisdom to give a law whose equity, righteousness, and holiness, should never be exemplified in obedience—should never be made to appear but in the punishment inflicted on its transgressors. Wherefore the original law of personal righteousness was not given solely nor primarily that men might suffer justly for its transgression, but that God might be glorified in its accomplishment. If this be not done, it is impossible that men should be restored to the glory of God. If the law be not fulfilled by obedience, man must suffer evermore for his disobedience, or God must lose the manifestation of his holiness therein. Besides, God had represented his holiness in that image of it which was implanted on our nature, and which was the principle enabling us to obedience. This also was rejected by sin, and therein the holiness of God despised. If this be not restored in our nature, and that with advantages above what it had in its first communication, we cannot be recovered to the glory of God.

The Satisfaction of Divine Justice

It was necessary that the disorder brought into the rule and government of God by sin and rebellion should be rectified. This could no otherwise be done but by the infliction of that punishment which, in the unalterable rule and standard of divine justice, was due thereunto. The dismission of sin on any other terms would leave the rule of God under unspeakable dishonour and confusion; for where is the righteousness of government, if the highest sin and provocation that our nature was capable of, and which brought confusion on the whole creation below, should for ever go unpunished? The first express intimation that God gave of his righteousness in the government of mankind, was his threatening a punishment equal to the demerit of disobedience, if man should fall into it: 'In the day you eatest thereof you shall die.' If he revoke and disannul this sentence, how shall the glory of his righteousness in the rule of all be made known? But how this punishment should be undergone, which consisted in man's eternal ruin, and yet man be eternally saved, was a work for divine wisdom to contrive. This, therefore, was necessary to the honour of God's righteousness, as he is the supreme governor and judge of all the earth

Satan Had to Be Despoiled

It was necessary that Satan should be justly despoiled of his advantage and power over mankind, to the glory of God; for he was not to be left to triumph in his success. And inasmuch as man was, on his part, rightfully given up to him, his deliverance was not to be wrought by an act of absolute dominion and power, but in a way of justice and lawful judgement; which things shall be afterward spoken to.

Without these things the recovery of mankind into the favour and to the enjoyment of God was utterly impossible, on the account of the concern of the glory of his divine perfections in our sin and apostasy.

How all this might be effected—how the glory of the holiness and righteousness of God in his law and rule, and in the primitive constitution of our nature, might be repaired—how his goodness, love, grace, and mercy, might be manifested and exalted in this work of the reparation of mankind—was left to the care and contrivance of infinite wisdom. From the eternal springs thereof must this work arise, or cease for ever.

To trace some of the footsteps of divine wisdom herein, in and from the revelation of it by its effects, is that which lies before us. And sundry things appear to have been necessary hereunto.

The Whole Work Had to Be Wrought in Our Nature

That all things required to our restoration, the whole work wherein they consist, must be wrought in our own nature—in the nature that had sinned, and which was to be restored and brought to glory. On supposition, I say, of the salvation of our nature, no satisfaction can be made to the glory of God for the sin of that nature, but in the nature itself that sinned and is to be saved. For whereas God gave the law to man as an effect of his wisdom and holiness, which he transgressed in his disobedience, wherein could the glory of them or either of them be exalted, if the same law were complied withal and fulfilled in and by a nature of another kind—suppose that of angels? For, notwithstanding any such obedience, yet the law might be unsuited to the nature of man, whereunto it was originally prescribed. Wherefore, there would be a veil drawn over the glory of God in giving the law to man, if it were not fulfilled by obedience in the same nature; nor can there be any such relation between the obedience and sufferings of one nature in the stead and for the disobedience of another, as that glory might ensue to the wisdom, holiness, and justice of God, in the deliverance of that other nature thereon.

The Scripture abounds in the declaration of the necessity hereof, with its condecency to divine wisdom. Speaking of the way of our relief and recovery, 'Verily,' says the apostle, 'he took not on him the nature of angels' (Heb. 2:16). Had it been the recovery of angels which he designed, he would have taken their nature on him. But this would have been no relief at all to us, no more than the assuming of our nature is of advantage to the fallen angels. The obedience and sufferings of Christ therein extended not at all to them—nor was it just or equal that they should be relieved thereby. What, then, was required to our deliverance? Why, says he, 'Forasmuch as the children are partakers of flesh and blood, he also himself likewise took part of the same' (v. 14). It was human nature (here expressed by flesh and blood) that was to be delivered; and therefore it was human nature wherein this deliverance was to be wrought. This the same apostle disputes at large (Rom. 5:12–19). The sum is, that 'as by one man's disobedience many were made sinners; so by the obedience of one' (of one man, Jesus Christ, verse 15) 'are many made righteous.' The same nature that sinned must work out the reparation and recovery from sin. So he affirms again (1 Cor. 15:21), 'For since by man came death, by man came also the resurrection of the dead.' No otherwise could our ruin be retrieved, nor our deliverance from sin with all the consequents of it be effected—which came by man, which were committed and deserved in and by our nature—but by man, by one of the same nature with us. This, therefore, in the first place, became the wisdom of God, that the world of deliverance should be wrought in our own nature—in the nature that had sinned.

A Nature Taken from the Same Root as Our Nature

That part of human nature wherein or whereby this work was to be effected, as to the essence or substance of it, was to be derived from the common root or stock of the same nature, in our first parents. It would not suffice hereunto that God should create a man, out of the dust of the earth or out of nothing, of the same nature in general with ourselves; for there would be no cognation or alliance between him and us, so that we should be any way concerned in what he did or suffered: for this advance depends solely hereon, that God 'has made of one blood all nations of men' (Acts 17:26). Hence it is that the genealogy of Christ is given us in the gospel—not only from Abraham, to declare the faithfulness of God in the promise that he should be of his seed, but from Adam also, to manifest his relation to the common stock of our nature, and to all mankind therein.

The first discovery of the wisdom of God herein was in that primitive revelation, that the deliverer should be of 'the seed of the woman' (Gen. 3:15). No other but he who was so could 'break the serpent's head,' or 'destroy the work of the devil,' so as that we might be delivered and restored. He was not only to be partaker of our nature, but he was so to be, by being 'the seed of the woman' (Gal. 4:4). He was not to be created out of nothing, nor to be made of the dust of the earth, but so 'made of a woman,' as that thereby he might receive our nature from the common root and spring of it. Thus 'he who sanctifies and they who are sanctified are all of one' (Heb. 2:11) — ἐξ ἑνὸς; that is, φυράματος — of the same mass, of one nature and blood; whence he is not ashamed to call them brethren. This also was to be brought forth from the treasures of infinite wisdom.

Yet Without Sin

This nature of ours, wherein the work of our recovery and salvation is to be wrought and performed, was not to be so derived from the original stock of our kind or race as to bring along with it the same taint of sin, and the same liableness to guilt, upon its own account, as accompany every other individual person in the world; for, as the apostle speaks, 'such a high priest became us' (and as a high priest was he to accomplish this work) 'as was holy, harmless, undefiled, separate from sinners.' For, if this nature in him were so defiled as it is in us — if it were under a deprivation of the image of God, as it is in our persons before our renovation — it could do nothing that should be acceptable to him. And if it were subject to guilt on its own account, it could make no satisfaction for the sin of others. Here, therefore, again occurs *dignus vindice nodus* — a difficulty which nothing but divine wisdom could expedite.

To take a little farther view hereof, we must consider on what grounds these things (spiritual defilement and guilt) do adhere to our nature, as they are in all our individual persons. And the first of these is — that our entire nature, as to our participation of it, was in Adam, as our head and representative. Hence his sin became the sin of us all—is justly imputed to us and charged on us. In him we all sinned; all did so who were in him as their common representative when he sinned. Hereby we became the natural 'children of wrath,' or liable to the wrath of God for the common sin of our nature, in the natural and legal head or spring of it. And the other is—that we derive our nature from Adam by the way of natural generation. By that means alone is the nature of our first parents, as defiled, communicated to us; for by this means do we become to appertain to the stock as it was degenerate and corrupt. Wherefore that part of our nature wherein and whereby this great work was to be wrought, must, as to its essence and substance, be derived from our first parents—yet so as never to have been in Adam as a common representative, nor be derived from him by natural generation.

The bringing forth of our nature in such an instance—wherein it should relate no less really and truly to the first Adam than we do ourselves, whereby there is the strictest alliance of nature between him so partaker of it and us, yet so as not in the least to participate of the guilt of the first sin, nor of the defilement of our nature thereby—must be an effect of infinite wisdom beyond the conceptions of any created understanding. And this, as we know, was done in the person of Christ; for his human nature was never in Adam as his representative, nor was he comprised in the covenant wherein he stood. For he derived it legally only from and after the first promise, when Adam ceased to be a common person. Nor did it proceed from him by natural generation—the only means of the derivation of its depravation and pollution; for it was a 'holy thing,' created in the womb of the Virgin by the power of the Most High. 'O the depths of the wisdom and knowledge of God!'

It was necessary, therefore, on all these considerations—it was so to the glory of the holy properties of the divine nature, and the reparation of the honour of his holiness and righteousness—that he by whom the work of our recovery was to be wrought should be a man, partaker of the nature that sinned, yet free from all sin, and all the consequent of it. And this did divine wisdom contrive and accomplish in the human nature of Jesus Christ.

No Task for a Mere Man

But yet, in the second place, on all the considerations before mentioned, it is no less evident that this work could not be wrought or effected by him who was no more than a mere man, who had no nature but ours—who was a human person, and no more. There was no one act which he was to perform, in order to our deliverance, but did require a divine power to render it efficacious. But herein lies that great mystery of godliness whereunto a continual opposition has been made by the gates of hell; as we manifested in the entrance of this discourse. But whereas it belongs to the foundation of our faith, we must inquire into it, and confirm the truth of it with such demonstrations as divine revelation accommodates us withal. And three things are to be spoken to.

1. We are to give in rational evidences that the recovery of mankind was not to be effected by any one who was a mere man, and no more, though it were absolutely necessary that a man he should be; he must be God also.
2. We must inquire into the suitableness or condecency to divine wisdom in the redemption and salvation of the church by Jesus Christ, who was God and man in one person [ch. 17].
3. Give a description of the person of Christ and its constitution, which suits all the ends of infinite wisdom in this glorious work [ch. 18].

The first of these falls under sundry plain demonstrations.

Obedience of Infinite Value Required

That human nature might be restored, or any portion of mankind be eternally saved to the glory of God, it was necessary, as we proved before, that an obedience should be yielded to God and his law, which should give and bring more glory and honour to his holiness than there was dishonour reflected on it by the disobedience of us all. Those who are otherwise minded care not what becomes of the glory of God, so that wicked, sinful man may be saved one way or other. But these thoughts spring out of our apostasy, and belong not to that estate wherein we loved God above all, and preferred his glory above all—as it was with us at the first, in the original constitution of our nature. But such an obedience could never be yielded to God by any mere creature whatever;—not by any one who was only a man, however dignified and exalted in state and condition above all others. For to suppose that God should be pleased and glorified with the obedience of any one man, more than he was displeased and dishonored by the disobedience of Adam and all his posterity, is to fancy things that have no ground in reason or justice, or are any way suitable to divine wisdom and holiness. He who undertakes this work must have somewhat that is divine and infinite, to put an infinite value on his obedience—that is, he must be God.

Obedience that Would Advantage Others Required

The obedience of such a one, of a mere man, could have no influence at all on the recovery of mankind, nor the salvation of the church. For, whatever it were, it would be all due from him for himself, and so could only profit or benefit himself; for what is due from any on his own account, cannot redound or be reckoned to the advantage of another. But there is no mere creature, nor can there be any such, but he is obliged for himself to all the obedience to God that he is capable of the performance of in this world; as we have before declared. Yea, universal obedience, in all possible instances, is so absolutely necessary to him, as a creature made in dependence on God, and for the enjoyment of him, that the voluntary omission of it, in any one instance, would be a criminal disobedience, ruinous to his own soul. Wherefore, no such obedience could be accepted as any kind of compensation for the disobedience of others, or in their stead. He, then, that performs this obedience must be one who was not originally obliged thereunto, on his own account, or for himself. And this must be a divine person, and none other; for every mere creature is so obliged. And there is nothing more fundamental in gospel principles, than that the Lord Christ, in his divine person, was above the law, and for himself owed no obedience thereunto; but by his own condescension, as he was 'made of a woman' for us, so he was 'made under the law' for us. And therefore, those by whom the divine person of Christ is denied, do all of them contend that he yielded obedience to God for himself, and not for us. But herein they bid defiance to the principal effect of divine wisdom, wherein God will be eternally glorified.

Propitiation for an Infinite Offence Required

The people to be freed, redeemed, and brought to glory, were great and innumerable; 'a great multitude, which no man can number' (Rev. 7:9). The sins which they were to be delivered, ransomed, and justified from—for which a propitiation was to be made—were next to absolutely infinite. They wholly surpass the comprehension of any created understanding, or the compass of imagination. And in every one of them there was something reductively infinite, as committed against an infinite Majesty. The miseries which hereon all these persons were obnoxious to were infinite, because eternal; or all that evil which our nature is capable to suffer was by them all eternally to be undergone.

By all these persons, in all these sins, there was an inroad made on the rule and government of God, an affront given to his justice, in the violation of his law; nor can any of them be delivered from the consequent hereof in eternal misery, without a compensation and satisfaction made to the justice of God. To assert the contrary, is to suppose, that upon the matter it is all one to him whether he be obeyed or disobeyed, whether he be honoured or dishonored, in and by his creatures; and this is all one as to deny his very being, seeing it opposes the glory of his essential properties. Now, to suppose that a mere man, by his temporary suffering of external pains, should make satisfaction to the justice of God for all the sins of all these persons, so as it should be right and just with him not only to save and deliver them from all the evils they were liable to, but also to bring them to life and glory, is to constitute a mediation between God and man that should consist in appearance and ostentation, and not be an effect of divine wisdom, righteousness, and holiness, nor have its foundation in the nature and equity of things themselves. For the things supposed will not be reduced to any rules of justice or proportion, that one of them should be conceived in any sense to answer to the other, that is, there is nothing which answers any rule, notions, or conceptions of justice—nothing that might be exemplary to men in the punishment of crimes—that the sins of an infinite number of men, deserving every one of them eternal death, should be expiated by the temporary sufferings of one mere man, so as to demonstrate the righteousness of God in the punishment of sin. But God does not do these things for show or appearance, but according to the real exigence of the holy properties of his nature. And on that supposition, there must be a proportion between the things themselves—namely, the sufferings of one and the deliverance of all.

Nor could the faith of man ever find a stable foundation to fix upon on the supposition before mentioned. No faith is able to conflict with this objection, that the sufferings of one mere man should be accepted with God as a just compensation for the sins of the whole church. Men who, in things of this nature, satisfy themselves with notions and fancies, may digest such suppositions; but those who make use of faith for their own delivery from under a conviction of sin, the nature and demerit of it, with a sense of the wrath of God, and the curse of the law against it, can find no relief in such notions or apprehensions. But it became the wisdom of God, in the dispensation of himself herein to the church, so to order things as that faith might have an immovable rock to build upon. This alone it has in the person of Christ, God and man, his obedience and sufferings. Wherefore, those by whom the divine nature of the Lord Christ is denied, do all of them absolutely deny also that he made any satisfaction to divine justice for sin. They will rather swallow all the absurdities which the absolute dismission of sin without satisfaction or punishment brings along with it, than grant that a mere man could make any such satisfaction by his temporary sufferings for the sins of the world. And, on the other hand, whoever truly and sincerely believes the divine person of Christ—namely, that he was God and man in one person, and as such a person acted in the whole work of mediation—he cannot shut his eyes against the glorious light of this truth, that what he did and suffered in that work must have an intrinsic worth and excellency in it, out-balancing all the evil in the sins of mankind—that more honour and glory accrued to the holiness and law of God by his obedience than dishonour was cast on them by the disobedience of Adam and all his posterity.

Man Could not Discharge the Office

The way whereby the church was to be recovered and saved, was by such works and acting as one should take on himself to perform in the way of an office committed to him for that end. For whereas man could not recover, ransom, nor save himself as we have proved, the whole must be wrought for him by another. The undertaking hereof by another must depend on the infinite wisdom, counsel, and pleasure of God, with the will and consent of him who was to undertake it. So also did the constitution of the way and means in particular whereby this deliverance was to be wrought. Hereon it became his office to do the things which were required to that end. But we have before proved, apart by itself, that no office to this purpose could be discharged towards God, or the whole church, by any one who was a man only. I shall not, therefore, here farther insist upon it, although there be good argument in it to our present purpose.

Man Had to be Restored to His Original Glory

If man be recovered, he must be restored into the same state, condition, and dignity, wherein he was placed before the fall. To restore him with any diminution of honour and blessedness was not suited to divine wisdom and bounty; yea, seeing it was the infinite grace, goodness, and mercy of God to restore him, it seems agreeable to the glory of divine excellencies in their operations, that he should be brought into a better and more honourable condition than that which he had lost. But before the fall, man was not subject nor obedient to any but to God alone. Somewhat less he was in dignity than the angels; howbeit he owed them no obedience—they were his fellow-servants. And as for all other things here below, they were made 'subject to him, and put under his feet,' he himself being in subjection to God alone. But if he were deemed and restored by one who was a mere creature, he could not be restored to this state and dignity; for, on all grounds of right and equity, he must owe all service and obedience to him by whom he was redeemed, restored, and recovered, as the author of the state wherein he is. For when we are 'bought with a price,' we are not our own, as the apostle affirms (1 Cor. 6:19–20). We are therefore his who has bought us; and him are we bound to serve in our souls and bodies, which are his. Accordingly, in the purchase of us, the Lord Christ became our absolute Lord, to whom we owe all religious subjection of soul and conscience (Rom. 14:7–9). It would follow, therefore, that if we were redeemed and recovered by the interposition of a mere creature—if such a one were our redeemer, saviour, and deliverer—into the service of a mere creature (that is, religious service and obedience) we should be recovered. And so they believe who affirm the Lord Christ to be a man, and no more. But, on this supposition, we are so far from an advancement in state and dignity by our restoration, that we do not recover what we were first instated in. For it belonged thereunto that we should owe religious service and obedience to him alone who was God by nature over all, blessed for ever. And they bring all confusion into Christian religion, who make a mere creature the object of our faith, love, adoration, invocation, and all sacred worship. But in our present restoration we are made subject anew, as to religious service, only to God alone. Therefore the holy angels, the head of the creation, do openly disclaim any such service and veneration from us, because they are only the fellow-servants of them that have the testimony of Jesus (Rev. 19:10). Nor has God put the 'world to come,' the gospel state of the church, into subjection to angels, or any other creature, but only to the Son, who is Lord over his own house, even he that made all things, who is God (Heb. 3:4–6). Wherefore, we are restored into our primitive condition, to be in spiritual subjection to God alone. He, therefore, by whom we are restored, to whom we owe all obedience and religious service, is, and ought to be, God also. And as they utterly overthrow the gospel who affirm that all the obedience of it is due to him who is a man, and no more—as do all by whom the divine nature of Christ is denied; so they debase themselves beneath the dignity of the state of redemption, and cast dishonour on the mediation of Christ, who subject themselves in any religious service to saints or angels, or any other creatures whatever.

Summary

On these suppositions, which are full of light and evidence, infinite wisdom did interpose itself, to glorify all the other concerned excellencies of the glory of God, in such a way as might solve all difficulties, and satisfy all the ends of God's glory, in the recovery and redemption of mankind. The case before it was as follows:

Man, by sin, had cast the most inconceivable dishonour on the righteousness, holiness, goodness, and rule of God; and himself into the guilt of eternal ruin. In this state it became the wisdom and goodness of God, neither to suffer the whole race of mankind to come short eternally of that enjoyment of himself for which it was created, nor yet to deliver any one of them without a retrieval of the eternal honour of his righteousness, holiness, and rule, from the diminution and waste that was made of it by sin. As this could no way be done but by a full satisfaction to justice and an obedience to the law, bringing and yielding more honour to the holiness and righteousness of God than they could any way lose by the sin and disobedience of man—so this satisfaction must be made, and this obedience be yielded, in and by the same nature that sinned or disobeyed, whereby alone the residue of mankind may be interested in the benefits and effects of that obedience and satisfaction. Yet was it necessary hereunto, that the nature wherein all this was to be performed, though derived from the same common stock with that whereof in all our persons we are partakers, should be absolutely free from the contagion and guilt which, with it and by it, are communicated to our persons from that common stock. Unless it were so, there could be no undertaking in it for others—it would not be able to answer for itself. But yet, on all these suppositions, no undertaking, no performance of duty, in human nature, could possibly yield that obedience to God, or make that satisfaction for sin, whereon the deliverance of others might ensue, to the glory of the holiness, righteousness, and rule of God.

In this state of things did infinite wisdom interpose itself, in that glorious, ineffable contrivance of the person of Christ—or of the divine nature in the eternal Son of God and of ours in the same individual person. Otherwise this work could not be accomplished—at least all other ways are hidden from the eyes of all living, no created understanding being able to apprehend any other way whereby it might so have been, to the eternal glory of God. This, therefore, is such an effect of divine wisdom as will be the object of holy adoration and admiration to eternity—as to this life, how little a portion is it we know of its excellency!

17

EVIDENCE OF DIVINE WISDOM

That which remains of our present inquiry, is concerning those evidences of divine condecency, or suitableness to infinite wisdom and goodness, which we may gather from the nature of this work, and its effects as expressed in divine revelation. Some few instances hereof I shall choose out from amongst many that might be insisted on.

CHRIST'S CONDESCENSION V. ADAM'S SELF-EXALTATION

Man was made to serve God in all things. In his person—in his soul and body—in all his faculties, powers, and senses—all that was given to him or intrusted with him—he was not his own, but every way a servant, in all that he was in all that he had, in all that he did or was to do. This he was made for—this state and condition was necessary to him as a creature. It could be no otherwise with any that was so; it was so with the angels, who were greater in dignity and power than man. The very name of creature includes the condition of universal subjection and service to the Creator. This condition, in and by his sin, Adam designed to desert and to free himself from. He would exalt himself out of the state of service and obedience absolute and universal, into a condition of self-sufficiency—of domination and rule. He would be as God, like to God; that is, subject no more to him, be in no more dependence on him—but advance his own will above the will of God. And there is somewhat of this in every sin; the sinner would advance his own will in opposition to and above the will of God. But what was the event hereof? Man, by endeavouring to free himself from absolute subjection and universal service, to invade absolute dominion, fell into absolute and eternal ruin.

For our recovery out of this state and condition, considering how we cast ourselves into it, the way insisted on was found out by divine wisdom—namely, the incarnation of the Son of God; for he was Lord of all, had absolute dominion over all, owed no service, no obedience for himself—being in the form of God, and equal to him. From this state of absolute dominion he descended into a condition of absolute service. As Adam sinned and fell by leaving that state of absolute service which was due to him, proper to his nature, inseparable from it—to attempt a state of absolute dominion which was not his own, not due to him, not consistent with his nature; so the Son of God, being made the second Adam, relieved us by descending from a state of absolute dominion, which was his own—due to his nature—to take on him a state of absolute service, which was not his own, nor due to him. And this being inconsistent with his own divine nature, he performed it by taking our nature on him—making it his own. He descended as much beneath himself in his self-humiliation, as Adam designed to ascend above himself in his pride and self-exaltation.

The consideration of the divine grace and wisdom herein the apostle proposes to us, 'Who, being in the form of God, thought it not robbery to be equal with God; but made himself of no reputation, and took upon him the form of a servant, and was made in the likeness of men; and being found in fashion as a man, he humbled himself, and became obedient to death, even the death of the cross' (Phil. 2:6–8). Adam being in the form—that is, the state and condition—of a servant, did by robbery attempt to take upon him the 'form of God,' or to make himself equal to him. The Lord Christ being in the 'form of God'—that is, his essential form, of the same nature with him—accounted it no robbery to be in the state and condition of God, to be 'equal to him;' but being made in the 'fashion of a man,' taking on him our nature, he also submitted to the form or the state and condition of a servant therein. He had dominion over all, owed service and obedience to none, being in the 'form of God,' and equal to him—the condition which Adam aspired to; but he condescended to a state of absolute subjection and service for our recovery. This did no more belong to him on his own account, than it belonged to Adam to be like to God, or equal to him. Wherefore it is said that he humbled himself to it, as Adam would have exalted himself to a state of dignity which was not his due.

This submission of the Son of God to an estate of absolute and universal service is declared by the apostle (Heb. 10:5). For those words of the Psalmist, 'My ears you have digged,' or bored (Ps. 50:6), he renders, 'A body you have prepared me.' There is an allusion in the words of the prophecy to him under the law who gave up himself in absolute and perpetual service; in sign whereof his ears were bored with an awl. So the body of Christ was prepared for him, that therein he might be in a state of absolute service to God. So he became to have nothing of his own—the original state that Adam would have forsaken; no not his life—he was obedient to the death.

This way did divine wisdom find out and contrive, whereby more glory did arise to the holiness and righteousness of God from his condescension to universal service and obedience who was over all, God blessed for ever, than dishonour was cast upon them by the self-exaltation of him who, being in all things a servant, designed to be like to God.

CHRIST'S POVERTY V. ADAM'S SELF-ENRICHMENT

Adam was poor in himself, as a creature must be. What riches he had in his hand or power, they were none of his own, they were only trusted with him for especial service. In this state of poverty he commits the robbery of attempting to be like to God. Being poor, he would make himself rich by the rapine of an equality with God. This brought on him and us all, as it was meet it should, the loss of all that we were trusted with. Hereby we lost the image of God—lost our right to the creatures here below—lost ourselves and our souls. This was the issue of his attempt to be rich when he was poor.

In this state infinite wisdom has provided for our relief, to the glory of God. For the Lord Jesus Christ being rich in himself, for our sakes he became poor, that we through his poverty might be rich (2 Cor. 8:9). He was rich in that riches which Adam designed by robbery; for 'he was in the form of God, and accounted it no robbery to be equal with God.' But he made himself poor for our sakes, with poverty which Adam would have relinquished; yea, to that degree that 'he had not where to lay his head'—he had nothing. Hereby he made a compensation for what he never made spoil of, or paid what he never took. In this condescension of his, out of grace and love to mankind, was God more glorified than he was dishonored in the sinful exaltation of Adam out of pride and self-love.

Christ's Obedience v. Man's Disobedience

The sin of man consisted formally in disobedience; and it was the disobedience of him who was every way and in all things obliged to obedience. For man—by all that he was, by all that he had received, by all that he expected or was farther capable of, by the constitution of his own nature, by the nature and authority of God, with his relation thereunto—was indispensably obliged to universal obedience. His sin, therefore, was the disobedience of him who was absolutely obliged to obedience by the very constitution of his being and necessary relation to God. This was that which rendered it so exceeding sinful, and the consequents of it eternally miserable; and from this obligation his sin, in any one instance, was a total renunciation of all obedience to God.

The recompense, with respect to the glory of God, for disobedience must be by obedience, as has been before declared.

And if there be not a full obedience yielded to the law of God in that nature that sinned, man cannot be saved without an eternal violation of the glory of God therein. But the disobedience of him who was every way obliged to obedience could not be compensated but by his obedience who was no way obliged thereunto; and this could be only the obedience of him that is God (for all creatures are obliged to obedience for themselves), and it could be performed only by him who was man. Wherefore, for the accomplishment of this obedience, he who, in his own person as God, was above the law, was in his human nature, in his own person as man, made under the law. Had he not been made under the law, what he did could not have been obedience; and had he not been in himself above the law, his obedience could not have been beneficial to us. The sin of Adam (and the same is in the nature of every sin) consisted in this—that he who was naturally every way under the law, and subject to it, would be every way above the law, and no way obliged by it. Wherefore it was taken away, to the glory of God, by his obedience, who being in himself above the law, no way subject to it, yet submitted, humbled himself, to be 'made under the law,' to be every way obliged by it (see Gal. 3:13, 4:4). This is the subject of the discourse of the apostle (Rom. 5, from verse 12 to the end of the chapter).

Unto the glory of God in all these ends, the person of Christ, as an effect of infinite wisdom, was meet and able to be a mediator and undertaker between God and man. In the union of both our natures in the same person he was so meet by his relation to both; unto God by filiation, or sonship; to us by brotherhood, or nearness of kindred (Heb. 2:14). And he was able from the dignity of his person; for the temporary sufferings of him who was eternal were a full compensation for the eternal sufferings of them who were temporary.

An Unencumbered Inheritance

God made man the lord of all things here below. He was, as it were, the heir of God, as to the inheritance of this world in present, and as to a blessed state in eternal glory. But he lost all right and title hereunto by sin. He made forfeiture of the whole by the law of tenure whereby he held it, and God took the forfeiture. Wherefore he designs a new heir of all, and vests the whole inheritance of heaven and earth in him, even in his Son. He appointed him 'the heir of all things' (Heb. 1:2). This translation of God's inheritance the apostle declares (Heb. 2:6–9); for the words which he cites from Psalm 8:4–6—'What is man, that you are mindful of him, and the son of man, that you visit him? For you have made him a little lower than the angels, and have crowned him with glory and honour. You made him to have dominion over the works of your hands; you have put all things under his feet'—do declare the original condition of mankind in general. But man forfeited the dominion and inheritance that he was intrusted withal; and God settles it anew, solely in the man Christ Jesus. So the apostle adds, 'We see not yet all things put under him;' but we see it all accomplished in Jesus (v. 8). But as all other inheritances do descend with theirs, so did this to him with its burden. There was a great debt upon it—the debt of sin. This he was to undergo, to make payment of, or satisfaction for, or he could not rightly enter upon the inheritance. This could no otherwise be done but by his suffering in our nature, as has been declared. He who was the heir of all, was in himself to purge our sins. Herein did the infinite wisdom of God manifest itself, in that he conveyed the inheritance of all things to him who was meet and able so to enter upon it, so to enjoy and possess it, as that no detriment or damage might arise to the riches, the revenue, the glory of God, from the waste made by the former possessor.

THE STRONGEST MOTIVES TO FAITH AND LOVE

Mankind was to be recovered to faith and trust in God, as also to the love of him above all. All these things had utterly forsaken our nature; and the reduction of them into it is a work of the greatest difficulty. We had so provoked God, he had given such evidences of his wrath and displeasure against us, and our minds thereon were so alienated from him, as we stood in need of the strongest motives and highest encouragements once to attempt to return to him, so as to place all our faith and trust in him, and all our love upon him.

Sinners generally live in a neglect and contempt of God, in an enmity against him; but whenever they are convinced of a necessity to endeavour a return to him, the first thing they have to conflict withal is fear. Beginning to understand who and what he is, as also how things stand between him and them, they are afraid to have anything to do with him, and judge it impossible that they should find acceptance with him. This was the sense that Adam himself had upon his sin, when he was afraid, and hid himself. And the sense of other sinners is frequently expressed to the same purpose in Scripture (see Isa. 33:14; Micah 6:6–7).

All these discouragements are absolutely provided against in that way of our recovery which infinite wisdom has found out. It were a thing delightful to dwell on the securities given us therein, as to our acceptance, in all those principles, acts, and duties wherein the renovation of the image of God consists. I must contract my meditations, and shall therefore instance in some few things only to that purpose.

What We Are to Believe—Delivered in Our Nature

Faith is not capable of greater encouragement or confirmation than lies in this one consideration—that what we are to believe to this end is delivered to us by God himself in our nature. What could confirm our faith and hope in God, what could encourage us to expect acceptance with God, like this ineffable testimony of his goodwill to us? The nature of things is not capable of greater assurance, seeing the divine nature is capable of no greater condescension.

This the Scripture proposes as that which gives a just expectation that, against all fears and oppositions, we should close with divine calls and invitations to return to God: 'Last of all he sent to them his son, saying, They will reverence my son' (Matt. 21:37)—they will believe the message which I send by him. He has 'spoken to us by his Son'—'the brightness of his glory, and the express image of his person' (Heb. 1:1–3). The consideration hereof is sufficient to dispel all that darkness and confusion which fear, dread, and guilt do bring on the minds of men, when they are invited to return to God. That that God against whom we have sinned should speak to us, and treat with us, in our own nature, about a return to himself, is the utmost that divine excellencies could condescend to. And as this was needful for us (though proud men and senseless of sin understand it not), so, if it be refused, it will be attended with the sorest destruction (Heb. 12:25).

Only New Sin Keeps Us from Christ

This treaty principally consists in a divine declaration, that all the causes of fear and dread upon the account of sin are removed and taken away. This is the substance of the gospel, as it is declared by the apostle (2 Cor. 5:18–21). Wherefore, if hereon we refuse to return to God—to make him the object of our faith, trust, love, and delight—it is not by reason of any old or former sin, not of that of our original apostasy from God, nor of the effects of it against the law, [but] by the means of a new sin, outdoing them all in guilt and contempt of God. Such is final unbelief against the proposal of the gospel. It has more malignity in it than all other sins whatever. But by this way of our recovery, all cause of fear and dread is taken away—all pretences of a distrust of the love and good-will of God are defeated; so that if men will not hereon be recovered to him, it is from their hatred of him and enmity to him—the fruits whereof they must feed on to eternity.

He Loved Us First

Whereas, if we will return to God by faith, we are also to return to him in love, what greater motive can there be to it than that infinite love of the Father and the Son to us, which is gloriously displayed in this way of our recovery? (see 1 John 4:9–10). 'Si amare pigebat, saltem redamare ne pigeat.'

A CONSPICUOUS PATTERN

The whole race of mankind falling into sin against God, and apostasy from him, there was no example left to them to manifest how excellent, how glorious and comely a thing it is, to live to God—to believe and trust in him—to cleave to him unchangeably by love; for they were utter strangers to what is done by angels above, nor could be affected with their example. But without a pattern of these things, manifesting their excellency and reward, they could not earnestly endeavour to attain to them. This is given us most conspicuously in the human nature of Christ (see Heb. 12:2–3). Hereby, therefore, everything needful for our encouragement to return to God is, in infinite wisdom, provided for and proposed to us.

CHRIST MAKES OBEDIENCE ATTRACTIVE

Divine wisdom, in the way of our recovery by Jesus Christ, God manifest in the flesh, designed to glorify a state of obedience to God, and to cast the reproach of the most inexpressible folly on the relinquishment of that state by sin. For, as God would recover and restore us; so he would do it in a way of obedience on our part—of that obedience which we had forsaken. The design of man, which was imposed on him by the craft of Satan, was to become wise like to God, knowing good and evil. The folly of this endeavour was quickly discovered in its effects. Sense of nakedness, with shame, misery, and death, immediately ensued thereon.

But divine wisdom thought meet to aggravate the reproach of this folly. He would let us see wherein the true knowledge of good and evil did consist, and how foolishly we had aspired to it by a relinquishment of that state of obedience wherein we were created.

Job 28, from verse 12 to the end of the chapter, there is an inquiry after wisdom, and the place of its habitation. All creatures give an account that it is not in them, that it is hid from them—only they have heard the fame thereof. All the context is to evince that it is essentially and originally only in God himself. But if we cannot comprehend it in itself, yet may we not know what is wisdom to us, and what is required thereunto? Yes, says he; for 'unto man he said, Behold, the fear of the Lord, that is wisdom; and to depart from evil is understanding' (v. 28). Man, on the other hand, by the suggestion of Satan, thought, and now of himself continues to think, otherwise; namely, that the way to be wise is to relinquish these things. The world will not be persuaded that 'the fear of the Lord is wisdom, and to depart from evil is understanding;' yea, there is nothing that the most of men do more despise and scorn, than thoughts that true wisdom consists in faith, love, fear, and obedience to God (see Ps. 14:6). Whatever else may be pleaded to be in it, yet sure enough they are that those who count it wisdom are but fools.

To cast an everlasting reproach of folly on this contrivance of the devil and man, and uncontrollably to evince wherein alone true wisdom consists, God would glorify a state of obedience. He would render it incomparably more amiable, desirable, and excellent, than ever it could have appeared to have been in the obedience of all the angels in heaven and men on earth, had they continued therein. This he did in this way of our recovery—in that his own eternal Son entered into a state of obedience, and took upon him the 'form' or condition 'of a servant' to God.

What more evident conviction could there be of the folly of mankind in hearkening to the suggestion of Satan to seek after wisdom in another condition? How could that great maxim, which is laid down in opposition to all vain thoughts of man, be more eminently exemplified—that 'the fear of the Lord, that is wisdom; and to depart from evil, that is understanding?' What greater evidence could be given, that the nature of man is not capable of a better condition than that of service and universal obedience to God? How could any state be represented more amiable, desirable, and blessed? In the obedience of Christ, of the Son of God in our nature, apostate sinners are upbraided with their folly in relinquishing that state which, by his susception of it, is rendered so glorious. What have we attained by leaving that condition which the eternal Son of God delighted in? 'I delight,' says he, 'to do your will, O my God;

yea, your law is in the midst of my bowels' (Ps. 40:8) — margin. It is the highest demonstration that our nature is not capable of more order, more beauty, more glory, than consists in obedience to God. And that state which we fell into upon our forsaking of it, we now know to be all darkness, confusion, and misery.

Wherefore, seeing God, in infinite grace and mercy, would recover us to himself; and, in his righteousness and holiness, would do this in a way of obedience — of that obedience which we had forsaken; it has an eminent impression of divine wisdom upon it, that in this mystery of God manifest in the flesh, the only means of our recovery, he would cast the reproach of the most inexpressible folly on our apostasy from a state of it, and render it amiable and desirable to all who are to return to him.

To bear the shame of this folly, to be deeply sensible of it, and to live in a constant prospect and view of the glory of obedience in the person of Christ, with a sedulous endeavour for conformity thereunto, is the highest attainment of our wisdom in this world — and whosoever is otherwise minded, is so at his own utmost peril.

No Second Forfeiture of Our Inheritance

God, in infinite wisdom, has by this means secured the whole inheritance of this life and that which is to come from a second forfeiture. Whatever God will bestow on the children of men, he grants it to them in the way of an inheritance. So the land of Canaan, chosen out for a representative of spiritual and eternal things, was granted to Abraham and his seed for an inheritance. And his interest in the promise is expressed by being 'heir of the world.' All the things of this life, that are really good and useful to us, do belong to this inheritance. So they did when it was vested in Adam. All things of grace and glory do so also. And the whole of the privilege of believers is, that they are heirs of salvation. Hence godliness has the 'promise of the life that now is, and of that which is to come' (1 Tim. 4:8). And the promise is only of the inheritance. This inheritance, as was before intimated, was lost in Adam, and forfeited into the hand of the great Lord, the great possessor of heaven and earth. In his sovereign grace and goodness he was pleased again to restore it—as to all the benefits of it—unto the former tenants; and that with an addition of grace, and a more exceeding weight of glory. But withal, infinite wisdom provides that a second forfeiture shall not be made of it. Wherefore the grant of it is not made immediately to any of those for whose use and benefit it is prepared and granted. They had been once tried, and failed in their trust, to their own eternal beggary and ruin, had not infinite grace interposed for their relief. And it did not become the wisdom and glory of God to make a second grant of it, which might be frustrated in like manner. Wherefore he would not commit it again to any mere creature whatever; nor would it safely have been so done with security to his glory.

Too Great a Trust for Any Mere Creature

It was too great a trust—even the whole inheritance of heaven and earth, all the riches of grace and glory—to be committed to any one of them. God would not give this glory to any one creature. If it be said it was first committed to Adam, and therefore to have it again is not an honour above the capacity of a creature; I say that the nature of the inheritance is greatly changed. The whole of what was intrusted with Adam comes exceedingly short of what God has now prepared as the inheritance of the church. There is grace in it, and glory added to it, which Adam neither had nor could have right to. It is now of that nature, as could neither be intrusted with, nor communicated by, any mere creature. Besides, he that has it is the object of the faith and trust of the church; nor can any be interested in any part of this inheritance without the exercise of those and all other graces on him whose the inheritance is. And so to be the object of our faith, is the prerogative of the divine nature alone.

Impossible to Secure by Any Mere Creature

No mere creature could secure this inheritance that it should be lost no more; and yet if it were so, it would be highly derogatory to the glory of God. For two things were required hereunto—First, That he in whom this trust is vested should be in himself incapable of any such failure, as through which, by the immutable, eternal law of obedience to God, a forfeiture of it should be made;—Secondly, That he undertake for them all who shall be heirs of salvation, who shall enjoy this inheritance, that none of them should lose or forfeit their own personal interest in it, or the terms whereon it is conveyed and communicated to them. But no mere creature was sufficient to these ends; for no one of them, in and by him in the constitution of his nature, is absolutely free from falling from God, himself. They may receive—the angels in heaven and the glorified saints have received—such a confirmation, in and by grace, as that they shall never actually apostatize or fall from God; but this they have not from themselves, nor the principles of their own nature—which is necessary to him that shall receive this trust. For so when it was first vested in Adam, he was left to preserve it by the innate concreated abilities of his own nature. And as to the latter, all the angels in heaven cannot undertake to secure the obedience of any one man, so as that the conveyance of the inheritance may be sure to him. Wherefore, with respect hereunto, those angels themselves though the most holy and glorious of all the creatures of God, have no greater trust or interest than to be 'ministering spirits, sent forth to minister for them who shall be heirs of salvation' (Heb. 1:14). So unmeet are they to have the whole inheritance vested in any of them.

But all this infinite wisdom has provided for in the great 'mystery of godliness God manifest in the flesh.' God herein makes his only Son the heir of all things, and vests the whole inheritance absolutely in him. For the promise, which is the court-roll of heaven—the only external mean and record of its conveyance—was originally made to Christ only. God said not, 'And to seeds as of many; but as of one, And to your seed, which is Christ' (Gal. 3:16). And we become again heirs of God only as we are joint heirs with Christ (Rom. 8:17); that is by being taken into a participation of that inheritance which is vested in him alone. For many may be partakers of the benefit of that whose right and title is in one alone, when it is conveyed to him for their use. And hereby the ends before mentioned are fully provided for.

Christ—the Only Capable Heir

He who is thus made the 'heir of all' is meet to be intrusted with the glory of it. For where this grant is solemnly expressed, it is declared that he is the 'brightness of the Father's glory, and the express image of his person' (Heb. 1:2–3); and that by him the worlds were made. He alone was meet to be this heir who is partaker of the divine nature, and by whom all things were created; for such things belong to it as cannot appertain to any other. The reader may consult, if he please, our exposition of that place of the apostle.

He Cannot Fail

Any failure in his own person was absolutely impossible. The subsistence of the human nature in the person of the Son of God, rendered the least sin utterly impossible to him; for all the moral operations of that nature are the acts of the person of the Son of God. And hereby not only is the inheritance secured but also an assurance that it is so is given to all them that do believe. This is the life and soul of all gospel comforts, that the whole inheritance of grace and glory is vested in Christ, where it can never suffer loss or damage. When we are sensible of the want of grace, should we go to God, and say, 'Father, give us the portion of goods that falls to us,' as the prodigal did, we should quickly consume it, and bring ourselves to the utmost misery, as he did also. But in Christ the whole inheritance is secured for evermore.

He Preserves Every Heir

He is able to preserve all those who shall be heirs of this inheritance, that they forfeit not their own personal interest therein, according to the terms of the covenant whereby it is made over to them. He can and will, by the power of his grace, preserve them all to the full enjoyment of the purchased inheritance. We hold our title by the rod—at the will of the Lord; and many failures we are liable to, whereon we are '*in misericordia Domini*,' and are subject to amercements. But yet the whole inheritance being granted to Christ is eternally secured for us, and we are by his grace preserved from such offences against the supreme Lord, or committing any such wastes, as should cast us out of our possession (see Ps. 89:27–32). Thus in all things infinite wisdom has provided that no second forfeiture should be made of the inheritance of grace and glory, which as it would have been eternally ruinous to mankind, so it was inconsistent with the glory and honour of God.

THE INCARNATION DESTROYS AND TORMENTS SATAN

The wisdom of God was gloriously exalted in the righteous destruction of Satan and his interest, by the incarnation and mediation of the Son of God. He had prevailed against the first way of the manifestation of divine glory; and therein both pleased and prided himself. Nothing could ever give such satisfaction to the malicious murderer, as the breach he had occasioned between God and man, with his hopes and apprehensions that it would be eternal. He had no other thoughts but that the whole race of mankind, which God had designed to the enjoyment of himself, should be everlastingly ruined. So he had satisfied his envy against man in his eternal destruction with himself, and his malice against God in depriving him of his glory. Hereon, upon the distance that he had made between God and man, he interposed himself, and boasted himself for a long season as 'The god of this world,' who had all power over it and in it. It belonged to the honour of the wisdom of God that he should be defeated in this triumph. Neither was it meet that this should be done by a mere act of sovereign omnipotent power; for he would yet glory in his craft and the success of it—that there was no way to disappoint him, but by crushing him with power, without respect to righteousness or demonstration of wisdom. Wherefore, it must be done in such a way as wherein he might see, to his eternal shame and confusion, all his arts and subtleties defeated by infinite wisdom, and his enterprise overthrown in a way of right and equity. The remark that the Holy Ghost puts on the serpent, which was his instrument in drawing man to apostasy from God—namely, that he was 'more subtle than any beast of the field'—is only to intimate wherein Satan designed his attempt, and from whence he hoped for his success. It was not an act of power or rage; but of craft, counsel, subtlety, and deceit. Herein he gloried and prided himself; wherefore the way to disappoint him with shame, must be a contrivance of infinite wisdom, turning all his artifices into mere folly.

This work of God, with respect to him, is expressed in the Scripture two ways—First, it is called the spoiling of him, as to his power and the prey that he had taken. The 'strong man armed' was to be bound, and his goods spoiled. The Lord Christ, by his death, 'destroyed him that had the power of death, that is, the devil.' He 'led captivity captive,' spoiling principalities and powers, triumphing over them in his cross. So Abraham, when he smote the kings, not only delivered Lot, who was their captive, but also took all their spoils. Again, it is expressed by the destruction of his works: 'For this cause was the Son of God manifested, that he might destroy the works of the devil.' The spoils which he had in his own power were taken from him, and the works which he had erected in the minds of men were demolished. The web which he had woven to clothe himself withal, as the god of this world, was unravelled to the last thread. And although all this seems to represent a work of power, yet was it indeed an effect of wisdom and righteousness principally.

For the power which Satan had over mankind was in itself unjust. For (1.) He obtained it by fraud and deceit: 'The serpent beguiled' Eve. (2.) He possessed it with injustice, with respect to God, being an invader of his right and possession. (3.) He used and exercised it with malice, tyranny, and rage;—so as that it was every way unjust, both in its foundation and execution. With respect hereunto he was justly destroyed by omnipotent power, which puts forth itself in his eternal punishment. But, on the other side, mankind did suffer justly under his power—being given up to it in the righteous judgement of God. For one may suffer justly what another unjustly inflicts; as when one causelessly strikes an innocent man, if he strikes him again, he who did the first injury suffers justly, but the other does unjustly in revenging himself. Wherefore, as man was given up to him in a way of punishment, he was a lawful captive, and was not to be delivered but in a way of justice. And this was done in a way that Satan never thought of. For, by the obedience and sufferings of the Son of God incarnate, there was full satisfaction made to the justice of God for the sins of man, a reparation of his glory, and an exaltation of the honour of his holiness, with all the other properties of his nature, as also of his law, outbalancing all the diminution of it by the first apostasy of mankind; as has been declared. Immediately hereon all the charms of Satan were dissolved, all his chains loosed, his darkness that he had brought on the creation dispelled, his whole plot and design defeated—whereon he saw himself, and was exposed to all the holy angels of heaven, in all the counsels, craft, and power he had boasted of, to be nothing but a congeries—a mass of darkness, malice, folly, impotency, and rage.

Hereon did Satan make an entrance into one of the principal parts of his eternal torments, in that furious self-maceration which he is given up to on the consideration of his defeat and disappointment. Absolute power he always feared, and what it would produce; for he believes that, and trembles. But against any other war he thought he had secured himself. It lies plain to every understanding, what shame, confusion, and self-revenge, the proud apostate was cast into, upon his holy, righteous disappointment of his design; whereas he had always promised himself to carry his cause, or at least to put God to act in the destruction of his dominion, by mere omnipotent power, without regard to any other properties of his nature. To find that which he contrived for the destruction of the glory of God—the disappointment of his ends in the creation of all things—and the eternal ruin of mankind, to issue in a more glorious exaltation of the holy properties of the divine nature, and an unspeakable augmentation of blessedness to mankind itself, is the highest aggravation of his eternal torments. This was a work every way becoming the infinite wisdom of God.

A Task for the Second Person of the Trinity

Whereas there are three distinct persons in the holy Trinity, it became the wisdom of God that the Son, the second person, should undertake this work, and be incarnate. I shall but sparingly touch on this glorious mystery; for as to the reason of it, it is absolutely resolved into the infinite wisdom and sovereign counsel of the divine will. And all such things are the objects of a holy admiration—not curiously to be inquired into. To intrude ourselves into the things which we have not seen—that is, which are not revealed—in those concerns of them which are not revealed, is not to the advantage of faith in our edification. But as to what is declared of them—either immediately and directly, or by their relation to other known truths—we may meditate on them to the improvement of faith and love towards God. And some things are thus evident to us in this mystery.

The Son Restored the Image We Lost by Sin

We had by sin lost the image of God, and thereby all gracious acceptance with him—all interest in his love and favour. In our recovery, as we have declared, this image is again to be restored to us, or we are to be renewed into the likeness of God. And there was a condecency to divine wisdom, that this work should, in a peculiar manner, be effected by him who is the essential image of God—that is, the Father. This, as we have formerly showed, was the person of the Son. Receiving his personal subsistence, and therewithal the divine nature, with all its essential properties, from the Father by eternal generation, he was thereon the express image of his person, and the brightness of his glory. Whatever is in the person of the Father is in the person of the Son, and being all received from the Father, he is his essential image. And one end of his incarnation was, that he might be the representative image of God to us. Whereas, therefore, in the work of our recovery, the image of God should be restored in us, there was a condecency that it should be done by him who was the essential image of God; for it consists in the communication of the effects and likeness of the same image to us which was essentially in himself.

The Son Made Us Sons Again

We were by nature the sons of God. We stood in relation of sons to him by virtue of our creation—the communication of his image and likeness—with the preparation of an inheritance for us. On the same accounts the angels are frequently called the sons of God. This title, this relation to God, we utterly lost by sin, becoming aliens from him, and enemies to him. Without a recovery into this estate we cannot be restored, nor brought to the enjoyment of God. And this cannot be done but by adoption. Now, it seems convenient to divine wisdom that he should recover our sonship by adoption, who was himself the essential and eternal Son of God.

The Father Loves—the Son Executes—the Spirit Perfects

The sum of what we can comprehend in this great mystery arises from the consideration of the order of the holy persons of the blessed Trinity in their operations; for their order herein follows that of their subsistence. To this great work there are peculiarly required, authority, love, and power—all directed by infinite wisdom. These originally reside in the person of the Father, and the acting of them in this matter is constantly ascribed to him. He sent the Son, as he gives the Spirit, by an act of sovereign authority. And he sent the Son from his eternal love—he loved the world, and sent his Son to die. This is constantly assigned to be the effect of the love and grace of the Father. And he wrought in Christ, and he works in us, with respect to the end of this mystery, with the 'exceeding greatness of his power' (Eph. 1:19). The Son, who is the second person in the order of subsistence, in the order of operation puts the whole authority, love, and power of the Father in execution. This order of subsistence and operation thereon is expressly declared by the apostle, 'To us there is but one God, the Father, of whom are all things, and we in him; and one Lord Jesus Christ, by whom are all things, and we by him' (1 Cor. 8:6). The Father is the original fountain and spring, ἐξ οὗ, from whom—whose original authority, love, goodness, and power—are all these things. That expression, 'from him,' peculiarly denotes the eternal origin of all things. But how are this authority, goodness, love, and power in the Father, whence all these things spring and arise, made effectual—how are their effects wrought out and accomplished? 'There is one Lord,' even Jesus Christ, a distinct person from the Father, δι' οὗ, 'by whom are all things.' He works in the order of his subsistence, to execute, work, and accomplish all that originally proceeds from the Father. By the Holy Spirit, who is the third person in order of subsistence, there is made a perfecting application of the whole to all its proper ends.

Wherefore, this work of our redemption and recovery being the especial effect of the authority, love, and power of the Father— it was to be executed in and by the person of the Son; as the application of it to us is made by the Holy Ghost. Hence it became not the person of the Father to assume our nature—it belonged not thereunto in the order of subsistence and operation in the blessed Trinity. The authority, love, and power whence the whole work proceeded, were his in a peculiar manner. But the execution of what infinite wisdom designed in them and by them belonged to another. Nor did this belong to the person of the Holy Spirit, who, in order of divine operation following that of his subsistence, was to perfect the whole work, in making application of it to the church when it was wrought. Wherefore it was every way suited to divine wisdom—unto the order of the holy persons in their subsistence and operation—that this work should be undertaken and accomplished in the person of the Son. What is farther must be referred to another world.

MOVING BEYOND SUPERFICIAL KNOWLEDGE

These are some few of those things wherein the infinite wisdom of God in this holy contrivance gives forth some rays of itself into enlightened minds and truly humbled souls. But how little a portion of it is heard by us! How weak, how low are our conceptions about it! We cannot herein find out the Almighty to perfection. No small part of the glory of heaven will consist in that comprehension which we shall have of the mystery of the wisdom, love, and grace of God herein.

Howbeit, we are with all diligence to inquire into it whilst we are here in the way. It is the very centre of all glorious evangelic truths. Not one of them can be understood, believed, or improved as they ought, without a due comprehension of their relation hereunto; as we have showed before.

This is that which the prophets of old inquired into and after with all diligence, even the mystery of God manifest in the flesh, with the glory that ensued thereon (1 Pet. 1:11). Yet had they not that light to discern it by which we have. The 'least in the kingdom of God,' as to the knowledge of this mystery, may be above the greatest of them. And ought we not to fear lest our sloth under the beams of the sun should be condemned by their diligence in the twilight?

This the angels bow down to look into, although their concerns therein are not equal to ours. But angels are angels, and prophets were prophets; we are a generation of poor, sinful men, who are little concerned in the glory of God or our own duty.

Is it not much to be lamented that many Christians content themselves with a very superficiary knowledge of these things? How are the studies, the abilities, the time, and diligence of many excellent persons engaged in, and laid out about, the works of nature, and the effects of divine wisdom and power in them, by whom any endeavour to inquire into this glorious mystery is neglected, if not despised! Alas! The light of divine wisdom in the greatest works of nature holds not the proportion of the meanest star to the sun in its full strength, to that glory of it which shines in this mystery of God manifest in the flesh, and the work accomplished thereby! A little time shall put an end to the whole subject of their inquiries, with all the concern of God and man in them for evermore. This alone is that which fills up eternity, and which, although it be now with some a nothing, yet will shortly be all.

Is it not much more to be lamented, that many who are called Christians do even despise these mysteries? Some oppose them directly with pernicious heresies about the person of Christ, denying his divine nature, or the personal union of his two natures whereby the whole mystery of infinite wisdom is evacuated and rejected; and some there are who, though they do not deny the truth of this mystery, yet they both despise and reproach such as with any diligence endeavour to inquire into it. I shall add the words used on a like occasion, to them who sincerely believe the mysteries of the gospel: 'But ye, beloved, building up yourselves on your most holy faith, praying in the Holy Ghost, keep yourselves in the love of God, looking for the mercy of our Lord Jesus Christ to eternal life.' And the due contemplation of this mystery will certainly be attended with many spiritual advantages.

STEADFASTNESS IN BELIEVING

It will bring in steadfastness in believing, as to the especial concerns of our own souls; so as to give to God the glory that is his due thereon. This is the work, these are the ends, of faith (Rom. 5:1–5). We see how many Christians who are sincere believers, yet fluctuate in their minds with great uncertainties as to their own state and condition. The principal reason of it is, because they are 'unskilful in the word of righteousness,' and so are babes, in a weak condition, as the apostle speaks (Heb. 5:13). This is the way of spiritual peace. When the soul of a believer is able to take a view of the glory of the wisdom of God, exalting all the other holy properties of his nature, in this great mystery to our salvation, it will obviate all fears, remove all objections, and be a means of bringing in assured peace into the mind; which without a due comprehension of it will never be attained.

Transformation into the Image of Christ

The acting of faith hereon is that which is accompanied with its great power to change and transform the soul into the image and likeness of Christ. So is it expressed by the apostle, 'We all, with open face beholding as in a glass the glory of the Lord, are changed into the same image, from glory to glory, even as by the Spirit of the Lord' (2 Cor. 3:18)—we all beholding—κατοπτριζόμενοι, not taking a transient glance of these things, but diligently inspecting them, as those do who, through a glass, design a steady view of things at a distance. That which we are thus to behold by the continued actings of faith in holy contemplation, is the 'glory of God in the face of Jesus Christ,' as it is expressed (2 Cor. 4:6); which is nothing but that mystery of godliness in whose explanation we have been engaged. And what is the effect of the steady contemplation of this mystery by faith? Μεταμορφούμεθα—'we are changed'—made quite other creatures than we were—cast into the form, figure, and image of Jesus Christ—the great design of all believers in this world. Would we, then, be like to Christ? Would we bear the image of the heavenly, as we have borne the image of the earthy? Is nothing so detestable to us as the deformed image of the old man, in the lusts of the mind and of the flesh? Is nothing so amiable and desirable as the image of Christ, and the representation of God in him? This is the way, this is the means of attaining the end which we aim at.

Frees Us from Earthly-mindedness

Abounding in this duty is the most effectual means of freeing us, in particular, from the shame and bane of profession in earthly-mindedness. There is nothing so unbecoming a Christian as to have his mind always exercised about, always filled with thoughts of, earthly things and according as men's thoughts are exercised about them, their affections are increased and inflamed towards them. These things mutually promote one another, and there is a kind of circulation in them. Multiplied thoughts inflame affections, and inflamed affections increase the number of thoughts concerning them. Nothing is more repugnant to the whole life of faith, nothing more obstructive to the exercise of all grace, than a prevalence of this frame of mind. And at this season, in an especial manner, it is visibly preying on the vitals of religion. To abound in the contemplation of this mystery, and in the exercise of faith about it, as it is diametrically opposed to this frame, so it will gradually cast it out of the soul. And without this we shall labour in the fire for deliverance from this pernicious evil.

PREPARES US TO ENJOY GLORY ABOVE

And hereby are we prepared for the enjoyment of glory above. No small part of that glory consists in the eternal contemplation and adoration of the wisdom, goodness, love, and power of God in this mystery, and the effects of it; as shall afterward be declared.

And how can we better or otherwise be prepared for it, but by the implanting a sense of it on our minds by sedulous contemplation whilst we are in this world? God will not take us into heaven, into the vision and possession of heavenly glory, with our heads and hearts reeking with the thoughts and affections of earthly things. He has appointed means to make us 'meet for the inheritance of the saints in light,' before he will bring us into the enjoyment of it. And this is the principal way whereby he does it; for hereby it is that we are 'changed' into the image of Christ, 'from glory to glory,' and make the nearest approaches to the eternal fulness of it.

> *God will not take us into heaven, into the vision and possession of heavenly glory, with our heads and hearts reeking with the thoughts and affections of earthly things.*

18

THE NATURE OF THE PERSON OF CHRIST

The nature or constitution of the person of Christ has been commonly spoken to and treated of in the writings both of the ancient and modern divines. It is not my purpose, in this discourse, to handle anything that has been so fully already declared by others. Howbeit, to speak something of it in this place is necessary to the present work; and I shall do it in answer to a double end or design.

First, to help those that believe, in the regulation of their thoughts about this divine person, so far as the Scripture goes before us. It is of great importance to our souls that we have right conceptions concerning him; not only in general, and in opposition to the pernicious heresies of them by whom his divine person or either of his natures is denied, but also in those especial instances wherein it is the most ineffable effect of divine wisdom and grace. For although the knowledge of him mentioned in the gospel be not confined merely to his person in the constitution thereof, but extends itself to the whole work of his mediation, with the design of God's love and grace therein, with our own duty thereon; yet is this knowledge of his person the foundation of all the rest, wherein if we mistake or fail, our whole building in the other parts of the knowledge of him will fall to the ground. And although the saving knowledge of him is not to be obtained without especial divine revelation (Matt. 16:17)—or saving illumination (1 John 5:20)—nor can we know him perfectly until we come where he is to behold his glory (John 17:24); yet are instructions from the Scripture of use to lead us into those farther degrees of the knowledge of him which are attainable in this life.

Secondly, to manifest in particular how ineffably distinct the relation between the Son of God and the man Christ Jesus is, from all that relation and union which may be between God and believers, or between God and any other creature. The want of a true understanding hereof is the fundamental error of many in our days. We shall manifest thereupon how 'it pleased the Father that in him should all fulness dwell,' so that in all things 'he might have the pre-eminence' (Col. 1:18–19). And I shall herein wholly avoid the curious inquiries, bold conjectures, and unwarrantable determinations of the schoolmen and some others. For many of them, designing to explicate this mystery, by exceeding the bounds of Scripture light and sacred sobriety, have obscured it. Endeavouring to render all things plain to reason, they have expressed many things unsound as to faith, and fallen into manifold contradictions among themselves. Hence Aquinas affirms, that three of the ways of declaring the hypostatic union which are proposed by the Master of the Sentences [Lombard], are so far from probable opinions, as that they are downright heresies. I shall therefore confine myself, in the explication of this mystery, to the propositions of divine revelation, with the just and necessary expositions of them.

What the Scripture represents of the wisdom of God in this great work may be reduced to these four heads:

1. The assumption of our nature into personal subsistence with the Son of God.
2. The union of the two natures in that single person which is consequential thereon.
3. The mutual communication of those distinct natures, the divine and human, by virtue of that union.

4. The enunciations or predications concerning the person of
Christ, which follow on that union and communion.

CHRIST ASSUMED OUR NATURE

The first thing in the divine constitution of the person of Christ
as God and man, is assumption. That ineffable divine act I intend
whereby the person of the Son of God assumed our nature, or
took it into a personal subsistence with himself. This the Scripture
expresses sometimes actively, with respect to the divine nature
acting in the person of the Son, the nature assuming; sometimes
passively, with respect to the human nature, the nature assumed.
The first it does, 'Forasmuch as the children are partakers of flesh
and blood, he also himself likewise took part of the same. For verily
he took not on him the nature of angels, but he took on him the
seed of Abraham' (Heb. 2:14, 16); 'Being in the form of God, he
took upon him the form of a servant' (Phil. 2:6–7); and in sundry
other places. The assumption, the taking of our human nature to
be his own, by an ineffable act of his power and grace, is clearly
expressed. And to take it to be his own, his own nature, can be
no otherwise but by giving it a subsistence in his own person;
otherwise his own nature it is not, nor can be. Hence God is said
to 'purchase his church with his own blood' (Acts 20:28). That
relation and denomination of 'his own,' is from the single person of
him whose it is. The latter is declared, 'The Word was made flesh'
(John 1:14); God sent 'his own Son in the likeness of sinful flesh'
(Rom. 8:3); 'Made of a woman, made under the law' (Gal. 4:4);
'Made of the seed of David according to the flesh' (Rom. 1:3).
The eternal Word, the Son of God, was not made flesh, not made
of a woman, nor of the seed of David, by the conversion of his
substance or nature into flesh; which implies a contradiction—and,
besides, is absolutely destructive of the divine nature. He could no
otherwise, therefore, be made flesh, or made of a woman, but in
that our nature was made his, by his assuming of it to be his own.
The same person—who before was not flesh, was not man—was
made flesh as man, in that he took our human nature to be his own.

This ineffable act is the foundation of the divine relation between the Son of God and the man Christ Jesus. We can only adore the mysterious nature of it—'great is this mystery of godliness.' Yet may we observe sundry things to direct us in that duty.

AN ACT OF THE DIVINE NATURE

As to original efficiency, it was the act of the divine nature, and so, consequently, of the Father, Son, and Spirit. For so are all outward acts of God—the divine nature being the immediate principle of all such operations. The wisdom, power, grace, and goodness exerted therein, are essential properties of the divine nature. Wherefore the acting of them originally belongs equally to each person, equally participant of that nature. (1.) As to authoritative designation, it was the act of the Father. Hence is he said to send 'his Son in the likeness of sinful flesh' (Rom. 8:3; Gal. 4:4). (2.) As to the formation of the human nature, it was the peculiar act of the Spirit (Luke 1:35). (3.) As to the term of the assumption, or the taking of our nature to himself, it was the peculiar act of the person of the Son. Herein, as Damascen observes, the other persons had no concurrence, but only κατὰ βούλησιν καὶ εὐδοκίαν—'by counsel and approbation.'

THE ONLY IMMEDIATE ACT

This assumption was the only immediate act of the divine nature on the human in the person of the Son. All those that follow, in subsistence, sustentation, with all others that are communicative, do ensue thereon.

DISTINCTIONS BETWEEN ASSUMPTION AND UNION

This assumption and the hypostatic union are distinct and different in the formal reason of them.

1. Assumption is the immediate act of the divine nature in the person of the Son on the human; union is mediate, by virtue of that assumption.

2. Assumption is to personality; it is that act whereby the Son of God and our nature became one person. Union is an act or relation of the natures subsisting in that one person.

3. Assumption respects the acting of the divine and the passion of the human nature; the one assumes, the other is assumed. Union respects the mutual relation of the natures to each other. Hence the divine nature may be said to be united to the human, as well as the human to the divine; but the divine nature cannot be said to be assumed as the human is. Wherefore assumption denotes the acting of the one nature and the passion of the other; union, the mutual relation that is between them both.

These things may be safely affirmed, and ought to be firmly believed, as the sense of the Holy Ghost in those expressions: 'He took on him the seed of Abraham'—'He took on him the form of a servant;' and the like. And who can conceive the condescension of divine goodness, or the acting of divine wisdom and power therein?

Hypostatic Union

That which follows hereon, is the union of the two natures in the same person, or the hypostatic union. This is included and asserted in a multitude of divine testimonies. 'Behold, a virgin shall conceive, and bear a son, and shall call his name Emmanuel' (Isa. 7:14, Matt. 1:23). He who was conceived and born of the virgin was Emmanuel, or God with us; that is, God manifest in the flesh, by the union of his two natures in the same person. 'Unto us a child is born, to us a son is given: and his name shall be called Wonderful, Counsellor, the mighty God, the everlasting Father, the Prince of Peace' (Isa. 9:6). That the same person should be 'the mighty God' and a 'child born,' is neither conceivable nor possible, nor can be true, but by the union of the divine and human natures in the same person. So he said of himself, 'Before Abraham was, I am' (John 8:58). That he, the same person who then spake to the Jews, and as a man was little more than thirty years of age, should also be before Abraham, undeniably confirms the union of another nature, in the same person with that wherein he spoke those words, and without which they could not be true. He had not only another nature which did exist before Abraham, but the same individual person who then spoke in the human nature did then exist (see to the same purpose, John 1:14; Acts 20:28; Rom. 9:5; Col. 2:9; 1 John 3:16).

This union the ancient church affirmed to be made ἀτρέπτως, 'without any change' in the person of the Son of God, which the divine nature is not subject to; ἀδιαιρέτως, with a distinction of natures, but 'without any division' of them by separate subsistences; ἀσυγχύτως, 'without mixture' or confusion; ἀχωρίστως, 'without separation' or distance; and οὐσιωδῶς, 'substantially,' because it was of two substances or essences in the same person, in opposition to all accidental union, as the 'fulness of the Godhead dwelt in him bodily.'

These expressions were found out and used by the ancient church to prevent the fraud of those who corrupted the doctrine of the person of Christ, and (as all of that sort ever did, and yet continue so to do) obscured their pernicious sentiments under ambiguous expressions. And they also made use of sundry terms which they judged significant of this great mystery, or the incarnation of the Son of God. Such are ἐνσάρκωσις, 'incarnation;' ἐνσωμάτωσις, 'embodying;' ἐνανθρώπησις, 'inhumanation;' ἡ δεσποτικὴ ἐπιδημία, καὶ παρουσία, ἡ οἰκονομία, to the same purpose; ἡ διὰ σαρκὸς ὁμιλία, 'his conversation in or by the flesh;' ἡ διὰ ἀνθρωπότητος φανέρωσις, 'his manifestation by humanity;' ἡ ἔλευσις, 'the advent;' ἡ κένωσις, 'the exinanition', or humiliation; ἡ τοῦ Χριστοῦ ἐπιφάνεια, 'the appearance' or manifestation 'of Christ;' ἡ συγκατάβασις, 'the condescension.' Most of these expressions are taken from the Scripture, and are used therein with respect to this mystery, or some concerns of it. Wherefore, as our faith is not confined to any one of these words or terms, so as that we should be obliged to believe not only the things intended, but also the manner of its expression in them; so, in as far as they explain the thing intended according to the mind of the Holy Ghost in the Scripture, and obviate the senses of men of corrupt minds, they are to be embraced and defended as useful helps in teaching the truth.

The Grace of Union

That whereby it is most usually declared in the writings of the ancients, is χάρις ἐνώσεως, '*gratia unionis*', the 'grace of union;'— which form of words some manifesting themselves strangers to, do declare how little conversant they are in their writings. Now, it is not any habitual inherent grace residing subjectively in the person or human nature of Christ that is intended, but things of another nature.

God's Free Grace towards the Man Christ Jesus

The cause of this union is expressed in it. This is the free grace and favour of God towards the man Christ Jesus—predestinating, designing, and taking him into actual union with the person of the Son, without respect to, or foresight of, any precedent dignity or merit in him (1 Pet. 1:20).

Hence is that of Augustine, '*Eâ gratiâ fit ab initio fidei suæ homo quicunque Christianus, quâ gratiâ homo ille ab initio factus est Christus*,' De Prædest. Sanct., cap. xv. For whereas all the inherent grace of the human nature of Christ, and all the holy obedience which proceeded from it, was consequent in order of nature to this union, and an effect of it, they could in no sense be the meritorious or procuring causes of it; it was of grace.

Unique Dignity

It is used also by many and designed to express the peculiar dignity of the human nature of Christ. This is that wherein no creature is participant, nor ever shall be to eternity. This is the fundamental privilege of the human nature of Christ, which all others, even to his eternal glory, proceed from, and are resolved into.

Unique Ability

The glorious meetness and ability of the person of Christ, for and to all the acts and duties of his mediatory office. For they are all resolved into the union of his natures in the same person, without which not one of them could be performed to the benefit of the church. And this is that 'grace of our Lord Jesus Christ,' which renders him so glorious and amiable to believers. To them 'that believe he is precious.'

The common prevalent expression of it at present in the church is the hypostatic union; that is, the union of the divine and human nature in the person of the Son of God, the human nature having no personality nor subsistence of its own.

UNLIKE ANY OTHER UNION

With respect to this union the name of Christ is called 'Wonderful,' as that which has the pre-eminence in all the effects of divine wisdom. And it is a singular effect thereof. There is no other union in things divine or human, in things spiritual or natural, whether substantial or accidental, that is of the same kind with it; — it differs specifically from them all.

The Trinity

The most glorious union is that of the Divine Persons in the same being or nature; the Father in the Son, the Son in the Father, the Holy Spirit in them both, and both in him. But this is a union of distinct persons in the unity of the same single nature. And this, I confess, is more glorious than that whereof we treat; for it is in God absolutely, it is eternal, of his nature and being. But this union we speak is not God; it is a creature—an effect of divine wisdom and power. And it is different from it herein, inasmuch as that is of many distinct persons in the same nature; this is of distinct natures in the same person. That union is natural, substantial, essential, in the same nature; this, as it is not accidental, as we shall show, so it is not properly substantial, because it is not of the same nature, but of diverse in the same person, remaining distinct in their essence and substance, and is therefore peculiarly hypostatic or personal. Hence Augustine feared not to say, that '*Homo potius est in filio Dei, quam filius in Patre*;' (*De Trin.*, lib. 1: cap 10). But that is true only in this one respect, that the Son is not so in the Father as to become one person with him. In all other respects it must be granted that the in-being of the Son in the Father—the union between them, which is natural, essential, and eternal—does exceed this in glory, which was a temporary, external act of divine wisdom and grace.

Soul and Body

The most eminent substantial union in things natural, is that of the soul and body constituting an individual person. There is, I confess, some kind of similitude between this union and that of the different natures in the person of Christ; but it is not of the same kind or nature. And the dissimilitudes that are between them are more, and of greater importance, than those things are wherein there seems to be an agreement between them. For—

1. The soul and body are so united as to constitute one entire nature. The soul is not human nature, nor is the body, but it is the consequent of their union. Soul and body are essential parts of human nature; but complete human nature they are not but by virtue of their union. But the union of the natures in the person of Christ does not constitute a new nature, that either was not or was not complete before. Each nature remains the same perfect, complete nature after this union.

2. The union of the soul and body constitutes that nature which is made essentially complete thereby—a new individual person, with a subsistence of its own, which neither of them was nor had before that union. But although the person of Christ, as God and man, be constituted by this union, yet his person absolutely, and his individual subsistence, was perfect absolutely antecedent to that union. He did not become a new person, another person than he was before, by virtue of that union; only that person assumed human nature to itself to be its own, into personal subsistence.

3. Soul and body are united by an external efficient cause, or the power of God, and not by the act of one of them upon another. But this union is effected by that act of the divine nature towards the human which we have before described.

4. Neither soul nor body have any personal subsistence before their union; but the sole foundation of this union was in this, that the Son of God was a self-subsisting person from eternity.

Mixtures of Composition

There are other unions in things natural, which are by mixture of composition. Hereon something is produced composed of various parts, which is not what any of them are. And there is a conversion of things, when one thing is substantially changed into another—as the water in the miracle that Christ wrought was turned into wine; but this union has no resemblance to any of them. There is not a κρᾶσις, 'a mixture,' a contemperation of the divine and human natures into one third nature, or the conversion of one into another. Such notions of these things some fancied of old. Eutyches supposed such a composition and mixture of the two natures in the person of Christ, as that the human nature at least should lose all its essential properties, and have neither understanding nor will of its own. And some of the Arians fancied a substantial change of that created divine nature which they acknowledged, into the human. But these imaginations, instead of professing Christ to be God and man, would leave him indeed neither God nor man; and have been sufficiently confuted. Wherefore the union we treat of has no similitude to any such natural union as is the effect of composition or mutation.

Artificial Unions

There is an artificial union wherewith some have illustrated this mystery; as that of fire and iron in the same sword. The sword is one; the nature of fire and that of iron different; and the acts of them distinct; the iron cuts, the fire burns; and the effects distinct; cutting and burning; yet is the agent or instrument but one sword. Something of this nature may be allowed to be spoken in way of allusion; but it is a weak and imperfect representation of this mystery, on many accounts. For the heat in iron is rather an accident than a substance, is separable from it, and in sundry other things diverts the mind from due apprehensions of this mystery.

The Spiritual Union between Christ and Believers

There is a spiritual union—namely, of Christ and believers; or of God in Christ and believers, which is excellent and mysterious—such as all other unions in nature are made use of in the Scripture to illustrate and represent. This some among us do judge to be of the same kind with that of the Son of God and the man Christ Jesus. Only they say they differ in degrees. The eternal Word was so united to the man Christ Jesus, as that thereby he was exalted inconceivably above all other men, though ever so holy, and had greater communications from God than any of them. Wherefore he was on many accounts the Son of God in a peculiar manner; and, by a communication of names, is called God also. This being the opinion of Nestorius, revived again in the days wherein we live, I shall declare wherein he placed the conjunction or union of the two natures of Christ—whereby he constituted two distinct persons of the Son of God and the Son of man, as these now do—and briefly detect the vanity of it. For the whole of it consisted in the concession of sundry things that were true in particular, making use of the pretence of them to the denial of that wherein alone the true union of the person of Christ did consist.

Nestorius' Notions

Nestorius allowed the presence of the Son of God with the man Christ Jesus to consist in five things.

Inhabitation

He said he was so present with him κατὰ παράστασιν, or by inhabitation, as a man dwells in a house or a ship to rule it. He dwelt in him as his temple. So he dwells in all that believe, but in him in a more especial manner. And this is true with respect to that fulness of the Spirit whereby God was with him and in him; as he is with and in all believers, according to the measures wherein they are made partakers of him. But this answers not that divine testimony, that in him dwelt 'all the fulness of the Godhead bodily' (Col. 2:9). The fulness of the Godhead is the entire divine nature. This nature is considered in the person of the Son, or eternal Word; for it was the Word that was made flesh. And this could no otherwise dwell in him bodily, really, substantially, but in the assumption of that nature to be his own. And no sense can be given to this assertion to preserve it from blasphemy—that the fulness of the Godhead dwells in any of the saints bodily.

Union of Affections

He allowed an especial presence, κατὰ σχέσιν, as some call it; that is, by such a union of affections as is between intimate friends. The soul of God rested always in that man; in him was he well pleased: and he was wholly given up in his affections to God. This also is true; but there is that which is no less true, that renders it useless to the pretensions of Nestorius. For he allowed the divine person of the Son of God. But whatever is spoken of this nature concerning the love of God to the man Christ Jesus, and of his love to God, it is the person of the Father that is intended therein; nor can any one instance be given where it is capable of another interpretation. For it is still spoken of with reference to the work that he was sent of the Father to accomplish, and his own delight therein.

By Dignity and Honour

He allowed it to be κάτ' ἀξίαν, by way of dignity and honour. For this conjunction is such, as that whatever honour is given to the

Son of God is also to be given to that Son of man. But herein, to recompense his sacrilege in taking away the hypostatic union from the church, he would introduce idolatry into it. For the honour that is due to the Son of God is divine, religious, or the owning of all essential divine properties in him, with a due subjection of soul to him thereon. But to give this honour to the man Christ Jesus, without a supposition of the subsistence of his human nature in the person of the Son of God, and solely on that account, is highly idolatrous.

Consent and Agreement

He asserted it to be κατὰ ταυτοβουλίαν, or on the account of the consent and agreement that was between the will of God and the will of the man Christ Jesus. But no other union will thence ensue, but what is between God and the angels in heaven; in whom there is a perfect compliance with the will of God in all things. Wherefore, if this be the foundation of this union, he might be said to take on him the nature of angels as well as the seed of Abraham; which is expressly denied by the apostle (Heb. 2:16–17).

Equivocal Denomination

Καθ᾽ ὁμωνυΐαν, by an equivocal denomination, the name of the one person, namely, of the Son of God, being accommodated to the other, namely, the Son of man. So they were called gods to whom the word of God came. But this no way answers any one divine testimony wherein the name of God is assigned to the Lord Christ—as those wherein God is said 'to lay down his life for us,' and to 'purchase his church with his own blood,' to come and be 'manifest in the flesh,'—wherein no homonymy or equivocation can take place. By all these ways he constituted a separable accidental union, wherein nothing in kind, but in degree only, was peculiar to the man Christ Jesus.

But all these things, so far as they are true, belong to the third thing to be considered in his person—namely, the communion or mutual communication of the distinct natures therein. But his personal union consists not in any of them, nor in all of them together; nor do they answer any of the multiplied testimonies given by the Holy Ghost to this glorious mystery. Some few of them may be mentioned.

'The Word was made flesh' (John 1:14). There can be but two senses of these words: Firstly, that the Word ceased to be what it was, and was substantially turned into flesh. Secondly, that continuing to be what it was, it was made to be also what before it was not. The first sense is destructive of the Divine Being and all its essential properties. The other can be verified only herein, that the Word took that flesh—that is, our human nature—to be his own, his own nature wherein he was made flesh; which is that we plead for. For this assertion, that the person of the Son took our nature to be his own, is the same with that of the assumption of the human nature into personal subsistence with himself. And the ways of the presence of the Son of God with the man Christ Jesus, before mentioned, do express nothing in answer to this divine testimony, that 'The Word was made flesh.'

'Being in the form of God, he took upon him the form of a servant, and became obedient' (Phil. 2:6–8). That by his being 'in the form of God,' his participation in and of the same divine nature with the Father is intended, these men grant; and that herein he was a person distinct from him Nestorius of old acknowledged, though it be by ours denied. But they can fancy no distinction that shall bear the denomination and relation of Father and Son; but all is inevitably included in it which we plead for under that name. This person 'took on him the form of a servant,'—that is, the nature of man in the condition of a servant. For it is the same with his being made of a woman, made under the law; or taking on him the seed of Abraham. And this person became obedient. It was in the human nature, in the form of a servant, wherein he was obedient. Wherefore that human nature was the nature of that person—a nature which he took on him and made his own, wherein he would be obedient. And that the human nature is the nature of the person of him who was in the form of God, is that hypostatic union which we believe and plead for.

'Unto us a child is born, to us a son is given; and his name shall be called The mighty God' (Isa. 9:6). The child and the mighty God are the same person, or he that is 'born a child' cannot be rightly called 'The mighty God.' And the truth of many other expressions in the Scripture has its sole foundation in this hypostatic union. So the Son of God took on him 'the seed of Abraham,' was 'made of a woman,' did 'partake of flesh and blood,' was 'manifest in the flesh.' That he who was born of the blessed Virgin was 'before Abraham,'—that he was made of the 'seed of David according to the flesh,'—whereby God 'purchased the church with his own blood,'—are all spoken of one and the same person, and are not true but on the account of the union of the two natures therein. And all those who plead for the accidental metaphorical union, consisting in the instances before mentioned, do know well enough that the true Deity of our Lord Jesus Christ is opposed by them.

THE COMMUNION OF DISTINCT NATURES

Concurrent with, and in part consequent to, this union, is the communion of the distinct natures of Christ hypostaticly united. And herein we may consider, 1. What is peculiar to the Divine nature; 2. What is common to both.

THREEFOLD COMMUNICATION

There is a threefold communication of the divine nature to the human in this hypostatic union.

1. Immediate in the person of the Son. This is subsistence. In itself it is ἀνυπόστατος—that which has not a subsistence of its own, which should give it individuation and distinction from the same nature in any other person. But it has its subsistence in the person of the Son, which thereby is its own. The divine nature, as in that person, is its suppositum.

2. By the Holy Spirit he filled that nature with an all-fulness of habitual grace; which I have at large explained elsewhere.

3. In all the acts of his office, by the divine nature, he communicated worth and dignity to what was acted in and by the human nature.

For that which some have for a long season troubled the church withal, about such a real communication of the properties of the divine nature to the human, which should neither be a transfusion of them into it, so as to render it the subject of them, nor yet consist in a reciprocal denomination from their mutual in-being in the same subject—it is that which neither themselves do, nor can any other well understand.

THREE CATHOLIC CONVICTIONS

Wherefore, concerning the communion of the natures in this personal union, three things are to be observed, which the Scripture, reason, and the ancient church, do all concur in.

1. Each nature preserves its own natural, essential properties, entirely to and in itself; without mixture, without composition or confusion, without such a real communication of the one to the other, as that the one should become the subject of the properties of the other. The Deity, in the abstract, is not made the humanity, nor on the contrary. The divine nature is not made temporary, finite, united, subject to passion or alteration by this union; nor is the human nature rendered immense, infinite, omnipotent. Unless this be granted, there will not be two natures in Christ, a divine and a human; nor indeed either of them, but somewhat else, composed of both.

2. Each nature operates in him according to its essential properties. The divine nature knows all things, upholds all things, rules all things, acts by its presence everywhere; the human nature was born, yielded obedience, died, and rose again.

But it is the same person, the same Christ, that acts all these things—the one nature being his no less than the other.

3. Wherefore, the perfect, complete work of Christ, in every act of his mediatory office—in all that he did as the King, Priest, and Prophet of the church—in all that he did and suffered—in all that he continues to do for us, in or by virtue of whether nature soever it be done or wrought—is not to be considered as the act of this or that nature in him alone, but it is the act and work of the whole person—of him that is both God and man in one person. And this gives occasion, —

How Scripture Speaks

Unto that variety of enunciations which is used in the Scripture concerning him; which I shall name only, and conclude.

Some things are spoken of the person of Christ, wherein the enunciation is verified with respect to one nature only; as—'The Word was with God, and the Word was God' (John 1:1); 'Before Abraham was, I am' (John 8:58); 'Upholding all things by the word of his power' (Heb. 1:3). These things are all spoken of the person of Christ, but belong to it on account of his divine nature. So is it said of him, 'Unto us a child is born, to us a son is given' (Isa. 9:6); 'A man of sorrows, and acquainted with grief' (Isa. 53:3). They are spoken of the person of Christ, but are verified in human nature only, and the person on the account thereof.

Sometimes that is spoken of the person which belongs not distinctly and originally to either nature, but belongs to him on the account of their union in him—which are the most direct enunciations concerning the person of Christ. So is he said to be the Head, the King, Priest, and Prophet of the church; all which offices he bears, and performs the acts of them, not on the singular account of this or that nature, but of the hypostatic union of them both.

Sometimes his person being denominated from one nature, the properties and acts of the other are assigned to it. So they 'crucified the Lord of glory.' He is the Lord of glory on the account of his divine nature only; thence is his person denominated when he is said to be crucified, which was in the human nature only. So God purchased his church 'with his own blood' (Acts 20:28). The denomination of the person is from the divine nature only—he is God; but the act ascribed to it, or what he did by his own blood, was of the human nature only. But the purchase that was made thereby was the work of the person as both God and man. So, on the other side, 'The Son of man who is in heaven' (John 3:13). The denomination of the person is from the human nature only—'The Son of man.' That ascribed to it was with respect to the divine nature only—'who is in heaven.'

Sometimes the person being denominated from one nature, that is ascribed to it which is common to both; or else being denominated from both, that which is proper to one only is ascribed to him (see Rom. 9:5; Matt. 22:42).

These kinds of enunciations the ancients expressed by ἐναλλαγή, 'alteration;' ἀλλοίωσις, 'permutation,' κοινότης, 'communion;' τρόπος ἀντιδόσεως, 'the manner of mutual position;' κοινωνία ἰδιωμάτων, 'the communication of properties,' and other the like expressions.

These things I have only mentioned, because they are commonly handled by others in their didactical and polemical discourses concerning the person of Christ, and could not well be here utterly omitted.

19

THE EXALTATION OF CHRIST

The apostle, describing the great mystery of godliness—'God manifest in the flesh'—by several degrees of ascent, he carries it within the veil, and leaves it there in glory—ἀνελήφθη ἐν δόξῃ (1 Tim. 3:16); God was manifest in the flesh, and 'received up into glory.' This assumption of our Lord Jesus Christ into glory, or his glorious reception in heaven, with his state and condition therein, is a principal article of the faith of the church—the great foundation of its hope and consolation in this world. This, also, we must therefore consider in our meditations on the person of Christ, and the use of it in our religion.

That which I especially intend herein is his present state in heaven, in the discharge of his mediatory office, before the consummation of all things. Hereon the glory of God, and the especial concern of the church, at present depends. For, at the end of this dispensation, he shall give up the kingdom to God, even the Father, or cease from the administration of his mediatory office and power, as the apostle declares (1 Cor. 15:24–8):

> Then comes the end, when he shall have delivered up the kingdom to God, even the Father; when he shall have put down all rule and all authority and power. For he must reign, till he

> has put all enemies under his feet. The last enemy that shall be destroyed is death. For he has put all things under his feet. But when he says, All this are put under him, it is manifest that he is excepted which did put all things under him. And when all things shall be subdued to him, then shall the Son also himself be subject to Him that put all things under him, that God may be all in all.

All things fell by sin into an enmity to the glory of God and the salvation of the church. The removal of this enmity, and the destruction of all enemies, is the work that God committed to his Son in his incarnation and mediation (Eph. 1:10). This he was variously to accomplish in the administration of all his offices. The enmity between God and us immediately, he removed by the blood of his cross, whereby he made peace (Eph. 2:14–16); which peace he continues and preserves by his intercession (Heb. 7:25; 1 John 2:1). The enemies themselves of the church's eternal welfare—namely, sin, death, the world, Satan, and hell—he subdues by his power. In the gradual accomplishment of this work—according as the church of the elect is brought forth in successive generations (in every one whereof the same work is to be performed)—he is to continue to the end and consummation of all things. Until then the whole church will not be saved, and therefore his work not be finished. He will not cease his work whilst there is one of his elect to be saved, or one enemy to be subdued. He shall not faint nor give over until he has sent forth judgement to victory.

For the discharge of this work he has a sovereign power over all things in heaven and earth committed to him. Herein he does and must reign. And so absolutely is it vested in him, that upon the ceasing of the exercise of it, he himself is said to be made subject to God. It is true that the Lord Christ, in his human nature, is always less than, or inferior to, God, even the Father. In that sense he is in subjection to him now in heaven. But yet he has an actual exercise of divine power, wherein he is absolute and supreme. When this ceases, he shall be subject to the Father in that nature, and only so. Wherefore, when this work is perfectly fulfilled and ended, then shall all the mediatory acting of Christ cease for evermore. For God will then have completely finished the whole design of his wisdom and grace in the constitution of his person and offices, and have raised up and finished the whole fabric of eternal glory. Then will God 'be all in all'. In his own immense nature and blessedness he shall not only be 'all' essentially and causally, but 'in all' also; he shall immediately be all in and to us.

This state of things—when God shall immediately 'be all in all'— we can have no just comprehension of in this life. Some refreshing notions of it may be framed in our minds, from these apprehensions of the divine perfections which reason can attain to; and their suitableness to yield eternal rest, satisfaction, and blessedness, in that enjoyment of them whereof our nature is capable. Howbeit, of these things in particular the Scripture is silent; however, it testifies our eternal reward and blessedness to consist alone in the enjoyment of God.

But there is somewhat else proposed as the immediate object of the faith of the saints at present, as to what they shall enjoy upon their departure out of this world. And Scripture revelations extend to the state of things to the end of the world, and no longer.

Wherefore heaven is now principally represented to us as the place of the residence and glory of Jesus Christ in the administration of his office; and our blessedness to consist in a participation thereof, and communion with him therein. So he prays for all them who are given him of his Father, that they may be where he is, to behold his glory (John 17:24). It is not the essential glory of his divine person that he intends, which is absolutely the same with that of the Father; but it is a glory that is peculiarly his own—a glory which the Father has given him, because he loved him: 'My glory, which you have given me; for you loved me.' Nor is it merely the glorified state of his human nature that he intends; as was before declared in the consideration of the fifth verse of this chapter, where he prays for this glory. However, this is not excluded; for to all those that love him, it will be no small portion of their blessed refreshment, to behold that individual nature wherein he suffered for them, undergoing all sorts of reproaches, contempts, and miseries, now unchangeably stated in incomprehensible glory. But the glory which God gives to Christ, in the phase of the Scripture, principally is the glory of his exaltation in his mediatory office. It is the 'all power' that is given him in heaven and earth; the 'name' that he has 'above every name,' as he sits on the right hand of the Majesty on high. In the beholding and contemplation hereof with holy joy and delight, consists no small part of that blessedness and glory which the saints above at present enjoy, and which all others of them shall so do who depart this life before the consummation of all things. And in the due consideration hereof consists a great part of the exercise of that faith which is 'the evidence of things not seen,' and which, by making them present to us, supplies the room of sight. This is the ground whereon our hope anchors—namely, the things 'within the veil' (Heb. 6:19), which directs us to the temple administration of the mediatory office of Christ. And it is for the strengthening of our faith and hope in God, through him, that we do and that we ought to inquire into these things.

The consideration of the present state of Christ in heaven may be reduced to three heads:

1. The glorification of his human nature; what it has in common with, and wherein it differs in kind from, the glory of all saints whatever.
2. His mediatory exaltation; or the especial glory of his person as mediator.
3. The exercise and discharge of his office in the state of things: which is what at present I shall principally inquire into [ch. 20].

I shall not speak at all of the nature of glorified bodies, nor of anything that is common to the human nature of Christ and the same nature in glorified saints; but only what is peculiar to himself. And hereunto I shall premise one general observation.

All perfections whereof human nature is capable, abiding what it was in both the essential path of it, soul and body, do belong to the Lord Christ in his glorified state. To ascribe to it what is inconsistent with its essence, is not an assignation of glory to its state and condition, but a destruction of its being. To affix to the human nature divine properties, as ubiquity or immensity, is to deprive it of its own. The essence of his body is no more changed than that of his soul. It is a fundamental article of faith, that he is in the same body in heaven wherein he conversed here on earth; as well as the faculties of his rational soul are continued the same in him. This is that 'holy thing' which was framed immediately by the Holy Ghost, in the womb of the Virgin. This is that 'Holy One' which, when it was in the grave, saw no corruption. This is that 'body' which was offered for us, wherein he bare our sins on the tree. To fancy any such change in or of this body, by its glorification, as that it should not continue essentially and substantially the same that it was is to overthrow the faith of the church in a principal article of it. We believe that the very same body wherein he suffered for us, without any alteration as to its substance, essence, or integral parts, and not another body, of an ethereal, heavenly structure, wherein is nothing of flesh, blood, or bones, by which he so frequently testified the faithfulness of God in his incarnation, is still that temple wherein God dwells, and wherein he administers in the holy place not made with hands. The body which was pierced is that which all eyes shall see, and no other.

CHRIST'S GLORIFIED HUMAN NATURE

On this foundation I willingly allow all perfections in the glorified human nature of Christ, which are consistent with its real form and essence. I shall, therefore, only in some instances inquire into the present glory of the human nature of Christ, wherein it differs either in kind or degree from the glory of all other saints whatever. For even among them I freely allow different degrees in glory; which the eternal order of things—that is, the will of God, in the disposal of all things to his own glory—requires.

DIFFERS IN NATURE FROM THE SAINTS' HUMAN NATURE

There is that wherein the present glory of the human nature of Christ differs, in kind and nature, from that which any other of the saints are partakers of, or shall be so after the resurrection. And this is—

Subsisting in the Person of the Son of God

The eternal subsistence of that nature of his in the person of the Son of God. As this belongs to its dignity and honour, so it does also to its inherent glory. This is, and shall be, eternally peculiar to him, in distinction from, and exaltation above, the whole creation of God, angels and men. Those by whom this is denied, instead of the glorious name whereby God calls him—'Wonderful, Counsellor, The mighty God,' &c.—do call him 'Ichabod,' 'Where is the glory?' or, there is none that is peculiar to him. But the mystery hereof, according to our measure, and in answer to our design, we have already declared. And this glory he had, indeed, in this world, from the first instant of his incarnation, or conception in the womb. But, as to the demonstration of it, 'he emptied himself,' and made himself of no reputation, under the form of a servant. But now the glory of it is illustriously displayed in the sight of all his holy ones. Some inquire, whether the saints in heaven do perfectly comprehend the mystery of the incarnation of the Son of God? I do not well understand what is meant by 'perfectly comprehend;' but this is certain, that what we have now by faith, we shall have there by sight. For as we live now by faith, so shall we there by sight. No finite creature can have an absolute comprehension of that which is infinite. We shall never search out the almighty to perfection, in any of his works of infinite wisdom. Wherefore this only I shall say, there is such a satisfactory evidence in heaven, not only of the truth, but also of the nature of this mystery, as that the glory of Christ therein is manifest, as an eternal object of divine adoration and honour. The enjoyment of heaven is usually called the beatifical vision; that is, such an intellectual present view, apprehension, and sight of God and his glory, especially as manifested in Christ, as will make us blessed to eternity. Wherefore, in the contemplation of this mystery a great part of our blessedness consists; and farther our thoughts cannot attain. This is that wherein the glory of the human nature of Christ does essentially excel, and differ from that of any other blessed creature whatever. And hereon other things do depend.

In How God Communicates with Christ's Human Nature

Hence the union of the human nature of Christ to God, and the communications of God to it, are of another kind than those of the blessed saints. In these things—namely, our union with God and his communications to us—do our blessedness and glory consist.

In this world, believers are united to God by faith. It is by faith that they cleave to him with purpose of heart. In heaven, it shall be by love. Ardent love, with delight, complacency, and joy, from a clear apprehension of God's infinite goodness and beauty, now made present to us, now enjoyed by us, shall be the principle of our eternal adherence to him, and union with him. His communications to us here are by an external efficiency of power. He communicates of himself to us, in the effects of his goodness, grace, and mercy, by the operations of his Spirit in us. Of the same kind will all the communications of the divine nature be to us, to all eternity. It will be by what he works in us by his Spirit and power. There is no other way of the emanation of virtue from God to any creature. But these things in Christ are of another nature. This union of his human nature to God is immediate, in the person of the Son; ours is mediate, by the Son, as clothed with our nature. The way of the communications of the divine nature to the human in his person is what we cannot comprehend; we have no notion of it—nothing whereby it may be illustrated. There is nothing equal to it, nothing like it, in all the works of God. As it is a creature, it must subsist in eternal dependence on God; neither has it anything but what it receives from him. For this belongs essentially to the divine nature, to be the only independent, eternal spring and fountain of all being and goodness. Nor can Omnipotency itself exalt a creature into any such condition as that it should not always and in all things depend absolutely on the Divine Being. But as to the way of the communications between the divine and human nature, in the personal union, we know it not. But whether they be of life, power, light, or glory, they are of another kind than that whereby we do or shall receive all things. For all things are given to us, are wrought in us, as was said, by an external efficiency of power. The glorious immediate emanations of virtue, from the divine to the human nature of Christ, we understand not. Indeed, the acting of natures of different kinds, where both are finite, in the same person, one towards the other, is of a difficult apprehension. Who knows how directive power and efficacy proceeds from the soul, and is communicated to the body, to every the least minute action, in every member of it—so as that there is no distance between the direction and the action, or the accomplishment of it? Or how, on the other hand, the soul is affected with sorrow or trouble in the moment wherein the body feels pain, so as that no distinction can be made between the body's sufferings and the soul's sorrow? How much more is this mutual communication in the same person of diverse natures above our comprehension, where one of them is absolutely infinite! Somewhat will be spoken to it afterward. And herein this eternal glory differs from that of all other glorified creatures whatever.

An Object of Worship

Hence the human nature of Christ, in his divine person and together with it, is the object of all divine adoration and worship (Rev. 5:13). All creatures whatever do forever ascribe 'blessing, honour, glory, and power, to the Lamb,' in the same manner as to him who sits on the throne. This we have declared before. But no other creature either is, or ever can be, exalted into such a condition of glory as to be the object of any divine worship, from the meanest creature which is capable of the performance of it. Those who ascribe divine or religious honour to the saints or angels, as is done in the Church of Rome, do both rob Christ of the principal flower of his imperial crown, and sacrilegiously attempt to adorn others with it—which they abhor.

All God's Glory Will Be Manifest in Christ

The glory that God designed to accomplish in and by him, is now made evident to all the holy ones that are about the throne. The great design of the wisdom and grace of God, from eternity, was to declare and manifest all the holy, glorious properties of his nature, in and by Jesus Christ. And this is that wherein he will acquiesce, with which he is well pleased. When this is fully accomplished, he will use no other way or means for the manifestation of his glory. Herein is the end and blessedness of all.

Wherefore the principal work of faith, whilst we are in this world, is to behold this glory of God, as so represented to us in Christ. In the exercise of faith therein is our conformity to Him carried on to perfection (2 Cor. 3:18). And to this end, or that we may do so, he powerfully communicates to our minds a saving, internal light; without which we can neither behold his glory nor give glory to him. He 'who commanded the light to shine out of darkness,' shines into our hearts, to give us 'the light of the knowledge of the glory of God in the face of Jesus Christ' (2 Cor. 4:6). The end, I say, why God communicates a spiritual, supernatural light to the minds of believers, is that they may be able to discern the manifestation and revelation of his glory in Christ; which is hid from the world (Eph. 1:17–19; Col. 2:2). Howbeit, whilst we are here, we see it but 'darkly as in a glass,' it is not evident to us in its own lustre and beauty. Yea, the remainder of our darkness herein is the cause of all our weakness, fears, and disconsolations. Want of a steady view of this glory of God, is that which exposes us to impressions from all our temptations. And the light of our minds therein is that whereby we are changed and transformed into the likeness of Christ.

But in heaven this is conspicuously and gloriously manifest to all the blessed ones that are before the throne of God. They do not behold it by faith in various degrees of light, as we do here below. They have not apprehensions of some impressions of divine glory on the person of Christ and the human nature therein, with the work which he did perform; which is the utmost of our attainment.

But they behold openly and plainly the whole glory of God, all the characters of it, illustriously manifesting themselves in him, in what he is, in what he has done, in what he does. Divine wisdom, grace, goodness, love, power, do all shine forth in him to the contemplation of all his saints, in whom he is admired. And in the vision hereof consists no small part of our eternal blessedness. For what can be more satisfactory, more full of glory to the souls of believers, than clearly to comprehend the mystery of the wisdom, grace, and love of God in Christ? This is that which the prophets, at a great distance, inquired diligently into—that which the angels bow down to look towards—that whose declaration is the life and glory of the gospel. To behold in one view the reality, the substance of all that was typified and represented by the beautiful fabric of the Tabernacle, and Temple which succeeded in the room thereof—of all the utensils of them, and services performed in them—all that the promises of the Old Testament did contain, or the declarations of the New—as it is the most satisfactory, blessed, and glorious state, that by the present light of faith we can desire or long for, so it evidences a glory in Christ of another kind and nature than what any creature can be participant in. I shall therefore state it to our consideration, with some few observations concerning it.

EVERY BELIEVER SEES THE GLORY OF CHRIST IN THIS LIFE. Every believer sees here in this life an excellency, a glory in the mystery of God in Christ. They do so in various degrees, unless it be in times of temptation, when any of them walk in darkness, and have no light. The view and prospect hereunto is far more clear, and accompanied with more evidence, in some than in others, according to the various degrees of their faith and light. The spiritual sight of some is very weak, and their views of the glory of God in Christ are much obscured with inevidence, darkness, and instability. This in many is occasioned by the weakness of their natural ability, in more by spiritual sloth and negligence—in that they have not habitually 'exercised their senses to discern good and evil,' as the apostle speaks (Heb. 5:14). Some want instruction, and some have their minds corrupted by false opinions. Howbeit, all true believers have the 'eyes of their understanding opened' to discern, in some measure, the glory of God, as represented to them in the gospel. To others it is foolishness; or they think there is that darkness in it whereunto they cannot approach. But all the darkness is in themselves. This is the distinguishing property and character of saving faith—it beholds the glory of God in the face of Jesus Christ; it makes us to discern the manifestation of the glory of God in Christ, as declared in the gospel.

THE SOURCE OF ALL OBEDIENCE AND HOPE. Our apprehension of this glory is the spring of all our obedience, consolation, and hope in this world. Faith discovering this manifestation of the glory of God in Christ, engages the soul to universal obedience, as finding therein abundant reason for it and encouragement to it. Then is obedience truly evangelic, when it arises from this acting of faith, and is thereon accompanied with liberty and gratitude. And herein is laid all the foundation of our consolations for the present and hope for the future. For the whole security of our present and future condition depends on the acting of God towards us, according as he has manifested himself in Christ.

LOVE TO GOD INFLAMED. From the exercise of faith herein does divine love, love to God, proceed; therein alone it is enlivened and inflamed. On these apprehensions does a believing soul cry out, 'How great is his goodness! how great is his beauty!' God in Christ reconciling the world to himself, is the only object of divine love. Under that representation of him alone can the soul cleave to him with ardent love, constant delight, and intense affections. All other notions of love to God in sinners, as we are all, are empty fancies.

LONGING TO SEE THE GLORY OF CHRIST. Wherefore, all believers are, or should be, conversant in their minds about these things, with longings, expectations, and desires after nearer approaches to them, and enjoyments of them. And if we are not so, we are earthly, carnal, and unspiritual; yea, the want of this frame—the neglect of this duty—is the sole cause why many professors are so carnal in their minds, and so worldly in their conversions. But this is the state of them who live in the due exercise of faith—this they pant and breathe after—namely, that they may be delivered from all darkness, unstable thoughts, and imperfect apprehensions of the glory of God in Christ. After these things do those who have received the 'first fruits of the Spirit,' groan within themselves. This glory they would behold 'with open face;' not, as at present, 'in a glass,' but in its own beauty. What do we want? What would we be at? What do our souls desire? It is not that we might have a more full, clear, stable comprehension of the wisdom, love, grace, goodness, holiness, righteousness, and power of God, as declared and exalted in Christ to our redemption and eternal salvation? To see the glory of God in Christ, to understand his love to him and valuation of him, to comprehend his nearness to God—all evidenced in his mediation—is that which he has promised to us, and which we are pressing after (see John 17:23–4).

SATISFIED IN HEAVEN. Heaven will satisfy all those desires and expectations. To have them fully satisfied, is heaven and eternal blessedness. This fills the souls of them who are already departed in the faith, with admiration, joy, and praises (see Rev. 5:9–10). Herein is the glory of Christ absolutely of another kind and nature than that of any other creature whatever. And from hence it is that our glory shall principally consist in beholding his glory, because the whole glory of God is manifested in him.

And, by the way, we may see hence the vanity as well as the idolatry of them who would represent Christ in glory as the object of our adoration in pictures and images. They fashion wood or stone into the likeness of a man. They adorn it with colours and flourishes of art, to set it forth to the senses and fancies of superstitious persons as having a resemblance of glory. And when they have done, 'they lavish gold out of the bag,' as the prophet speaks, in various sorts of supposed ornaments—such as are so only to the vainest sort of mankind—and so propose it as an image or resemblance of Christ in glory. But what is there in it that has the least respect thereunto—the least likeness of it? Nay, is it not the most effectual means that can be devised to divert the minds of men from true and real apprehensions of it? Does it teach anything of the subsistence of the human nature of Christ in the person of the Son of God? Nay, does it not obliterate all thoughts of it! What is represented thereby of the union of it to God, and the immediate communications of God to it? Does it declare the manifestation of all the glorious properties of the divine nature in him? One thing, indeed, they ascribe to it that is proper to Christ—namely, that it is to be adored and worshipped; whereby they add idolatry to their folly. Persons who know not what it is to live by faith—whose minds are never raised by spiritual, heavenly contemplations, who have no design in religion but to gratify their inward superstition by their outward senses—may be pleased for a time, and ruined for ever, by these delusions. Those who have real faith in Christ, and love to him, have a more glorious object for their exercise.

And we may hereby examine both our own notions of the state of glory and our preparations for it, and whether we are in any measure 'made meet for the inheritance of the saints in light.' More grounds of this trial will be afterward suggested; these laid down may not be passed by. Various are the thoughts of men about the future state—the things which are not seen, which are eternal. Some rise no higher but to hopes of escaping hell, or everlasting miseries, when they die. Yet the heathen had their Elysian fields, and Mohammed his sensual paradise. Others have apprehensions of I know not what glistering glory, that will please and satisfy them, they know not how, when they can be here no longer. But this state is quite of another nature, and the blessedness of it is spiritual and intellectual. Take an instance in one of the things before laid down. The glory of heaven consists in the full manifestation of divine wisdom, goodness, grace, holiness—of all the properties of the nature of God in Christ. In the clear perception and constant contemplation hereof consists no small part of eternal blessedness. What, then, are our present thoughts of these things? What joy, what

The glory of heaven consists in the full manifestation of divine wisdom, goodness, grace, holiness—of all the properties of the nature of God in Christ.

satisfaction have we in the sight of them, which we have by faith through divine revelation? What is our desire to come to the perfect comprehension of them? How do we like this heaven? What do we find in ourselves that will be eternally satisfied hereby? According as our desires are after them, such and no other are our desires of the true heaven—of the residence of blessedness and glory. Neither will God bring us to heaven whether we will or no. If, through the ignorance and darkness of our minds—if, through the earthliness and sensuality of our affections—if, through a fulness of the world, and the occasions of it—if, by the love of life and our present enjoyments, we are strangers to these things, we are not conversant about them, we long not after them—we are not in the way towards their enjoyment. The present satisfaction we receive in them by faith, is the best evidence we have of an indefeasible interest in them. How foolish is it to lose the first fruits of these things in our own souls—those entrances into blessedness which the contemplation of them through faith would open to us—and hazard our everlasting enjoyment of them by an eager pursuit of an interest in perishing things here below! This, this is that which ruins the souls of most, and keeps the faith of many at so low an ebb, that it is hard to discover any genuine working of it.

DIFFERS IN DEGREES FROM THE SAINTS' HUMAN NATURE

The glory of the human nature of Christ differs from that of the saints after the resurrection, in things which concern the degrees of it.

The Glory of His Body Is the Pattern

The glory of his body is the example and pattern of what they shall be conformed to: 'Who shall change our vile body, that it may be fashioned like to his glorious body, according to the working whereby he is able even to subdue all things to himself' (Phil. 3:21). Our bodies were made vile by the entrance of sin; thence they became brothers to the worms, and sisters to corruption. To death and the grave, with rottenness and corruption therein, they are designed. At the resurrection they shall be new-framed, fashioned, and moulded. Not only all the detriment and disadvantage they received by the entrance of sin shall be removed, but many additions of glorious qualifications, which they had not in their primitive, natural constitution, shall be added to them. And this shall be done by the almighty power of Christ—that working or exercise of it whereby he is able to subdue all things to himself. But of the state whereinto we shall be changed by the power of Christ, his own body is the pattern and example. A similitude of it is all that we shall attain to. And that which is the idea and exemplar in any state, is the rule and standard to all others. Such is the glory of Christ; ours consists in conformity thereunto; which gives him the pre-eminence.

Greater Grace in the Glorified Christ

As the state of his body is more glorious than ours shall be, so will that of his soul in itself be made appear to be more excellent than what we are capable of. For that fulness of the Spirit without measure and of all grace, which his nature was capacitated for by virtue of the hypostatic union, now shines forth in all excellency and glory. The grace that was in Christ in this world is the same with that which is in him now in heaven. The nature of it was not changed when he ceased to be viator, but is only brought into a more glorious exercise now he is comprehensor. And all his graces are now made manifest, the veil being taken from them, and light communicated to discern them. As, in this world, he had to the most neither form nor comeliness for which he should be desired—partly from the veil which was cast on his inward beauty from his outward condition, but principally from the darkness which was on their minds, whereby they were disenabled to discern the glory of spiritual things; (notwithstanding which, some then, in the light of faith, 'beheld his glory, as the glory of the only-begotten of the Father, full of grace and truth;')—so now the veil is removed, and the darkness wholly taken away from the minds of the saints, he is in the glory of his grace altogether lovely and desirable. And although the grace which is in believers be of the same nature with that which is in Christ Jesus, and shall be changed into glory after the likeness of his; yet is it, and always shall be, incomprehensibly short of what dwells in him. And herein also his glory gradually excels that of all other creatures whatever.

But we must here draw a veil over what yet remains. For it does not yet appear what we ourselves shall be; much less is it evident what are, and what will be, the glories of the Head above all the members—even then when we shall 'be made like to him.' But it must be remembered, that whereas, at the entrance of this discourse, we so proposed the consideration of the present state of the Lord Christ in heaven, as that which should have an 'end at the consummation of all things;' what has been spoken concerning the glory of his human nature in itself, is not of that kind but what abides to eternity. All the things mentioned abide in him and to him for evermore.

His Mediatory Exaltation

The second thing to be considered in the present state and condition of Christ is his mediatory exaltation. And two things with respect thereunto may be inquired into:

1. The way of his entrance into that state above;
2. The state itself, with the glory of it.

'Received Up into Glory'

The way of his entrance into the exercise of his mediatory office in heaven is expressed, he was 'received up into glory' (1 Tim. 3:16), or rather gloriously; and he entered 'into his glory' (Luke 24:26). This assumption and entrance into glory was upon his ascension, described Acts 1:9–11. 'He was taken up into heaven,' ἀνελήφθη ἐν δόξῃ, by an act of divine power; and he went into heaven, εἰσελθεῖν εἰς τὴν δόξαν, in his own choice and will, as that which he was exalted to. And this ascension of Christ in his human nature into heaven is a fundamental article of the faith of the church. And it falls under a double consideration (1.) As it was triumphant, as he was a King; (2.) As it was gracious, as he was a Priest. His ascension, as to change of place, from earth to heaven, and as to the outward manner of it, was one and the same, and at once accomplished; but as to the end of it, which is the exercise of all his offices, it had various respects, various prefigurations, and is distinctly proposed to us with reference to them.

As a King

In his ascension, as it was triumphant, three things may be considered: First, the manner of it, with its representation of old; secondly, the place whereinto he ascended; thirdly, the end of it, or what was the work which he had to do thereon.

TRIUMPHANT & GLORIOUS. As to the manner of it, it was openly triumphant and glorious. So is it described, 'When he ascended up on high, he led captivity captive, and gave gifts to men' (Eph. 4:8). And respect is had to the prefiguration of it at the giving of the law, where the glory of it is more fully expressed, 'The chariots of God are twenty thousand, even thousands of angels: the Lord is among them, as in Sinai, in the holy place. You have ascended on high, you have led captivity captive' (Ps. 68:17–18). The most glorious appearance of God upon the earth, under the Old Testament, was that on Mount Sinai, in the giving of the law. And as his presence was there attended with all his glorious angels, so, when, upon the finishing of that work, he returned or ascended into heaven, it was in the way of a triumph with all that royal attendance. And this prefigured the ascent of Christ into heaven, upon his fulfilling of the law, all that was required in it, or signified by it. He ascended triumphantly after he had given the law, as a figure of his triumphant ascent after he had fulfilled it. Having then 'spoiled principalities and powers, he made a show of them openly, triumphing over them' (Col. 2:15). So he led captivity captive; or all the adverse powers of the salvation of the church, in triumph at his chariot wheels. I deny not but that his leading 'captivity captive' principally respects his spiritual conquest over Satan, and the destruction of his power; yet, whereas he is also said to 'spoil principalities and powers, making a show of them openly,' and triumphing over them, I no way doubt but Satan, the head of the apostasy, and the chief princes of darkness, were led openly, in sight of all the holy angels, as conquered captives—the 'seed of the woman' having now bruised the 'head of the serpent.' This is that which is so emphatically expressed (Ps. 47 throughout). The ground and cause of all the triumphant rejoicing of the church, therein declared, is, that God was 'gone up with a shout, the Lord with the sound of a trumpet' (v. 5), which is nothing but the glorious ascent of Christ into heaven, said to be accompanied with shouts and the sound of a trumpet, the expressions of triumphant rejoicing, because of the glorious acclamations that were made thereon, by all the attendants of the throne of God.

ON HIGH. The place whither he thus ascended is on high. 'He ascended up on high' (Eph. 4:8)—that is, heaven. He went 'into heaven' (Acts 1:11)—and the 'heaven must receive him' (Acts 3:21); not these aspectable heavens which we behold—for in his ascension 'he passed through them' (Heb. 4:14), and is made 'higher than they' (Heb. 7:26)—but into the place of the residence of God in glory and majesty (Heb. 1:3, 8:1, 12:2). There, on 'the throne of God' (Rev. 3:21)—'on the right hand of the Majesty on high,'—he sits down in the full possession and exercise of all power and authority. This is the palace of this King of saints and nations. There is his royal eternal throne (Heb. 1:8). And 'many crowns' are on his head (Rev. 19:12)—or all dignity and honour. And he who, in a pretended imitation of him, wears a triple crown, has upon his own head thereby, 'the name of blasphemy' (Rev. 13:1). There are before him his 'sceptre of righteousness,' his 'rod of iron,'—all the regalia of his glorious kingdom. For by these emblems of power the Scripture represents to us his sovereign, divine authority in the execution of his kingly office. Thus he ascended triumphantly, having conquered his enemies; thus he reigns gloriously over all.

TO CONQUER & RULE. The end for which he thus triumphantly ascended into heaven, is twofold.

First, the overturning and destruction of all his enemies in all their remaining powers. He rules them 'with a rod of iron,' and in his due time will 'dash them in pieces as a potter's vessel' (Ps. 2:9); for he must 'reign until all his enemies are made his footstool' (1 Cor. 15:25–6; Ps. 110:1). Although at present, for the most part, they despise his authority, yet they are all absolutely in his power, and shall fall under his eternal displeasure.

Secondly, the preservation, continuation, and rule of his church, both as to the internal state of the souls of them that believe, and the external order of the church in its worship and obedience, and its preservation under and from all oppositions and persecutions in this world. There is in each of these such a continual exercise of divine wisdom, power, and care—the effects of them are so great and marvellous, and the fruits of them so abundant to the glory of God—that the world would 'not contain the books that might be written' of them; but to handle them distinctly is not our present design.

As a High Priest

His ascension may be considered as gracious, as the ascent of a High Priest. And herein the things before mentioned are of a distinct consideration.

ON BEHALF OF HIS PEOPLE. As to the manner of it, and the design of it, he gives an account of them himself (John 20:17). His design herein was not the taking on him the exercise of his power, kingdom, and glorious rule; but the acting with God on the behalf of his disciples. 'I go,' says he, 'to my Father, and to your Father; to my God, and to your God,'—not his God and Father with respect to eternal generation, but as he was their God and Father also. And he was so, as he was their God and Father in the same covenant with himself; wherein he was to procure of God all good things for them. Through the blood of this everlasting covenant—namely, his own blood, whereby this covenant was established, and all the good things of it secured to the church—he was 'brought again from the dead' that he might live ever to communicate them to the church (Heb. 13:20–21). With this design in his ascension, and the effects of it, did he often comfort and refresh the hearts of his disciples, when they were ready to faint on the apprehensions of his leaving of them here below (John 14:1–2, 16:5–7). And this was typified by the ascent of the high priest to the temple of old. The temple was situated on a hill, high and steep, so as that there was no approach to it but by stairs. Hence in their wars it was looked on as a most impregnable fortress. And the solemn ascent of the high priest into it on the day of expiation, had a resemblance of this ascent of Christ into heaven. For after he had offered the sacrifices in the outward court, and made atonement for sin, he entered into the most holy place—a type of heaven itself, as the apostle declares (Heb. 9:24)—of heaven, as it was the place whereinto our High Priest was to enter. And it was a joyful ascent, though not triumphant. All the Psalms, from the 120th to the 134th inclusively, whose titles are שִׁיר הַמַּעֲלוֹת, 'Songs of Degrees,' or rather ascents or risings—being generally songs of praise and exhortations to have respect to the sanctuary—were sung to God at the resting-places of that ascent. Especially was this represented on the day of jubilee. The proclamation of the jubilee was on the same day that the high priest entered into the holy place; and at the same time—namely, on the 'tenth day of the seventh month' (Lev. 16:29, 25:9). Then did the trumpet sound throughout the land, the whole church; and liberty was proclaimed to all servants, captives, and such as had sold their possessions that they might return to them again. This being a great type of the spiritual deliverance of the church, the noise of the trumpet was called 'The joyful sound' (Ps. 89:15), 'Blessed are the people that know the joyful sound; they shall walk, O Lord, in the light of your countenance.' Those who are made partakers of spiritual deliverance, shall walk before God in a sense of his love and grace. This is the ascent of our High Priest into his sanctuary, when he proclaimed 'the acceptable year of the Lord, and the day of vengeance of our God; to comfort all that mourn; to appoint to them that mourn in Zion, to give to them beauty for ashes, the oil of joy for mourning, the garment of praise for the spirit of heaviness; that they might be called Trees of righteousness, The planting of the Lord, that he might be glorified' (Isa. 61:2–3). For in this ascension of Christ, proclamation was made in the gospel, of mercy, pardon, peace, joy, and everlasting refreshments, to all that were distressed by sin, with a communication of righteousness to them, to the eternal glory of God. Such was the entrance of our High Priest into heaven, with acclamations of joy and praise to God.

ENTERING THE TABERNACLE. The place whereinto he thus entered was the sanctuary above, the 'tabernacle not made with hands' (Heb. 9:11). It was into heaven itself, not absolutely, but as it is the temple of God, as the throne of grace and mercy-seat are in it; which must farther be spoken to immediately.

TO APPEAR FOR US. The end why the Lord Christ thus ascended, and thus entered into the holy place, was 'to appear in the presence of God for us,' and to 'make intercession for all that come to God by him' (Heb. 7:26–27, 9:24–5).

He ascended triumphantly into heaven, as Solomon ascended into his glorious throne of judgement described 1 Kings 10:18–20. As David was the type of his conquest over all the enemies of his church, so was Solomon of his glorious reign. The types were multiplied because of their imperfection. Then came to him the queen of Sheba, the type of the Gentile converts and the church; when נְדִיבֵי עַמִּים, the 'voluntaries of the people,' (those made willing in the day of his power (Ps. 110:3), 'gathered themselves to the people of the God of Abraham,' and were taken in his covenant (Ps. 47:9). But he ascended graciously, as the high priest went into the holy place; not to rule all things gloriously with mighty power, not to use his sword and his sceptre—but to appear as an high priest, in a garment down to the foot, and a golden girdle about his paps (Rev. 1:13)—as in a tabernacle, or temple, before a throne of grace. His sitting down at the right hand of the Majesty on high adds to the glory of his priestly office, but belongs not to the execution of it. So it was prophesied of him, that he should be 'a priest upon his throne' (Zech. 6:13).

It may be added hereunto, that when he thus left this world and ascended into glory, the great promise he made to his disciples—as they were to be preachers of the gospel, and in them to all that should succeed them in that office—was, that he would 'send the Holy Spirit to them,' to teach and guide them, to lead them into all truth—to declare to them the mysteries of the will, grace, and love of God, for the use of the whole church. This he promised to do, and did, in the discharge of his prophetical office. And although his giving 'gifts to men' was an act of his kingly power, yet it was for the end of his prophetic office.

From what has been spoken, it is evident that the Lord Christ 'ascended into heaven,' or was received up into glory, with this design—namely, to exercise his office of mediation in the behalf of the church, until the end should be. As this was his grace, that when he was rich, for our sakes he became poor; so when he was made rich again for his own sake, he lays forth all the riches of his glory and power on our behalf.

The Glory of His State of Exaltation

The glory of the state and condition whereinto Christ thus entered is the next thing to be considered; for he is set down at the right hand of the Majesty on high. And as his ascension, with the ends of it, were twofold, or of a double consideration, so was his glory that ensued thereon. For his present mediatory state consists either in the glory of his power and authority, or, in the glory of his love and grace—his glory as a King, or his glory as a Priest. For the first of these, or his royal glory, in sovereign power and authority over the whole creation of God—all in heaven and earth, persons and things, angels and men, good and bad, alive and dead—all things spiritual and eternal, grace, gifts, and glory;—his right and power, or ability to dispose of all things according to his will and pleasure, I have so fully and distinctly declared it, in my exposition on Hebrews 1:3, as that I shall not here again insist upon it. His present glory, in the way of love and grace—his glory as a Priest—will be manifested in what ensues.

20

THE MEDIATORIAL OFFICE OF CHRIST

The third and last thing which we proposed to consideration, in our inquiry into the present state and condition of the person of Christ in heaven, is the exercise and discharge of his mediatory office in behalf of the church—especially as he continues to be a 'minister of the sanctuary, and of the true tabernacle, which the Lord pitched, and not man.'

All Christians acknowledge that his present state is a state of the highest glory—of exaltation above the whole creation of God, above every name that is or can be named; and hereon they esteem their own honour and safety to depend. Neither do they doubt of his power, but take it for granted that he can do whatever he pleases; which is the ground of their placing all their confidence in him. But we must show, moreover, that his present state is a state of office-power, work, and duty. He leads not in heaven a life of mere glory, majesty, and blessedness, but a life of office, love, and care also. He lives as the Mediator of the church; as the King, Priest, and Prophet thereof. Hereon do our present safety and our future eternal salvation depend. Without the continual acting of the office-power and care of Christ, the church could not be preserved one moment. And the darkness of our faith herein is the cause of oft our disconsolations, and most of our weaknesses in obedience. Most men have only general and confused notions and apprehensions of the present state of Christ, with respect to the church. And by some, all considerations of this nature are despised and derided. But revealed things belong to us; especially such as are of so great importance to the glory of God and the saving of our own souls—such as this is, concerning the present state of the person of Christ in heaven, with respect to his office-power and care.

Thus he is at once represented in all his offices, 'And I beheld, and, lo, in the midst of the throne and of the four living creatures, and in the midst of the elders, stood a Lamb as it had been slain, having seven horns and seven eyes, which are the seven Spirits of God sent forth into all the earth' (Rev. 5:6). The whole representation of the glory of God, with all his holy attendants, is here called his 'throne;' whence Christ is said to be in the 'midst' of it. And this he is in his kingly glory; with respect also whereunto he is said to have 'seven horns,' or perfect power for the accomplishment of his will. And with respect to his sacerdotal office, he is represented as a 'Lamb that had been slain;' it being the virtue of his oblation that is continually effectual for the salvation of the church. For, as the 'Lamb of God,'—in the offering of himself—he 'takes away the sin of the world.' And as a prophet he is said to have 'seven eyes,' which are 'the seven Spirits of God;' or a perfect fulness of all spiritual light and wisdom in himself, with a power for the communication of gifts and grace for the illumination of the church.

The nature of these offices of Christ, what belongs to them and their charge, as was before intimated, I have declared elsewhere. I do now no farther consider them but as they relate to the present state and condition of the person of Christ in heaven. And because it would be too long a work to treat of them all distinctly, I shall confine myself to the consideration of his priestly office, with what depends thereon. And with respect thereunto the things ensuing may be observed.

CHRIST ENTERED HEAVEN

The Lord Christ entered into heaven, the place of the residence of the glory of God, as into a temple, a tabernacle, a place of sacred worship. He did so as the high priest of the church (Heb. 9:24). He 'is not entered into the holy places made with hands, which are the figures of the true; but into heaven itself, now to appear in the presence of God for us.' He is entered into heaven, as it was figured by the tabernacle of old; which was the place of all sacred and solemn worship. And therefore is he said to enter into it 'through the veil' (Heb. 6:19–20, 10:19–20); which was the way of entrance into the most holy place, both in the tabernacle and temple. Heaven is not only a palace, a throne, as it is God's throne (Matt. 5:34); but it is a temple, wherein God dwells, not only in majesty and power, but in grace and mercy. It is the seat of ordinances and solemn worship. So is it represented (Rev. 7:15, 17). It is said of the whole number of the saints above that have passed through the tribulations of this world, that they are 'before the throne of God, and serve him day and night in his temple, and he that sits on the throne shall dwell among them;' and 'the Lamb which is in the midst of the throne shall feed them, and lead them to living fountains of water.' See also chapter 8:1–4. The worship of the church below may also be herein comprised; but it is by virtue of communion with that above. This is that heaven which the souls of believers do long for an entrance into. Other apprehensions of it are but uncertain speculations.

A HIGH PRIEST IN THE REAL PRESENCE OF GOD

In this temple, this sanctuary, the Lord Christ continues gloriously to minister before the throne of grace, in the discharge of his office (see Heb. 4:14–16, 9:24). As the high priest went into the holy place to minister for the church to God, before the ark and mercy-seat, which were types of the throne of grace; so does our High Priest act for us in the real presence of God. He did not enter the holy place only to reside there in a way of glory, but to do temple-work, and to give to God all that glory, honour, and worship, which he will receive from the church. And we may consider, both (1.) What this work is, and (2.) How it is performed.

THE WORK ITSELF

In general; herein Christ exerts and exercises all his love, compassion, pity, and care towards the church, and every member of it. This are we frequently called to the consideration of, as the foundation of all our consolation, as the fountain of all our obedience (see Heb. 2:17–18, 4:15–16, 5:2). Thoughts hereof are the relief of believers in all their distresses and temptations; and the effects of it are all their supplies of grace, enabling them to persevere in their obedience. He appears for them as the great representative of the church, to transact all their affairs with God. And that for three ends.

First, to make effectual the atonement that he has made for sin. By the continual representation of it, and of himself as a 'Lamb that had been slain,' he procures the application of the virtues and benefits of it, in reconciliation and peace with God, to their souls and consciences. Hence are all believers sprinkled and washed with his blood in all generations—in the application of the virtues of it to them, as shed for them.

Secondly, to undertake their protection, and to plead their cause against all the accusations of Satan. He yet accuses and charges them before God; but Christ is their advocate at the throne of grace, effectually frustrating all his attempts (Rev. 12:10; Zech. 3:2).

Thirdly, to intercede for them, as to the communication of all grace and glory, all supplies of the Spirit, the accomplishment of all the promises of the covenant towards them (1 John 2:1–2). This is the work of Christ in heaven. In these things, as the high priest of the church, does he continue to administer his mediatory office on their behalf. And herein is he attended with the songs and joyful acclamations of all the holy ones that are in the presence of God, giving glory to God by him.

As to the manner of this glorious administration, sundry things are to be considered.

An Interim Service

That this transaction of things in heaven, being in the temple of God, and before the throne of grace, is a solemn instituted worship at present, which shall cease at the end of the world. Religious worship it is, or that wherein and whereby all the saints above do give glory to God. And it is instituted worship, not that which is merely natural, in that it is God's especial appointment, in and by Christ the mediator. It is a church-state which is constituted hereby, wherein these glorious ordinances are celebrated; and such a state as shall not be eternal, but has its time allotted to it. And believers at present have, by faith, an admission into communion with this church above, in all its divine worship. For we 'are come to mount Zion, and to the city of the living God, the heavenly Jerusalem, and to an innumerable company of angels, to the general assembly and church of the first born, which are written in heaven, and to God the Judge of all, and to the spirits of just men made perfect, and to Jesus the mediator of the new covenant, and to the blood of sprinkling, that speaks better things than that of Abel' (Heb. 12:22–4). A church-state does the apostle most expressly represent to us. It is Zion, Jerusalem, the great assembly—the names of the church state under the Old Testament. And it is a state above, the heavenly Jerusalem, where are all the holy angels, and the spirits of just men made perfect in themselves, though not in their state as to the restitution of their bodies at the resurrection. And a holy worship is there in this great assembly; for not only is Jesus in it as the mediator of the covenant, but there is the 'blood of sprinkling' also, in the effectual application of it to the church. Hereunto have we an entrance. In this holy assembly and worship have we communion by faith whilst we are here below

(Heb. 10:19–22). O that my soul might abide and abound in this exercise of faith!—that I might yet enjoy a clearer prospect of this glory, and inspection into the beauty and order of this blessed assembly! How inconceivable is the representation that God here makes of the glory of his wisdom, love, grace, goodness, and mercy, in Christ! How excellent is the manifestation of the glory and honour of Christ in his person and offices!—the glory given him by the Father! How little a portion do we know, or can have experience in, of the refreshing, satiating communications of divine love and goodness, to all the members of this assembly; or of that unchangeable delight in beholding the glory of Christ, and of God in him—of that ardency of affections wherewith they cleave to him, and continual exultation of spirit, whereby they triumph in the praises of God, that are in all the members of it! To enter into this assembly by faith—to join with it in the assignation of praises to 'him that sits on the throne, and to the Lamb for evermore,'—to labour after a frame of heart in holy affections and spiritual delight in some correspondence with that which is in the saints above—is the duty, and ought to be the design, of the church of believers here below. So much as we are furthered and assisted herein by our present ordinances, so much benefit and advantage have we by them, and no more. A constant view of this glory will cast contempt on all the desirable things of this world, and deliver our minds from any dreadful apprehensions of what is most terrible therein.

Conspicuous Glory

This heavenly worship in the sanctuary above, administered by the High Priest over the house of God, is conspicuously glorious. The glory of God is the great end of it, as shall be immediately declared; that is, the manifestation of it. The manifestation of the glory of God consists really in the effects of his infinite wisdom, goodness, grace, and power—declaratively, in the express acknowledgement of it with praise. Herein, therefore, the solemn worship of God in the sanctuary above consists—setting aside only the immediate acting of Christ in his intercession. It is a glorious, express acknowledgement of the wisdom, love, goodness, grace, and power of God, in the redemption, sanctification, and salvation of the church by Jesus Christ, with a continual ascription of all divine honour to him in the way of praise. For the manner of its performance, our present light into it is but dark and obscure. Some things have an evidence in them.

First, that there is nothing carnal in it, or such things as are suited to the fancies and imaginations of men. In the thoughts of heaven, most persons are apt to frame images in their minds of such carnal things as they suppose they could be delighted withal. But they are far remote from the worship of this holy assembly. The worship of the gospel, which is spiritually glorious, makes a nearer approach to it than that of the Temple, which was outwardly and carnally so.

Secondly, it is not merely mental, or transacted only in the silent thoughts of each individual person; for, as we have showed, it is the worship of a church assembly wherein they have all communion, and join in the performance of it. We know not well the way and manner of communication between angels and the spirits of just men made perfect. It is expressed in the Scripture by voices, postures, and gestures; which, although they are not of the same nature as absolutely ours are, yet are they really significant of the things they would express, and a means of mutual communication. Yea, I know not how far God may give them the use of voice and words whereby to express his praise, as Moses talked with Christ at his transfiguration (Matt. 17:3). But the manner of it is such as whereby the whole assembly above do jointly set forth and celebrate the praises of God and the glory hereof consists in three things.

BEAUTIFUL ORDER. The blessed and beautiful order of all things in that sanctuary. Job describes the grave beneath to be a 'place without any order, and where the light is as darkness' (Job 10:22). All above is order and light—every person and thing in its proper place and exercise.

1. Heaven itself is a temple, a sanctuary, made so by the especial presence of God, and the ministration of Christ in the tabernacle of his human nature.

2. God is on the throne of grace, gloriously exalted on the account of his grace, and for the dispensation of it. To the saints above he is on the throne of grace, in that they are in the full enjoyment of the effects of his grace, and do give glory to him on the account thereof. He is so, also with respect to the church here below, in the continual communications of grace and mercy through Christ.

3. The Lord Christ, in his human nature, is before the throne, acting his mediatory office and power in behalf of the church.

4. All the holy angels, in the various orders and degrees of their ministration, are about the throne continually.

5. So are the spirits of just men made perfect, in the various measures of light and glory.

And these things were obscurely represented in the order of the church at its first erection in the wilderness; for the ordinances of God among them were patterns or figures of heavenly things (Heb. 9:23):

1. In the midst was the tabernacle or sanctuary—which represented the sanctuary or temple above.

2. In the most holy place were the ark and mercy-seat—representatives of the throne of grace.

3. The ministry of the high priest—a type of the ministry of Christ.

4. The Levites, who attended on the priest, did represent the ministry of angels attending on Christ in the charge of his office.

5. Round about them were the tribes in their order.

CLEAR APPREHENSIONS OF THE GLORY OF GOD. In the full, clear apprehensions which all the blessed ones have of the glory of God in Christ, of the work and effects of his wisdom and grace towards mankind. These are the foundation of all divine worship. And because our conceptions and apprehensions about them are dark, low, obscure, and inevident, our worship is weak and imperfect also. But all is open to the saints above. We are in the dust, the blood, the noise of the battle; they are victoriously at peace, and have a perfect view of what they have passed through, and what they have attained to. They are come to the springs of life and light, and are filled with admiration of the grace of God in themselves and one another. What they see in God and in Jesus Christ, what they have experience of in themselves; what they know and learn from others, are all of them inconceivable and inexpressible. It is well for us, if we have so much experience of these things as to see a real glory in the fulness and perfection of them. The apprehensions by sight, without mixture of unsteadiness or darkness, without the alloy of fears or temptations, with an ineffable sense of the things themselves on their hearts or minds, are the springs or motives of the holy worship which is in heaven.

GLORIOUS IN PERFORMANCE. In the glorious manner of the performance of it. Now, whereas it arises from sight and present enjoyment, it must consist in a continual ascription of glory and praise to God; and so it is described in the Scripture (see Rev. 4:9–11, with Isa. 6:3). And how little a portion of the glory of these things is it that we can apprehend!

Worship Made Acceptable

In this solemn assembly before the throne of grace, the Lord Jesus Christ—the great High Priest—does represent and render acceptable to God the worship of the church here below. So it is expressed (Rev. 8:3–4):

> And another angel came and stood at the altar, having a golden censer; and there was given to him much incense, that he should offer it with the prayers of all saints upon the golden altar which was before the throne. And the smoke of the incense which came with the prayers of the saints, ascended up before God out of the angel's hand.

It is a representation of the high priest burning incense on the golden altar on the day of atonement, when he entered into the most holy place; for that altar was placed just at the entrance of it, directly before the ark and mercy seat, representing the throne of God. This angel, therefore, is our High Priest; none else could approach that altar, or offer incense on it, the smoke whereof was to enter into the holy place. And the 'prayers of all saints' is a synecdochical expression of the whole worship of the church. And this is presented before the throne of God by this High Priest. And it is not said that their prayers came to the throne of God, but the smoke of the incense out of the hand of the angel did so; for it is the incense of the intercession of Christ alone that gives them their acceptance with God. Without this, none of our prayers, praises, or thanksgivings, would ever have access into the presence of God, or to the throne of grace. Blessed be God for this relief, under the consideration of the weakness and imperfection of them! Wherefore, in him and by him alone do we represent all our desires, and prayers, and whole worship to God. And herein, in all our worship, do we ourselves 'enter into the most holy place' (Heb. 10:19). We do it not merely by faith, but by this especial exercise of it, in putting our prayers into the hand of this High Priest.

There are three things in all our worship that would hinder its access to God, and acceptance with him, as also keep off comfort and peace from our consciences. The first is, the sin or iniquity that cleaves to it; secondly, the weakness or imperfection that at best is in it; and, thirdly, the unworthiness of the persons by whom it is performed. With reference to these things the law could never consummate or perfect the consciences of them that came to God by the sacrifices of it. But there are three things in the sacerdotal ministration of Christ that remove and take them all away, whereon we have access with boldness to God. And they are— (1.) the influence of his oblation; (2.) the efficacy of his intercession; and (3.) the dignity of his person. Through the first of these he bears and takes away all the iniquity of our holy things, as Aaron did typically of old, by virtue of the plate of gold with the name of God (a figure of Christ) on his forehead (Exod. 28:36–38). He has made atonement for them in the blood of his oblation, and they appear not in the presence of God. Through the second, or the efficacy of his intercession, he gives acceptance to our prayers and holy worship, with power and prevalence before God. For this is that incense whose smoke or sweet perfume comes up with the prayers of all saints to the throne of God. Through the third, or the dignity of his person, wherein he appears as the representative of his whole mystical body, he takes away from our consciences that sense of our own vileness and unworthiness which would not suffer us to approach with boldness to the throne of grace. In these things consists the life of the worship of the church—of all believers; without which, as it would not be acceptable to God, so we could have neither peace nor consolation in it ourselves.

The Church Above Loves the Church Below

Herein has the church that is triumphant communion with that which is yet militant. The assembly above have not lost their concern in the church here below. As we rejoice in their glory, safety, and happiness, that having passed through the storms and tempests, the temptations, sufferings, and dangers, of this life and world, they are harboured in eternal glory, to the praise of God in Christ; so are they full of affections towards their brethren exercised with the same temptations, difficulties, and dangers, which they have passed through, with earnest desires for their deliverance and safety. Wherefore, when they behold the Lord Jesus Christ, as the great high priest over the house of God, presenting their prayers, with all their holy worship to him, rendering them acceptable by the incense of his own intercession, it fills them with satisfaction, and continually excites them to the assignation of praise, and glory, and honour to him. This is the state of the saints above, with respect to the church here below. This is all which may be herein ascribed to them; and this may safely be so. What some have fancied about their own personal intercession, and that for particular persons, is derogatory to the honour of Jesus Christ, and inconsistent with their present condition; but in these things consists their communion with the church here below. A love they have to it, from their union with it in the same mystical body (Eph. 1:10). A sense they have of its condition, from the experience they had of it in the days of their flesh. A great concern they have for the glory of God in them, and a fervent desire of their eternal salvation. They know that without them they shall not be absolutely consummate, or made perfect in their whole persons (Rev. 6:11). In this state of things they continually behold the Lord Jesus Christ presenting their prayers before the throne of grace—making intercession for them—appearing to plead their cause against all their adversaries—transacting all their affairs in the presence of God—taking care of their salvation, that not one of them shall perish. This continually fills them with a holy satisfaction and complacency, and is a great part of the subject-matter of their incessant praises and ascriptions of glory to him. Herein lies the concern of the church above in that here below; this is the communion that is between them, whereof the person of Christ, in the discharge of his office, is the bond and centre.

WITHIN THE VEIL

There is herein a full manifestation made of the wisdom of God, in all the holy institutions of the tabernacle and temple of old. Herein the veil is fully taken off from them, and that obscure representation of heavenly things is brought forth to light and glory. It is true, this is done to a great degree in the dispensation of the gospel. By the coming of Christ in the flesh, and the discharge of his mediatory office in this world, the substance of what they did prefigure is accomplished; and in the revelations of the gospel the nature and end of them is declared. Howbeit, they extended their signification also to things within the veil, or the discharge of the priestly office of Christ in the heavenly sanctuary (Heb. 9:24). Wherefore, as we have not yet a perfection of light to understand the depth of the mysteries contained in them; so themselves also were not absolutely fulfilled until the Lord Christ discharged his office in the holy place. This is the glory of the pattern which God showed to Moses in the mount, made conspicuous and evident to all. Therein especially do the saints of the Old Testament, who were exercised all their days in those typical institutions whose end and design they could not comprehend, see the manifold wisdom and goodness of God in them all, rejoicing in them for evermore.

A Priest on His Throne

All that the Lord Christ receives of the Father on the account of this holy interposition and mediation for the church, he is endowed with sovereign authority and almighty power in himself to execute and accomplish. Therefore is he said, as a priest, to be 'made higher than the heavens;' and as a 'priest to sit down at the right hand of the majesty on high' (Heb. 8:1). This glorious power does not immediately belong to Him on the account of his sacerdotal office, but it is that qualification of his person which is necessary to the effectual discharge of it. Hence it is said of him, that he should 'bear the glory,' and 'sit and rule upon his throne,' and should be 'a priest upon his throne' (Zech. 6:13). A throne is *insigne regium*, and properly belongs to Christ with respect to his kingly office (Heb. 1:8–9). Howbeit the power accompanying and belonging to his throne being necessary to the effectual discharge of his priestly office, as he sits and rules on his throne, so it is said that he is a 'priest on his throne' also.

This is one instance of the present state of Christ in heaven, and of the work which he there performs, and the only instance I shall insist upon. He was made a priest 'after the power of an endless life,'—the life which he now leads in heaven;—and 'lives for ever to make intercession for us.' He was dead, but is alive, and lives for evermore, and has the keys of hell and death—all power over the enemies of his church. God on a throne of grace; Christ, the high priest, so on his right hand in glory and power as yet to be 'before the throne' in the virtue of his sacerdotal office, with the whole concern of the church on his hand, transacting all things with God for them; all the holy angels and the 'spirits of just men made perfect' encompassing the throne with continual praises to God, even the Father, and him, on the account of the work of infinite wisdom, goodness, and grace, in his incarnation, mediation, and salvation of the church thereby;—himself continuing to manage the cause of the whole church before God, presenting all their prayers and services to him perfumed with his own intercession—is that resemblance of heaven and its present glory which the Scripture offers to us. But, alas! how weak, how dark, how low, are our conceptions and apprehensions of these heavenly things! We see yet as through a glass darkly, and know but in part. The time is approaching when we shall see these things 'with open face,' and know even as we are known. The best improvement we can make of this prospect, whilst faith supplies the place of future sight, is to be stirred up thereby to holy longings after a participation in this glory, and constant diligence in that holy obedience whereby we may arrive thereunto.

WHY CHRIST'S MEDIATORIAL OFFICE CONTINUES

What remains yet to be spoken on this subject has respect to these two ensuing propositions:

First, all the effects of the offices of Christ, internal, spiritual, and eternal, in grace and glory—all external fruits of their dispensation in providence towards the church or its enemies—are wrought by divine power; or are the effects of an emanation of power from God. They are all wrought 'by the exceeding greatness of his power,' even as he wrought in Christ himself when he raised him from the dead (Eph. 1:19). For all the outward works of God, such as all these are, which are wrought in and for the church, are necessarily immediate effects of divine power—nor can be of another nature.

Second, upon supposition of the obedience of Christ in this life, and the atonement made by his blood for sin, with his exaltation thereon, there is nothing in any essential property of the nature of God—nothing in the eternal, unchangeable law of obedience—to hinder but that God might work all these things in us to his own honour and glory, in the eternal salvation of the church and the destruction of all its enemies, without a continuance of the administration of the offices of Christ in heaven, and all that sacred solemnity of worship wherewith it is accompanied.

These things being certain and evident, we may inquire thereon, whence it is that God has ordered the continuation of all these things in heaven above, seeing these ends might have been accomplished without them, by immediate acts of divine power.

The great 'works of the Lord are sought out of them that have pleasure in them' (Ps. 111:2). This, therefore, being a great work of God, which he has wrought and revealed to us, especially in the effect and fruit of it, and that for the manifestation of his wisdom and grace, it is our duty to inquire into it with all humble diligence; 'for those things which are revealed belong to us and our children,' that we may do the will of God for our good.

For God's Own Glory

God would have it so, for the manifestation of his own glory. This is the first great end of all the works of God. That it is so is a fundamental principle of our religion. And how his works do glorify him is our duty to inquire. The essential glory of God is always the same—eternal and immutable. It is the being of God, with that respect which all creatures have to it. For glory adds a supposition of relation to being. But the manifestations of his glory are various, according to the pleasure of his will. Wherefore, that which he chooses to manifest his glory in and by at one time, he may cease from using it to that end at another; for its being a means of the manifestation of his glory may depend on such circumstances, such a state of things, which being removed, it ceases to be. So of old he manifested and represented his glory in the tabernacle and temple, and the holy pledges of his presence in them, and was glorified in all the worship of the law. But now he ceases so to do, nor is any more honoured by the services and ceremonies of religion therein prescribed. If the whole structure of the temple and all its beautiful services were now in being on the earth, no glory would redound to God thereby—he would receive none from it. To expect the glory of God in them would be a high dishonour to him. And God may at any time begin to manifest his glory by such ways and means as he did not formerly make use of to that purpose. So is it with all gospel ordinances: which state will be continued to the consummation of all things here below, and no longer; for then shall they all cease—God will be no more glorified in them or by them. So has God chosen to glorify himself in heaven by this administration of all things in and by Jesus Christ; whereunto also there is an end determined.

And in the continuance of this holy worship in the sanctuary above, God manifests his glory on many accounts, and rests thereto. First, he does it in and to the saints who departed this life under the Old Testament. They came short in glory of what they now enter into who die in the faith of our Lord Jesus Christ. For—not to dispute about nor determine positively, what was their state and condition before the ascension of Christ into heaven, or what was the nature of the blessed receptacle of their souls—it is manifest that they did not, they could not, behold the glory of God, and the accomplishment of the mystery of his wisdom and will, in Jesus Christ; nor was it perfectly made known to them. Whatever were their rest, refreshment, and blessedness—whatever were their enjoyments of the presence of God; yet was there no throne of grace erected in heaven—no High Priest appearing before it—no Lamb as it had been slain—no joint ascription of glory to him that sits on the throne, and the Lamb, for ever; God 'having provided some better thing for us, that they without us should not be made perfect' (see Eph. 3:9–10).

This was that, and this was that alone, so far as in the Scripture it is revealed, wherein they came short of that glory which is now enjoyed in heaven. And herein consists the advantage of the saints above them, who now die in faith. Their state in heaven was suited to their faith and worship on the earth. They had no clear, distinct knowledge of the incarnation and mediatory office of Christ by their revelations and services; only they believed that the promise of deliverance, of grace and mercy, should be in and by him accomplished. Their reception into heaven—that which they were made meet and prepared for by their faith and worship—was suited thereunto. They had a blessed rest and happiness, above what we can comprehend; for who knows what it is to be in the glorious presence of God, though at the greatest distance? They were not immediately surprised with an appearance of that glory which they had no distinct apprehensions of in this world. Neither they nor the angels knew clearly either the sufferings of Christ or the glory that should ensue. But they saw and knew that there was yet something farther to be done in heaven and earth, as yet hid in God and the counsels of his will, for the exaltation of his glory in the complete salvation of the church. This they continued waiting for in the holy place of their refreshment above. Faith gave them, and it gives us, an entrance into the presence of God, and makes us meet for it. But what they immediately enjoyed did not in its whole kind exceed what their faith directed to. No more does ours. Wherefore they were not prepared for a view of the present glory of heaven; nor did enjoy it. But the saints under the New Testament, who are clearly instructed by the gospel in the mysteries of the incarnation and mediation of Christ, are, by their faith and worship, made meet for an immediate entrance into this glory. This they long for, this they expect and are secured of, from the prayer of our Saviour—that they be, when they leave this world, where he is, to behold his glory.

But now, upon the entrance of Christ into the heavenly sanctuary, all those holy ones were admitted into the same glory with what the saints under the New Testament do enjoy. Hereon with open face they behold the use and end of those typical services and ordinances wherein these things were shadowed out to them. No heart can conceive that ineffable addition of glory which they received hereby. The mystery of the wisdom and grace of God in their redemption and salvation by Christ was now fully represented to them; what they had prayed for, longed for, and desired to see in the days of their flesh on the earth, and waited for so long in heaven, was now gloriously made manifest to them. Hereon did glorious light and blessed satisfaction come into and upon all those blessed souls, who died in the faith, but had not received the promise—only beheld it afar off. And hereby did God greatly manifest his own glory in them and to them; which is the first end of the continuation of this state of things in heaven. This makes me judge that the season of Christ's entrance into heaven, as the holy sanctuary of God, was the greatest instance of created glory that ever was or ever shall be, to the consummation of all things. And this as for other reasons, so because all the holy souls who had departed in the faith from the foundation of the world, were then received into the glorious light of the counsels of God, and knowledge of the effects of his grace by Jesus Christ.

Want of a due apprehension of the truth herein has caused many, especially those of the Church of Rome, to follow after vain imaginations about the state of the souls of the faithful, departed under the Old Testament. Generally, they shut them up in a subterranean limbus, whence they were delivered by the descent of Christ. But it is contrary to all notions and revelations of the respect of God to his people—contrary to the life and nature of faith—that those who have passed through their course of obedience in this world, and finished the work given to them, should not enter, upon their departure, into blessed rest in the presence of God. Take away the persuasion hereof, and the whole nature of faith is destroyed. But into the fulness of present glory they could not be admitted; as has been declared.

Moreover, God hereby manifests his glory to the holy angels themselves. Those things wherein it consists were hid in himself even from them, from the foundation of the world—hidden in the holy counsels of his will (Eph. 3:9). Wherefore to these 'principalities and powers in heavenly places the manifold wisdom of God was made known by the church' (v. 10). The church being redeemed by the blood of Christ, and himself thereon exalted in this glory, they came to know the 'manifold wisdom of God' by the effects of it; which before they earnestly desired to look into (1 Pet. 1:12). Hereby is all the glory of the counsels of God in Christ made conspicuous to them; and they receive themselves no small advancement in glory thereby. For in the present comprehension of the mind of God, and doing of his will, their blessedness consists.

Heaven itself was not what it is, before the entrance of Christ into the sanctuary for the administration of his office. Neither the saints departed nor the angels themselves were participant of that glory which now they are. Neither yet does this argue any defect in heaven, or the state thereof in its primitive constitution; for the perfection of any state has respect to that order of things which it is originally suited to. Take all things in the order of the first creation, and with respect thereunto heaven was perfect in glory from the beginning. Howbeit there was still a relation and regard in it to the church of mankind on the earth, which was to be translated thither. But by the entrance of sin all this order was disturbed, and all this relation was broken. And there followed thereon an imperfection in the state of heaven itself; for it had no longer a relation to, or communion with, them on earth, nor was a receptacle meet for men who were sinners to be received into. Wherefore, by the 'blood of the cross,' God 'reconciled all things to himself, whether they be things in earth, or things in heaven' (Col. 1:20) — or gathered all things into one in him, 'both which are in heaven, and which are on earth' (Eph. 1:10). Even the things in heaven so far stood in need of a reconciliation, as that they might be gathered together in one with the things on earth; the glory whereof is manifested in this heavenly ministration. And the apostle affirms that the 'heavenly things themselves' were purified by the sacrifice of Christ (Heb. 9:23). Not that they were actually defiled in themselves, but without this purification they were not meet for the fellowship of this mystery in the joint worship of the whole society in heaven and earth, by Jesus Christ. Hence, therefore, there is a continual manifestation of the glory of God to the angels themselves. They behold his manifold wisdom and grace in the blessed effects of it, which were treasured up in the holy counsels of his will from eternity. Hereby is their own light and blessedness advanced, and they are filled with admiration of God, ascribing praise, honour, and glory to him for evermore; for the beholding of the mystery of the wisdom of God in Christ, which is here so despised in the dispensation of the gospel, is the principal part of the blessedness of the angels in heaven, which fills them with eternal delight, and is the ground of their ascribing praise and glory to him for evermore.

This is that manifestative glory wherewith God satisfies himself, until the end determined shall be. On the account hereof he does and will bear with things in this world, to the appointed season. For whilst the creation is in its present posture, a revenue of glory must be taken out of it for God; and longer than that is done it cannot be continued. But the world is so full of darkness and confusion, of sin and wickedness, of enmity against God—is so given up to villany, to all the ways whereby God may be dishonoured—that there is little or no appearance of any revenue of glory to him from it. Were it not on the secret account of divine wisdom, it would quickly receive the end of Sodom and Gomorrah. The small remnant of the inheritance of Christ is shut up in such obscurity, that, as to visible appearance and manifestation, it is no way to be laid in the balance against the dishonour that is done to him by the whole world. But whilst things are in this posture here below, God has a solemn honour, glory, and worship above, in the presence of all his holy ones; wherein he rests and takes pleasure. In his satisfaction herein he will continue things in this world to all the ends of his wisdom, goodness, righteousness, and patience, let it rage in villainy and wickedness as it pleases. And so, when any of the saints who are wearied, and even worn out, with the state of things in this world, and, it may be, understand not the grounds of the patience of God, do enter into this state, they shall, to their full satisfaction, behold that glory which abundantly compensates the present dishonour done to God here below.

For the Glory of Christ

This state of things is continued for the glory of Christ himself. The office of Mediator was committed by God the Father to his only-begotten Son—no other being able to bear or discharge it (see Isa. 9:6; Rev. 5:1–5). But in the discharge of this office it was necessary he should condescend to a mean and low condition, and to undergo things difficult, hard, and terrible (Phil. 2:6–8). Such were the things which our Lord Jesus Christ underwent in this world;—his undergoing of them being necessary to the discharge of his office; yea, it consisted therein. Herein was he exposed to reproach, contempt, and shame, with all the evils that Satan or the world could bring upon him. And besides, he was, for us and in our stead, to undergo the 'curse of the law,' with the greatest of terror and sorrows in his soul, until he gave up the ghost. These things were necessary to the discharge of his office, nor could the salvation of the church be wrought out without them. But do we think that God would commit so glorious an office to his only Son to be discharged in this manner only? Let it be granted that after he had so accomplished the will of God in this world, he had himself entered into glory; yet if he should so cease the administration of his office, that must be looked on as the most afflictive and dolorous that ever was undergone. But it was the design of God to glorify the office itself; as an effect of his wisdom, and himself therein; yea, so as that the very office itself should be an everlasting honour to his Son as incarnate. To this end the administration of it is continued in glory in his hand, and he is exalted in the discharge of it. For this is that glory which he prays that all his disciples may be brought to him to behold. The time between his ascension and the end of all things is allotted to the glory of Christ in the administration of his office in the heavenly sanctuary. And from hence the apostle proves him, 'as a high priest,' to be far more glorious than those who were called to that office under the law (Heb. 8:1–3). Herein it is manifest to angels and men, how glorious a thing it is to be the only king, priest, and prophet of the church. Wherefore, as it behoved Christ, in the discharge of his office, to suffer; so, after his sufferings in the discharge of the same office, he was to enter into his glory (Rev. 1:18).

For the Church Triumphant

God has respect herein to those who depart in the faith, in their respective generations, especially those who died betimes, as the apostles and primitive Christians. And sundry things may be herein considered.

The Service of Christ Continues in Heaven

There are two things which believers put a great price and value on in this world, and which sweeten every condition to them. Without them the world would be a noisome dungeon to them, nor could they be satisfied with a continuance therein. The one is the service of Christ. Without an opportunity of being exercised herein, they could not abide here with any satisfaction. They who know it not so to be, are under the power of worldly-mindedness. The meanest service of Christ has refreshment in it. And as to those who have opportunities and abilities for great instances of service, they do not know on just grounds, nor are able to determine themselves, whether it be best for them to continue in their service here below, or to enter into the immediate service of Christ above;—so glorious, so excellent is it to be usefully serviceable to the Lord Jesus. So was it with the apostle (Phil. 1:21–6); so may it be with others, if they serve him in the same spirit, with the same sincerity, though their ability in service be not like to his. For neither had he anything but what he received. Again, they have the enjoyment of Christ in the ordinances of gospel worship. By these means do they live—in these things is the life of their souls.

In this state of things God will not call them hence to their loss; he will not put an end to these privileges, without an abundant recompense and advantage. Whatever we enjoy here, yet still to depart hence and to be with Christ shall be far better (Phil. 1:23).

First, although service here below shall cease, and be given over to other hands who are to have their share herein; yet, on the continuance of this state of things in heaven, there is also a continuation of service to Christ, in a way inexpressibly more glorious than what we are in this life capable of. Upon their admittance into this state of things above, they are before the throne of God, and serve him day and night in his temple; and he that sits on the throne shall dwell among them (Rev. 7:15). The whole state of the glorious worship of God before described is here respected; and herein is a continual service performed to him that sits on the throne, and to the Lamb. Wherefore it is so far from being loss, in being called off from service here below, as that, in point of service itself, it is an inconceivable advancement.

Secondly, the enjoyment of Christ in and by the ordinances of his worship, is the immediate fountain and spring of all our refreshments and consolations in this world (Ps. 87:7); but what is it to the blessed immediate enjoyment of him in heaven! Hence the blessedness of the state above is described, by being with Christ, being with Christ for ever—in the presence and immediate enjoyment of him. The light of the stars is useful and relieving in a dark night as we are on our way; but what are they when the sun arises! Will any man think it a loss that, upon the rising of the sun, they shall not enjoy their light any more, though in the night they knew not what to have done without it? It may be we cannot conceive how it will be best for us to forego the use of sacraments, ministry, and the Scripture itself. But all the virtue of the streams is in the fountain; and the immediate enjoyment of Christ unspeakably exceeds whatever by any means we can be made partakers of here below.

In this blessed state have the holy apostles, all the primitive martyrs and believers, from the time of their dissolution, enjoyed full satisfaction and solace, in the glorious assembly above (Rev. 7:15–17).

Continued Communion for the Church Above and Below

Hereby there is a continuation of communion between the church triumphant above and that yet militant here below. That there is such a communion between glorified saints and believers in this world, is an article of faith. Both societies are but one church, one mystical body, have one Head, and a mutual concern in each other. Yea, the spring and means of this communion is no small part of the glory of the gospel. For—before the saints under the Old Testament had the mystery of the glory of God in Christ, with our redemption thereby, revealed to them, in the way before declared—the communion was very obscure; but we are now taken into the light and glory of it, as the apostle declares (Heb. 12:22–4).

I know some have perverted the notions of the communion to idolatrous superstition; and so have all other truths of the gospel been abused and wrested, to the destruction of the souls of men; all the Scriptures have been so dealt withal (2 Pet. 3:16). But they deceived themselves in this matter—the truth deceives none. Upon a supposition of communion, they gathered that there must of necessity be an immediate communication between them above and us below. And if so, they knew no way for it, no means of it, but by our praying to them, and their praying for us. But they were under the power of their own deceivings. Communion does not require immediate mutual communication, unless it be among persons in the same state, and that in such acts as wherein they are mutually assisting and helpful to one another. But our different states will admit of no such intercourse; nor do we stand in need of any relief from them, or can be helped by any acts of their love, as we may aid and help one another here below. Wherefore the centre of this communion is in Christ alone and our exercise of it is upon him only, with respect to them.

Yet hereon some deny that there is any such communion between the members of the church or the mystical body of Christ in these diverse states. And they suppose it is so declared in that of the prophet, 'Doubtless you are our Father, though Abraham be ignorant of us, and Israel acknowledge us not' (Isa. 43:16). But there is nothing of any such importance in these words. The church, under a deep sense of its present state, in its unworthy walking and multiplied provocations, profess themselves to be such, as that their forefathers in covenant could not own them as their children and posterity in the faith. Hereupon they appeal to the infinite mercy and faithfulness of God, which extend themselves even to that condition of unworthiness which was enough to render them utterly disowned by the best of men, however otherwise concerned in them. But to suppose the church above, which has passed through its course of faith and obedience in afflictions, tribulations, and persecutions, to be ignorant of the state of the church here below in general, and unconcerned in it—to be without desires of its success, deliverance, and prosperity, to the glory of Christ—is to lay them asleep in a senseless state, without the exercise of any grace, or any interest in the glory of God. And if they cry for vengeance on the obdurate persecuting world (Rev. 6:10), shall we suppose they have no consideration nor knowledge of the state of the church suffering the same things which they did themselves? And, to put it out of question, they are minded of it in the next verse by Christ himself (v. 11).

But that which at present I alone intend, is the joint communion of the whole church in the worship of God in Christ. Were all that die in the Lord immediately received into that state wherein God 'shall be all in all,'—without any use of the mediation of Christ, or the worship of praise and honour given to God by him—without being exercised in the ascription of honour, glory, power, and dominion to him, on the account of the past and present discharge of his office—there could be no communion between them and us. But whilst they are in the sanctuary, in the temple of God, in the holy worship of Christ and of God in him, and we are not only employed in the same work, in sacred ordinances suited to our state and condition, but, in the performance of our duties, do by faith 'enter in within the veil,' and approach to the same throne of grace in the most holy place, there is a spiritual communion between them and us. So the apostle expresses it (Heb. 12:22–4).

To Prepare the Saints Above for the Eternal State

It is the way that God has appointed to prepare the holy souls above for the enjoyment of that eternal state which shall ensue at the end of all things. As we are here, in and by the Word and other ordinances, prepared and made meet for the present state of things in glory; so are they, by the temple-worship of heaven, fitted for that state of things when Christ shall give up the kingdom to the Father, that God may be all in all.

For the Church Militant

Respect is had herein to the faith of the church yet militant on the earth, and that, among others, in two things.

To Encourage Their Faith

For the encouragement of their faith. God could, as we have observed, upon the supposition of the atonement and reconciliation made by the blood of Christ, have saved the church by mere sovereign act of power. But whereas it was to his glory that we should be saved in the way of faith and obedience, this way was necessary to our encouragement therein. For it is in the nature of faith, it is a grace suited to that end, to seek for and receive aid, help, and relief, from God continually, to enable us to obedience.

For this end the Lord Christ continues in the discharge of his office, whereby he is able to save us to the uttermost, that we may receive such supplies by and from him. The continual use that faith makes of Christ to this purpose, as he gloriously exercises his mediatory office and power in heaven, cannot fully be declared. Neither can any believer, who is acted by present gospel light and grace, conceive how the life of faith can be led or preserved without it. No duties are we called to—no temptation are we exercised withal—no sufferings do we undergo—no difficulties, dangers, fears, have we to conflict withal—nothing is there in life or death, wherein the glory of God or our own spiritual welfare is concerned—but faith finds and takes relief and encouragement in the present mediatory life and power of Christ in heaven, with the exercise of his love, care, and compassion therein. So he proposes himself to our faith (Rev. 1:17–18).

To Guide Our Faith

That our faith may be guided and directed in all our accesses to God in his holy worship. Were nothing proposed to us but the immensity of the divine essence, we should not know how to make our approaches to it. And thence it is that those who are unacquainted with the glory of this dispensation, who know not how to make use of Christ in his present state for an access to God, are always inventing ways of their own (as by saints, angels, images) for that end; for an immediate access to the divine essence they cannot fancy. Wherefore, to end this discourse in one word—all the present faith and worship of God in the church here on earth, all access to him for grace, and all acceptable ascriptions of glory to his divine majesty, do all of them, in their being and exercise, wholly depend on, and are resolved into, the continuation of the mediatory actings of Christ in heaven and glory.

ETERNAL ASPECTS

I shall close this discourse with a little review of somewhat that passed before. From the consideration of that place of the apostle wherein he affirms, that at the end Christ shall give up the kingdom to the Father, I declared that all the state of things which we have described shall then cease, and all things issue in the immediate enjoyments of God himself. I would extend this no farther than as to what concerns the exercise of Christ's mediatory office with respect to the church here below, and the enemies of it. But there are some things which belong to the essence of this state which shall continue to all eternity.

First, I do believe that the person of Christ, in and by his human nature, shall be for ever the immediate head of the whole glorified creation. God having gathered all things to a head in him, the knot or centre of that collection shall never be dissolved. We shall never lose our relation to him, nor he his to us.

Secondly, I do therefore also believe, that he shall be the means and way of communication between God and his glorified saints for ever. What are, what will be, the glorious communications of God to his saints for ever, in life, light, power, joy, rest, and ineffable satisfaction (as all must be from him to eternity), I shall not now inquire. But this I say, they shall be all made in and through the person of the Son, and the human nature therein. That tabernacle shall never be folded up, never be laid aside as useless. And if it be said, that I cannot declare the way and manner of the eternal communications of God himself to his saints in glory by Christ; I shall only say, that I cannot declare the way and manner of his communications of himself in grace by Christ to the souls of men in this world, and yet I do believe it. How much more must we satisfy ourselves with the evidence of faith alone in those things which, as yet, are more incomprehensible. And our adherence to God, by love and delight, shall always be through Christ. For God will be conceived of to eternity according to the manifestation that he has made of himself in him, and no otherwise. This shall not be by acting faith with respect to the actual exercise of the mediation of Christ, as now we cleave to God; but it shall be by the all-satisfying acting of love to God, as he has manifested himself, and will manifest himself in Christ.

Thirdly, the person of Christ, and therein his human nature, shall be the eternal object of divine glory, praise, and worship. The life of glory is not a mere state of contemplation. Vision is the principle of it, as faith is of the life of grace. Love is the great vital acting of that principle, in adherence to God with eternal delight. But this is active in it also. It shall be exercised in the continual ascription and assignation of glory, praise, and honour to God, and the glorious exercise of all sorts of grace therein;—hereof the Lamb, the person of Christ, is the eternal object with that of the Father and the Spirit; the human nature in the Son, admitted into the communion of the same eternal glory.

Other books of interest in the
Christian Heritage imprint

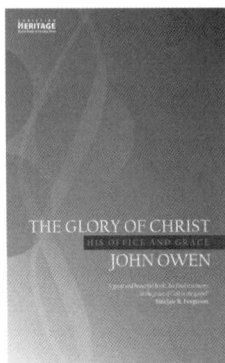

THE GLORY OF CHRIST
HIS OFFICE AND GRACE
JOHN OWEN

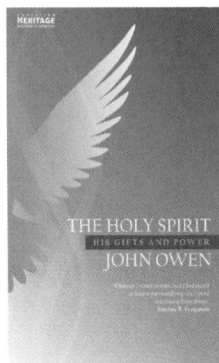

THE HOLY SPIRIT
HIS GIFTS AND POWER
JOHN OWEN

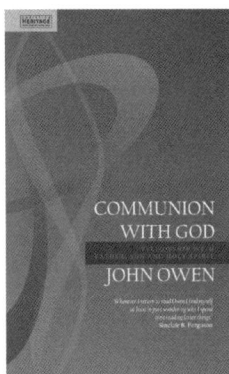

COMMUNION
WITH GOD
JOHN OWEN

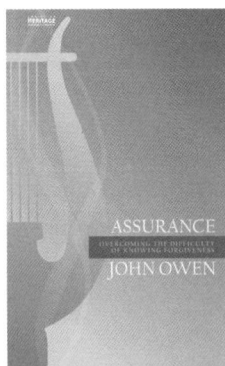

ASSURANCE
OVERCOMING THE DIFFICULTY
OF KNOWING FORGIVENESS
JOHN OWEN

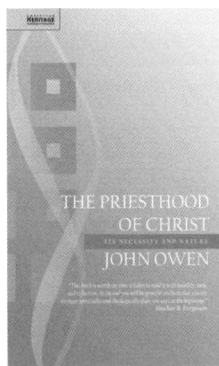

THE PRIESTHOOD
OF CHRIST
HIS NECESSITY AND NATURE
JOHN OWEN

THE GLORY OF CHRIST
His Office and Grace
ISBN 978-1-85792-474-9

THE HOLY SPIRIT
His Gifts and Power
ISBN 978-1-85792-475-6

COMMUNION WITH GOD
Fellowship with the Father, Son and Holy Spirit
ISBN 978-1-84550-209-6

ASSURANCE
Overcoming the Difficulty of Knowing Forgiveness
ISBN 978-1-84550-974-3

THE PRIESTHOOD OF CHRIST
Its Necessity and Nature
ISBN 978-1-84550-599-8

The Pleasantness of a Religious Life

Life as good as it can be

• • •

MATTHEW HENRY

INTRODUCTION BY J. I. PACKER

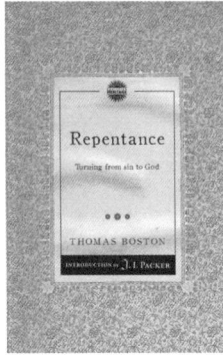

Repentance

Turning from sin to God

• • •

THOMAS BOSTON

INTRODUCTION BY J. I. PACKER

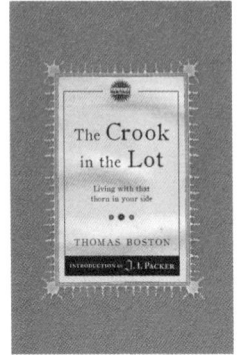

The Crook in the Lot

Living with that thorn in your side

• • •

THOMAS BOSTON

INTRODUCTION BY J. I. PACKER

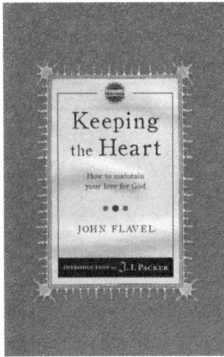

Keeping the Heart

How to maintain your love for God

• • •

JOHN FLAVEL

INTRODUCTION BY J. I. PACKER

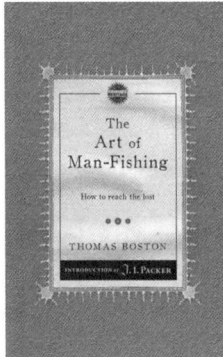

The Art of Man-Fishing

How to reach the lost

• • •

THOMAS BOSTON

INTRODUCTION BY J. I. PACKER

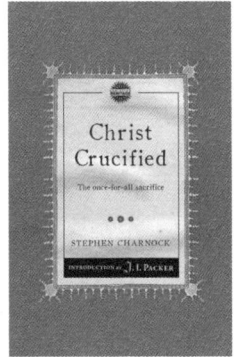

Christ Crucified

The once-for-all sacrifice

• • •

STEPHEN CHARNOCK

INTRODUCTION BY J. I. PACKER

The Heavenly Footman

How to get to Heaven

• • •

JOHN BUNYAN

INTRODUCTION BY J. I. PACKER

The Life of God in the Soul of Man

Real Religion

• • •

HENRY SCOUGAL

INTRODUCTION BY J. I. PACKER

The Mortification of Sin

Dealing with sin in your life

• • •

JOHN OWEN

INTRODUCTION BY J. I. PACKER

THE PLEASANTNESS OF THE RELIGIOUS LIFE
Life as good as it can be
Matthew Henry
ISBN 978-1-84450-651-3

REPENTANCE
Turning from sin to God
Thomas Boston
ISBN 978-1-84450-975-0

THE CROOK IN THE LOT
Living with that thorn in your side
Thomas Boston
ISBN 978-1-84550-649-0

KEEPING THE HEART
How to maintain your love of God
John Flavel
ISBN 978-1-84550-648-3

THE ART OF MAN-FISHING
How to reach the lost
Thomas Boston
ISBN 978-1-78191-108-2

CHRIST CRUCIFIED
The once-for-all sacrifice
Stephen Charnock
ISBN 978-1-84550-976-7

THE HEAVENLY FOOTMAN
How to get to Heaven
John Bunyan
ISBN 978-1-84550-650-6

THE LIFE OF GOD IN THE SOUL OF MAN
Real Religion
Henry Scougal
ISBN 978-1-78191-107-5

THE MORTIFICATION OF SIN
Dealing with sin in your life
John Owen
ISBN 978-1-84550-977-4

HISTORY HM MAKERS

JOHN OWEN

IM

PRINCE OF PURITANS
Andrew Thomson

ISBN 978-1-85792-267-7

JOHN OWEN

Prince of Puritans

Andrew Thomson

John Owen (1616-1683) was one of the defining theologians in the Christian era. His books have been continually in print and are still influential today. Educated at Queen's College, Oxford, he was a moderate Presbyterian who became a Congregationalist after reading a book by John Cotton. He later helped draw up the Savoy Declaration, the Congregational Basis of Faith.

During the English Civil War Owen was wholly on the side of the Parliamentarians, accompanying Cromwell on expeditions to Scotland and Ireland as Chaplain. Owen was influential in national life and was made Vice-Chancellor of Christ Church Oxford. After the Restoration of the Monarchy he was ejected from this position and devoted his energies to developing 'godly and learned men', in writing commentaries and devotional books, and in defending nonconformists from state persecution.

Andrew Thomson uses various sources for this biography including Owen's adversaries 'who could not be silent on so great a name or withhold reluctant praise.'

Christian Focus Publications

Our mission statement –

STAYING FAITHFUL

In dependence upon God we seek to impact the world through literature faithful to His infallible Word, the Bible. Our aim is to ensure that the Lord Jesus Christ is presented as the only hope to obtain forgiveness of sin, live a useful life and look forward to heaven with Him.

Our books are published in four imprints:

CHRISTIAN
FOCUS

Popular works including biographies, commentaries, basic doc-trine and Christian living.

CHRISTIAN
HERITAGE

Books representing some of the best material from the rich heritage of the church.

MENTOR

Books written at a level suitable for Bible College and seminary students, pastors, and other serious readers. The imprint includes commentaries, doctrinal studies, examination of current issues and church history.

CF4•K

Children's books for quality Bible teaching and for all age groups: Sunday school curriculum, puzzle and activity books; personal and family devotional titles, biographies and inspirational stories – because you are never too young to know Jesus!

Christian Focus Publications Ltd,
Geanies House, Fearn, Ross-shire,
IV20 1TW, Scotland, United Kingdom.
www.christianfocus.com